THE LITERARY COLD WAR,
1945 TO VIETNAM

In memoriam Lena Piette, who escaped Russia in 1917

For Diane, Jessica and Lauriane

THE LITERARY COLD WAR,
1945 TO VIETNAM

Adam Piette

EDINBURGH UNIVERSITY PRESS

© Adam Piette, 2009

Edinburgh University Press Ltd
22 George Square, Edinburgh

Typeset in Sabon and Gill Sans
by Servis Filmsetting Ltd, Stockport, Cheshire, and
printed and bound in Great Britain by
CPI Antony Rowe, Chippenham and Eastbourne

A CIP record for this book is available from the British Library

ISBN 978 0 7486 3527 6 (hardback)

The right of Adam Piette
to be identified as author of this work
has been asserted in accordance with
the Copyright, Designs and Patents Act 1988.

CONTENTS

Acknowledgements   vii

Introduction   1
1 The Special Relationship and the British Hypothesis: 19
  The Black Laurel, The Third Man, Cold War Vienna and Berlin
2 Cold War on the 1930s and Sacrificial Naming: 47
  John Dos Passos and Josephine Herbst
3 DEW Line, Uranium and the Arctic Cold War: 74
  Ginsberg's *Kaddish* and Nabokov's *Lolita*
4 Cold War Sex War, Or the Other Being Inside: Burroughs, Paley,   106
  Plath, Hughes
5 The Sacrificial Logic of the Asian Cold War: Greene's *The Quiet*   152
  American and McCarthy's *The Seventeenth Degree*
Conclusion   209
Bibliography   215

Index   234

ACKNOWLEDGEMENTS

This book would not have seen the light of day without the support, advice and example of a number of colleagues at the Universities of Glasgow and Sheffield, in particular John Coyle, John Gardner, Richard Cronin, the late Stephen Johnson, David Pascoe, Alex Houen and Duco Van Oostrum. I would also like to thank Holger Nehring and Erica Sheen for their help in creating the Cold War Cultures network, which energized the last year or so of the research. My greatest gratitude is to Neil Corcoran and Mark Rawlinson, who helped me selflessly with the final stages of the project at a critical time.

The Leverhulme Foundation generously funded three years' research leave and gave me the chance to travel to the States to pursue research crucial to the book. The Major Research Fellowship was fundamental to the project.

I would also like to thank the librarians and staff of the research libraries consulted for the book, in particular the team at the Harry Ransom Humanities Research Center (University of Texas) for their superb efficiency and forbearance over two visits, the last as Mellon fellow. I am also grateful to the librarians at the Berg collection at the New York Public Library, the Beinecke Rare Book and Manuscript Library at Yale, the National Security Archives at Washington, the Library of Congress, and the Ginsberg collection at the University of Columbia.

I would like to thank the publishers Faber & Faber, Weidenfeld & Nicolson and Harcourt Trade Publishers for their consideration. Every effort has been made to trace copyright holders and the publisher would be pleased to rectify any errors.

A broader debt is to the women who ran Women Strike for Peace through the dark days of the 1960s. I dedicate this book to their activism.

INTRODUCTION

In June 2004, I took my daughters down 'Scotland's Secret Bunker' at Troywood, Anstruther, in Fife. Disguised as a Scottish farmhouse, and concealed underground at the end of a 150m tunnel, it was built in the 1950s as one of the regional government HQs for the Scottish secretary and his ministry in case of nuclear emergency. As we walked through the spooky bunkered spaces with their antique machinery of war communications, my young daughters shrank from the sinister horror of it all. They refused to leave the only sunny space down there, a concrete room given over to the anti-nuclear movement, with colourful Campaign for Nuclear Disarmament (CND) posters, rainbows and chains of friendly hands. Their reaction made me ashamed of the boyish thrill that had led me to lure my family down there in the first place, all the allure of wartime technology, the rockets and guns on display, the blastproof doors, the Ops room intricacies, the labyrinthine underworld with its concrete imagining of survival by the very few.

By strange coincidence, the week of our visit saw a spectral enactment of my own shame in the form of Ronald MacDonald, a homeless paranoid schizophrenic. On 8 June he used a JCB digger to crash into the bunker after midnight – he stayed down there, in what the papers were to call the Bunker Siege, for two whole days and nights. He dressed in the display uniforms, played with the weapons, caused £100,000 of damage before being coaxed out by police. Inspector Jenks of the local constabulary said 'the complex nature of the building was creating operational issues for the police, who were playing a "long game" with the aim of bringing matters to a safe conclusion'.[1] The long game of detente played as if to tame and contain the imaginary psychotic event of nuclear emergency was being allegorized at Troywood. On the Scottish news, CCTV images of Mr MacDonald were broadcast, broken mind at play among the machinery of the nuclear security state. Dr Strangelove's militarized world was being playacted there, Cold War citizen paranoia as nightmare in an underground to which one could retreat and play among dream weapons, acting the uncivil avenging ghost of all those destined to die in the long nuclear endgame. The dream citizen had broken into the sacred spaces of the chosen few in command, releasing CND energies from the bunkered display and into schizophrenic flicker on CCTV.

Mr MacDonald's desire to go underground may also have been an act of weird nostalgia, a homing in on the forbidden zones of the past, acting out my own tourist zest for the sinister menace and glamour of Cold War technology. I have appropriated his two-day wonder at Troywood for my daughters as much as for myself, as an acknowledgement of, even as protection from, the contagious forces of the Cold War since 1989 – which they shrank from as if from something pestilential. For the peace of the Cold War relied on the deaths of very many in the hot wars between Communist- and NATO-sponsored powers around the world. And the Cold War continues to live and thrive within our collective imaginations as a security state hysteria, as a paranoid field of fantasies which draw whole populations in their wake in the organized states of mind marshalled by other more recent wars.

Nostalgia for the Cold War takes on many strange and twisted forms, including Don DeLillo's analytic historicism in *Underworld*, described by Martin Amis as his 'wake for the cold war' where the 'cosmic might' of nuclear weapons changed the relations between state and citizen in the West for ever: 'the State', Amis paraphrases, 'was your enemy's enemy; but nuclear logic decreed that the State was no longer your friend'.[2] The hostile pseudo-friend of the state targets its own citizens in the long game of deterrence and nuclear logic, as though by concrete interpellation.

The nostalgia is articulated in *Underworld* by the artist Klara, with her B-52 graveyard project and her obscure longing for the stabilities of the nuclear stand-off and its fixed ideological confrontation:

> Power meant something thirty, forty years ago. It was stable, it was focused, it was a tangible thing. It was greatness, danger, terror, all those things. And it held us together, the Soviets and us. Maybe it held the world together. You could measure things. You could measure hope and you could measure destruction.[3]

The desire is not only for the return of those times of grim measurement, but for the tranquillizing fantasy possession of the sudden secret world revealed once the Cold War is over. As the garbage guerrilla Jesse Dewilter tells Sims in the book: 'Don't underestimate our capacity for complex longings. Nostalgia for the banned materials of civilization, for the brute force of old industries and old conflicts' (*Underworld*, p. 286). The Cold War generated complex longings of a terrifying kind whilst it lasted, then this new state of rapt nostalgia in its aftermath. And it is a longing, most perniciously, for a direct link between private fantasies and the military–industrial complex running the world. Taking his cue from Pynchon, with the fantastic coincidence of rocket weaponry and a citizen's random sexual desire in *Gravity's Rainbow*, DeLillo ponders and unpicks this most powerful of dreams: that the big world of the Cold War has an entranced relationship with the citizen's unconscious. It is there in the conspiracy theorist Marvin's attachment to the Cold War in the waning days of Gorbachev: 'You don't know that every privilege in your life and every thought in your mind depends on the ability of the two great powers to hang a threat over the planet?' (*Underworld*, p. 182).

Marvin's addiction to this relationship mimics the state–private relations that constituted the Cold War's warfare state economy during the long forty-year game.[4] It also reinscribes as nostalgia the paranoia that typified fantasy reactions to the Cold War. Pynchon's phallic equation between the rockets of the Cold War and male sexual desire, the penile rodeo horse ridden by Major 'King' Kong – and its links to Jack D. Ripper's paranoid fantasy of Communist control over his 'precious bodily fluids' – in *Dr. Strangelove*, are transformed into complex longings for state-controlled desire in Marvin's nostalgia: 'When the cold war goes out of business, you won't be able to look at some woman in the street and have a what-do-you-call-it kind of fantasy the way you do today' (*Underworld*, p. 182). The Cold War was, DeLillo argues, a set of forces 'rooting from the gut' (p. 133), aligning the most intimate and repressed fantasies of the subject with their global-destructive equivalents.

Nostalgia in the United States post-1989 has concrete manifestations too: the Trinity and the Nevada test sites, for instance, have become tourist zones. Strategic Air Command sites are being put on the National Register of Historic Places by the US Army Corps of Engineers: the airborne alert facilities, airborne command posts, the sci-fi sea-stations like the Texas Towers, the extraordinary DEW and Pinetree Lines. The Department of Energy showcases atomic culture at the National Atomic Museum in Albuquerque, New Mexico. Titan missiles are on show at the Titan Missile Museum at Sahuarita, Arizona. There is a Minuteman Missile Site museum at Philip, South Dakota. At the Peterson Air and Space Museum, the HAWK, BOMARC, GENIE, NIKE HERCULES and AJAX missiles are on display – you can even 'Adopt-A-Missile' and opt to spend workdays cleaning the Nike Ajax. The folk nostalgia is matched by burgeoning Cold War material culture initiatives: in 2002, Colleen Beck and Bill Johnson undertook an archaeological mission to survey the atomic test-site installations worthy of preservation, sponsored by the Department of Energy and the Desert Research Institute.

The preservation nostalgia is matched by the heritage industry in the UK. English Heritage's Monuments Protection Programme (MPP) under the tutelage of John Schofield has commandeered all the old rusting Cold War military installations across the country and moved to preserve the most important – the National Trust has taken on similar sites, such as the enormous Orford Ness, choosing to present the Cold War there not as theme park, but as powerfully evocative ruin.[5] English Heritage's publication *Cold War: Building for Nuclear Confrontation, 1946–1989* maps and describes each testing site, early warning unit, RAF nuclear bomb base, from the monumental Atomic Weapons Research Establishment sites to the discreet Royal Observer Corps monitoring posts in the fields. The authors, Wayne Cocroft and J.C. Thomas, describe the installations as 'secret and closed worlds',[6] conflict archaeology revealing how the Cold War built its mystique on the geopolitical alliance of nuclear power with state secrecy.[7]

The traces of the gravitational pull generated by the alliance of power and secrecy have motivated a series of poets, writers and artists to reflect on the menace and mystery of the abandoned sites in the post-Cold War. W.G. Sebald was drawn to the ruins of Orford Ness in *The Rings of Saturn* (which he journeys to as if to the realm of the dead) because they enticed him to experience 'the remains of our own civilization after its extinction in some future catastrophe'.[8] Installation artist Louise K. Wilson, following Sebald's lead, used acoustic experiments to sound out the traces and sonic unconscious of the Cold War in work on Orford Ness. For her, the recordings enact a deep listening to the 'echoes' within politically unsettling spaces, gauging the compelling fascination of the Cold War uncanny through haunted sounding out of the militarized landscape. Orford Ness generates 'this atmosphere of secrecy, strangeness and renewed "occupation"' because of its dual role as atomic bomb environmental testing site (it tested all Britain's bombs from Blue Danube to Polaris) and its electronic surveillance role: it harboured a listening post that tuned in to Sputnik, and then in the 1970s hosted the Cobra Mist project using backscatter radar to spy on the Soviet Union. Her deep listening mimics this Cold War surveillance whilst 'testing' the power ratios left as echoey traces in the ruined centrifuges and vibration test cell 'pagodas'.[9] Cold War nostalgia is, at this level of attention, exorcism and fascination entwined together as a strategic-symptomatic act of historical witnessing, activating the old sites in order to register and counter the prevailing energies in the body politic. As Louise Wilson notes, 'this place is so decayed and historical, you have to keep reminding yourself that what was happening here still continues – that's why there is still so much secrecy. It's not as if an endpoint has been reached' (*Record of Fear*, p. 114). An education in the forms secrecy took in the Cold War gives some insight into the control systems governing contemporary culture.

Literary criticism and theory have been relatively slow to follow developments in the discipline of history which have attempted to move the discipline out of the zone of international diplomatic relations. A useful summary of the current state of affairs in Cold War history is given in the introduction to Rana Mitter and Patrick Major's 2003 collection of essays *Across the Blocs: Cold War Cultural and Social History*. They read their own field as itself shaped by Cold War ideology, Cold War history's predominant interest in international relations and foreign policy being an extension of the Cold War academy's 'policy-driven concerns of political science and area studies, once devoted to Kremlinology'.[10] Their interest lies in the expansion of the field 'from the state to include state–private networks [. . .] to de-centre the focus of attention even more radically away from government and diplomacy, towards society and culture as autonomous spheres of historical interest, and to establish the Cold War "home front" as a sub-field in its own right' (p. 3). The specific topics that Mitter and Major argue Cold War cultural history might concern itself with have very much shaped this book: adversary-otherness and mirroring mechanisms and the drive against neutral positions in the new global thinking (fuelled by the new concepts of nuclear self-destruction and species preservation) (pp. 7–8); the role played by the Second World War in the construction of the Cold War; understanding the Cold War as a non-European set of conflicts with East Asia as 'a faultline region in the era' (p. 8); the psychological effects of Cold War propaganda, especially in home fronts and during the era's hot wars (p. 9); the social consequences of the ideological struggle between anti-Communism and anti-Americanism; the interplay between atomic destruction and civil defence, the psychology of mass terror, including studies of peace movements; anxieties about technology and the space race as new frontier; cultural realities within countries divided by the Cold War ('In some countries a cold civil war was being waged, whereby international confrontations were simultaneously domestic conflicts, often with inter-war roots' (p. 12)).

History has been leading the way, in other words, with literary studies sometimes bafflingly indifferent to the importance of the Cold War in shaping cultures in the postwar. There have been, however, significant contributions to the field of the literary Cold War, substantial enough to constitute a well-established field.

Nuclear criticism in the 1980s was one of the first serious attempts to deal with the textual culture created by the Cold War, specifically the relations between representation and nuclear weapons.[11] Nuclear criticism had three main effects on subsequent Cold War criticism, as Bryan Taylor argues: it theorized the textual nature of Cold War culture, based on Derrida's analysis of the incommensurability and impossibility of any post-nuclear thinking. It showed how the Cold War was both overtly and covertly discursive in nature in legitimizing certain social practices and demonizing others. And it showed how radical and polemical forms of textual resistance could operate against those nuclear practices through demonstration of the covert-overt structures of the security state. Ken Ruthven's fine book *Nuclear Criticism* (1993) revived the nuclear critical terms and arguments for potential application to the post-Cold War.

Paul Boyer's *By the Bomb's Early Light: American Thought and Culture at the Dawn of the Atomic Age* (1985) showed how nuclear weapons and the idea of nuclear warfare had been internalized by the American public, thereby affecting almost every area of American life. Boyer's redefinition of nuclear culture did a lot to open up the enormous archive of texts, history and material culture for the field.[12] *By the Bomb's Early Light* led directly to a number of highly significant books in the 1990s once the Wall and Soviet Russia fell – stimulated by the declassification of archives, by the dwindling of the doomsday terror of nuclear weapons following decommissioning. The collective imaginary closure of the Cold War led to a plethora of works focusing on the cultural history of the period. General studies like Stephen Whitfield's key *The Culture of the Cold War* (1991) focused on the First Cold War and defined Cold War culture as the self-righteous anti-Communism spawned by McCarthyite and House Committee Investigating Un-American Activities (HUAC) propaganda. US superpower ideology was generated on the back of the basic moral binary opposition between East and West, and 1960s counterculture could be said to have been stimulated by the corrosion of that differential – Whitfield's book was the one of the first to see the pivotal importance of Kubrik's *Dr. Strangelove* in bringing the First Cold War to an ideological close.

Published earlier in the same year, it was Thomas Hill Schaub's *American Fiction in the Cold War* (1991) which really launched Cold War literary criticism. Schaub expertly dissects the shift to anti-political ideology amongst writers in the 1940s and 1950s (his case studies are Mailer, Ellison, O'Connor and Barth), and gives the first convincing and detailed account of the key role played by the non-Communist left in the general withdrawal from New Deal-style progressive politics and radical activist writing. The ex-Trotskyite *Partisan Review* and the New York intellectuals are a key focus, with keen and satirical accounts of the new 'tragic' angst of the alienated individual that is such a feature of the reactionary existentialism of the period.

The Cold War became a regular feature of readings of late twentieth-century American fiction after Schaub. Single-author studies married close reading and cultural history, as with Jon Lance Bacon's *Flannery O'Connor and Cold War Culture* (1994), which tracked the metaphorical force of containment in O'Connor's prose. Bacon's work inspired concentrated attention to specific authors and their Cold War trajectories, as with Steven Gould Axelrod's article on 'Robert Lowell and the Cold War' (1999) and Robin Peel's *Writing Back:*

Sylvia Plath and Cold War Politics (2002), both key works. The texts revealed how extensively a writer's work and reputation change once the Cold War context is properly re-established, in terms of activist and/or reactionary temptations, specific and detailed historicist occasions, and deep rhetorical tropes in the writing. It was Steffen Hantke's *Conspiracy and Paranoia in Contemporary American Fiction* (1994) which made the critical link between postmodernism and the Cold War through a lively and politically astute analysis of the conspiracy theories in McElroy and DeLillo. This was accompanied by a more rigorous and theoretical cultural history from American studies scholars such as Guy Oakes, with his *The Imaginary War: Civil Defense and American Cold War Culture* (1994), which demonstrates how the US government linked family values to national security objectives in the home front civil defence promotional propaganda. Oakes shows how possible it is to read the official texts of the Cold War directorates, from George Kennan's 1946 long telegram to the protect-and-survive leaflets of the 1950s, with a literary-critical eye for the rhetoric of persuasion. The literary forms taken by the Cold War should include, in other words, the fictions generated by the state security systems in persuading citizens to pay the price necessary for effective deterrence and possible failure of deterrence.

The initial phase was crowned by Alan Nadel's indispensable *Containment Culture* (1995). Nadel retraces Oakes' trajectory through Kennan's telegram but has a sharper focus on the precise lineaments of that rhetoric: following Bacon, containment is shown to spread out from the policy of geopolitical restraint advocated by Kennan to the most diverse areas, from Disney and *Playboy* through to Cecil B. DeMille and the Bond films. Of particular interest are the impressive readings of John Hersey's *Hiroshima* and the comparison between Salinger's *Catcher in the Rye* and Heller's *Catch-22*. It is the attention paid to the fantasy tropes disguised within popular and textual forms which has influenced this study: Nadel reveals how these fantasy tropes are themselves unstable and conflicted containment strategies for the marketing of the essential relation between the national pursuit of a geopolitical agenda in the world and the local policing of subversive social energies in the domestic sphere.

It was work by Nadel and others which gave Ann Douglas the material with which to write her important position paper 'Periodizing the American Century: Modernism, Postmodernism, and Postcolonialism in the Cold War' (1998) – it argues convincingly that neither postmodernism nor postcolonialism can be properly understood without the concept of the Cold War. For the Cold War superpowers' ideological machinery taught writers like Pynchon the intricate discursive mindgames postmodernists associated with *mise en abyme* language and fiction, whilst the Cold War's principal battlegrounds were the decolonizing Third World.

Following Nadel, the late 1990s and early 2000s saw media studies covering the popular culture of the Cold War with depth and precision. The role TV played in the popularization of the Cold War, in the rise and fall of McCarthyism and in the disseminating of the technological sublime is charted by Michael Curtin's *Redeeming the Wasteland* (1995) and Thomas Doherty's *Cold War, Cool Medium* (2003). Christine Klein published the excellent Said remake *Cold War Orientalism* (2003) with trenchant analyses of the geopolitical work done by popular culture in educating Americans about their imperial responsibilities in the Far East, in chapters on Mitchener's travel writing, *The King and I* and *South Pacific*. Tony Shaw's *Hollywood's Cold War* (2007) is essential reading for the teasing out of the micro-histories of the relations between the state and cinema's private networks, especially the cultural propaganda work done by the United States Information Agency (USIA). His earlier book *British Cinema and the Cold War* (2006) included astonishing new research into the screening of Orwell and the making of *Dr. Strangelove*. Genre writing was covered with comparable authority by several key texts, including Keith Booker's *Monsters, Mushroom Clouds and the Cold War* (2001), Woody Haut's *Pulp Culture* (1996), David Seed's *American Science Fiction and the Cold War* (1999) and Julia Mickenberg's *Learning from the Left: Children's Literature, the Cold War and Radical Politics in the United States* (2005). David Caute single-handedly provided a detailed general history of the culture and arts in the West during the Cold War in *The Dancer Defects* (2003).

Genre-specific studies followed suit. Edward Brunner's *Cold War Poetry* (2000) reassessed mainstream poetry of the 1950s in terms of the bomb and the growing instability of state authority. His work was accompanied by Deborah Nelson's ground-breaking *Pursuing Privacy in Cold War America* (2002), which uses law and literature theory to analyse the legal redefinition of privacy performed within the confessional poetry genre in the 1950s. Mark Carroll's *Music and Ideology in Cold War Europe* (2003) is an essential American studies text on the working of the Congress for Cultural Freedom in United States Cold War cultural propaganda. Bruce McConachie's magisterial *American Theater in the Culture of the Cold War* (2003) took Nadel and Bacon's containment thesis and showed the trope at work in the most extraordinarily elaborate forms in the staging histories of plays by Gaddo, Williams, Miller, Axelrod, MacLeish and Martha Graham. McConachie has superb accounts of a whole ecosystem of Cold War ideas and practices: nuclear bomb anxieties, the 'Freudian Fifties' therapeutic inward turn, Momism, civil rights Popular Front radicalism, military machismo, containment liberalism, McCarthyite confessional, nuclear godhead theology and the H-bomb bunker mentality.

Specific histories and methodologies also produced significant work at the millennium: Robert J. Corber's excellent gender analysis of the Cold War in *Homosexuality in Cold War America* (1997) led to Suzanne Clark's excoriating dissection of the masculinist rhetoric of the Cold War in her *Cold Warriors* (2000) and Michael Davidson's shrewd analysis, in his *Guys Like Us* (2003), of the exclusionary homosociality structuring Cold War progressive poetry. Ron Robin's *The Making of the Cold War Enemy* (2001) looked at the recruitment of the behavioural sciences to the Cold War in the US in the analysis of the enemy. The history of civil rights in America has been thoroughly reassessed in Cold War cultural terms. Building on Gerald Horne's work on radical African-American culture during the Cold War, especially his *Black and Red* (1985), Mary Dudziak's *Cold War Civil Rights* (2000) has been influential in demonstrating how Soviet and Third World pressures on the US – to resolve the flat contradiction between their advocacy of freedom abroad and the existence of racist states in the South – helped energize the civil rights breakthroughs. Dudziak's work, with that of others in the Cold War race history field such as Thomas Borstelmann,[13] has helped consolidate some very fine work on African-American literature and the Cold War from authors such as James Smethurst.[14]

Perhaps the most essential books underlying this study, with its focus on the relations between textual representations and the covert state in the Cold War UK and US, are Peter Hennessy's *The Secret State* and Frances Stonor Saunders' *Who Paid the Piper?* Hennessy's dissection of the British government's extraordinary war plans during the Cold War builds on whistle-blowing anti-nuclear activist texts from during the Cold War, especially Duncan Campbell's *War Plan UK* (1982), but with the added authority of declassified archive material. The result is an astonishing insight into the fiction-generating machine at the heart of the Cold War: the plans are 'scenarios' which play zero-sum games with the Soviet enemy and its fellow travellers and satellites; imagine the most apocalyptic forms of social collapse; and try to outwit public panic and unrest. Campbell had shown how the war plans were designed to suppress dissent, their primary concern being 'with an *internal* enemy'.[15] Hennessy's work in the archives reveals the full baroque, Gothic horror of some of the planning decisions, with civil servants worrying about omnicidal cock-ups, as with 'the classical "destruction of Russia by mistake" situation', to quote Frank Motterhead, MOD deputy secretary responsible for the War Book in 1961.[16]

The grim scenarios in anti-nuclear docudrama films such as Peter Watkins' *The War Game* (banned by the BBC after consultation with Whitehall) and Barry Hines' BBC TV documentary *Threads* is revealed as falling not far short of the truth. Hennessy shows how the government, after the assessment by William Strath (head of the Central War Plans Secretariat in 1955) of the devastating effects of a thermonuclear strike on Britain, decided that there would be little point trying to impose any centralized control over a post-nuclear UK. The government would be bunkered down in the vast Corsham bunker in Wiltshire *for its own safety* and not in order to govern at all.

The situation in the US is as surreal. The RAND ('R & D') organization was set up after the Second Word War to ally game theory with systems analysis to run nuclear and containment strategy, beginning by correlating weapon efficiency with, in the words of David R. Jardini of the *RAND Review*, the '[mathematizing of] conflict in two-person, zero-sum games'.[17] The story of the move from war games to real war strategy in Vietnam with the RAND-friendly McNamara in charge is told in *Soldiers of Reason* by Alex Abella (2008).[18] The whole unholy mix of social science, cybernetic systems theory and war management through Operations Research in the rule of McNamara's guilt-ridden RAND experts in Vietnam is important both methodologically and historically to the later chapters of this book.

Cold War literary studies would not have taken the form they have since 1999 were it not for Stonor Saunders' *Who Paid the Piper?*. Her revelation of the extent of CIA funding of the arts in the postwar through the Congress for Cultural Freedom (CCF), headed by Michael Josselson, and including as one of its apparatchiks Vladimir Nabokov's cousin Nicholas Nabokov, has influenced many of the historians working on Cold War culture. The CCF was set up at the Titania Palace in Berlin in 1950 in direct response to the Soviet-sponsored peace movement launched at the Waldorf-Astoria Hotel in New York the year before.[19] Stonor Saunders detailed what the Congress handlers called the 'convergence' between the CIA and intellectuals in Europe, especially the non-Communist left (known as the NCL to the CIA), funding ex-Communists such as Silone and Koestler, promoting literary and artistic festivals and events with prominent anti-Communist thinkers and dissidents. Though only a close inner circle then knew for certain of the secret funding by the CIA's International Organizations Division (IOD), it had become practically public knowledge by the 1960s. What had passed as necessary propaganda and anti-Stalinist fervour in the 1940s now seemed corruption and dirty tricks to an America made suspicious and cynical after the series of blunders from the Bay of Pigs and Cuban missile crisis to Vietnam. Stonor Saunders unravels the web of the IOD's *Kulturkampf* with astonishing depth and imagination, revealing the complicity of the NCL intellectuals in the cultural Cold War at its most amoral and blatantly US-imperialist. The reputation of many who were caught up in the enormous scandal following the *Ramparts* exposé in 1967 of the funding of the Congress and *Encounter* by the CIA (Silone, Muggeridge, Lasky, Bell, Aron) has hardly recovered since. And the most naive victim of them all, Stephen Spender, one of the editors of *Encounter* when the news broke, did penance for his sins by offering his house in France to the *soixante-huitards*, and by setting up the rigorously independent anti-censorship body *Article 19*. Stonor Saunders' book raises questions about the broader forms of complicity in the cultural Cold War on the part of all writers. This book attempts to address some of those questions.

In 1974, John Le Carré equated the secret services with the unconscious of the nation: the 'secret services', says Bill Haydon in *Tinker, Tailor, Soldier, Spy*, are 'the only real measure of a nation's political health, the only real expression of its subconscious'.[20] Hennessy and Stonor Saunders have informed this book's attempts to probe the collective political unconscious, backed up by the findings of the indefatigable Cold War intelligence historian Richard Aldritch, whose journal *Intelligence and National Security* and book *The Hidden Hand: Britain, America and Cold War Secret Intelligence* (2001) have done so much to establish the importance of agencies like the USIA, the UK's Information Research Department (IRD) and British Information Services in the propaganda war.[21]

This emergent field has provided me with various strands and forms of advocacy. From nuclear criticism, I have absorbed the discursive nature of the Cold War and the need to identify the textual nodes of resistance occurring *during* the Cold War. From Schaub's work came the decision to concentrate some of the research attention on the former Trotskyite intellectuals (Dos Passos, McCarthy) and to probe with the Herbst chapter the extent to which the war was covertly a war on the 1930s. Hantke's *Conspiracy and Paranoia* is behind the desire to see how far the paranoia sketched in Cold War postmodernism is traceable back to earlier texts. Nadel and Bacon's work revealed how effective the parsing of a complex textual and psycho-geopolitical trope like containment can be in the analysis of certain forces and drives within culture and the collective imagination. Coupled with Oakes' close readings of official prose, the Nadel methodology justified a dual reading of literary and culturally contemporary texts. McConachie's book has been most influential in the sheer range of topics and texts covered as well as the colour and wit of the delivery. The present study's interest in Cold War uses of Freud and their relation to Cold War tropes of anxiety is indebted to *American Theater in the Culture of the Cold War*. The cultural and intelligence historians outlined above have been critical in shaping the decision to write the book about the special relationship, and to concentrate on texts which negotiate the underground, covert Anglo-American spaces discovered by Hennessy, Stonor Saunders and Aldritch in the declassified archives.

This book attempts to tease out a cluster of Cold War fantasies from the outset of the Cold War in the late 1940s up to the Vietnam War. This is a book about Cold War culture, looking at writers working at the hazy borders between aesthetic project and political allegory, with specific attention being paid to Vladimir Nabokov and Graham Greene as Cold War writers. The book looks at the special relationship as a form of paranoid plotline governing key Anglo-American texts from Storm Jameson to Sylvia Plath and Ted Hughes, as well as examining the figure of the non-aligned neutral observer caught up in the sacrificial triangles structuring Cold War fantasy. The observer is the dissenting citizen as liberal victim caught between the (Janus) faces of the enemy construct generated by Cold War ideology. The sacrificial logic is played out in different formations according to the phases of the early Cold War, from anxieties about the captive European city in the late 1940s, through nuclear fears fuelled by the arms race in the 1950s, to the bombing nightmares created by Vietnam. I will be looking at writers engaged in projects which cross psychological and political fields: examples include Graham Greene using Freud in Vienna to plot the political-allegorical love triangle in *The Third Man*; Nabokov encoding fantasized dreams of uranium in his novel to signal Lolita as Cold War sacrificial victim; Sylvia Plath and Ted Hughes acting out a self-destructive sex war at the level of psychic system and bodily cell under radioactive attack. The aim of the book is to sketch out the secret, obsessive and paranoid story of the mind under the compulsions of the Cold War, to graph the triangulated nuclear anxieties of the citizen in the postwar security state. Using some of the wealth of material unearthed by historians and cultural theorists, the book hopes to redefine the literary postwar period, 1945–89, as Cold War. It also hopes to explore the special relationship as an example of Cold War sacrificial logic to ground an argument linking British decolonization to American assumption of superpower.

Some justification of the curious structure of the chapters might be helpful here. The scheme of combining pairs of texts/authors in each chapter came partly as a result of the methodology chosen, a combination of a pragmatic historicism with creative close writing, my term for the merging of creative procedures for research writing with close reading practices. It had also to do with the emergent topic of the whole book: the developing story of gender relations in the structuring of the sacrificial logic of Cold War fantasy. I wanted to tell the story of the relations between men and women, and the chapters reflect that in their structure and pairings. Each chapter pitches male alongside and sometimes against female, in varying ratios of approach, victimization and menace. Each chapter has a double structure to test and exemplify the gendered nature of the conflict within the triangulated paranoid Cold War history internalized by desiring citizens. The weaving together of literary criticism and historical-cultural information becomes increasingly involved as the book progresses, with a view to performing as well as substantiating the escalating power of Cold War politics over the stories of the relations between the genders.

A paradigmatic form of those compromised stories takes place literally at the frontier between East and West on the Berlin Wall with John Le Carré's *The Spy Who Came in from the Cold*. Liz Gold is shot, effectively sacrificed between the two superpowers, to seal the secret pact that preserves the identity of the neo-fascist spy being used by the British secret service. Liz's sacrifice reprises the killing of the Jewish Jens Fiedler, underlining Le Carré's dark sense of the unholy choices made in the denazification era in Germany that led to the creation of NATO. Taking the secret service as the expression of the nation's subconscious, the secret of secrets is the 'unconscious' fascism at the core of the British establishment, and the sacrifices of Fiedler and Liz Gold are fantasy re-enactments of the appeasement sacrifices made before and during the Second World War. The German Stasi, for Leamas, is indistinguishable from his own secret service in the quasi-divine surveillance and scope of their power: 'they would expect him to be afraid; for his service pursued traitors as the eye of God followed Cain across the desert' (p. 62). This paranoid sense of the secret service is matched by the Communist system as ideologized by its apparatchiks: 'The Party knows more about us than we know about ourselves' (p. 203). For Le Carré, the Cold War was a continuation of the Second World War by other means, with power multiplied exponentially by technology, by life-and-death secrecy and the necessary ruthlessness demanded by the urgency of the situation ('everywhere the air of conspiracy' (p. 65)).

The two superpowers of the Cold War are figured as two colossi or giants that threaten the citizen on either side. What is being enacted in the death of Liz is the nightmare of citizenship in the newly emergent national security state, figured as the all-seeing beam of the searchlight: 'the watchtower's searchlight began feeling along the wall towards them' (p. 217). Liz's death (and Leamas' subsequent self-sacrifice) has the logic of a political nightmare, a ritual sacrifice to the *polis* god of security, who turns out not to be an East–West hybrid, but a Janus fashioned from the overt/covert formations within the West. It is clear that what is fuelling the sacrificial logic, for the West's secret agent Mundt at least, is a fascist masculinity that identifies women and Jews as victims. In mimicking Stasi ruthlessness, the British secret service is 'unconsciously' taking that sacrificial logic into its own control systems. As Control tells Leamas, 'you can't be less ruthless than the opposition' (p. 19). Liz as a soft Communist is represented as naive not because she is Communist, but because she fails to see that the individual who must be crushed by her party according to the political propaganda she has ingested ('history, individuals must bow to it, be crushed by it if necessary' (p. 160)) is *her*. In the nightmare court scene, Liz is subject to the malignant gaze of the court and the treacherous gaze of Leamas on her back. Once in this zone of the political unconscious, neither Liz or Leamas can extricate themselves from the median zone of the Cold War.

The fantasy of the woman under sacrificial pressure from two sinister male presences is the trope this study discovers and pursues through its various different guises, from the kidnapping of Lolita by Humbert Humbert and Quilty through the psychoanalytic dreamwork in Plath's poetry to Mary McCarthy facing American bombs in Hanoi. Its avatar might be Iphigenia, targeted as 'daughter' of the Cold Warrior, sacrificed by the good father/bad father as exemplary proxy victim to guarantee male transport to a misguided war. Iphigenia plays a coded role in Nabokov's Cold War text *Pale Fire*, there as the site of Shade's lectures on the afterlife ('I.P.H., a lay / Institute (I) of Preparation (P) / For the Hereafter (H)'), very like the front organizations used by the CIA to fund Nicholas Nabokov's Congress, but within the economy of the novel/ poem signifying Hazel, Iphigenia-victim of the Cold War fantasy constructed by the patriarch double act of Shade and Kinbote.

I use the term 'sacrifice' relatively loosely, and only according to the folk forms it takes in the contexts discovered. My argument is, though, that the paranoid sacrificial narratives are dependent on something substantial in Cold War politics, namely the fusion between the patriotic rhetoric of bellicose propaganda (as in L.B. Johnson's celebrated farewell television speech: 'a vigilant America stands ready tonight to defend an honoured cause, whatever the price, whatever the burden, whatever the sacrifice that duty may require') and the real doctrine of proxy sacrifice whereby it is others who pay the price for the Cold War's ordeals (from the same speech: 'Peace will come because Asians were willing to work for it and to sacrifice for it – and to die by the thousands for it').[22] The political form of sacrificial rhetoric blends in with obscure self-sacrificial drives within the citizen imagination, following the logical sequence sketched out by René Girard's theory of the scapegoating mechanism in Western culture. The mimetic escalation between the USSR and US in the nuclear arms race and struggles over the Third World is matched by what Girard calls internal mediation, whereby the (paranoid) citizen imagines herself as emissary victim, target and necessary *pharmakon* in the obscure drama of nuclear fear. Girard's theory of the scapegoat could not have been conceived outside the Cold War: the theory's elaborate structures of copycat violence, the close relationship it sets up between ideas of political sacrifice and the need to bury the news of the real death toll, the talk of escalation and emulation of the enemy, the mimetic desire written into the collective will, all these features imitate the oppositional configurations of the Cold War imaginary.[23] The surrogate victim, in the forms of Cold War sacrifice imagined in this study, channels the war's eerie violence so as (seemingly) to avert nuclear catastrophe, simultaneously obscuring the uncanny truth: that the Cold War *is* a scapegoating mechanism.

The sacrificial trope depends, clearly, on the relevance of embedded psychological fantasy narratives in the texts under consideration here: Cold War psychoanalysis is therefore necessarily a recurrent concern. Cold War uses of Freud in the United States have been the focus of a significant body of critical and theoretical work, due in the first place to the historical recruitment of psychology and psychiatry to the anti-Communist cause. Ellen Herman in her monograph *The Romance of American Psychology* (1995) revealed the military's deployment of academic psychologists, psychiatrists and social scientists in the domains of psychological warfare, propaganda and public opinion formation. Covert analysis and manipulation of opinion abroad, as with the ill-fated Project Camelot in Chile in 1964, were virtually counterinsurgency by means of operations research. Herman also shows how these defence and psy-war projects had a knock-on effect in psychologizing the analysis of culture. This chimed in with the Freudian attachments of the New York intellectuals, particularly Trilling. Mark Krupnick's *Lionel Trilling and the Fate of Cultural Criticism* argued that intellectuals in the 1950s adapted psychoanalysis to their own agenda, effectively uncoupling Freud from Marx, whilst using him as a tool for social conformism and against revolutionary creeds. This was deliberately quietist, as Cyndy Hendershot has shown in her fine book on Cold War horror movies, *I Was a Cold War Monster* (2001). She looks at Philip Rieff's *Freud: the Mind of a Moralist* (1959) – Freud, for Rieff, had discovered a 'brilliant formula with which to shrink the revolutionary character – as basically a revolt against [the] father' (quoted in *I Was a Cold War Monster*, p. 94). As Hendershot comments, 'because Freudian theory forces the individual to resign himself or herself to a constant inner war between id and superego, it causes the individual to accept things as they are' (p. 94).

Deviance from this normative pressure is itself psychologically controlled by being labelled as neurotic; or more specifically as conspiratorial paranoia. There have been excellent studies of paranoia in the Cold War inspired by the Cold War postmodernism of Pynchon and DeLillo, most usefully for this study Mark Fenster's *Conspiracy Theories* (1999) and Timothy Melly's *Empire of Conspiracy* (1999). The Cold War had the curious effect of institutionalizing the paranoid system conjured by Freud's Schreber (whose God acted as chief persecutor of his victims using an intricate network of rays to act on their nervous system) as the social order controlled by the military–industrial complex. For professional paranoiacs like William Burroughs, the compulsion to read chance events as political signs issues from a surrealist hunch that unconscious desires are also what must be coordinating the secret state's systems and fictions. The dispiriting effect, though, of this use of Freud to compel countercultural suspicion is that the secrets intuited by this Cold War form of Dali's paranoiac-critical method must still be contained within the psychodynamic sphere of the individual citizen: the suspicions are still primarily symptoms, not collectively valid readings; fantasies, not evidence.[24]

If Freudian psychoanalysis informs both the establishment intellectuals and the counterculture, it is also found shaping the fantasies of citizens suffering mental disorder in the high Cold War. R.D. Laing treated a young woman convinced she harboured a nuclear weapon in her womb, a fantasy Laing refused to downgrade to mere schizophrenia. Hannah Segal had a patient who imagined Britain as peopled by zombies protected by a ring of nuclear bombs triggered as if by tripwire by any intruder. Another, subject to bouts of self-violence and severe persecution mania, admitted she 'wouldn't mind a nuclear war' as long as 'she and her child would die immediately'; but she was in truth already living psychologically in a post-nuclear-war world of perpetual fallout: 'the diffuse experience of persecution in a large part of the session', Segal explains, 'was like the fall-out'.[25] These Cold War persecutory symptoms reinforce the death-instinctual self-sacrificial narratives embedded in the literary texts I examine, and are a significant feature of the imaginative work done by literary artists during the Cold War. The most celebrated instance of this, Plath's *The Bell Jar*, has been analysed by David Seed in his excellent *Brainwashing* (2004). The clinical setting of Esther's electric shock treatment conjures up the Janus persecutor in the form of the walleyed nurse who places the electrodes on her head: the first treatment is an 'act of technological and institutional violence' on the part of a split enemy carer. Pat Macpherson argues that the nurse is 'disconcertingly double, mother and electrocutioner, relief and torturer, escape and fate'.[26]

The double fabricated by the paranoid victim is a fantasy counterpart, therefore, to the polarized enemies of the Cold War, and also to the covert/overt contradictions of the West. In the Cold War, the Freudian split subject mimics the split political world because the superpowers treat their citizens, under nuclear and ideological compulsion, as infantilized neurotics in need of the authority of their parentally styled injunctions. The forms this Cold War Freudian patriarchal bullying takes rely on the knowledge that citizens have already internalized political forces as versions of the superego in any case, with the state playing the transferential role of split analyst to the citizen analysand. A spectacular confirmation of this was Freud's Wolf-Man, on whom constant psychoanalytic care was lavished during the Cold War. The Wolf-Man, an émigré White Russian, in a Vienna still divided by the early Cold War into zones, wandered into the Russian sector on the anniversary of his sister's suicide. As George Dimock argues, in an article that rewrites Freud's case study as a story about Pankejeff's fusional bond with his sister (accused of being the seducer in the wolf dream analysis) as depicted in a photograph of the two together:

> It is at least plausible to interpret [Pankejeff's] abandonment of Freud's Vienna in favour of the Russian sector as an unconscious defection to the world of his childhood and his bond with his sister. The solidarity expressed in their double portrait finds quasi-suicidal expression within a matrix of cold-war politics. He situates himself between conflicting regimes – analyst versus sister, Western versus Soviet bloc, psychological autonomy versus family history – and seeks punishment in both camps.[27]

The Soviets kept the Wolf-Man in custody for two days before returning him to the West. This story of Pankejeff's impulsive, quasi-suicidal nostalgia, of his transferential identification with the Soviet enemy, of his neurotic mourning for his sister as figure for all the victims of the world, and his adoption of the structural oppositions of the Cold War into his psyche may be taken as emblematic of the fantasy formations this book concentrates on. It can also stand as a symbolic story for the more liminal citizens of the Cold War *The Literary Cold War* is particularly interested in: the Russian-Americans like Ginsberg and Paley, the

White Russian émigrés like Nabokov, the ex-Communist and ex-Trotskyite Cold Warriors like Dos Passos, oddities like the Catholic-Communist agent/ double agent Greene, the CCF liberals turned anti-American by the Vietnam War like McCarthy. These harbour the most extreme forms of bi-fold Cold War fantasies, staged textually as fictions generated by the constant inner war within all citizens of the Cold War security states.

The book stretches from the earliest manifestations of the Cold War, with texts written in the late 1940s exploring the captive cities at the borders of the Eastern Bloc in Cold War Europe, forward to the Vietnam War, the Cold War's longest hot war, in order to examine the proposition that there is an oblique and secret relationship between British ceding of power to the US and the ways the Americans fought that terrible war. Between the Cold War Europe and Vietnam chapters, the book looks at three different episodes: McCarthyite naming and contestation of 1930s radicalism; fantasies and paranoid plotlines generated by the nuclear arms race; and the radiation scare created by the atmospheric tests in the late 1950s and early 1960s. The book's main work will be a weaving together of historical and political material with close literary textual analysis, demonstrating how forcefully and intricately these major literary texts are woven into their specific Cold War cultural contexts. I have chosen authors and texts which either explicitly or implicitly engage with political events and situations in a variety of psychological ways. They have either insider knowledge of Cold War systems (Graham Greene as spy, as political journalist; Nabokov's sense of Russo-American anti-Communism as propaganda through his cousin Nicholas Nabokov, key figure in the CCF), or experience of victim status (Josephine Herbst's grey-listing in the 1950s; Mary McCarthy protesting the Vietnam War with her trip to Hanoi). Their texts engage in a variety of different ways with the same Janus-faced enemy, with comparable sacrificial procedures, at the Cold War-Freudian level of literary paranoia. My book hopes to do justice to these extraordinary texts and the ambition characteristic of their exploration of the Cold War literary imagination.

NOTES

1. Fife's *Courier*, 9 June 2009.
2. Review, *New York Times*, 5 October 1997.
3. DeLillo, *Underworld* (1997), p. 76.
4. Cf. Laville and Wilford, *Freedom's Crusade*.
5. John Schofield headed the MPP after 2000 and built on Colin Dobinson's studies of twentieth-century fortifications for English Heritage. For works written during the Cold War on these complexes, cf. Dewar, *Defence of the Nation*; Laurie, *Beneath the City Streets*; and Spaven, *Fortress Scotland*.
6. Cocroft and Thomas, *Cold War*, p. 1.
7. Cf. Arrowsmith, 'View from Orford Castle', in *On the Brink*, p. 13.
8. Sebald, *The Rings of Saturn*, p. 237. German original first published 1995.
9. Wilson, *A Record of Fear*, pp. 10–11.

10. Mitter and Major, 'East is East and West is West? Towards a Comparative Socio-Cultural History of the Cold War', in Mitter and Major, *Across the Blocs*, p. 3. Cf. Hanimäki and Westad, *The Cold War*.
11. Cf. Bryan C. Taylor, 'Nuclear Pictures and Metapictures', p. 567. Cf. also Derrida, 'No Apocalypse, Not Now'; Richard Klein and Warner, 'Nuclear Coincidence'; Richard Klein, 'The Future of Nuclear Criticism'; Royle, 'Nuclear Piece'.
12. Cf. Arne Axelsson's comprehensive survey of military novels from the 1940s to the 1960s, *Restrained Response* (1990). Cf. also Seed, 'The Debate over Nuclear Refuge' (2003).
13. Borstelmann, *Apartheid's Reluctant Uncle* and *The Cold War and the Color Line*.
14. Smethurst, *The New Red Negro* and the edited collection (with Bill Mullen and James Edward Smethurst) *Left of the Color Line*.
15. Campbell, *War Plan UK*, p. 28.
16. Cf. Hennessy, *The Secret State*, pp. 122–3.
17. Jardini, 'Out of the Blue Yonder'.
18. Cf. also Edwards, *The Closed World* (1997).
19. Cf. Nicholas Nabokov, *Le Cosmopolite*.
20. Le Carré, *Tinker, Tailor, Soldier, Spy*, p. 354.
21. For the IRD in particular, cf. also Defty, *Britain, America and Anti-Communist Propaganda, 1945–1953*.
22. Speech to nation on Vietnam on not seeking re-election, delivered 31 March 1968. The speech is available through the American Rhetoric website. www.american-rhetoric.com/speeches/lbjvietnam.htm, accessed 25 July 2008.
23. Cf. Markus Mueller, interview with René Girard.
24. Cf. Melly, 'Paranoid Modernity and the Diagnostics of Cultural Theory'.
25. Segal, 'On the Clinical Usefulness of the Concept of the Death Instinct', *Psychoanalysis, Literature and War: Papers 1972–95*, p. 16.
26. Quoted in Seed, *Brainwashing*, p. 181.
27. Dimock, 'Anna and the Wolf-Man: Rewriting Freud's Case History', p. 70.

THE SPECIAL RELATIONSHIP AND THE BRITISH HYPOTHESIS:
THE BLACK LAUREL, THE THIRD MAN, COLD WAR VIENNA AND BERLIN

In Storm Jameson's 1947 novel *The Black Laurel*, set in 1945 Berlin, the American philanthropist Scorel is shown busy in the rubble, cellars and internment camps of the ruined city, offering gifts, medicine and hearty work-ethic advice to the tormented survivors. He sees himself as the good doctor for Europe, vast hospital of invalids, acting with a child's egoism and generosity, a bully but a good man.[1] He is viewed by the English in Berlin with a mixture of politeness, respect and derision for his naivety and 'unmisgiving ignorance' (Jameson, *The Black Laurel*, p. 127). The military view of the man is tinged with ill-concealed contempt for the country he represents: 'A nation that lets its chiefs of staff run its foreign policy' (p. 48). Scorel is a minor character in this dense, ambitious novel, yet his status as typical charitable Yank in war-torn Europe ramifies beyond his brief though regular appearances. His doctoring role is keyed in to a network of references to diseased, tortured and dead flesh in the book which trope the city ruins as the flayed 'body of Europe' (p. 35). The collapsed streets have suffered internal trauma within that body, predicated as a form of 'intestinal rupture' (p. 36).

The topography of the city is not only politically zoned between the four powers, but psychogeographically zoned too: the business of international intrigue, crime, conspiracy and expediency takes place on a precarious surface, floors balanced dangerously above empty space and rubble (p. 68). Beneath that surface is the realm of the scarcely surviving Berliners, but also the zone of the unburied dead, releasing the stench of rotting flesh into the everyday air. Jameson registers this 'sickening smell of the unnumbered crowd of buried alive' (p. 327) in four different ways: first, as signifying the destruction of innocent victims which is the main theme of the book, poor slaves subject to the anguish and death inflicted by power and history.

She also develops its meanings to represent the return of repressed memories and histories from the amnesias, lies and repressions of the postwar world. The underground is a 'cave of echoes' (p. 19), a ruined cellar of memories (p. 124), a dark space of anguished voices chattering of the cultures forgotten and destroyed. Out of the stricken earth issue voices seeking a purer darkness and release from 'the hell of memory which in 1945 is Europe' (p. 130). *Angst*, we are told by the German sage Lucius Gerlach, mouthpiece for Jameson's political existentialism, springs from what we have forgotten (p. 224). The 'blind lunar desert' of the modern city (p. 256) is a mere treacherous surface away from the primitive 'sub-soil of anguish' (p. 62), seedbed for the return of repressed story.

The third cluster of meanings for the dead underground of ruined Berlin is more purely existential: it signifies the void underlying the fragile being of the human species. Kalb, the Jewish sacrificial victim of the novel, intuits the void as a 'vacancy' sucking him down into the ruins, a death force of annihilation consuming 'all living men, the dead' (p. 78). The existential void is what the war has taught European minds to understand and feel: the war's absolutes of destruction of all value and tradition have exposed the nothingness underlying all social structures. The Nazi art crook, Leist, relishing the wiping out of 'monuments' and 'structures of the mind' by the German forces in Warsaw, suddenly senses the 'void open[ing] under his feet' (p. 96).[2]

Its fourth set of meanings is the dark inversion of the first three: the sewer smell from the heaps of dust is an infection, contaminating the world with the disease of Nazi fascism still operative in the smashed and defeated city. Seemingly destroyed forever by the bombs of war, the ideology lives on as a viral emanation from the polluted ground. 'The madness breeding in ruined cities' (p. 76) spreads fascist totalitarian violence as an infection of the imagination (p. 54), caught from the ruined cellars and killing chambers of the Third Reich.

Working in parallel to the spatial rhetoric of the city, Jameson's historic sense reads the Berlin cellars as a darkly contradictory Gothic temporal zone. Those who descend into the cellars move back in time to a medieval world, meeting figures emerging from the dark ages of the mind. Candles underground give the Berliners 'the look of a gothic relief cut in wood' (p. 129). Lucius Gerlach is a 'gothic St Francis' in his bombed-out rooms (p. 158). The ruins figure the whole city as a Gothic body, 'nerves exposed and torn, the fractured bones, the nails rotted, decomposing flesh, a death terrible, sordid, poisoned'. Yet why, the English pilot Arnold (who'd bombed Berlin during the war) self-evadingly asks himself, 'regret it more than anyone regrets the Middle Ages?' (p. 35).

The Gothic theme is as twisted as the smell of the dead: it serves at once to trope the Berliners as the 'Gothic' victims of all history – 'the ruins were of any age [. . .] Berlin was inhabited by sleep-walkers, lost in their dream of ruins' (p. 133) – and as the carriers of the Nazi disease, a barbaric medievalism of torture, expediency and violence. The SS in Warsaw are 'gothic purists' (p. 84), the Reich a regime accentuating and releasing the more apocalyptic energies of German medievalizing culture. As Lucius puts it:

> We, Germans, are still tormented by the Middle Ages: with us they were an infection – violence, cruelty, indefensible frontiers, invasions, famine; we carry the mark in our imaginations to this day. Burned in. The cruelty of our fairy-tales, the energy – sensuous at its most intellectual – of our music – safety-valves. But too weak. Our imaginations themselves are infected. (Jameson, *The Black Laurel*, p. 54)

The Second World War had inaugurated a second Middle Ages in Europe, smashing modernity back to a fascist dark age. The new medieval territory is still visible beneath the Berlin streets, sanctuary for starving saints, holy fools, insane warriors and fanatics from the Gothic hinterland of the infected Teutonic imagination, as well as a full compliment of sadists still inflamed by Nazi propaganda, SS sacrificial violence, the evils of genocidal anti-semitism.

The historical and spatial zoning of Berlin come together in Jameson's idea of the postwar subject. The fascist-Gothic imagination seeping from the cellar spaces of Europe is characteristic not only of the city as psychopolitical zone, but of the individual body and mind. Each subject as she roams the streets is possessed by the city's psychogeography, transforming the relations between conscious and unconscious. Kalb as he walks through the stinking ruins falls into a trance; a dark stream flows behind his eyes, a stream full of floating voices (p. 47). Leist stalking through the horrors of wartime Warsaw has a vision of medieval battles and begins to panic, a 'panic of his body as if it were not his own' (p. 98). The underzones of the body are panic-possessed by the political and cultural unconscious beneath the politicized territory of the nation and city. The fascist city's repressions, temptations, anguishes and bad dreams occupy the spaces of the citizen's interiority, infection through indoctrination.

The citizen imagination and body in post-fascist Berlin is in suspension between the indoctrinated body of the war years and the broken mind which dreams of the peace of forgetting. But that state of suspense is itself politicized by the balance of power of the emergent Cold War, and that balance of power, since the powers must establish it within the most troubled area of the early Cold War, wartorn Europe, is likely to be itself infected by the Gothic-somatic miasma still oozing from the ruins. This terrible feedback effect is the real story of the novel, and the huge task of representing the complexity of its angles, scope and effects very nearly breaks the back of Jameson's narrative.

The Gothic symbolic and historical spatialization of Berlin is partly a response, Jameson would argue, to the ways its future was being bargained for in the Cold War's Byzantine zoning of the city. The bargaining going on in the corridors of power, in the military bases, law courts, backrooms and camps, had all to do with political forms of remembering and forgetting. If Nuremberg constituted the legal execution of necessary remembering, then the shady denazification deals taking place across Germany were in many cases acts of expedient forgetting. For Jameson, in Berlin as observer and journalist in 1945, wise with a long experience as president of English PEN and activist for German refugees, the yawning gap between justice and expediency in the Allies' dealings with ex-Nazis bordered on the criminal or criminally naive. The novel was written to advertise her shock, but also to unpick the complex impact of the emergent Cold War on the denazification procedures and the emergent new order heralded by what Churchill christened the special relationship in March 1946.

The novel's plot turns on the sacrifice of a Jewish innocent scapegoat, executed on a trumped-up charge of looting and murder, as a result of the superheated Cold War bargaining going on in the city. The German survivors are being recruited to the Cold War in various ways throughout the novel, and many are actively selling themselves to the new masters. War-maimed ex-soldiers, represented in the book by crippled friends of Rudi Gerlach, try to teach the young English newcomer, Arnold, about the new political landscape of the postwar. Everything is measured in power units, they say; the English, though civilized, are paupers, soon to be crushed between the Americans and the Russians (p. 70). German cruelties may prove of use to the new powers if on the same side (p. 72). The soldiers play on Arnold's guilt over the excessive bombing of Germany, forcing him to relive Hamburg and Dresden, to acknowledge his own role in bombing Berlin. It is a kind of belated propaganda, and acts on Arnold with something of the force of somatic indoctrination: leaving Rudi's flat, he feels strangely restless, an obscure desire for violent action, a desire correlated with knowing intimately 'what [the Germans] were talking about' (p. 75). That knowledge is troped as an animal instinct, fusing the propaganda with his own interiority: 'It had sprung on him in the darkness, but from a hiding-place in himself, as though he housed an animal or a lunatic' (p. 75).

The courting of the British by the Germans in the Cold War re-inscription of the city's Gothic underground is in response to British courting of influential Germans in the very same game. The English venture capitalist Gary is seeking recruits for his quasi-fascistic new order, an 'aristocracy of brains and finance' aiming to control the masses with a propaganda of infantilizing consumerism and fake United Nations rhetoric of peace. He needs a philosopher to dress up the propaganda – so seeks out Lucius Gerlach – and dirty German money for its influence in neutral Europe and the United States – so seeks out the Nazi collaborator steel baron von Rechberg. Lucius Gerlach is put under intense pressure to choose between rival bids – as Germany's leading dissident philosopher, a blend of Tillich and Barth, he is subject to medieval temptation by three men of power. Gary wants him as pet propagandist for a British new world order; Scorel wants him as an American university professor; von Rechberg wants him to go Soviet, as part of a cynical conspiracy to revivify the Third Reich.

The political allegory is strained and melodramatic, partly because Jameson is so patently boosting British influence in Berlin with the sinister figure of Gary. The wishful thinking is there in the dream of Gary's fabulous wealth, when most of the novel is lucid about the UK's pauper status in the late 1940s. The boosting is evident too in the representation of the occupying powers – predominantly British throughout. Jameson is ingenious, however, in her decomposition of the varieties of British efforts in Germany, from the coldly self-seeking West, the self-deluding and over-ambitious power-monger Gary, the stickler for justice and fair play Brett, the self-devouring intelligence officer Renn, the bomber-guilty Arnold. As a composite, these figures come together to form a curiously self-negating complex, as though the desire to do good in the desolate zones of Europe is doomed to failure since interpreted *by the British themselves* as so cynically a symptom of war-sickened illusions about power. The war had exhausted and bankrupted Britain, but more chillingly it had sucked credibility out of all liberal values, turned British minds into sarcastic cynics about world politics, with something of the hard edge of the defeated in their tones and projects. Many of the British in *The Black Laurel* sound eerily like the Germans moaning and scoffing in their broken-down world, cheering themselves up with dreams of old power redeemed.

Jameson looks long and hard at this loser cynicism, sleep-walking *Realpolitik* and angry cold-heartedness in British attitudes, and suggests four sources for it: the costs of the long war, persistence of the military mind's ruthless hard-headedness and pragmatism into the postwar, the shock of the camps and the bomb, the recognition of second-class status in the new Cold War world order.

If Brett is right in thinking Germany to be 'Europe's bad conscience, a mediterranean of monsters' (p. 324), then Berlin in the book is also a rough translation of British bad conscience, its monsters nightmare projections of the creatures generated by the bombed-out dreams of empire. Indeed, it could be said to be working, subliminally in its cave of echoes, as a dark twin to bombed and battered London. Gerlach's temptations are the temptations facing Attlee and his government: act with the Soviets, the US, or invent a crazy anarchist British foreign policy to perpetuate prewar imperial ambitions into the postwar. Lucius' own solution – risk annihilation at the hands of the German pro-Soviets in order to preserve integrity, preaching poverty and penance to the young – stands as a sharp allegory of pauper Britain, having to do penance for the crimes of Dresden and failure to save the European Jews,[3] tempted towards a solitary isolationism, unrecruitable, untouchable, incorruptible, refusing the Cold War's blandishments, doing nothing in the world. Lucius' murder shadows the sacrifice of Kalb to Cold War machinations: Jameson is warning London that glorious little-Englander seclusion could prove fatal in the new era of industrial genocide and atom bomb.[4]

The political allegory of London projected by 1945 Berlin may be only a minor relay effect of the novel's representations – its project is clearly more ambitious, an existential exploration of Europe – yet it serves to explain the soul-searching undergone by most of the British figures in the book. At the heart of that soul-searching is the combined failure of the three good men on the British side, Arnold, Renn and Brett, to act with justice in a Cold War contaminated by the Second World War's Gothic infection. Arnold is haunted by his part in the raids on Germany and mesmerized by Gary's glamour; Brett ruins his chances by speaking truth to power; Renn is corrupted by having worked for too long in the underworld of intelligence. It is Renn above all who provides the key to the Berlin/London code. As a secret agent working for the 'Special Branch' of the 'Political Investigation Division', he has operated in the zone of the political unconscious, in the 'dense shadows behind lives' (p. 38). The effect of the work is to turn the bad conscience of his own nation in on himself. To Brett, Renn's scruples have obliterated his face; he is 'one of your self-devourers', living 'meagrely on his own entrails' (p. 189). As a result of this self-devouring bad conscience, everything seen and heard in the cellars of Europe is incorporated into his own guilty insides.[5] It is with him that we visit the worst places of the postwar, and hear the most unbearable stories, as he searches for his Eurydice, Maria: compacted into his somatic unconscious are the visions and voices of Terezin and Pancrac, the dark centres of *The Black Laurel*, acts of guilty belated witness Jameson had herself undergone.[6]

This terrible knowledge gives Renn a Gothic understanding of the Cold War choices faced by London as a broken political power in Europe. It is he who meets the representative Russian, Kalitin, in the Soviet zone: admiring his energy and freedom, seeing through the easy lies and politicking, he fears the dangerous power he can wield. It is Renn who builds up a dossier on von Rechberg, the extent of his collaboration with the Nazi Reich, the secret links with American finance, his cynical trafficking with the Soviets over East Germany. It is Renn who understands the futile self-aggrandizing ambitions of Gary, how complicit such a covert British move would be with the amnesty whitewashing manoeuvres structuring denazification, how tempted by totalitarian scientism and dictatorship. And it is through Renn's secret agency that the special relationship is held up to judgement.

If Scorel represents the benevolent side to US involvement in Europe, a Marshall-Planning Victor Gollancz of good conscience and preparedness to heal and forgive, then the shady financiers speculating on von Rechberg as necessary ally in the emergent Cold War against the Soviet Union are its dirty secret. They never appear, of course – this as symptom, perhaps, of Jameson's own Cold War liberal discretion.[7] But they do have an advocate: it is Gary. Gary is the voice of atomic power in the world of the book, the promoter of Cold War values *à l'état pur*. For him, the Middle Ages of the Third Reich will be followed by a second Renaissance, with himself as post-atomic messiah preaching peace and Cold War – 'history, power, enough power [. . .] in the hands of men who want peace in the world' (p. 56) – to the ruined postwar of 'human atoms and atomic bombs' (p. 248). His atomic perspective on Europe may superficially distance itself from America as resented ally – he believes German 'self-satisfaction and greedy wish to embrace the world' have infected the United States (p. 113) – but it is clear from his own megalomania that he is the primary channel for just such an infected greedy wish. Renn's understanding of Gary's covert links with ex-Nazis in Berlin is as secretly a knowledge of exactly who Gary really represents: the United States as emergent Cold War superpower infected by Nazi-Gothic political desire. He is an Englishman not merely artificially to boost British power-brokering: it is because it was the British who were most vociferously lobbying for the United States to play its old superpower role in the Cold War.

Gary as coded metonym for the US as British-directed superpower serves to explain the otherwise inexplicable role Scorel plays: his recruitment of Leist, his references to 'my Germans' (p. 317). Scorel's benevolence is too close to Gary's recruitment drive for comfort – the British may be inviting in not only good American money but bad. The fear that the invitation might have a double edge underscores the network of resentful references to the States in the novel: von Rechberg's dream of ending up a rich man in New York, Barbe's desire to emigrate there, the occasional glimpses of the conspicuous consumption of American soldiers, Renn's cynicism about Auden and Isherwood: 'perhaps something new will come out of America. Why not? The rats of culture are already leaving us to go there' (p. 330). Gary/Scorel in Berlin forms a composite portrait of American superpower dreamed up by a poverty-stricken London imagination.

If Scorel/Gary is the United States melodramatized, von Rechberg is a nightmare version of the Cold War politics the UK might be tempted to play. He resents the English for handing over half of his country to the Soviets, so is prepared to rally to the USSR to bully the British into supporting him in his secret deals with American finance (p. 295). To Gary, he is an incompetent Talleyrand, playing off East and West without genius or feeling for Europe (p. 330), a charge which serves to break off their relations. The breakdown of relations has something of a purgative effect, neutralizing the Gary–von Rechberg conspiracy, leaving just Scorel as the good chap doing good work in Europe, a proleptic imagining of the Marshall Plan. What the allegory suggests is that Britain must act to eradicate the expediency of American Cold War denazification in order to preserve the benevolent Roosevelt-liberal projects: in other words, the UK should blow the US cover in order to transform that cover into a practical reality.

The Black Laurel is a fiction about the special relationship as European Gothic, testing out the possibilities of third-force *Realpolitik* for both a US–UK combine, or for an anarchic Anglo-German secret bargain. Both third-force initiatives are infected by Berlin because, Jameson argues, the Cold War's two forces, the USSR and US, are recruiting in their different ways the victimization procedures of Nazi politics. Between the two forces, Britain, with only its own self-devouring, war-bankrupt imagination to play with, must choose a special relationship purged of those procedures. But in the depressed and infected miasma of Berlin, the very act of purgation necessitates a sacrifice, a sacrifice which threatens to bury beneath the streets of Berlin/London the very liberal ideals the purgation was designed to preserve.

Graham Greene recalled his wartime work for the British secret service at Ryder Street in St. James': 'Security was a game we played less against the enemy than against the allies on the upper floor.'[8] The allies in question were the American Office of Strategic Services (OSS), and we can catch a glimpse here of the anti-Americanism which so shaped Greene's postwar career as both writer and Third World journalist. Anti-Americanism is at the same time an occluded and inverted form of Americanism. The Lime personality created by Greene's attitudes is drawn directly from the US metropolis, his instincts for treachery learned on the mean streets of hard-boiled American fictions. The covert admiration for the Yankee gangster as player of the game of security, Al Capone as the new Machiavel, betrays rueful envy towards the new superpower whose dirty tricks on the international scene are tellingly stripped of the camouflage of propagandized convictions.

It is now a matter of public knowledge that *The Third Man* was a project that issued out of Greene's contacts in the covert world of intelligence. His war work for Philby's section V in the Secret Intelligence Service (SIS), or MI6, brought him into contact with producer Alexander Korda and sealed the collaborations with Carol Reed. Peter Wollen has shown how it was Korda's desire for a spy story set in Four-Power-divided Vienna which was the driving force behind *The Third Man*. It was Korda's inside knowledge of the emergent Cold War, through his secret service work in the United States and friendship with William Donovan of the OSS, which is the covert context of the project; and it was the same background which provided Greene with the contacts in Vienna which furnished the plot of the film treatment novella. It was Korda, through Elizabeth Montague, who introduced Greene to the secret agent Hans

Peter Smolka, source of the penicillin racket tale and much else: Greene gave Major Calloway's driver the name Smolka as sly acknowledgement of the covert knowledge driving his script (Peter Wollen, 'Spies and Spivs', p. 142).

The covert background does raise the question, though, as to its subdued anti-Americanism. Greene's novelette and draft script for *The Third Man* are much more pointedly anti-American than the final film product was allowed to be. David Selznick, who was funding the film alongside Alexander Korda, complained about the bias:

> the script is written as though England were the sole occupying power of Vienna, with some Russians vaguely in the distance; with an occasional Frenchman walking around; and with, most important from the stand-point of this criticism, the only American being an occasional soldier who apparently is merely part of the British occupying force [. . .] And just to make matters worse, the American hero, apparently, is completely subject to the orders and instructions of the British authorities.[9]

Greene had already had to concede an important change with his villains: the creepy Tyler, one of Lime's conspirators and 'attached loosely to an American cultural mission', according to the script list of characters, is 'apparently trustwor-thy, with tousled grey hair and kindly long-sighted humanitarian eyes; one would have said a really good American type'.[10] Under pressure from the American backers and Carol Reed, Greene agreed to turn Tyler into the more acceptable Cold War stereotype, the smooth hypocrite from Romania, Popescu.

To answer Selznick's criticism about Holly Martins' subjection to British authority, Greene and Reed rather lamely made him a Canadian, though this does not affect the script in any real way, aside from Martins taking his pass-port to the 'Canadian passport office' in the opening scene. For Greene, Lime was supposed to be an internationalized Englishman, as he and Martins first meet at a British school. In the original Greene–Reed script, Martins muses: 'It seems like yesterday – that school corridor and the cracked bell and all those British children kidding me about my accent' (*The Third Man*, ed. Sinclair, p. 25). This was cut from the film in production, though, perhaps because Reed felt it would be more interesting to raise questions about exactly which country Lime came from. Welles' drawl may be British expat transatlantic or East Coast lazy or maybe somewhere in between like Canada.

In Greene's original novel, written to provide raw material for the first script, Calloway is narrator and both Lime and Martins were Englishmen.[11] The point of the film would have been to set these English types loose onto the treacherous terrain of Cold War Vienna, each subject to different forms of American culture – Martins as purveyor of American pulp fiction, Lime as the hard-boiled double-crossing gangster. Vienna, as James Naremore has pointed out, stands as 'one of the cradles of both modernism and Hitlerian fascism,

[. . .] reduced by the war to a kind of "Greeneland"'.[12] In 1949, it was the most easterly outpost of the Western powers, jutting deep into Soviet satellite territory. It is a terrain which the British know only too well, as instanced by the cool know-how of the head of the team investigating Lime's penicillin racket, Colonel Calloway. In Greene's original, it is American subversive propaganda which is the secret engine running the racket, through Cooler (the original name for Tyler) with his interest in black-market deals and connections with the 'cultural mission'. The racket is a thinly veiled metonym for the dark deals of the Cold War as totalitarian *Realpolitik*: 'A racket', Calloway, the narrator of Greene's novel, says, 'works very like a totalitarian party' (*The Third Man & The Fallen Idol*, p. 87).

The concept was therefore to be a film about the tough choices Britain had to make in the postwar in cooperating with the US. One choice would be to act according to the corrupting, subversive and 'totalitarian' amorality of the secret Cold War. American-sponsored black propaganda seduces the English subject into their post-fascist racket – in the novel, Lime's flat in Vienna was previously owned by a Nazi, and Anna Schmidt is the daughter of a Nazi – playing a hard and loose mimetic game with the totalitarian politics of the equally treacherous Soviets in their zone (Lime's hideout is there). Or the choice would be to act ethically with the British forces (Colonel Calloway in the book) to stamp the racket out. The point of the Lime persona is that he has become Americanized in a postwar where the *noir* racketeer of American prewar pulp fiction has had his head turned by the fascist ruthlessness still operating in post-Nazi Vienna. The English amateur detective-outsider cooperates with the newly wised-up wartime soldier-policeman to police the new Europe subject to Cold War racketeering.

In the final film version, though, both Martins and Lime have to be American to accord with the Hollywood star system. Lime and Martins, in Reed's film, now stand for two ideas of American males: one the clumsy Candide, Joseph Cotten, the innocent, the boyishly idealistic writer of Westerns, someone who really *is* kindly, humanitarian and a really good American type; the other the dangerously amoral charmer and boy-killer, dandy gangster, 'light, amusing, ruthless' (*The Third Man*, ed. Sinclair, p. 7), a rakish Hemingway narcissist.

Lime is therefore still the product of US underground complicity with the 'fascist' remnants of the war, but this time *as* an American. His main cover is his own faked demise, tricked up as the accidental death of a prewar American hero. What really has died is any form of old-fashioned American belief system: Martins' silly love for the prewar Lime is connected with the lowbrow heroics and values of the Westerns he writes. In the crude Cold War dynamics of the first script, Tyler and Lime are prepared to sell off Eastern Europe (in the form of Anna) to the Russians in exchange for the drug cartel business in the new international zones of wartorn Europe. This corrupt deal has to be eliminated by the joint Anglo-American initiative, Martins–Calloway, to clear space for an ethical Europe. The downside of the initiative is that Martins must betray his own alter ego, his friend and his lover's lover, must sacrifice both ideas of the American male, the prewar idealist and cynical *noir* hero, on the altar of the new, clear-headed and pragmatic Anglo-American Cold War. Anna, compound of romantic clichés about Eastern Europe, rejects the Anglo-American move as treacherous and harsh, and is presumably resigned to being absorbed into the ominous Soviet bloc.

The real power in Vienna is figured in Reed's extraordinary shots of the rococo statuary in the bombed city: stony gods looking down on the poor and wasted population, dying or maddened like the children poisoned by Lime's penicillin. Reed had worked from a hint in Greene's original novel: '[Martins] caught sight of the Titans on the Hofburg balancing great globes of snow above their heads' (*The Third Man & The Fallen Idol*, p. 71). These Titanic gods source their power from the underground network underlying the city, figured in the miles of sewers – where Lime, the Cold War subversive, must be tracked down and killed. Their gaze on the population is cruel and superpowerful – it is a gaze Lime adopts on the Prater Wheel, significantly in the Russian zone, a stone's throw away from Kurtz's apartment: 'Would you really feel any pity if one of those dots stopped moving for ever? [. . .] In these days, old man, nobody thinks in terms of human beings. Governments don't, so why should we?' (*The Third Man*, ed. Sinclair, pp. 97–8). The clever, if slightly melodramatic, analogy Greene makes between Lime's resurrection from the grave as ghost and the Catholic subtext is telling. The Titans of the new world order at the meeting point of Soviet and American subversive activity are dark parodies of the Catholic godhead, ruling the metropolis from the air, with power over life, death and resurrection, sourcing their power from the supernatural realm of death beneath the streets.

The Prater viewpoint on the Cold War city is identified with cynical knowledge of the underground machinations of the Titans, knowledge Greene correlates with a toxic nuclear culture. When Martins learns of the racket from Calloway in the novel, his memories of his friendship with Lime are poisoned as by radioactive waste: 'every shared experience was simultaneously tainted, like the soil of an atomised town' (*The Third Man & The Fallen Idol*, p. 89). The nuclear effect is achieved in the film with Robert Krasker's cinematography, a Gothic chiaroscuro conjuring a de Chirico dream of an atomized cityscape, a bombed-out night city swept clean of its population, leaving only predators and victims, their atomic shadows on the walls, spied on by the film crew, with crazy Dutch angles and savage backlighting, as though by insane secret gods of stone.

But it is the underground sewer network which steals the show and makes the film. With the economy of quick genius, Greene had identified the huge Vienna sewers as the scene and trope for the political unconscious of postwar Europe beneath the international zones of the surface streets. There is something potentially superficial about this move – it scripts Lime and his kind as *noir* dirty rats eating away at the social fabric, living off the city's waste products, dragging bodies down to their Plutonian realm. Yet in the specifics of the actual Viennese sewers, the trope gains uncanny power: the rush of waters, the waste-landish scum, the echoey corridors, tunnels, ladders, ramps and vaults specify the site as a modern political Hades, a crypt of voices and secret identities that ramifies deep into the body of the emergent national security state the Cold War was generating at or from its contact zones.[13]

John Le Carré equated the secret services with the unconscious of the nation: the 'secret services are the only real measure of a nation's political health, the only real expression of its subconscious' (*Tinker, Tailor, Soldier, Spy*, p. 354). In the underground world of ruined Vienna, Lime is a corrupt form of double agent whose criminal identity associates him with the Cold War enemies in the Soviet zone: Lavrenti Beria's NKVD (People's Commissariat for Internal Affairs) headquarters was just outside the city at Baden.[14] The penicillin racket is a vicious parody of the nuclear secret poisoning the soil of atomized towns, for it attacks the body as fake cure, a *Pharmakos* fabricated as cover for the real deal. This structurally shadows the ways the shifting alibis exploited by Lime and Cooler–Tyler–Popescu – the relief organization, the cultural mission, alibis which appeal to Martins' sentimental illusions – are 'literary' guises concealing the harsh and ruthlessly trafficked knowledge underground.

The act of concealment is a multiple inversion of the alibi, as though the cover must rhyme according to some strict convention with the crime, and the convention may well abide by the techniques of condensation, displacement and elaboration governing dreamwork, here in the city of the dead exile Freud. Indeed, the three identities of Lime – trickster stone-hearted god on the wheel, ghost on the streets, killer rat underground – map Freud's topics onto the 'espionage' network of the city: the superego as totalitarian *Realpolitik* and high Cold War strategy, the ego as sham cover organization, the id as the counterintelligence networks underground. The relations between the three topics is unreal and stylized, like a film projecting Freud's screen memories, like an elaborate surrealist drama of coincidences, yet the very literariness of the relations is a sign, at least, that elaboration of some kind is at work. It is as though the very fact the wheel–street–sewer connections are so fantastic must imply that something *else* is structuring the contact interactions between the Cold War zones of policy, propaganda and secret operations.

The quiet joke behind the title, *The Third Man*, is that Plato's baffled self-interrogation about the dangers of infinite regress involved in his theory of forms in *Parmenides*, the so-called Third Man Argument (TMA to philosophers – and it was known as the Third Man Argument in Aristotle's day), may have a political analogue in the Cold War world of the new national security states. Socrates is forced by Parmenides to admit that his theory of the ideal forms governing self-identity and predication is locked into an endless cycle of regressive dialectic which must invent ever higher forms and superforms in order to satisfy the conditions by which any quality can be said to be sufficient unto itself. This nightmare regress sketched in the TMA is the fate of any argument about the relation of particulars in the world to the abstract concepts they may participate in simply because every thought must, Parmenides insists, have an analogue beyond itself out there. If the forms must be real and substantial, then the game of likeness and unlikeness must be played and replayed until some unreal limit is reached, a form which is entirely separate from the particulars it governs and yet which rules their appearances with a necessary collectivizing logic.

The TMA is played out in *The Third Man* with the figure of Harry Lime, third man at his own assassination, surviving as ghost form of himself, yet destined to be transcended again by the life-and-death game of dark politics being played on, above and beneath the streets of Vienna. He transcends himself on the Prater wheel, hinting at the higher, more ghostly and insubstantial forms of himself up there in the ether, the Cold War governments who will replace him as superpower superforms. But the nightmare regress has set in, maybe for a thousand years, a Reich of impositions and superimpositions, of endless fake ascriptions, bogus predicates and sham dialectic trumping themselves in cycles of propaganda and counterpropaganda, intelligence and counterintelligence, till the doomsday of nuclear death.

For Greene, the TMA does not issue in an ascent of desire towards ever higher Forms of power, but in a descent or fall into the political unconscious of death. It is within this realm that the relations between abstract superpower politics and citizen-agents become entangled. This death zone is internalized as film dreamwork in a fantasy of regress along the endless tunnels of the city sewer system, tunnels which are facsimiles of the secret passageways of the body, its bloodstream and nerve fibres and intestinal tracts:

> What a strange world unknown to most of us lies under our feet: we live above a cavernous land of waterfalls and rushing rivers, where tides ebb and flow as in the world above. [. . .] The main sewer, half as wide as the Thames, rushes by under a huge arch, fed by tributary streams: these streams have fallen in waterfalls from higher levels and have been purified in their fall, so that only in these side channels is the air foul. The main stream smells sweet and fresh with a faint tang of ozone, and everywhere in the darkness is the sound of falling and rushing water. (*The Third Man & The Fallen Idol*, p. 127)

In the film, the roar of waters is deafening, and into the dark hellish system pour the sewer police in white protective suits, like white antibodies zooming in on an antigen. Reed elaborates on Greene's spectral body zone with the soundtrack: the sewers are full of voices, echoes of German along the channels and tributaries. The echoing language recalls the long passages of pure German elsewhere in the film, a language Martins does not understand. The sewers stage the involvement of the Americans in the city as a nightmare transgression into the post-fascist spaces of Europe, as into the alien territories of a foreign language spoken by the ghosts of evil men of power. The journey through the four-zoned Vienna of the Cold War in Greene's narrative was a fall into the body politic's secret 'strange world'; for Reed it is a psycholinguistic transgression of borders into a crypt of rival tongues and whispering discourses, brute shouts and barked orders, an underground system of secrets and coded knowledge that echoes with the Cold War metropolis' internal dream voices chattering above the roar of the city's waste waters.

But precisely because this is so, precisely because it so successfully dramatizes the censored material of the Cold War as encrypted, as death-entranced, as a rival jabber of tongues, as embodied in ghost forms of predatory energy within each citizen's body, we are invited to translate the film against the grain of its own purposes and elaborations. For, according to Freud, the authority who rules over the tropes of *The Third Man*, if the film is the dream, then its concrete screenings may be manifestations of the suppressed material, but only in a form scrambled by the 'frontier-censorship' operating at the contact zones of psychic levels.[15]

The whole plot of the film comes from Freud: the narrative of a man mourning a dead childhood friend who turns into a bitter enemy whom he must kill is an elaboration of Freud's *non vixit* dream in *The Interpretation of Dreams*. In it Freud meets the *revenant* of a dead colleague P. and a third man, his friend Fleiss, at a café in Vienna: the dead man P., under Freud's gaze and after Freud has uttered the magic words *non vixit*, 'becomes pale and blurred, and his eyes turn a sickly blue – and at last he dissolves'. Freud's interpretation of the dream tells us that the phrase *non vixit* must have come from 'the pedestal of the statue of the Emperor Joseph in the Vienna Hofburg' which has the inscription 'Saluti patriae vixit / non diu sed totus' ('He lived for the security of his country / not for one day but always').[16] He remembers his sour satisfaction at turning the inscription against itself by stressing 'vixit non' together ('he lived not'): 'That fellow has nothing to say in the matter, he is not really alive.' Freud goes on to add that there must be an embedded allusion to *Julius Caesar*: he is acting like Brutus in wishing both to weep for Caesar's love and to slay him for his ambition, for this has the shape and cadence of the dream narrative: 'As my friend P. has deserved well of science, I erect a memorial to him: as he has been guilty of a malicious wish (expressed at the end of the dream), I annihilate him.' Freud had acted Brutus as a boy of fourteen, with a nephew, a year older than he, 'who had come to us from England – and was thus a *revenant*', a boy he both loved and hated. P. is a reincarnation of his nephew John as Caesar.[17]

Later in 'The Dream-Work', Freud returns to the *non vixit* dream, reflects on the presence of the third man, Fleiss, at the scene, and speculates that condensed into the narrative are other memories: of being stared at by his mentor Brücke's annihilating blue eyes, blabbing secrets to two old friends, and anxiety about Fleiss's health. The dreamwork accomplishes a complex splitting and projection of elements to disguise wish fulfilments. For instance, Brücke's gaze is scrambled: 'it leaves the blue eyes to the other man, but it gives me the part of the annihilator' (Freud, *Basic Writings*, p. 450). All this is preamble to the wonderful paragraph about his childhood enmity with his nephew John:

> My present trivial annoyance at the injunction not to divulge secrets draws reinforcement from springs that flow far beneath the surface, and so swells to a stream of hostile impulses towards persons who are in reality dear to me. The source which furnishes the reinforcement is to be found in my childhood. I have already said that my warm friendships as well as my enmities with persons of my own age go back to my childish relations to my nephew, who was a year older than I. In these he had the upper hand, and I early learned how to defend myself, but at times, as the statements of older persons testify, we used to squabble and *accuse* one another. In a certain sense, all my friends are incarnations of this figure; they are all *revenants*. My nephew himself returned when a young man, and then we were like Caesar and Brutus. An intimate friend and a hated enemy have always been indispensable to my emotional life; I have always been so closely approached that friend and enemy have coincided in the same person; but not simultaneously, of course, nor in constant alternation, as was the case in my early childhood. (Freud, *Basic Writings*, p. 451)

Freud's Caesar-*revenant*, the nephew from England, returns split into two other ghosts in his *non vixit* dream, as the dead rival and the threatened friend, both subject to his wish-fulfilling, annihilating gaze. The cycle of incarnations suggests another emotional dream dialectic to rival Plato's TMA, constantly generating substitute forms of the original friend-and-enemy third man.[18]

Freud's dream of lethal rivalry with a childhood enemy is imprinted on *The Third Man* in the choice of location for the murder of Harbin, substitute for the killing of the third man, Lime: Reed and Greene opted for the pavement beneath the statue of the Emperor Franz Josef with its 'vixit / non' inscription. The contradictory compound of memorialization and murder is played out in the two funeral scenes, in the struggle between Martins' love for Lime and Calloway's hatred, and in his dual incarnation in the film as charming, smiling Orson Welles and killer of children, as the spirit of the stone statues of the city and the dead rat in the sewers. He is the *revenant* in the doorway, the concrete manifestation of the intimate friend and hated enemy who must be killed again to enable the cycle of unconscious dream forms to continue to act out their

TMA drama for the Brutus in us all. '*It is dark on the stairs and we cannot make out the face. By now we are prepared to see in all strangers, in all mysterious figures, the possible features of the third man.*'[19]

Furthermore, it is Freud who has created the three levels of Cold War Vienna under frontier-censorship, a space run according to 'the injunction not to divulge secrets', the espionage culture of the emergent national security state. The injunction not only 'draws reinforcement from' but could be said to fabricate the ghostly space beneath our feet or within the body, the underground zone of 'springs that flow far beneath the surface', swelling, under the pressure of Cold War enmities, propaganda and subversion, 'to a stream of hostile impulses towards persons who are in reality dear to me'. The friend-enemy Lime, initially an Americanized Englishman as fascist playboy-gangster, is now a rogue American counterintelligence operative, gargoyle and neo-totalitarian narcissist, he who must be killed to free up space for the impossibly compromised dream of a British-directed Cold War. The TMA regressive dialectic between hostility and friendship typifies the contradictory impulses of the special relationship between the UK and the US, troping with the help of Freud and Vienna the pull either towards a client relationship, with the USSR as common and externalized arch-enemy (Martins and Calloway working together against traitors to the West), or towards a politics of deep resentment at superpower privilege, profoundly suspicious of American policies abroad, secretly wishing for the demise of the US Cold War, in the underground espionage spaces beneath the monuments of old Europe.

Both choices indulge in clichés about America. On the one hand, the client relationship figures the Martins/US as naive, ignorant and idealistic: it must be stripped of its illusions about the political world, especially concerning its so-called friends and allies, and patiently taught how to do the world's policing by Calloway/UK, for the old superpower must needs hand over its secret knowledge to the new master.

On the other, Lime/US is a corrupt and corrupting robber nation, disguising its operations abroad under the cover of universal benevolence, but covertly in league with its Cold War enemy, the Soviet Union, in carving up the secret territories of Europe under their power, prepared to sacrifice the continent and its peoples to nuclear destruction for the sake of their 'interests'. Vienna had suffered a holocaust by bombs that not only served as a reminder of the ferocity of American night-time bombing raids on Europe, but also, proleptically, gave a dreamy sketch view of what European cities might look like after nuclear strike. Only the British, with their experience of imperial world control (infinitely more ethical than the new empires), can hope to stop the nuclear cycle escalating in TMA-like leaps and bounds – by appealing to the surviving cohorts of American liberals, providing them with the knowledge and technology necessary to put a stop to the killing of the next generation of Europe's children.

The secret urge to *annihilate* the rival United States, though, takes the argument a step further into morbid delusional fantasy. The desire may be the real secret in the crypt, streaming with hostile impulses beneath the edifices of the special relationship. At the same time, it is an urge which is being generated by the very superpower it aims to corner along its underground ratlines. For the imaginary sewer-space beneath the Cold War metropolis took on form as a result of the national security state so feared by liberal civilians such as Greene. The secret state beneath the state, transforming *saluti patriae* into national security, also fabricated inside spaces within the citizen imagination, political body zones haunted by the tropes of underground intelligence and counterintelligence networks, covert surveillance technology and the treacherous traffic of alien communication systems between East and West.

The film captures something of the double bind in which Attlee's government found itself with regard to the emergent superpower status of the United States. Greene had hinted at the game of anti-Americanism being played in the corridors of the secret service during the war. That game continued in the late 1940s to near-disastrous effect. John Ranelagh has shown how intense was the rivalry between the American and British security establishments, especially in the run-up to the 1947 National Security Act and the creation of a civilian CIA. William Donovan's OSS had been embarrassingly branded a British agency by Hoover-sponsored critics of the CIA plan in newspaper headlines in 1945. It had been modelled on the British SIS: in its previous incarnation, as the Co-ordinator of Information (COI), the British had actually trained most of the operatives. The Americans had had to work as second in command in most of the joint wartime operations, largely dependent on the British for European operations once Ultra had been cracked,[20] and many feared the OSS had been penetrated by British agents. This was untrue, but behind the scenes, Donovan had been manipulated by the SIS and Special Operations Executive (SOE), notably in 1941, when the British forged a map of Nazi plans for South America and sold it to Donovan as real. The map was crucial propaganda used by Roosevelt to convince American public opinion to repeal the Neutrality Act.[21]

In the context of the immediate postwar, the struggle in America over national security turned on rival perceptions of the USSR. For Roosevelt and Wallace, the British Empire was the real rival, and Russia a more obvious candidate for postwar alliances. Those suspicious of the USSR included Donovan himself, who had known the Cold War would be inevitable from early 1944: he had kept secret copies of Russian codes taken from the Finns, and knew, from the material of his research and analysis people, about Russian plans for Eastern Europe.

When Roosevelt died in April 1945, Truman had to decide which camp to opt for. Initially, he leaned towards a Roosevelt line: 'Gentlemen,' he had said to senators soon after becoming president, 'it is not Soviet communism I fear, but rather British imperialism' (Ranelagh, *The Agency*, p. 122). By 1946, Truman was distancing himself from the position: he sacked Wallace for his outspoken speech in September which had contrasted the British and the Soviets:

> To make Britain the key to our foreign policy would, in my judgement, be the height of folly. Make no mistake about it: the British imperial policy in the Near East alone, combined with Russian retaliation, would lead the United States straight to war [. . .] The real peace treaty we now need is between the United States and Russia. (quoted in Ranelagh, *The Agency*, p. 125)

Wallace's speech was aimed at British anti-Soviet propaganda which he saw unduly influencing Truman's policies in Iran and Turkey. When the Russians failed to withdraw from Iran, breaking the Tehran agreement, the British had sent a brigade to Basra on the Iraq–Iran border and Truman had backed up the threat: the Soviets backed down. The British were also more than supportive of the decision to send a task force to Istanbul to protect the Dardanelles and the north-eastern provinces from Stalin's demands.

It is clear that the Cold War was decided for, crucially, by British warnings about the state of European affairs. The so-called 'British hypothesis' amongst historians argues that it was primarily UK assessments of the dangers faced by Europe which determined the shift of policy towards Cold War containment and Marshall-Plan kinds of investment in the world. Peter J. Taylor, for instance, argues that it was the British government that convinced the United States to get involved in Europe and the Middle East in an effort to resolve the UK's strategic and economic crises in the immediate postwar.[22] The paradox was that Britain, 'in order to stay a first-class power, had to adopt the ways of a second-class one, begging favours in Washington'.[23] In particular, it was Greece and Turkey and the need for aid in countering the Communist incursions which served as a clincher for the vacillating Truman.

In February 1947, the famous two messages from Britain about the countries were delivered to the State Department, and it was Dean Acheson's speech to Congress which most shaped the Truman Doctrine. Acheson was a key supporter of George Kennan's analysis of Soviet plans for expansion, and was powerfully influenced by Churchill's Iron Curtain warnings about the Russian menace.[24] In Acheson's own paraphrase of the speech:

> Like apples in a barrel infected by one rotten one, the corruption of Greece would infect Iran and all to the east. It would also carry infection to Africa through Asia Minor and Egypt, and to Europe through Italy and France, already threatened by the strongest domestic Communist parties in Western Europe. The Soviet Union was playing one of the greatest gambles in history at minimal cost. It did not need to win all the

possibilities. Even one or two offered immense gains. We and we alone were in a position to break up the play. These were the stakes that British withdrawal from the eastern Mediterranean offered to an eager and ruthless opponent. (quoted in Ranelagh, *The Agency*, p. 124)

Intelligence issues were influential in firming up Truman's anti-isolationist resolve: Gouzenko's revelations of the infiltration of Canada in 1945, Elizabeth Bentley's 90-page confession in the same year, British physicist Alan Nunn May's arrest in 1946, information from the Venona transcripts, growing FBI evidence pertaining to Fuchs and the nuclear spies, and the findings of the HUAC committee in April 1947, based partly on the testimonies of Hiss and Chambers, all pointed to an alarming picture of massive Soviet networks within the West. The espionage material not only fostered HUAC anti-Communism, but gave concrete fifth-column form to the metaphor used by Kennan in his 1946 Long Telegram, published as 'The Sources of Soviet Conduct' in a 1947 issue of *Foreign Affairs*: 'Its political action is a fluid stream which moves constantly, wherever it is permitted to move, toward a given goal. Its main concern is to make sure that it has filled every nook and cranny available to it in the basin of world power.'

The spy cases and Kennan's telegram coalesced with Churchill's 'Sinews of Peace' Fulton speech on 5 March 1946 (Truman was on the platform), which had put at the heart of the idea of the Cold War not just the concept of the iron curtain, but, crucially, the idea of the captive capital city within the Soviet sphere:

> From Stettin in the Baltic to Trieste in the Adriatic, an iron curtain has descended across the continent. Behind that line lie all the capitals of the ancient states of central and eastern Europe. Warsaw, Berlin, Prague, Vienna, Budapest, Belgrade, Bucharest and Sofia, all these famous cities and populations around them lie in the Soviet sphere and all are subject in one form or another, not only to Soviet influence but to a very high and increasing measure of control from Moscow.[25]

For Churchill, the only possible resistance to the threat to those cities, and from 'Communist fifth columns', lay in 'the fraternal association of the English-speaking peoples. This means a special relationship between the British Commonwealth and Empire and the United States':

> If the population of the English-speaking Commonwealth be added to that of the United States, with all that such cooperation implies in the air, on the sea, all over the globe, and in science and in industry, and in moral force, there will be no quivering, precarious balance of power to offer its temptation to ambition or adventure. On the contrary there will be an overwhelming assurance of security. (Churchill, 'Sinews of Peace')

It was this powerful vision of the Soviet threat, particularly at the city frontier zones in Europe, and the imagining of a containing counterforce in the form of an Anglo-American Cold War – a special relationship designed to assure *security* rather than balance of power – which shaped the Truman Doctrine, the National Security Act, the Marshall Plan and the creation of the CIA, with its dirty tricks offshoot, the OPC (Office of Policy Coordination) and OSP (Office of Special Operations).

If the idea of Cold War national security issued from overt British prompts, the early formation of security operations was also a joint Anglo-American affair, especially in the area of covert intelligence. For instance, in terms of signals intelligence, the core move into anti-Soviet operations was achieved by agreements coordinating Government Communications Headquarters (GCHQ) and the US Army Security Agency efforts against the common enemy, culminating in the UK–USA Communications Intelligence Agreement (UKUSA), June 1948.[26] At the same time, the spy cases, notably the Alan Nunn May case in 1946, dogged UK–USA relations, especially with regard to nuclear secrets. As Richard Aldrich has argued:

> In February 1946 the United States was rocked by public revelations of Soviet espionage within the wartime allied atomic programme by Alan Nunn May, a British scientist. Fear of inadequate British security, along with ignorance of wartime agreements on co-operation, prompted the United States Congress to pass the McMahon Act 1946, which imposed drastic restrictions upon the exchange of all atomic information with foreign states. This had a severe impact on the exchange of intelligence relating to Soviet strategic developments, the very area which, as we have seen, the British COS [Chief of Staff Committee] had designated the top priority for GCHQ's postwar effort.[27]

The decision by Attlee and his cabinet to develop an independent nuclear deterrent in January 1947 was the direct result of the McMahon Act and the accompanying refusal by the US to supply nuclear weapons to the UK. The British decision to go nuclear became public knowledge in May 1948. The United States thought there had been an intelligence leak and breach of the McMahon Act. As a result, the British were refused access to US testing sites, forcing them to appeal to the Australians and negotiate an agreement to test the British bomb at the Monte Bello Islands off the northwest coast of Australia.[28]

Again, the difficulties underlying the special relationship can be gauged at the secret service level, specifically in the role played by the British Cold War propaganda organization, the Information Research Department. As W. Scott Lucas and C. J. Morris have shown, the department went through three phases between the war and 1949.[29] Before 1948, it saw its mission as producer of defensive propaganda projecting British moral and ideological superiority and of offensive propaganda against the Soviets in areas where they directly threatened British interests (Lucas and Morris, 'A Very British Crusade', p. 86). The second stage envisioned a third-force strategy in 1948, as a result of the situation produced by the McMahon Act and the government's pursuit of an independent nuclear deterrent: 'a new tenet of British foreign policy, the "positive" projection of the "Third Force", a British-led Western European bloc linked to the Empire and the Commonwealth and independent of both the Soviet Union and the USA'. But by 1949, 'Britain had dismissed the viability of the "Third Force" and accepted a long-term commitment to the Atlantic Pact' (Lucas and Morris, 'A Very British Crusade', p. 87).

With these considerations, one can begin to see how canny an allegory *The Third Man* is. The Cold War is launched primarily through the prompts supplied by Calloway/UK's attempts to involve a dangerously naive, isolationist Martins/America in its interpretation of the situation in Europe – as such, *The Third Man* is a film about the special relationship as 'British hypothesis'. The British hypothesis colours the early Cold War as overtly an affair of national security (a Churchillian monumental *saluti patriae*), covertly as a matter of secret communications intelligence aimed at subverting Soviet influence at the border zone cities in Europe (UK/USA and Churchill's iron curtain capital cities; the chatter of secrets in the Viennese sewers). The special relationship in *The Third Man* is also Churchillian in the way it scripts the cooperation between the waning Empire and the emergent superpower as a solid bond of friendship going back years which will be stretched over the new postwar world like a net or web, 'in the air, on the sea, all over the globe, and in science and in industry, and in moral force'. The special relationship between Martins and Lime bears traces of this: they are both in Vienna for propaganda purposes, friends reunited in their gestures of relief to the wartorn world.

But that network conceals dark 'Freudian' enmities underground: the Roosevelt–Wallace fear of the imperial rival finds expression in the Truman administration's mistrust of British security, witnessed by the direct causal relationship between the Nunn May case and the rescinding of exchange of nuclear technology and information written into the McMahon Act. In *The Third Man*, American distrust of the British is articulated through the suspicion and contempt felt by Martins for Calloway. The metonymical relation between the penicillin racket and nuclear secrets is another factor making *The Third Man* a film about the McMahon Act and its consequences for the special relationship. Conversely, the UK conceals deep resentments about the new power: *The Third Man* is as much about the secret 'third force' policy favoured by British propagandists in 1948, playing Europe off against the Americans and Soviets alike, as it is about the inevitable UK/USA NATO collusion (Martins–Calloway) which the British had to accept in 1949. The attempts to contain what Kennan defined as the 'fluid stream' of the common enemy's subversion (the sewers allow Lime to move between the international Inner Stadt and the Soviet zone) turns into the ambiguous 'stream of hostile impulses' aimed at the rival friend's CIA operations.[30] The penicillin racket under these lights becomes the dark side of the Cold War, figuring beneath the Communist corruption and infection in the apple barrel of Acheson's Europe the toxic poison of US nuclear culture. The sewer is a network of ratlines signalling covert UK/USA Comint antagonisms, a site of mutual Anglo-American hostility as the secret of the UK political unconscious. It playfully figures forth as TMA Form of Forms the national security state's illicit 'inner' space beneath the monuments to Churchill's special relationship.

There is a further underground subtext to *The Third Man*: the ghosting of Vienna by that other international city, core of the early Cold War in Europe, Berlin. The film was made during the Berlin airlift (26 June 1948 to 12 May 1949), and its zones are haunted by those more celebrated zones. Berlin had brought the United States and Britain closer than ever before, scene of heroic cooperation in the extraordinary air bridge, supplying 2 million people with a flight every ninety minutes for eleven months.[31] But freedom for West Berlin was bought at a heavy price: specifically, B-29s based on a quasi-permanent basis in East Anglia. Yet as Peter Hennessy has demonstrated, the Americans had been *invited in* by Bevin. Hennessy quotes General Leon Johnson, who led the bombers over: 'never before in history has one first-class Power gone into another without an agreement. We were just told to come over and "we shall be pleased to have you."'[32] The Americans had been staggered by the idea, which had originated from an RAF officer, Air Commodore Waite, backed by General Robertson in Berlin, 'keen to buttress his arguments', Hennessy remarks, 'against Clay's impulse to despatch an armed convoy east down the autobahn' (Hennessy, *Never Again*, p. 354). The only people Bevin consulted were the cabinet's Berlin Committee – the rest of the cabinet learned of it from the newspapers. The B-29s were not nuclear capable, but during the crisis everyone assumed they were. The deployment of nuclear weapons was also understood to be entirely in the hands of the Americans: the British government had ceded all rights to be consulted in January 1948. In return, the British were tacitly allowed a free hand in the development of their own nuclear capability, civil and military.

The important issue here is that it was the UK that invited the bombers onto British soil, just as it was the British government that had had to lobby hard for the Truman administration to assume its Cold War responsibilities. *The Third Man*, a film set in a city dark with the machinations of the Cold War, zoned according to the psychopolitical topography and coordinates of the British hypothesis, is a dream of Berlin as the crisis which saw Calloway/UK inviting the Americans, with the full panoply of their nuclear power, penicillin-toxic *saluti patriae*, into the most private landscape of the UK post-imperial worldview. That invitation is a measure not only of the crucial role played by Britain in initiating and sustaining US Cold War commitments, but also of the new client relationship the United States' nuclear superpower status demanded of the UK. The client relationship was as much a thing of clandestine deals, of top secret UK–USA agreements about classified information – undisclosed, unaccountable, 'underground' bartering of sovereignty and security – as it was a matter of overt haggling for money by the bankrupt nation from the US with its Marshall Plan largesse.

The client relationship also bred a counterforce as secret as those deals, an anti-Americanism of grudge and Brutus-like betrayal, already traceable in the outcry against the siting of the bombers on British soil, but also in the dependency resentment which dreamt of destruction of the friend-enemy with the force of Freud's annihilating gaze, dissolving the ghost returned from over the Atlantic sea with a magical *non vixit* of wishful thinking. Berlin and the siting of the B-29s had been perhaps a *Luftbrucke* too far, and contributed to these third-man contradictions within the structure of the special relationship. In an exchange in the film script that hit the cutting-room floor, Greene had dramatized the third-man fears generated by Berlin after Bevin's invitation, in an exchange between Martins and the plausible American Tyler, soon to metamorphose into Cold War slimebag Popescu:

> TYLER: I guess we all have to get together against the common enemy.
> MARTINS: Who's that, Mr. Tyler? (*The Third Man*, ed. Sinclair, p. 73)

For both Jameson and Greene, the special relationship is haunted by anti-American suspicions that lie deep in the political unconscious of post-imperial Britain. For both, the captive cities in the contact zones of the US and USSR in Europe are battlegrounds for the relationship which, because they still harbour the miasmic after-effects of the Nazi black market of death and vicious sacrifice of victims, tempt the Cold War allies into re-enacting sacrificial rituals aimed at purging the new war of liberal commitments to the weak and powerless. The third-force possibilities open to the UK after the Second World War are reduced by circumstances to inviting the Americans in to the zone and working alongside them. This entails, for Jameson, a choice between Marshall-Plan benevolence and CIA-sponsored dirty war, but the choice itself leads to a complicitous sacrifice of the good Germans like Gerlach, and of the surviving victims of the war such as Kalb. For Greene, the choice lies between a purgative police operation which will rid the special relationship of Nazi-inspired deals and 'nuclear' expediencies.

For Greene/Reed and Jameson, the issue turns on the psychoanalytic-existential unconscious running the special relationship, and both *The Black Laurel* and *The Third Man* are deeply pessimistic about the likely outcome. Between the imaginary two men of the United States and USSR, the third man of independent polity haunts the underground realm of political secrecies, and is shown to be a monstrous false friend who must be killed to preserve even the shreds of the possibility of a working special relationship. In Jameson's novel, between the rival forces of Soviet and American powers, the British improvise a purgative journey through the nightmare of Nazi Europe to attempt to learn the tough and self-humbling lessons of poverty which the Cold War has forced upon a war-bankrupt Empire. But in those underground zones too, the English learn only how complicit they must be in the new vicious and potentially species-destructive politics of sacrifice which is the only mode of warfare the two forces have learned after the bitter struggle with German fascism.

But there is a further analogy which can be drawn between the texts, and this is the way both *The Black Laurel* and *The Third Man*, though so lucid and powerful about the economy of sacrifice running the Cold War as a result of its infection by the Second World War, themselves indulge in versions of those sacrifices which tarnish them, perhaps making them in the process even more exemplary as Cold War documents.

The strain of the Janus-faced predicament before the UK in *The Black Laurel* – soliciting American money and power into Berlin to counter Soviet influence, fearful of the Nazi infection, resentful of the very power and money being solic-ited, playing the Talleyrand game to disengage Cold War justice from Cold War expediency – shows not only in the self-devouring intricacy and melodrama of Jameson's style, but also in the only representation she had to get right but did not. Kalb, the Jewish scapegoat sacrificed to the ex-Nazis, suffers a fate which replays the holocaust: his death by guillotine resembles the executions in Pancrac.[33] It is crucial to Jameson's novel that Kalb is forced to replay this role, since so much of the book turns on the creeping infection of the Cold War by the remnants of Nazi fascism enlisted to the cause. If fascism is recruited by the United States, then US atomic power will trigger a third world war.

Yet Jameson's portrayal of Kalb is itself infected by Nazi anti-Semitism. He is weak, a Kafka insect, a born victim despised by everybody, British included, whose last words are the incredible 'There are no victims!' In an annihilating review of the book for the Jewish review *Commentary* in 1948, Heinz Politzer wrote:

> If his last outcry – 'There are no victims!' – makes any sense at all, it must mean that he replies only with self-hatred to the hostility everybody in this book – and the author herself – seems to feel towards him. [...] Significantly enough, she does not fit her Jew into the pattern offered her by tolerance and enlightenment, pale and dated as that might be. She conjures up, instead, the shadow of the Eternal Jew, that time-honoured nightmare whom she wraps in the threadbare coat of progressive decency. A nightmare it is – and Miss Jameson [sic] behaves in the end like the child who meets a ghost. She runs away from it.[34]

For Politzer, the abject failure to resist anti-semitism – which the novel, in its progressive decency, aims to analyse in the Cold War dynamic – is a failure both of liberalism and of British power in the postwar. Liberalism is under severe strain from the onset of the Cold War:

> Liberalism, as a creative force, has not recovered from the shocks it suffered during the war and its aftermath. The emergence of another totalitarian threat hard on the heels of the vanquished Nazis has deeply shaken its self-confidence. (Politzer, 'The Liberal Novel', p. 95)

British power is tangled up in the history of its marginalization of the Jewish question during the war, and in the history of its own involvement in the Middle East. However unfair this must strike one as being about Storm Jameson, whose efforts for European Jews before and during the war were admirable, and however ignorant it is about British efforts since Balfour to establish a Jewish homeland in Palestine, Politzer's attack does strike home against the particular target, the representation of Kalb in *The Black Laurel*. If the British Cold War were to be the good and active conscience guiding the United States in its new role as anti-Soviet reconstructor of Europe, helping it resist the temptation to recruit ex-Nazis in the struggle, then it was of the utmost moment to demonstrate that the chief Gothic evil infecting the Third Reich, its war against the Jews, could play no part in the new arrangements. *The Black Laurel* drifted too close to the enemy it warned the world about, conjuring Kalb from the nightmare of Europe, revealing the dark underground ideology still at work in even the most progressive of British Cold War liberal consciences. The sacrificial logic of the Cold War's two men of power turns not only the British but Jameson herself, as UK's Third Force of representation, into complicitous bystanders to the expedient killing of the victim, Kalb.

The dynamic of sacrifice which the 'two men' of the Cold War superpowers have inherited, as if by contagion, from the Nazi regime is here at work within Storm Jameson's analysis of the special relationship. Similarly, in Greene and Reed's film, the Gothic attention to the need for a sacrificial victim in forging an ethical Cold War special relationship between a resentful UK and newly all-powerful US not only structures the ways the third man must be killed, but also feeds into the ways the other taboo victim of the encounter of the two forces of the Cold War is represented.

Marc Ferro has shown how Carol Reed turned Greene's initial plans for the film into an uncompromising political allegory, pro-British, anti-Soviet, and critical of the USA. In particular, Ferro argues, Reed insisted on a greater and more complex role for Anna, making her a Czech citizen trying to escape from the Soviets rather than the daughter of a Hungarian Nazi, and changing Greene's craven happy ending.[35] Anna walks contemptuously by the guilty Martins, condemning the new Allied project as vicious betrayal.

Implicit in the final film version is a baffled and difficult questioning of this British dream of the special relationship. If Brutus must kill Caesar to preserve British-style freedoms in the West, then there really is nothing to distinguish Cold War imperial liberals from the totalitarian ruthlessness the new security state was designed to counter. Implicit too in Reed's rewrite is a guilt never to be assuaged in all the years of the Cold War, guilt over the fate of Eastern Europe, bargained away at Yalta and Potsdam. More specifically, the reason for the change of Anna's nationality, Ferro suggests, was to allude to the 1948 Prague coup, which took place during the planning period of the film. Stalin had forced the Czech Third Republic to refuse the American Marshall Plan and encouraged the Czech Communists to purge non-Communists from the security forces, and Benes was finally required to replace protesting non-Communist cabinet ministers with their pro-Soviet counterparts. Lime's aid to Anna becomes an encrypted form of the Marshall Plan in Ferro's allegory – deeply compromised by the alliance with the Soviet Union during the war, and, as John and Sylvia Crane have shown, favouring German industry over Czech to such an extent that the British ambassador reported that the common people 'were blaming the West, particularly the United States, for putting them in a position of having to choose between East and West, and were even talking in terms of a second Munich'.[36]

Anna's contempt for the warped politics of the Calloway–Martins combine reflects secret British fears about the fate of moderates in the Soviet satellites, whose emblem was Masaryk's suicide by defenestration from the Foreign Ministry, 10 March 1948. Martins' gaze from the Vienna window down at the street where Lime once lay dead alludes by twisted guilty inversion to the scene of Masaryk's death in Prague. The guilt is the hard, knotty centre of *The Third Man* because of the sheer incoherence of the political allegory. Anna's attachment to Lime is at the core of the plot, yet it hardly stands examination in abstract political terms. The allegory that had seen a third-man dynamic forcing the UK to mime the sacrificial logic of the Cold War ends up itself consuming Anna as victim of its representations. The allegory falls down at the secret faultline of the British idea of the Cold War: sheer, helpless and delusional fetishizing of the peoples Stalin stole from the West.

NOTES

1. Jameson, *The Black Laurel*, pp. 48, 154, 349. Written between January 1946 and April 1947. There is relatively little criticism on the novel, but I am indebted to the work of Birkett, '"Waiting for the Death Wind"', Lassner, 'A Cry for Life', and Maslen, *Political and Social Issues*.
2. The whole of Berlin is ghosted by the memories of Warsaw – like Warsaw, the city signifies the innocent war dead and existential nothingness: 'the ossuary, the *nothing*, that had been Berlin' (Jameson, *The Black Laurel*, p. 81). Berlin also houses the guilt over Warsaw in more political senses: German fear of the dead

they have buried in the ruins of Warsaw is figured as a hatred rising from the soil (p. 82), a hatred linked to fear of the Russians over the border – both fears have their ghostly complement in Cold War Berlin.

3. And also for the fate of Poland – the Pole Gierymski admonishes the British for living in their comfortable room in the house of Europe while the Poles pay the price in their draughty ante-chamber. He advises them to learn the habit of loss, and to take that habit into their nerves: again the stress on a somatic ingesting of war guilt into the entrails of the British political unconscious (p. 123).

4. The Lucius temptation to resist the dark atomic age with the freedom of 'the medieval wandering scholar' affected Jameson as a novelist too. As she writes in 'The Novelist Today' in 1949: 'The temptations, especially in America, to write for the most glittering rewards ever offered to writers are enormous. Perhaps only the new method needed is to take vows of poverty and simplicity, and refuse bribes. It sounds simple' (Jameson, 'The Novelist Today', p. 574).

5. The entrail motif pops up again – linked to the dispossession of one's own insides by Cold War culpability – when Rudi Gerlach begins to feel guilt for the murder of Lucius; he suffers an attack of Sartrean nausea 'as if his entrails wanted to leave him' (p. 285).

6. She uses direct quotations of whole paragraphs from Renn's experiences at Pancrac and other camps in her autobiography, *Journey from the North*, vol. 2.

7. The discretion is clear from her 1949 article about her visit to the States, 'Why I Can't Write About America'. There she is aware of the unstoppable force of US superpower: 'This country may not want to conquer the world, I thought – probably doesn't – but it will by sheer weight and impetus roll over Europe, unless we can rebuild our broken walls' (Jameson, 'Why I Can't Write About America', p. 381).

8. 'Security in Room 51'.

9. Quoted in Falk, *Travels in Greeneland*, pp. 81–2. Cf. Evans, 'The Third Man (1949): Constructions of the Self', pp. 40–1. The criticism of *The Third Man* that has been most useful for me has been Wollen's 'Spies and Spivs' chapter in his *Paris Hollywood* for the espionage background; Beer's 'The Third Man' and 'Early CIA Reports'; Drazin's *In Search of the Third Man*; Carpenter's '"I Never Knew the Old Vienna"'; Robert Murphy's 'British Cinema and the Cold War'; Adamson's *Graham Greene and the Cinema*; McFarlane's 'The Third Man: Context, Text and Intertextuality'; and Brown's 'Making the Third Man Look Pale'.

10. Graham Greene, *The Third Man*, ed. Sinclair, p. 9.

11. *The Third Man & The Fallen Idol* (1972).

12. Naremore, *More than Night: Film Noir in its Contexts*, p. 77.

13. For an analysis of underground spaces in the Cold War, cf. Lutz, 'Epistemology of the Bunker: The Brainwashed and Other New Subjects of Permanent War'.

14. Policework in the novel and film is a thinly disguised metonym for intelligence activity. In Greene's novel, Calloway informs Martins that 'this kind of police work is very similar to secret service work: you look for a double agent whom you can really control' (*The Third Man & The Fallen Idol*, p. 88). Vienna had long been a hotbed of espionage activities. The Comintern in Vienna had been the organization which first recruited Philby before the war.

15. Freud, *The Interpretation of Dreams*, in *Basic Writings*, p. 539.

16. Freud made a slip in transcribing the inscription: it should read 'publicae' not 'patriae'. The patricide hinted at in the substitution is perhaps too Oedipal for comfort.

17. 'The Dream-Work', section F, in *Basic Writings*, pp. 406–8.

18. For Greene's own schoolboy enemy, Lionel Carter, cf. Sherry, *The Life of Graham Greene*, vol. 2, p. 67. Sherry suggests he pops up as 'T' in 'The Destructors'.

19. Cancelled direction in script, *The Third Man*, ed. Sinclair, p. 72.

20. The British had also been bemused by the lack of security in the American camp. The German spy, Gisevius, had told the Americans their codes had been broken by the Abwehr. 'The British', Ranelagh remarks, 'already knew this (they had also broken the American codes), which was one of the reasons why they were always anxious to protect their communications intelligence sources from the Americans' (Ranelagh, *The Agency*, p. 77).
21. Ranelagh, *The Agency*, footnote pp. 95–6.
22. Peter J. Taylor, *Britain and the Cold War*.
23. Adamthwaite, review of Taylor's book, p. 1036.
24. Churchill's speech on 12 May 1945 was the first time he used the term 'iron curtain', a speech which had been all about European security: 'I am profoundly concerned about the European situation. What will be the position in a year when the British and American armies have melted' (quoted in Ranelagh, *The Agency*, p. 128).
25. The Churchill Centre website, www.winstonchurchill.org, accessed 7 August 2008.
26. Cf. Aid, 'The National Security Agency and the Cold War'.
27. Aldrich, 'Secret Intelligence for a Post-War World', p. 37.
28. Gowing and Arnold, *Independence and Deterrence*; Cain, 'Missiles and Mistrust: US Intelligence Responses to British and Australian Missile Research', p. 6.
29. Lucas and Morris, 'A Very British Crusade'.
30. Marc Ferro argues that Holly Martins is Reed's portrait of a typical gaffe-prone American during the Second World War: 'nervy, naïve, needing guidance, confusing police and military police, "free" world and "Communist" world; as if the police of the former ought not to be bothering with the crime or crimes committed by the Soviets, allies by necessity, with whom it is important to find common ground nevertheless, whilst remaining vigilant, more than the Americans had at Yalta' (my trans., Ferro, 'Un Combat dans le film', p. 180).
31. The record daily delivery was on 16 April 1949, when 1,398 flights by the American and British air forces brought in 12,940 tons. 'The tallies for 321 days of operation were a total of 227,655 passengers flown either in or out of Berlin; 2,323,067 tons of mostly food and coal delivered at a cost of $345 million to Americans, 17 million pounds to the English, and 150 million Deutschmarks to the Germans. There was a greater price, however. Seventy-five American and British lives were lost in the operation' (Glines, 'Operation Vittles').
32. Hennessy, *Never Again*, p. 353.
33. The Pancrac execution chamber with its curtained-off guillotine and kangaroo court judges is also reprised in Lucius' murder – it takes place in a cellar with judges and a curtained-off area where Rudi lurks.
34. Politzer, 'The Liberal Novel'.
35. Ferro, 'Un Combat dans le film', pp. 175–83.
36. John D. Crane and Sylvia Crane, *Czechoslovakia*, p. 297.

2

COLD WAR ON THE 1930s
AND SACRIFICIAL NAMING:
JOHN DOS PASSOS
AND JOSEPHINE HERBST

In his 1946 wartime memoir, *Tour of Duty*, John Dos Passos as war correspondent for *Life Magazine* recalls one of the most extraordinary sights to be seen in the Pacific theatre of war, the floating base at Ulithi:

> As we slow down to approach the entrance to the anchorage, radar grids and gray masts and stacks and turrets bristling with guns rise out of the sea. We begin to make out a line of battleships and beyond them the great barns of aircraft carriers, planes with folded wings crowded close on their decks as bees swarming on a hive. There is a tangle of destroyers hull down far to the south behind ranks of long low tankers. In the broad lanes between whaleboats, bluntnosed landing craft of every size and description, tugs, destroyer escorts, patrol boats, stagger in a chain of white water through choppy seas. It's like steaming into a great port, New York or Liverpool, except there's no land, only a few drowned islets fringed with coconut palms along the reef.[1]

Dos Passos' awe at this mirage of a floating metropolis in the middle of the vast Pacific – he's as staggered as those little boats at the immense chain of ships in their lines and ranks – is tempered by his faint efforts to domesticate the scene with his farmyard allusions to hive and barn. Yet the vision commands his prose, summoning chains of assonance and alliteration along his lines ('grids', 'gray', 'guns'; 'carriers . . . crowded close on their decks'; 'tangle', 'ranks', 'tankers'; 'long low', 'lanes') to mimic the sudden symmetries of this sea-city Pandemonium, rising like a vast and mechanical Venus out of the sea, for it is a beautiful sight to see. From his interviews with the men involved in running this mind-boggling logistical miracle, the Seabees, beachmaster, port director, atoll commander, PR man etc., Dos Passos learns that Ulithi provides refuelling, resupplying anchorage for ships lying *eighteen miles by eight* thick, population over a third of a million men: floating bases are Nimitz's secret weapon, 'a system of supply undreamed of in naval history', key to the defeat of the Japanese (Dos Passos, *Tour of Duty*, p. 114).

Dos Passos overhears a British admiral as staggered as he: '"By Jove", he was saying in awed tones as he cast his eye along the ranks of ships, row on row as far as you could see in every direction. "I've never seen anything like it since the Imperial German Fleet lay at anchor at Scapa Flow"' (p. 113). The remark is pertinent, for Ulithi is incontrovertible evidence that the United States has assumed the imperial power once wielded by the Germans and the British, a godlike capacity to conjure an American metropolis anywhere in the world, Rome built in a day. If the vision of the floating base is so beautiful and troubling to Dos Passos it is only partly because it proves that the imperial role will continue the pioneering spirit of nineteenth-century America, moving 'on west' to adopt the Pacific, then Europe, tomorrow the world. It is also because, obscurely, Ulithi manufactures a mechanical, monstrous-metropolitan and giant bureaucratic substitute for the radical working-class communities many had hoped and worked for in the 1930s before the war in Spain killed the dream. Those dreams had also sought to forge links between the farmyard – the radicalized farming communities in the Midwest – and the international scene – the internationalist 'Lincoln Brigades' of progressive Americans abroad. Ulithi's barns and bees summon up those Depression farms; the weathered and leathery Seabees are recruited from the democratic workers of the Popular Front ('Damn little ranks in the seabees . . . We built every damn thing on this island' (pp. 106–7)), just as the floating base's moving on west into the world of the war establishes American freedom as internationalist, revolutionizing, globally liberating. Ulithi is a vision of the new superpower metropolis as mighty military–industrial Venusberg for the disillusioned left liberal.

Dos Passos remembers Ulithi in his sour and bitter 1949 novel about New Deal Washington and Communist infiltration of the farming lobbies, *The Grand Design*, last of the *District of Columbia* trilogy. In one of the italicized choric interchapters which preludes each section, Dos Passos itemizes the new techniques Americans learnt as they waged this new total war:

> *We learned. There were things we learned to do.*
> *[. . .]*
> *We invented the floating base.*

> *By reorganizing the notion of the bridge of ships; – keep the supply-line dense; an army travels on its transports; – we changed the rules of war.*
>
> *Sea war was the engagement of carrierbased planes. Capital ships hid behind the bulge of the globe. In the Coral Sea the issue was doubtful, but by the time of the great three day battle of Midway Island our torpedo planes and dive bombers were ready to inflict on the Japs a decisive defeat.*[2]

Dos Passos is alive to the comic slippage in his pronouns: the collective American 'we' is at once psychologically passive ('We learned') and active ('We invented') as if the subject position were a fruitful interchange between war's circumstance and military know-how initiative. Yet the 'we' is quickly swamped by the anonymous processes and machines supposedly servicing the collective will. 'Sea war' changes the meaning of the pronoun so that it becomes little more than a genitive-dependent patriotic predicate to war's technology ('our torpedo planes and dive bombers'). Political change in war's context becomes a matter less of collective agency than of 'reorganizing the notion' of the rules governing imperial enterprise, like bees following deep instinctual commands from the hive network. Spliced into Dos Passos' prose are intimations of the giant techno-bureaucracies that now constitute national and international power. Ulithi is the Nineveh of the new arrangements, the notional imperial city reorganized as the movable feast of Cold War ideology.

It is a Cold War city because of the logic of the history of the Second World War. Riding the US army's dense supply-line from Ulithi, Dos Passos in *Tour of Duty* moves on west through the defeat of the Japanese into the heart of liberated Europe, newly divided by the Allied powers. It is in Vienna, carved up like Berlin into rival Allied zones, that Dos Passos glimpses the new Cold War city-frontier that would define the postwar. As a good prodigal politico,[3] he gives credence to the rumours in Vienna that excoriate Soviet deviousness and superpower machinations in the 'great international poker game' of the brand-new Cold War, and links this new revelation to Ulithi:

> whoever thought up the plan of placing the quadripartite governments of Berlin and Vienna in zones ruled by the Russians certainly deserves a red star from the Kremlin. [. . .] In optimistic mood men would tell you that, even if we failed completely in accomplishing whatever we were trying to accomplish in Europe, we would at least have trained some army officers and some civilian officers in the art of international poker, Russian style. It was a game we could learn as well as we had learned to build airfields or to organize supply. If we were to keep our heads up as a nation in the very peculiar world we had inherited from the political defeats of World War Two, we damn well had to learn it. (*Tour of Duty*, pp. 286–7)

Here again Dos Passos muddies the collective pronoun, the 'we' only there passively to learn the game being played by the new arch-enemy, exactly on the lines of the lessons learnt at Ulithi ('to organize supply'). Agency is reduced to the aping of the conspiratorial, shadowy and unnamed experts in the anti-Communist game, those 'men', the 'they' who are themselves merely mimicking the poker-face ludic secrecies of the fictionalized, semi-legendary giants of world power (the 'Big Three', the Kremlin, Hitler, 'the Russians').

It becomes clear in the later chapters of *Tour of Duty* that the invisible structure of relations that is doing the teaching is the shadowy totalitarian regime of the Soviet Union with its unprecedented experiments in massive social engineering. At Nuremberg, Dos Passos is chastened out of his admiration for international justice by an unidentified man from Eastern Europe who accuses the Americans of betraying the new satellite states:

> What have the Nazis done that compares with your handing-over of Poland, your own ally, into the hands of the darkest totalitarian tyranny in history? I need not mention Estonia, Latvia, Lithuania. Perhaps you have not visited Jugoslavia? (*Tour of Duty*, p. 309)

In Berlin, Dos Passos becomes obsessed by news of the Soviet zone, source of the new notions the United States must now learn to reorganize, and begins to fear that Yalta and Potsdam may very well prove to be the Versailles of the Cold War era.

Depressed by the nightmare of Berlin's ruins and the horror of the stories of Soviet atrocities in their zone, Dos Passos moves on west to Paris, returning to the city he had been detained in as a soldier at the end of the First World War. In a curious fantasy sequence, he reflects on his own prodigal politico trajectory, staging an encounter on the Pont des Arts between his present fifty-year-old self and the twenty-five-year-old radical he had been at Versailles (here nominally a *Stars and Stripes* reporter interviewing the grand old man). They squabble over the intentions and realities of the Soviet Union, but the real debate is over the possible afterlife of 1930s revolutionary radicalism. 'Aren't the Russians right in insisting that we stamp out Fascism in Europe?' asks the young Dos Passos:

> 'The only cure for Fascism is liberty. The Englishspeaking peoples at least have developed a system that assures the individual a certain amount of liberty and that carries within it the machinery for peaceable adaptations to change . . . It's one of the ironies of history that you young fellows should be losing faith in it just at the moment when the world needs it most.'
>
> 'Don't forget, sir, that we were products of the Depression. How can we have faith in Congress and the lynching politicians and the greedy monopoly of big business? Better make a clean sweep like the Russians did.'

'The trouble is we would find out as the Russians did that we had made a clean sweep of civilization too. There are no short cuts to democracy. You've just got to go home and work it out little by little.'

'Have you ever thought, sir, what you'd think of yourself? I mean what your old self that was in Paris while they were making the Peace of Versailles would think of your new self that is here writing for the monopoly interests?'

'You mean I'd think I was an old reactionary . . . No, I don't think so . . . I have changed and so have the times. After all, we've got the sample of Communism to look at. In those days the Soviet Union was a dream. Now it's a reality.'

'They don't pretend to have Communism yet. The standard of life there will improve as the effects of the war wear off.'

'How do you know it will? . . . I think you young fellows are the reactionaries . . . You can't build a free society from the Kremlin down. It's got to come up from selfgovernment. The individual man has got to be strong enough socially and economically to stand on his own hindlegs and to talk back to his Government if he has to. No man has ever lived who can be trusted with absolute power.' (*Tour of Duty*, pp. 328–9)

This auto-dialogue stages, bluntly and melodramatically, a mini radio drama of Cold War liberal schizophrenia. Unengagingly populist, slightly hammy and wooden, the two selves perform a creaky allegory of memory and conscience in a postwar Paris shadowed, as if by heavy *noir* Klieg lights, by the Versailles of the past. The comedy of its very awfulness might make a reader mistake the older Dos Passos for a real voice, when the whole point, surely, of the antiphonal exchange is to question the viable unity and integrity of the 'individual man'. If the only hope for Cold War culture lies with the socially and economically strong individual man, then the auto-dialogue presents a voice split down the middle. And if it has to be a man, then why must that man be a hangdog begging for reward from its owner ('to stand on his own hindlegs')? There is a circularity in the question and answer between the younger and older selves, tantamount to self-entanglement, a self-entrancedness that is strangling, as when the younger self refers to himself as 'your old self', his older opposite number as 'your new self'. The confusion is there also in the tiny repetitions, as with 'thought', 'think' in 'Have you ever thought, sir, what you'd think of yourself?' Tweedledum and Tweedledee in the nursery dressing up for (cold) war, tangled up in sheets, in each other, an unfunny Mutt-and-Jeff double act who can't tell themselves apart despite political differences, a bogus Beckettian pseudo-couple playing out the sitcom clichés of generation-gap scrap between pop and son, the two Dos Passos can't quite count to *dos* without seriously knotting the threads.

Slipping through the nets of the clunky comedy, though, is real anxiety about presidential power in the world of the Ulithi metropolis. It is not so much the devious Russians and the Popular Front clones among the deluded younger generation who are the danger to civil liberties in the Cold War world spawned by the two world wars. It is the unlimited power given to the president and the president's men in the awesome struggle to defeat the fascists and counter Stalin: the temptation to slide towards mimetic dictatorship in order to defend the West may prove too great to the incumbent.

The comedy is telling in other ways – if individual citizens are autobiographically split into prewar and postwar selves by the spectacle of absolute power, then what is to stop the individual man elected president from becoming similarly divided between New Deal liberal and Cold War dictator? This fear – that the Ulithi power base necessarily offered the president so that the world can be defended at the 'level of the leaders' is a *de facto* corruption of individual liberties – colours the growling apocalyptic suspicions of *The Grand Design*:

> *War is a time of Caesars.*
>
> *The President of the United States was a man of great personal courage and supreme confidence in his powers of persuasion. He never spared himself a moment, flew to Brazil and Casablanca, Cairo to negotiate at the level of the leaders; at Teheran the triumvirate without asking anybody's leave got to meddling with history; without consulting their constituents, revamped geography, divided up the bloody globe and left the freedoms out.*
>
> *And the American People were supposed to say thank you for the century of the Common Man turned over for relocation behind barbed wire so help him God.*
>
> *We learned. There were things we learned to do but we have not learned, in spite of the Constitution and the Declaration of Independence and the great debates at Richmond and Philadelphia how to put power over the lives of men into the hands of one man and to make him use it wisely.* (*The Grand Design*, pp. 364–5)

Dos Passos's libertarian contempt for the presidential system has a Burroughs-like sarcasm that turns on the new power relations which have redefined 'individual man'. The American concentration camps, euphemistically called relocation centres, now house dissidents from the system, the Common Man of Wallace's New Deal rhetoric. The citizen of the Revolution has been sold down the river by the new man Caesar, war leader Roosevelt, '*an ageing man, an ill man*' who can yet '*play on a man like a violin*' (p. 364), '*a man of great personal courage*' who can run the world without consulting the constituent persons of the electorate, the '*one man*' cancelling out the '*Common Man*' with a stroke of the pen at Teheran.

If the interchapter generic voice sounds grumpy and crabbed, too backwoods *personal*, this might have something to do with the erosion of the grounds of the possibility of the collective common man voice that Dos Passos thought he had mastered in the grand old books of the interwar. And if the individual man is reduced to a propaganda item in power's liberal rhetoric, then this must have had a prehistory in the conversion of the presidential system from the New Deal network managing enlightened domestic policies in the 1930s into the war machine which helped divide the globe. This is the project of *The Grand Design*, to detail the backroom deals which crippled the New Deal, to analyse the foundations of the wartime bureaucracies and power-broking techniques which tempted America to imitate the totalitarian regimes it was up against.

The book's grand design is to hunt out the real culprits of the Cold War in its prewar prehistory, and singles out the way the Popular Front and the alliance with the Soviet Union during the war encouraged Communist conspirators in Washington to become key vectors in the radical cryptologizing of the New Deal administration. Their subterfuge infects the administration, introducing the notion of a secret other war into the ways and means of domestic and international policy. The administration's servants are effectively split in two, their allegiances doubled and divided against themselves by the multiplication of intentions and motivations generated by the fifth column. If every citizen is (in the popular sense) schizophrenic in Cold War America, it is because, *The Grand Design* argues, Soviet spies turned the government into a dual system of public liberalism and secret machination in the corridors of power during the transition from New Deal to the Second World War. The theme is given harsh and unremitting substance in the novel in the allegory of the death of the left liberal conscience: the suicide of Georgia.

Caught in the no man's land between increasingly desperate New Dealers in the administration seeing the fruit of their progressive work being frittered away as the administration gears itself for war, and cynical Communist conspirators playing their secret games, Georgia is driven into anxiety and depression. She is asked by each wing to spy on the other and on her own government in the new double game of treachery. The Communist Jed wants her to steal lists of War Production Board (WPB) agents in South America off Paul Graves' desk, and when she refuses, accuses her of craven political naivety:

> 'Which side are you on anyway, George?' He got to his feet and talked down at her with his hands on the back of the chair. 'We're fightin' two wars in this town. In the shortterm war we're allied to the Squire of the White House and his big business friends but in the longterm war they are our most dangerous enemies.' (*The Grand Design*, p. 346)

Paul Graves himself accuses her of being the source of dangerous leaks of government activities to the Communists, and he talks about a double war too, between the New Dealers and the hardline Realpolitikos in the State Department:

> 'it turns out we've got two wars to fight . . .' Funny, a little voice whispered inside her head, Jed said the same thing. My wasn't Paul being prosy, the little voice jeered . . . 'One war against all our various and assorted enemies and one against Jerry Evans and his allies in the State Department. [. . .] Actually these leaks aren't of any great importance in the real war', his drawling gentle voice went on. 'After all, we are allies . . . . But they can be used with real effect in the Battle of Washington. Jerry's got plenty of good friends in the investigation bureau who would be ready enough to believe as Jerry would tell 'em that Millard's a dangerous visionary who has let himself be taken for a ride by the comrades . . . and after all some of our commie operatives were all too chummy with the Nazis a year or so ago . . . . A very nasty little report could be placed on the President's desk and that would be the end of the New Deal in global strategy and the end of all our efforts to make sense out of our war aims.' (*The Grand Design*, pp. 353–5)

The political thinking is complex: Dos Passos sets the Jed–Paul comparison up in order to double up our interpretation of the already complicated case Paul is making. Paul asserts that the New Deal is a hostage to dark forces in the White House that can exploit the links of its left wing to the Communist party activists in Washington. The very existence of those links (e.g. Georgia's relations with Jed) could be interpreted as political espionage in order to scupper the New Dealer's hopes for progressive reform of foreign policy. The little voice in Georgia's head, though, articulates the comparison with Jed's own 'Russki' politics of subterfuge – defined by Paul as 'espionage and counter-espionage and countercounter espionage ad infinitum' (p. 354) – and another interpretation unfolds: that the Battle of Washington between right and left is calqued on the Communist party's system of bi-fold subversive politics – the war against fascism and for progressive common man policies becomes a mere propaganda front concealing the real civil war at home, inaugurating the home front Cold War. The espionage system breeds a politics of concealment, isolating the president within a paranoid White House which no longer holds true to its public policy statements, and as a consequence leaving the incumbent prey to all the Ulithi-metropolitan temptations of secret dictatorial power. Stalin's secret services and Communist infiltration techniques are the real mimetic source of political hypocrisy as power management, secret activism or politics as 'schizophrenic' secrecy, the cryptic energy running the Ulithi supply-line of superpower.

Georgia is the left liberal scapegoat victim of the dirty double war, powerless in the nightmare middle ground between Jed and Paul, between Communist espionage and accusation of Communist espionage. The two players police her into submission with disciplinary authority: Jed talks *down at* her from behind, holding the back of her chair as if to compel her to sit on the left side of the fence, but also to become pure voice in her head, to replace her own inner voice with the hush-hush voice of conspiracy, like some paranoid-political version of a bullying analyst.

Paul plays on their sexual history together to manipulate her responses – the interview takes place in the all-American, infantilizing space of the drugstore. Paul talks to her in familiar old ways, as expert to woman of experience 'in the same low quick voice', yet the body language is crudely sexual: he looks her full in the eyes, acting the adolescent teenager: 'opposite her Paul wound his long legs around the legs of the chair and teetered back and forth on it as he talked' (p. 353). It is an exercise in New Dealy propaganda, sincere, authentic, all-American, wide open, passionate, gauche and adolescent: yet what the voice does is to accuse her not only of being a spy for the Russians, but of scuppering the whole New Deal *because* of the very same sexual naivety Paul is at such pains to arouse in her. The technique is effective in so far as it reduces Georgia to tears, turning her into the weak emotional creature Paul now secretly thinks she is or desires her to be, and this despite Paul's progressive egalitarianism, all his gushing flattery of her ('I trust your judgement' etc.). Just as Communist conspiracy opens up a gulf between stated policy and secret power, so does Jed's courting of Georgia as sexual pawn tempt Paul to indulge in secret misogyny whilst spouting the catchwords of the feminist new man.

Forced to occupy the treacherous subject position of sexual pawn in the double game, Georgia retreats into a suicidal self-watchfulness, a psychic division that mimics the double-crossed secret civil war in the city: 'it was like the iron maiden. Outside there was a metal shell that went on with automaton gestures [. . .] while inside the crushed ruins of herself screamed out in agony' (p. 349). Even her own internal voice, 'the narrator inside her head' (p. 50), seems no longer her own after Jed's brainwashing techniques: it is merely 'a little voice', mouthpiece of her own shrunken and annexed subjectivity.

Agreeing to a sailing trip with Jed down the Potomac, Georgia goes through the hellish motions towards her own self-destruction. They sail down river on the rickety little cruiser, the *Niña*, from Alexandria, past Mount Vernon, cross over to a creek on the Maryland shore where they drop anchor for the night, but Georgia steals away in a tender, takes pills, rows into the heart of the channel and slips herself into the water. The whole episode is narrated soberly and dreamily by Dos Passos, contrasting Jed's patronizing, joshing, self-involved patter with her death-wish trance. It is the topography of the suicide which shifts the narrative into allegory, which Dos Passos alerts us to with Georgia's reminiscence of sailing on Lake Erie with her father reading 'passages from the Odyssey' and her memories of her younger self dreaming of liquid death: 'that sensation of being all transparent, the itchy thwarting of clothes and commands and hurt feelings melting away till she was clear as the lake, slicing through the bright world cool and clear as the lake water, swelling with the sunset to the immense stillness of the lake and the sky' (p. 358). Part allusion to Chopin's *The Awakening*, part establishing of Georgia as scion of an old and ancient liberal tradition (her father's attachment to nineteenth-century liberalism is noted, connected to his learning in the classics and knowledge of Europe), the allegorizing of the lake as death also hints at another set of parallels.

The suicide in the Potomac is carefully concerted so as to allude, *sotto voce*, as if in secret, to George Washington. Starting from Alexandria with its Washington connections, they sail down the 'Nation's River', the Potomac, surveyed by Washington for the choice of the capital city, past the Parkway, which must be the George Washington Parkway, past Mount Vernon, the family estate. To die in the Potomac within view of the Mount is to die within sight of the first president's presiding genius.[4] Or rather, it is to die *as* the spirit of Washington. Georgia is referred to as George throughout the novel. Her surname, Washburn, conjures up and cancels 'Washington' with (red?) fire. Her childhood in the north-west was the scene of Washington's surveying career, which included schemes for Lake Erie. Her father, nicknamed Père, resembles a latterday Pierre l'Enfant, designer of Washington. Living in Alexandria makes the identification uncomfortably close. Visiting Communists hate Georgia for it: Alexandria makes Jane Sparling's flesh creep:

> 'It was George Washington's home town, wasn't it?' Joe asked vaguely.
> 'George Washington was the first American Fascist', Jane came back at him in her most scornful tone. (*The Grand Design*, p. 254)

The journey from Alexandria past Mount Vernon to transparency and death rewinds Washington's life story, dismantling the accumulated inheritance of all the presidents since, an allegory of the suicide of 'social-fascist' Washington as (s)he slips off the ship of state now run secretly by the Communists. Washington the city of the New Deal commits suicide too, as George disappears beneath the waves, the Battle of Washington lost as the last lonely progressive passes away.

If it is the ideals of the Revolution which drown during the Second World War for Dos Passos, these include the ideals of revolutionary city, liberal presidency and progressive democracy which all sink beneath the river of the nation in the name of George. The spirit of George Washington, feminized and brainwashed by the hard left in the gangster plots and schemes of the 1930s, darkened in mind and spirit by the terrorism in international politics, enslaved by the civil war in the White House conspiracies, enters the cold waters of the Cold War to die.

On 3 June 1952, Dos Passos received a visit from two FBI special agents investigating 'Security Matter-C', an obscure matter related to a possible Communist cell in Shanghai. The visit was not designed to trap Dos Passos since the Bureau were fairly certain of his anti-Communist credentials – they were rather concerned to interview 'the subject regarding his Communist Party, Communist front and Trotskyite activities' before the war.[5] It was, then, a fact-finding mission. Dos Passos, as Ray Lewis White has shown, was more than happy to spill the beans about acquaintances involved in the Sacco-Vanzetti case, *New Masses*, the Harlan, Kentucky mine strike, the Group Theater, various front organizations such as the American Committee for Relief of Russian Children, the movie projects in the Spanish Civil War, the American Friends of Spanish Democracy, the Robles assassination, the Abraham Lincoln Brigade, the campaigning for Trotsky in Mexico and the John Dewey Committee, the civil rights work for the American Civil Liberties Union, and his trip to the Soviet Union in 1929. The interview in its transcript form is a tedious and farcical sheep-and-goats division of his large acquaintance. Apart from the organizations themselves, the specific naming strategy adopted by Dos Passos clears roughly thirteen individuals of Communist affiliations and accuses thirteen, in a clear and vicious example of 'even-handedness' with this unluckiest of odd numbers. A handful escape the procedure because Dos Passos cannot recall them. Some are merely incidentally smeared – he recalls meeting radical journalist and writer Anna Louise Strong in Russia and describes her as 'a stupid woman'.[6] One person however is named, cleared of Communist party membership, yet accused at the same time. In connection to Communist activities in the Spanish Civil War, '[Dos Passos] recalled also seeing Josephine Herbst in Spain and he believed that she was not a Communist but was greatly sympathetic to their cause' (White, 'John Dos Passos and the Federal Bureau of Investigation', p. 107): coded euphemism for 'fellow-traveller'.

Elinor Langer, in her fine biography of Herbst, though unaware of Ray Lewis White's findings, does give some indication of the reasons Dos Passos may have shopped Herbst. During the Spanish Civil War, in the Spring of 1937, Herbst, it seems, was told that the Communists had killed Robles by a ministry official who had vowed her to secrecy – she kept the news from Dos Passos whilst he sought for information about his friend in Madrid. She eventually told Hemingway, who seems the real source of her keeping quiet – he thought any enquiries after Robles might attract dangerous attention and wreck the chances of the film project *The Spanish Earth*.

> Agreeing with Hemingway that Dos Passos' inquiries were breeding suspicions, yet reluctant to break her promise to her informant, she contrived a story with Hem by which Dos Passos could be told indirectly. At a luncheon that day to which all three were invited Hemingway told Dos Passos that he had learned from a German correspondent whom he could not name that Robles was dead, that Josie had been told, and that

more than that they were not free to say. Watching Dos Passos across the table Josie knew from his expression that he had been told, and when afterward he approached her 'with a little coffee cup in hand . . . and in an agitated voice asked why it was that he couldn't meet the man who had conveyed the news, why couldn't he speak to him, too?', she could think of little to say.[7]

The source of Dos Passos' naming strategy is concealed in the excruciating agonies of the Robles affair, the secret contrived story about a contrived source 'whom [Hemingway] could not name' masking an unnameable and powerful secret informant, the fiction twisted round the telling of names and conspiratorial gagging of freedom to name, tell, say, speak ('that Josie had been told, and that more than that they were not free to say'). The triad John–Josie–Hem is an eerie anticipation of the Paul–Georgia–Jed triangle: in both cases, the woman is torn between fellow-travelling duplicity and the dangerous responsibilities demanded by liberal ethics. The triangle in *The Grand Design* is designed to replay the duplicities and ruthless fictions Dos Passos had suffered in 1937 Madrid, but this time with a vengeance. This time, Josie/Georgia gets it in the neck, sacrificed to the greater good of the nation she had betrayed with her sympathies, punished also for *failing* fully to betray with her seductions. The casual naming of Josephine Herbst to the FBI is venomous because it uses her inevitably double-dealing position between two powers (Hem and Dos Passos in Madrid, Communists and liberals in the 1930s) to accuse her in the Cold War ('not a Communist but . . . greatly sympathetic to their cause'). Dos Passos had geared himself up for this betrayal of her treacherously middling role with *The Grand Design*'s melodramatic allegorizing of the ominously named Georgia Washburn's suicide, as though preparing the victim for sacrifice. The plangent metonymical transformation of Josephine Herbst into trope for the self-betraying, gullible progressives in New Deal Washington is at once an exculpatory tactic which will justify Dos Passos' stance in the Cold War, and a form of preparatory manoeuvre initiating the FBI naming strategy.[8]

Nowhere is the fictionalizing of Herbst more devious than in the scripting of Georgia's subjectivity as self-destructive and suicidally depressed. The politicizing seduces her into welcoming her own death by casting a pall over her somatic and psychic interiority: 'the bitter misery that was spreading through her mind and body the way ink spreads through water' (*The Grand Design*, p. 261). The ink Dos Passos spills in writing Georgia into the role of Washingtonian self-sacrificial victim stains the textual waters of her insides, scripting their transformation into the dark waters in which she must die. She must die, says the text as the ink spreads, because her interiority recognizes that she must: the 'bitter misery' is, after all, *hers*. Dos Passos' identification of Georgia with the city of Washington is not merely a textual matter, however. It works, by insinuation, because the real named victim of the FBI interview, Josephine Herbst, was so embroiled in the Communist infiltration of 1930s Washington.

Her partner John Herrmann worked for the Hal Ware group in 1934, involved in farm research for the New Deal's agricultural policies. Herbst was also engaged, accompanying economist and journalist Webster Powell in a tour of farms in Iowa, Nebraska, and North and South Dakota in 1934, research which Dos Passos fictionalizes in *The Grand Design* in 'The Working Farmer' episode where Georgia and Paul visit farms in the Midwest. Ware was also working as a Communist information-gatherer, and Herrmann helped him in this, in particular acting as courier, shuttling documents between Communist Party of the United States of America (CPUSA) officials in Washington and New York – Langer surmises this must have been predominantly information 'about the administration's agricultural program that could be used politically by the Communist Party' (Langer, *Josephine Herbst*, p. 173). Herbst found the secrecy and hugger-mugger antics of the men involved faintly risible:

> Sometimes when she was in the apartment the telephone would ring or a visitor would come and John would ask her, in a voice thick with innuendo, to leave: other times she was permitted to remain: but either way: staying or leaving: she was close enough to whatever transactions were taking place to witness what she regarded as a lot of self-important revolutionary hocus-pocus and she was irritated by it in the extreme. (Langer, *Josephine Herbst*, p. 173)

The self-important and empty innuendo of Langer's obsessive colons is witty, as though each little phrase were heavy with hocus-pocus implicatures and unspoken connections. Nevertheless, the wit cannot disguise how damning all this would appear to future Cold War prying eyes, especially when one of the more self-important revolutionaries met with at this time in 1934 was the mysterious 'Karl', none other than Whittaker Chambers.

In 1949, Herbst was interviewed twice by the FBI for details about 'Karl' as part of the investigations for the Hiss trial. She was also interviewed by Hiss' lawyers as a possible witness, but she annoyed them with her blanket condemnation of the trial – there was nothing illegal about being a revolutionary. They reported her as saying 'revolutions had been going on for hundreds of years and referred to a volume of Lamartine, "Revolution of the Girondistes", which she was then reading. She indicated that the trouble with us was that we did not understand history' (Langer, *Josephine Herbst*, p. 302). Chambers talked about Herrmann and Herbst to the FBI in 1949, testifying in private that he'd photographed secret documents in their Washington apartment, that he and Hiss had been invited to Herbst's Erwinna farm, and that both Herbst and Herrmann had been members of the CPUSA, though Herbst had recently defected, making her a potentially valuable witness for the prosecution. In the second interview with the Bureau in November 1949, Herbst had to deny these allegations:

> JOSEPHINE FREY HERBST interviewed at Erwinna, Pennsylvania. [. . .] She stated no photographic work done by CHAMBERS when she was present in Washington apartment. She advised she has never met ALGER or PRISCILLA HISS. She stated it was impossible for HISS to have been at her Erwinna home around Easter, 1934 or 1935. She advised she was very sympathetic to Communism from 1932 to 1934. (quoted in Langer, *Josephine Herbst*, p. 304)

Herrmann and Herbst had separated in 1934 and lived separate lives. Herrmann had had to leave the US at the beginning of the Hiss investigations, and lived the rest of his life with his new partner, till his death by heart attack in 1959, in Mexico, one of many Cold War progressive exiles there. Anxious to protect him, appalled by Hiss' special pleading, yet concealing what she knew of Hiss and Chambers, Herbst's attitude during the Hiss investigations is at once defiant and necessarily sly. As Langer puts it:

> As the case continued to dominate and somehow even to symbolize the war of the 1950s against the 1930s she stood outside of it, critical of Hiss for his excessive denials of commitments which she believed ought to have been affirmed, sympathetic to Chambers if only because of the extraordinary vilification heaped upon him by others, contemptuous of the lawyers for their soulless re-creation of events that had so little to do with their reality. Yet she never revealed what she knew. 'I think the Hiss case was handled wrongly; he should have been more frank, as indeed I suggested to his lawyers all along', she hinted to her friend Clair Laning immediately after the first trial, in one of the few comments about it she ever seems to have permitted herself. 'He should have boldly admitted to certain ideas now termed subversive but which were only honestly enlightened and leftish in the '30s. Instead he took too pure a stand, denied too much, admitted nothing. A jury isn't made up of lawyers, who in my opinion are verbal fools, they sense the truth [. . .]. You suspect a man who denies everything and is a pinnacle of proper conduct [. . .]. Admitting small things would have validated major denials. Any novelist could have told them that.' (Langer, *Josephine Herbst*, pp. 305–6)

What to make of the fact that it was a novelist, Dos Passos, who was writing and publishing a fictionalized version of her 1930s progressive collusion with the CPUSA in the very same year?[9] The fiction not only prepares Herbst for future sacrifice in the FBI interview in 1952, but slots into a dangerous conspiracy of novelists against novelists since the war, since 1943 when Herbst had been investigated by the FBI over her trips to the Soviet Union and forced to abandon her work for the war propaganda agency in Washington following Katherine Anne Porter's secret denunciation of Herbst to the Bureau in 1942, outlined at length in Langer's biography.

The war of the 1950s against the 1930s has its origins in the reinterpretation of the New Deal that took place as a result of the Spanish Civil War and the Nazi–Soviet Pact during the Second World War. As Herbst wrote in a letter in 1957 to Edgar Branch about James Farrell and the thirties:

> The period of the thirties has been a good deal maligned. [. . .] The thirties actually might have developed into something far better if the Nazi–Soviet pact, the war and the cold war had not evolved. These events ushered in the Southern School and the trend towards personalism and the neurotic hero.[10]

There is direct causal link, in other words, between the withdrawal from politics brought on by the Cold War and the dominance of New Critical psychologism and libertarian individualism.[11] The shift to the right, towards Freud, towards neurosis and personalism, and into apolitical small questions had been spearheaded by the New York intellectuals at the *Partisan Review* as a direct consequence of their dialectical movement from anti-Stalinist to non-Communist to anti-political stances. The knock-on effect on the literary writing championed at the *Review* was the gradual disengagement of text from radical politics, a soft Freudianizing of modernist aesthetics, and a New Critical atomistic view of the artist. As we can see from Dos Passos' writing, the concept of the political novel changes form too: in the Cold War, it becomes a fantasy screen for the projection of the paranoid drama of informants, anti-Communist accusations and counteraccusations that constituted the public sphere after the Dies Committee (later HUAC) had begun the hunt for Communists in 1938. The literary text becomes an Alice-in-Wonderland Hiss case, complete with judge, jury, accused and accusers, an *ad hoc* HUAC investigation re-imagining and re-inscribing the secret stories of prewar history, a textual field where the naming strategies forced upon recanting left liberals and ex-Progressives re-emerge transformed and distorted as sacrificial *romans à clef*.

In her own quiet way, Herbst attempted to resist Dos Passos' representation of her in *The Grand Design*. If the lawyers defending Hiss were compromised as verbal fools who misunderstood history, then *The Grand Design* could equally be attacked as verbal trickery misconstruing history for the sake of a good Cold War story. If Dos Passos' novel returns to the 1930s to condemn the surviving progressives of the late 1940s in an orgy of sacrifice of their 'honestly enlightened and leftish' ideas on the altar of Cold War subversion, then Herbst would trump that card. In 1954, two years after Dos Passos talked to the FBI, Herbst published her odd little book about the eighteenth-century botanists John and William Bartram, *New Green World*. Its account of their

Enlightenment faith in the joy of the natural world, its advocacy of their sturdy communal ethic of work and the inquiring individual, seems at first reading the last place one would go for a *Crucible*-like denunciation of Cold War witch-hunts. Though written in a kind of environmentalist code, it is nevertheless clear about its 1950s intentions: a defence of the youthful idealism of the New Deal's agricultural-utopian progressive project, a history lesson which relates that project to the ideals of the American Revolution. Recalling the writing of the book in 1965, Herbst wrote: '*New Green World* was written as a kind of rescue work for myself, for it was during the McCarthy period, when I felt so sunk, that I decided to recall the intransigent Bartrams and their group of wonder-seekers' (quoted in Langer, *Josephine Herbst*, p. 317). The Bartrams represent a liberated and progressive international community, dream of the 1930s and of the early *Partisan Review* – a synopsis of the novel in her archive reads: 'In this curious free society of banned men a great interplay of communicated ideas and a lively correspondence broke down national barriers and set up an international kingdom of the spirit.'[12] If Dos Passos had quite literally 'sunk' her fictional image in the waters of the Potomac, then the Bartrams might counter his McCarthyite allegory.

Herbst uses as epigraph to the text a quotation from a poem by Jean Garrigue, her lover in the 1950s, to identify the botanists' story with the Edenic faith of 1930s Erwinna: 'It was all in the shades of the vines and meadows / Where Adam delves, in the green fables / Of the dogdays, in early youth.' The choice of subject is determined by the location of Erwinna:

> John Bartram, Eighteenth Century botanist and explorer of the wilderness, lived his long, good life in the State of Pennsylvania, some thirty-five miles from the place where I now live.[13]

The 'green fables' of pre-revolutionary America are the fables underwriting Progressive Era and Cold War Erwinna as farmhouse and writerly retreat, fables which depend on an organic theory of the subject long since blasted by the forces of modernity:

> The little coterie of men who devoted their lives to what was then known as natural history, for it included stones and turtles as well as trees and flowers, were whole men confronting a whole world, not human beings floating in a culture medium. When a man said 'I' he meant exactly 'I', not an ego or a super-ego lost in a soup of determinants. The mistake about the 'I' only came later when by saying 'I' one meant nothing but one's fragmented self alone in a world divided into pieces, abstract and aloof. (*New Green World*, p. 2)

The members of the little coterie of Erwinna in the 1930s had also been intransigent in their devotion to the green world of human rights,[14] as passionate in their explorations of the unknown world as the Bartrams, Herbst travelling to the hinterlands of Cuba, Russia, Spain and Germany in search of the rare species of embattled workers' democracies and resistance. The translation of those species into the neutral, Disneyfied forms of 'stones and turtles as well as trees and flowers' is a measure of the censorship that pertained in McCarthy's USA.

Equally the defence of the unified eighteenth-century self against the predation of pseudo-Freudian modernity subtly parries and parodies the libertarian individualism and Enlightenment-Romantic pessimistic psychologism being used by Dos Passos and the right to sink progressive history. The utopian naivety of the Edenic Erwinna synthesized from the Bartrams' story is strategic, in other words, anticipating R.W.B. Lewis' use of the Edenic in his 1955 *The American Adam* to critique the hard-headed 'new hopelessness' and vulgar Freudianism of the Cold War liberals.[15] Herbst was keen to provide her own cipher for decoding *New Green World*. In 1956, after the worst of McCarthyism was over, she wrote a brief but pungent piece for the *Nation*, 'The Ruins of Memory', extremely useful for translating *New Green World* back into the language of the Cold War. The Bartram natural-historical working self as opposed to the idea of 'human beings floating in a culture medium' is revealed as covertly contemporary:

> If past history is any guide, the present phase that tends to the compulsive presentation of people as isolated moral atoms without any sensible relation to society or the ideas of their time ought to have departed before this. For literary epochs come and go but this wave seems to have frozen in the cold war.[16]

New Critical ahistoricism, in other words, has been frozen fast by the ideological forces of the Cold War, masking its patently anti-radical agenda, its cult of the atomized author/reader. Past history has to be used as a guide to unthaw the wave of literary change: *New Green World* had been just such an exercise in past history.

The identification of the Bartrams with a rival tradition of free thought is hinted at in the brief but telling narrative of John Bartram's investigation by a local Quaker committee for heresy. Bartram had denied Christ's divinity and the Darby committee was appointed 'to treat with him on account of his said unbelief' (*New Green World*, p. 12). For fifteen months, Bartram was plagued by visits from the committee, remonstrating with him, threatening disownment. Bartram simply refused to bargain with them, acting as if nothing had happened, taking his seat at the meeting house regardless. 'In his eyes', writes Herbst, 'the action of the Quaker brethren could only be discreditable and childish':

> He would pay no more attention to it than he would the antics of a mischievous infant. His well known sentiments were emphasized for all

visitors to see in 1770 when he affixed over his study window a stone slab with the words cut deep into the rock:

> It is God alone, Almyty Lord,
> The Holy One by Me Ador'd
> John Bartram 1770

His clear mind and firm will thus asserted itself. In stone. It had to be stone, longer lasting than mortal man, more enduring than the congregation of the living who had made a puny attempt to abase his deepest convictions. (*New Green World*, p. 12)

Herbst's historical writing, *New Green World* and her postwar memoirs, would inscribe her convictions and sentiments in the 'stone' of longer-lasting and enduring textual memorials. The work would rescue her from the suicidal-sacrificial oblivion of Potomac censorship by the Cold War, the Dies, HUAC and McCarthyite committees running the public sphere. It would serve as a coded act of witness to the true idealism of the 1930s against the censorship and misrepresentations of those committees. As she remarked in 'The Ruins of Memory': 'The reaction in the forties, the Second World War, the new cynicism, the new prosperity and the new smugness put the thirties, its work and the sources of its potential, into a time capsule where it has been effectively isolated' (p. 302). As a painstaking act of historical reconstruction, *New Green World* allegorizes the Cold War's freezing of the 1930s into an isolated time capsule with a symptomatic satirical mimicry of its procedures (the 1930s are as distant and dead as the eighteenth century), at the same time as it resists the whole process of deadening anti-historical historicism by revivifying the life and human textures of the work done in the 1930s, the decade's potential sourced in foundational American-revolutionary idealism.

Herbst's technique is one of innocent reversal of the accusations levelled against her and her progressive generation, just as she had to counter the FBI investigators' reports. The reversal seems simplistic, a simple switching device, as when Dos Passos' key term 'design' is turned on its head. In *New Green World*, the term is divested of political connotation and made to signify Bartram's innocent policy of exploration, fructification and hybridization: '[Bartram's] grand design to which he was committed' (*New Green World*, p. 164). The innocence of the design is not as naive as it appears: Herbst knows the connection between eighteenth-century botany and the 'ulterior purposes' of empire, trade and colonialism (p. 200), just as she does not clear Bartram of all reproach – she goes to great lengths to criticize his prejudice against Native Americans, the 'Reds' of his day, and to praise his son William for his selfless and heroic attempts to live among, record and defend Native American culture. She is equally at pains to broaden the senses and scope of the word 'design' to stand for a complex ethic of research in adverse circumstance.

On one page of her history, Herbst uses 'design' three times, first to signify the range of interests of the botanists she is bearing witness to:

> the botanists maintained a continuity of design that passed from rash love of growing things to a scientific appraisal, in one direction; in another direction, to the imaginative flights of creative minds in the latter part of the Eighteenth Century. (*New Green World*, p. 135)

This continuity of design is made possible by the extravagant optimism of the botanists' faith in the world, their love of the world as benignly designed, even whilst the flora and fauna being recorded are under threat from the ferocity of the wars against the Native American tribes:

> In the midst of wars, the botanists kept their bearings and recorded their findings, trusting to some enormous intention within the universe, some miracle of design, to which each man hoped to contribute his part. (*New Green World*, p. 135)

If there is clear reference to Herbst's own sense of the continuity between her activism in the anti-fascist wars of her time and the creative writing of her inter-war novels, then the trust of the botanists is also self-referential. The progressive intellectuals of the 1930s were as credulous as their counterparts, trusting in the benign 'enormous intention' of history as revolutionary process. History is for Herbst the true grand design, collective rather than concentrated in corporations, White House and witch-hunting libertarians: 'this intricate design at work altering the social, economic and imaginative patterns of the period' (p. 135).

A similar reversal of the enemy's emphases occurs with Herbst's play with the naming strategies of the anti-Communist liberal front. In place of naming as accusation, Herbst praises the innocent taxonomical order of the naturalists: 'the name, the name! Oh, to name the world and hold it tight, to pin it down from vaporous wanderings!' (pp. 166–7). Such naming aims not to destroy a reputation, but to perfect a loving bond between mind and the thing it loves: 'Oh, most exact description, not only of a plant, but of a living relationship between a man and his object. This is love wholly occupied with the object' (p. 167). To name is to glorify the Edenic citizenship of the world, not to deny citizenship to the dissenter:

> The name, the name! To give each plant its citizenship, its ancestry and heritage. With the rising sense of the rights of man went a profound quest for identification of every species. Stones found their ancestors in that exploring period of exploring minds and animals a name and history. (*New Green World*, p. 86)

The sacrificial naming that poisons *The Grand Design* is answered by this reversal of its terms, a return to the classificatory euphoria of the revolutionary period: as such it is a defence of a different tradition of citizenship in history, a defence of the rights and ancestry of the 1930s Popular Front of exploring minds.

This 'innocent' reversal of Dos Passos' key term may strike one now as special pleading of a peculiarly green and *faux naif* kind. It might be helpful to remember that to turn the terms of the enemy inside out may have been the only appropriate response to the special pleading and misquotation of the accusers. It was the accusers who had taught her the technique, as she recalled in her account of the 1943 interrogation by the FBI in Washington:

> [The FBI investigators] could take *It is Reported that in Madrid, in 1937, you broadcast on behalf of the Spanish Loyalists*, turn it inside out, and find me involved in a conspiracy, where I saw only evidence of my own well-grounded reasons of the heart.[17]

The reverse switching of terms – as in Herbst's reappropriation of Dos Passos' translation of the New Deal's 'grand design' into a global conspiracy at the 'level of the leaders' – turns the inside-out language of the accusers inside out. In so doing, it works both as a counter-restorative reinstating the true imaginative history of the past, and as a satirical thrust which reveals the HUAC-FBI procedures of the congregation of the living. The code reversal is a struggle over the meaning of history: the shrivelling facts and reports and paranoia of the anti-Communists countermanded by Herbst's commitment to story, to a binding together of 'rash love', 'scientific appraisal' and 'imaginative flights of creative minds'. It is also a struggle over genre: Herbst's humble memoir set against Dos Passos' historical fiction. At the root is a skirmish over language:

> My Interlocutors and I spoke the same tongue but lacked the elements of a common language. On my native soil, I was in a kind of no-man's-land, more strange than I had been when I first went to Germany and loved to drift anonymously with the crowd. ('Yesterday's Road', p. 111)

The Cold War had effectively exiled her, as a feminist writer, internationalist, socialist, activist, within her own private skin, blood and memory, speaking a once common collective language made foreign in a land of no man. As she put it to Stanley Burnshaw: '*New Green World* is a biographical study of the Bartrams and of more – of a climate of opinion and a way of life that I admired and that had vanished in the McCarthy era and in a universal way, for all time. I wrote it to remind myself that it still persisted, if only in memory.'[18]

New Green World might be accused of falsifying the political urgencies of the 1930s by dressing them up as benign, natural, eco-friendly, green innocence. This would be to forget the local intricacy of Herbst's account: John Bartram is complicit in the racism levelled against Native Americans. His botany is in service to the modish aristocracy of the British Empire. His commitment to the natural world is nevertheless fraught with the pressing necessity of a struggle against time and modernity: 'The green world will melt away: it will slowly vanish and he will not be able to bear witness' (*New Green World*, p. 175). In a world of hostile witnesses and their science of accusation, the ability to bear witness is more than a gesture of judicial self-defence. William Bartram, as a young Romantic, is even further compromised, desperately struggling to record human and natural cultures under ultimate menace, 'caught in indecision, trapped by events' (p. 182), vainly advocating 'an artist's approach to his material and his life' (p. 183) against the ruthless scientism of technology and modern economics. The generational shift from the Enlightenment optimism of the father to the embattled Romanticism of the son not only counters the versions of liberalism running America in the 1950s, but serves as a confession and defence of the shifting circumstances and convictions endured by Herbst's generation's inheritance of earlier forms of American radicalism.

As Herbst was to discover in 1952, previous convictions could lead to real convictions in court. This was the year Dos Passos named her in his interview, the year she was routinely interrogated by the FBI, the year she was forced to defend her friend Robert Coe, Atomic Energy Commission (AEC) physicist at Oak Ridge, by testifying before a government hearing board in Washington for which she had to prepare 'a kind of dossier documenting her attitude to the Communist Party at various critical junctures by reference to both her private correspondence and her published writing between 1931 and 1948' (Langer, *Josephine Herbst*, p. 319). The next year, she had to intervene in the McCarthyite process again, this time helping another friend, Harvey O'Connor, defend himself against the congressional committee, writing the powerful defence of freedom of thought in the Emergency Civil Liberties pamphlet 'Mind of Your Own' (Langer, *Josephine Herbst*, pp. 319–20).[19] Langer suspects the time spent in these interviews, interrogations and writing of dossiers and pamphlets, coupled with the 'grey-listing' she suffered as a known radical, took a terrible toll on Herbst's ability to write fiction and memoir. That it did so is incontrovertible. As she put it in a letter in 1959 to Stanley Burnshaw:

> I can only wish that there were more ways to break the cement walls. For there are walls, and stupid ones. But this kind of clamor that goes up, the pressures exerted by forces one does not even respect, silences voices. If I have not written much in recent years as I should, something of this is part of the climate that has made it difficult. Not difficult to do but difficult to be convinced that it will be heard. That leads to retreat.[20]

But equally those pressures allowed her a glimpse into the mechanics of hostile history, the 'secret laws at cross-purposes with my own' that had dogged her since Spain, the 'gentle, clerklike' forms of mind-control that the United States had inherited from the fratricidal fascist–anti-fascist civil wars that had shaped the Cold War.[21] Those forms of mind-control, she wrote to Burnshaw in 1963, had revealed the structure of the imagination to her, the division of the composing mind as 'seeing eye' into 'victim', 'judge' and 'sharer' – a succinct description of the (self-)sacrificial triangular dynamics of the Cold War. Freudian topics are transformed into writerly terms that have become paranoid-political, the Janus-faced powers of the superego judge and unconscious secret sharer at dark work upon the ego-victim. But the same forces deprived the imagination of the will to compose: 'If it had not been for the long Cold War and all the blind alleys following I probably would have written many books in the last decade. [. . .] the whole revolting impasse since the last war, the retreats, the mumblings and apologies simply atrophied the will to care about all that.'[22]

The grey-listing she underwent during the high Cold War and the convolutions it drove her to in her defence of the 1930s in the *New Green World* had some traumatic effects. In a strange short story written in 1954, 'Hunter of Doves', the name Bartram crops up again, this time as the pseudonym of a dead author, Alec Barber (based on Nathaniel West), author of 1930s novels.[23] A young journalist interviews Bartram's old friend, Constance Heath (a writer very like Herbst), for a piece on Bartram, but without any real sense of the urgencies of the 1930s. The Heath–Barber–Bartram personas play out both Herbst's exile from her past in Cold War culture, the similar strategic renaming she had acted out in *New Green World*, and intimations of the dark naming in McCarthyite America. The Bartram here is not the ecologically friendly alter ego from the eighteenth century, but a progressive pessimist from the 1930s whose mind has gone dark through the encroachments of history: Nathaniel West as *Miss Lonelyhearts*; John Dos Passos as Glenn Spotswood.

The Bartram name gives us a clue as to Herbst's own deeper feelings about the naming subterfuges forced upon 1930s radicals by the psychologizing Cold War. The fictions generated by the imagination become false fronts, sacrificial masks, hopelessly compromised journeys into the atomized mind. At the heart of the brave project to resist the naming strategies of the accusers, Herbst felt her *New Green World* could be hijacked by revisionists like Dos Passos and construed as a lonely, eccentric retreat into a nightmare of Cold War America. Bartram, her ecological alter ego, becomes a Cold Warrior killer of doves, a neuroticized imagination drawn to the sacrifice of the defenceless, to the killing of peace in this world, to a Siberianizing of America according to the dictates of McCarthyite emulation: 'he was writing an American journey', Constance Heath says, 'into a Siberia of the human spirit. His people, if you call them that, were lopped-off criminals or impaled saints. Exiles, everyone of them. Surrounded, moreover, by crucified animals' ('Hunter of Doves', p. 317).

Josephine Herbst *had* once nearly drowned off the eastern seaboard of the United States. It was back in the 1920s, the week Sacco and Vanzetti's execution was announced to the world, on the longboat John Herrmann had converted and named *Josy*. In late August 1927, *Josy* was caught in a terrific two-day hurricane off Porpoise Harbor, limping through deep fog into Portland, Maine, where Herrmann and Herbst learnt of the execution. The pair abandoned the boat and returned to New York. Dos Passos and Katherine Anne Porter had been deeply involved in the defence of the two anarchists. And it was Dos Passos who was to look up the beached *Josy* a few years later and tell them it would take what to them would be a small fortune to sail again.

The experience of the storm and fog is curious to Herbst because it was not the storm which was dangerous, but being becalmed and drifting through the impenetrable fog, through treacherous waters 'filled with shoals and hidden reefs, sudden islands and mysterious currents':

> Because it was so calm, I was more at ease than I had a right to be. Out of pure ignorance. On other days, in the deep trough of an iron wave, I had been sick with fear, petrified in the cabin, where stretched out on a bunk I would expect to be plunged to the bottom in the black coffin of the *Josy*. John, of course, was an expert swimmer. I could not swim [...] You were inside some vast cocoon, and it was sticky with wetness that soaked the skin. It clung to your hair like damp bees. We might have been alone, except for the sound of the foghorns mooing in the distance of watery pastures. But the fog warped the view of immediate objects; the masts soared to twice their size, to be caught in the swathing vapours; as in one of the crazy mirrors at Coney Island, John's six-foot stature elongated to a giant's. [...] Once we came about fast at the sound of breakers and, edging off, saw the fanged tusks of a great slimy rock loom green to port. [...] At five o'clock we were still moving through the white visceral matter of some monster sheep's brain.[24]

The account of the fog is a twisted vision of a political space inaugurated by the Sacco and Vanzetti trial. The space at the offshore margins of America is treacherously ambiguous, at once a pastoral zone signifying the apolitical, carefree playground of the 1920s intellectual, and at the same time a region of hidden threat, mystificatory violence, concealed death. Herbst's prose summons the ghosts of this monstrous pastoral, with its bees, mooing foghorns and sheep's-brain fog. The looking-glass childishness of the vision, caught in the Coney Island image, is a form of confession of the callow naivety of her holidaying twenties persona. At the same time, there is a sharp, paranoid recognition that the fanged tusks of the dangers threatening *Josy* are real enough to kill her. This offshore zone may be the new world she will have to learn to navigate from Sacco and Vanzetti through to the Cold War. The fog signifies not merely the indefensible apolitical recreation of her twenties self, but the treacherous and lethal margins of America where dissenters must live, work and survive.

On shore, the couple are about to learn of the execution of the anarchists, and it is John, the Communist male, who teaches her the frightening swimming lesson for these new waters:

> 'You remember how Sacco said, "Kill me or set me free"?' I said.
>
> 'I guess they'll kill him, all right', John said. 'They seem to think they have to purify the city with a sacrifice. Like in old Athens, where they led out two of the most debased citizens: as an offscouring, they called it. To get rid of a pestilence or a famine. What was it they called them? *Pharmakos*. First they gave them cheese and a barley cake. Then they beat them with branches from the wild fig tree, then they burned them. Scattered the ashes into the sea and to the winds as a general cleanup. That's the way they did it.'
>
> 'You think we are any smarter?' ('A Year of Disgrace', p. 96)

The lesson is not simply that the state decides to scapegoat the couple to generate communal authority over its citizens, by warding off the evil of those who are deemed to be abject and debased by their acts of dissent against its authority. It is that the city is founded on and continually sustained by this sacrifice. Pastoral America and its City (Washington, or Boston where the execution of Sacco and Vanzetti took place) needs the sacrifice of its *Pharmakos* (meaning remedy and poison) as purifying antidote, a dose of limited violence in order to establish the distinction between its civic revolutionary virtues and the new revolutionary doctrines, anarchism and Communism, which mimetically threaten it.

Learning of the execution, Herrmann and Herbst begin to register the filiations between the political events fogging the United States and their near-fatal experience on *Josy*:

> Without saying a word, we both felt it and knew that we felt it: a kind of shuddering premonition of a world to come. But what it was to be we could never have foreseen. Not the density of the fog, the bewildering calls from deceptive buoys, the friends lost in the mist, the channels marked for death. The port harder to find than the eye of any needle. [. . .] As far as I am concerned, what had been the twenties ended that night. We would try to penetrate the fogs to come, to listen to the buoys, to read the charts. ('A Year of Disgrace', pp. 96–7)

If 23 August 1927 ends the 1920s and initiates writers into the world of politics, becoming the activists, dissenters, progressives and Communists of the 1930s, it is also a foundational moment for the struggle over the meaning of the 1930s for the Cold War. This is why the near-death experience in the fog of obfuscatory politics is central both to Herbst's Cold War memoirs and to Dos Passos' *The Grand Design*. For Herbst, the sacrificial *Pharmakos* narrative threatens the marriage of male and female, Communist and progressive, singling them out as the next scapegoat pair to fuel the 1930s long war between anti-Stalinists and Popular Front progressives,[25] a war developed to extraordinary intensity in the Cold War: Herrmann exiled and sent to his death in Mexico; Herbst greylisted and silenced by the slow attrition of accusation and quiet censorship.

For Dos Passos, Herbst did not escape death off Portland. She died as soon as she gave in to the seductions of the CPUSA, destroyed as sacrificial victim in the machinations which were to corrupt the New Deal, lost in the mist of power politics and factional Ware-group subversion of the ideals of the City. The *Josy* becomes the *Niña*, sly reference to Herbst's little-girl gullibility in Spain. Herbst's fog becomes a luminous, dazzling mist muffling the world on the Potomac, figure for the suicidal trance of her indoctrinated mind: 'She couldn't see the shore. All around her was a dazzle of mist' (*The Grand Design*, p. 362). The drift and danger of the move through the waters is less to do with the paranoid projection of a concealed political power than with this drugged, self-victimizing state of mind: '"Hey for cryin' out loud the buoy's over there," Jed's gruff voice rasped as he pushed her away from the wheel' (p. 358). The antidotal *Pharmakos* as remedy/poison drug turns up as the codeine tablets Georgia takes to ensure her own death in the Potomac. Instead of the double *Pharmakos*, we have a single female victim, caught between the dual recruiting forces of Jed at the wheel and failing New Dealer Paul Graves.

In one sense, Dos Passos did get this right. Herbst's first account of the experience on the *Josy*, in the 1930 short story 'A Bad Blow', had emphasized the wife's fear of drowning in the coffin-cabin while the husband exults in his male power on deck.[26] Mary Ann Rasmussen reads the tale as evidence of Herbst's 'repressed anger and disappointment with the inegalitarian terms of her "romantic" marriage'.[27] She links this anger to Herbst's resistance to the left's abandonment of 'prewar radicalism's socialist-feminist legacy' and the 'sexual egalitarianism and [. . .] companion love ideal' which it had advocated (p. xviii). There is a trace of this in the 1961 memoir: 'John, of course, was an expert swimmer. I could not swim.'

At the same time, Herbst resists her own 1930s feminism in the 1960s, not so much to paper over the clash of class and gender that made the Popular Front difficult for radical women as to counter the use of the feminist angle in texts like *The Grand Design*. Dos Passos had suggested in the suicide narrative that it was the left's masculinist bullying which did for Georgia. 'A Year of Digrace' begs to disagree: the issue was more starkly about the state's lethal 'pharmaceutical' fog-machine. Its victims were men and women, indiscriminately, Sacco and Vanzetti, but also the Rosenbergs, the Herbst-Herrmanns. Georgia did not commit suicide on her own. *Both* John and Josephine were marked out for judicial censorship by false accusers, pastoralized into non-existence as writers along 'the channels marked for death'. To navigate the 'shoals and hidden reefs, sudden islands and mysterious currents' of the Cold War, Herbst had not only to resist the 1950s war against the 1930s, she had to try and imagine a world without the dense fog and deceptive buoys of state propaganda and Ulithi-FBI-HUAC-Dos Passos misrepresentation and sacrificial naming. Like Collinson in her *New Green World*, she 'refuses to blur [her] green horizon with the cloud of [their] politics' (*New Green World*, p. 173). For that cloud of false politics had been generated, she knew, by the sacrificial burning of the histories, testimonies and reputations of the progressive 1930s: 'No one', she wrote in 1956, 'can seek for new clues or discover the actual world when it becomes clouded with the smoke of penitents burning the past.'[28]

NOTES

1. Dos Passos, *Tour of Duty*, pp. 93–4.
2. *The Grand Design*, pp. 363–4. The *District of Columbia* trilogy opens with *Adventures of a Young Man* (1939), followed by *Number One* (1943). Useful to me in my readings of *Tour of Duty* and *The Grand Design* have been Belkind, *Dos Passos*; Diggins, *Up from Communism*; Edmund Wilson, *Shores of Light*; Aaron, 'The Riddle of John Dos Passos' and *Writers on the Left*; and Bloom, *Prodigal Sons*.
3. Thomas Doherty's term for fellow-travelling Popular Fronters who recanted to become good Cold Warriors (*Cold War, Cool Medium*, p. 29).
4. Reprising the suicide of Clotel in William Wells Brown's 1854 *Clotel, or The President's Daughter*, where the daughter of Thomas Jefferson, pursued as a slave, commits suicide in the Potomac within sight of Mount Vernon.
5. White, 'John Dos Passos and the Federal Bureau of Investigation', p. 99. The Dos Passos file consulted by White (pp. 97–110) contains eighty-two pages, 'many of them mere checklists for references to Dos Passos in other Bureau files and all heavily censored by the Bureau for reasons of national defense, unwarranted invasion of privacy, and protection of confidential sources' (p. 97).
6. Author of the 1925 pro-Soviet *Children of Revolution* and *The First Time in History* with its Trotsky preface, as well as radical Eleanor Roosevelt New Dealer with her *Remaking an American* and *I Change Worlds*. The Bureau would have been interested in her because of her work in China: she interviewed Mao in 1946, for instance.
7. Langer, *Josephine Herbst*, pp. 245–6.
8. Josephine Herbst is surreptitiously 'named' in the novel too in a triangle of references: the Wallace figure, Walker Watson, has a wife named Josephine, who dies and is replaced in his affections by the scheming Jo Powers as his dream of the century of the common man dies; Georgia's first Communist boyfriend is named Joe Yerkes. And of course, the naive progressive figure who runs through the whole Columbia trilogy, suffering humiliation at a Communist rally in *The Grand Design*, is called Herbert.
9. There are ten letters from Dos Passos to Herbst amongst her papers at the Beinecke Library. The last two letters simply say he is too busy to see her – the very last is dated 16 April 1949. Beinecke Rare Book and Manuscript Library, Yale Collection of American Literature: Josephine Herbst Papers – Correspondence – Dos Passos.

10. Beinecke Rare Book and Manuscript Library, Yale Collection of American Literature: Josephine Herbst Papers – Herbst letter to Edgar Branch, 4 February 1957.
11. Josephine Herbst Papers – Series II: B Memoirs [Mss-M-New World], Notes, p. 5.
12. Josephine Herbst Papers – Series II: B box 12: *New Green World*.
13. Josephine Herbst, *New Green World*, p. 1. For criticism of Herbst's writing, I am indebted to Hubler, 'Josephine Herbst's *The Starched Blue Sky of Spain*'; Foley, *Radical Representations*; Ehrhardt, *Writers of Conviction*; and Nora Ruth Roberts, *Three Radical Writers*.
14. Related in Herbst's mind to the ecological concerns of 1920s radicalism, as remembered by Stanley Burnshaw: 'To be a communist was also to be a conservationist, because if "the people" could own the world, they would treat the green earth itself with as much love and decency and veneration as they would treat its men and women and children' (Harry Ransom Center, University of Texas at Austin, Stanley Burnshaw Papers – Stanley Burnshaw letter to Christina Stead, 16 July 1973, p. 3).
15. Cf. Schaub, *American Fiction in the Cold War*, pp. 22–4. Schaub calls the new realism and neo-Freudian cult of original sin advocated by Trilling and others 'the pessimism of revisionist liberalism' (p. 24).
16. 'The Ruins of Memory', p. 303.
17. 'Yesterday's Road', in *The Starched Blue Sky of Spain*, p. 107. First published after Herbst's death in the *New American Review* in 1968.
18. Harry Ransom Center, University of Texas at Austin, Stanley Burnshaw Papers – letter to Stanley Burnshaw, 27 March 1963.
19. The defence has its own rhetorical means of countering the naming of names: O'Connor 'has made an honored name for himself'; 'No attempt to erase the blackboard of history can wipe out all those names' ('Mind of Your Own: Harvey O'Connor's Stand', written for Emergency Civil Liberties Committee, 22 October 22 1953 – Beinecke Rare Book and Manuscript Library, Yale Collection of American Literature: Josephine Herbst Papers – Series III: A, Publications by Herbst III – box 31).
20. Harry Ransom Center, University of Texas at Austin, Stanley Burnshaw Papers – letter to Stanley Burnshaw, 7 July 1959.
21. 'Yesterday's Road', pp. 110–11.
22. Harry Ransom Center, University of Texas at Austin, Stanley Burnshaw Papers – letter to Stanley Burnshaw, 27 March 1963.
23. A good account of the story is given in Nora Ruth Roberts, *Three Radical Writers*, pp. 159–63.
24. 'A Year of Disgrace', in *The Starched Blue Sky of Spain*, pp. 93–4. First published in Saul Bellow and Keith Botsford's journal *Noble Savage* in 1961.
25. Cf. Kutulas, *The Long War*, p. 240.
26. In the story, the *Josy* becomes *Becky* and the Herbst character, also called Becky, is forced into a sullen and subservient position whilst the husband Dick skippers the boat. The tale is a thinly veiled political allegory: Dick would like to identify the *Becky* with the working-class fishing boats, not the capitalist pleasure yachts, all marooned in harbour whilst the storm blows. He manages to leave port with the fishing vessels despite the dangerous swell. This political success is earned at Becky's expense, however – her point of view is resented and ignored, and she has to suffer Dick's bravado even if means risking their lives.
27. Introduction to first of Herbst's Trexler trilogy, *Pity is Not Enough*, p. xxxv.
28. 'The Ruins of Memory', p. 303.

3

DEW LINE, URANIUM AND THE ARCTIC COLD WAR: GINSBERG'S *KADDISH* AND NABOKOV'S *LOLITA*

In May 1955, Allen Ginsberg began training as a Military Sea Transport Service yeoman-storekeeper in order to fund a trip to Europe. He served on the cargo ship USNS *Sgt. Jack J. Pendleton*, which, after several short trips along the Eastern seaboard, would eventually sail to the Arctic Circle. Just before leaving for the north, Ginsberg's mother, Naomi, died, on 9 June 1956, and it is a poignant fact that the journey to the polar regions coincided with his difficult mourning for his Russian mother, for the journey took him through the Bering Strait, the contact point between American Alaska and the Soviet Union.

From the very beginning, indeed, the fact of his engagement in the US Navy became nightmarishly embroiled with his attempts properly to perform the necessary Kaddish for his mother's spirit. Unable to attend her funeral on 11 June, he was distressed to learn from his father that there had not been enough men at the graveside to have a Kaddish read – the service demands at least ten men; there were only seven in the cortege.[1] Ginsberg decided he would have to write one himself, but found the Cold War was getting in the way. In a journal entry that month, Ginsberg wrote:

> Everything changes toward death. My mother. Myself. The asphalt pavement of the dock I am sitting on. The chair I am sitting on is labeled consigned for scrap. Along the dock, blue water, blue sky. USNS Kern sits on water, being charged for Arctic trip. Iron bulkheads disappearing and replaced by different walls. Then later mothballs. Then rust. Then salvage.

Whole navies float across the waters. To disappear. A man walks along the dock in grimy clothes, head bent down, carrying dead lunch. The pavement boils in the sun. The dock is already old and battered. My childhood is gone with my mother. My memory becomes less clear. My body will go. There is no me left. Naomi is memory. Naomi is a memory. My 30 years is a memory to me. Memory will be nothing. Memory changes toward death. Toward death, memory changes. Memories. Memory. Mors. M.....[2]

The changes toward death are rung out in the reduction of word to phoneme *m*, as the words 'mother', 'myself', 'man', 'memory', 'me' are stripped of their differences, their burden of semantic charge, mumming now merely their common denominator, the *m* of death (*mors*) and the elliptical series of fatal full stops. What the ellipsis periods fail entirely to erase, however, is how strangely and uncannily 'Naomi' has become identified with disappearing 'navies'. The rusting hulks of the wartime ships will sail over the horizon toward the death-zone of the Arctic, their freight, history, function and crew forgotten, unsalvageable, disappeared. 'Where e'er I went,' the next journal entry reads, 'I went & said one fucked up Kaddish for her soul' (Ginsberg, *Journals Mid-Fifties*, p. 260). Instead of the ten Kaddish mourners, Ginsberg only has himself, a disintegrating body and mind, with the only community those rusting ships, ambiguous companions to the lost Naomi.

Ginsberg's difficulty saying Kaddish turns, then, on the loss of the communal voice accompanying the little death of his mourning body and mind, and its spectral substitution by the relics of the US war machine. The voice of community had once nourished Naomi Ginsberg, in the form of Communism, and then tormented her in her madness in the form of psychotic possession by enemy voices, as Ginsberg's *Kaddish* relates. The communal voice in Ginsberg's own writings in the early months of the compositional prehistory of *Kaddish* is similarly tormented by alien voices, the alien voices of Cold War ideology. The journey north, towards his mother's homeland, is troped as a haunting by the secret Cold War purposes running the USNS *Sgt. Jack J. Pendleton,* as his recorded dreams reveal.

On July 5, 1956, Ginsberg narrates 'S.S. Pendleton, deep dream – aboard ship':

> Working on the Tally Cards for the national machine, under duress, in Moscow for a visit, I have the chance to sneak away and see the country – as in a science fiction dream – I'm in Moscow – I've been filling on cards the names of the streets of Russia – Carl Tilley is my superior he is also a spy [. . .] The question is, what are the points of interest to visit, where are the Franciscan Skid Rows of Moscow – how to we get there? This is all a deep political secret & mystery – I am willing to go anywhere & break all rules to see – I ask Tilley, who is evasive, but indicates that all the information is down there recorded on my tally cards. I am elated by

having the information. Woke up realizing it is my first nostalgic dream of Russia. (*Journals Mid-Fifties*, p. 270)

The tally cards yeoman Ginsberg would have been filling in, itemizing the storeroom stock, become secret communications about the Soviet Union, potentially transforming Moscow into San Francisco, identifying the two cities' underground street networks, the 'secret living places of the artists and the Damned & the queers & the poor' (p. 271). Yet the possibly liberating feeling this might give Ginsberg's dream self is disturbed by the possibility that the tally cards are secret service intelligence documents. He may be fulfilling the secret purposes of the national machine of the CIA and FBI. What the *Pendleton* hides in its stores is Cold War information about the secret Russia within dead Naomi's memories, within the subversive desires of the Beat Ginsberg, betrayed by the *Pendleton* Ginsberg, recruited to the national machine monitoring un-American dreams.

Further complicating the Cold War infiltration of his imagination on board ship is a set of psychoanalytic anxieties that trouble the process of Ginsberg's mourning for his mother. The journey to the Bering Strait had a dry run in a trip the *Pendleton* made along the Columbia river past Beaver Point to Seattle on 20–1 June – the ship sailed through the Straits of Juan de Fuca, the names Beaver and Fuca igniting an incestuous dream:

> In a motel of familiar visiting quarters, ran into [Naomi], settled down for the night – She undressed and I saw she had a large dull fleshly cock and a cluster of 6 genitals attached to her body by a piece of web-like flesh tube. (*Journals Mid-Fifties*, p. 268)

Waking up in horror, Ginsberg falls asleep again and dreams he meets his father, Louis, whom he tries to convince that Naomi is a mutant:

> Dreamed it was in 288 Graham Ave. house, in the living room talking to Louis, told him my dream, horrified, he shrugged it off, I said 'She's a mutant' – remembering from earlier dream the look of her face, extremely high dome hair, like a stovepipe curved or bowler hat shape, with french-block oily glistening shock of hair all over her, neatly and artificially arranged, black, as on a window dressing dummy, & blank black eyes & pallid skin, as if a robot or a mutant – the peculiar look on the face I ascribed in dream to the lobotomy. So Louis shrugged while I pleaded, 'She's a mutant', afraid, and then I went into the living room – she was *there*! Where did you come from? How long have you been here? I asked, afraid she had heard my complaint conversation – She smiled evilly & busied herself with preparations for bed? – 'I've been here all along, it's my home, isn't it? I wrote my name on the pillow here, right here (pointing to the pillow overhanging the edge of the couch), I wrote my name in the pillow so I wouldn't be forgotten or get lost.' (*Journals Mid-Fifties*, pp. 268–9)

The male–mother mutant is a creature both of the atomic paranoia of Cold War science fiction and of the folk-psychoanalytic crises of ego-identity foisted on the homosexual community in the 1950s. The atomic paranoia concentrates into the dead mother's body a mutated version of the external threat posed by Soviet nuclear missiles: as a Russian Communist émigreé, Naomi must, according to the Hooverist dictates of US Cold War home front propaganda, harbour the mutant energies a nuclear strike will, fantasmatically, wreak upon the American nuclear family home (note the shift from motel to 288 Graham Avenue in the double dream).[3] In service to a powerfully censoring male environment – one of Ginsberg's dreams is about the captain forbidding him to embrace his lover, Peter Lafcadio (pp. 310–11) – on board a ship fulfilling a Cold War agenda, Ginsberg is incapable of performing the Kaddish for a mother who, for the dominant culture of 1950s America, is at once a mutant US 'Soviet' and a matrix of deviant Oedipal energies. The dream occurs going through straits not only because the enemy is straight ideology, but because Ginsberg knows that his ship will soon be approaching the straits which liminally define the geopolitical spatialization of the Cold War. Sailing towards the border dividing the States from the Soviet Union, mourning a Russian Communist, the homosexual Ginsberg was also travelling in the wake of Hoover and McCarthy's witch-hunting campaigns, the *Pendleton* a vehicle for the nation's hysterical definitions of political-sexual deviance.[4]

On 27 July 1956, the *Pendleton* passed through the Bering Strait:

> Passing thru the Bering Strait – out on deck in unnecessary coat, sad, dull day, nothing of the meeting of Asia & America visible, continents shrouded in lighted mist, earlier in the morning waking saw the blue sky, sun brilliant in a lite low mist, 3/4 declining moon, and a rainbow with 2 white albatrosses flying cross the bulge of light in the blue air.
>
> Many birds flying passages between the continents, the sea choppy tho clear, the air immediately around clear, further away a bleak white haze blinds the sight of the two worlds apart almost touching – centuries shrouded in white mist. (*Journals Mid-Fifties*, p. 287)

The Cold War polarity of US (United States) and SU (Soviet Union) remains unreadable, shrouded in mystery, mystified by the 'conspiracy of secrecy & love' (p. 284) which Ginsberg identified with private desire. The freedom of the birds in their passage between the two continents figures the private poet's freedom to forget the Cold War, as though there might be a private American sublime which, through the departed shade of Naomi, might negotiate a rainbow covenant between the Cold-Warring superpowers. Ginsberg does not need to acknowledge the Cold War – he does not feel the cold ('unnecessary coat'). The two worlds are only artificially separate – in the mist they are undifferentiated. Naomi's death, its white shroud, enables a deconstruction of the geopolitical polarity that haunts the Strait.

In the poem he wrote about the experience, 'Bering Strait Blues' (uncollected but in the journal, *Journals Mid-Fifties*, pp. 289–90), Ginsberg is less sure of himself. Though birds still cross freely between the two continents ('Little birds with white stomachs / cross from invisible Russia to Alaska'), the sight of the ships, engaged in the rising, falling rhythm of their Cold War business, generates a real cold he feels:

> Ugly, unsettled ships, loughing up & down
>   sinking & rising on the waters,
> familiar sperm flecked moveable sea.
> Shapes in shrouds, high breasted bloated
>   suffering prideful boats
>   My fingers are cold.
>
>   (p. 289)

The border space is no longer an amnesiac American sublime, but inflected by Melvillean instabilities fabricated by the 'unsettled ships', an uncanny seascape bloated by the 'deep political secret & mystery' of the Cold War. For Ginsberg is aware that it is the *Pendleton*'s 'iron' mission which has supplied him with this freak insight into the sublimities of superpower politics: 'Vast area of cold & water & mist – it takes an iron ship to get here / Girded for ice & dead to pain of cold waves & skinless under inhuman skies in long bleak latitudes' (p. 290). It is the theatre of the Cold War which produces the white shrouds of mist that render its own operations at once secret and sublime: 'The ship a theatre surrounded by curtains of impenetrable ghostly air' (p. 291). Again the threat of hermaphrodite confusion ('familiar sperm . . . high breasted') is written into the cold Ginsberg feels, as though mutant Naomi were haunting the ships and movable sea. For this is also the space, still, where Ginsberg must begin the Kaddish for his mother: 'Forgot to say I threw 7¢ into Bering Strait to leave something of me in remembrance of Naomi, so near her Russia' (p. 291). The crux of his anxiety, forgetting to say Kaddish, prefaces this admission, as though Ginsberg recognizes that the poem 'Bering Strait Blues' has fabricated a mutant surrogate lost object out of the Arctic mist, Cold War ships and geopolitical border zone. Naomi's shade has been replaced/possessed by the shapes in shrouds of the imaginary dead of this other imaginary war.

What is secretly structuring Ginsberg's writing is the knowledge that his body and mind, suffering the deathlike evacuation of subjectivity triggered by the mourning process, is *on board*, recruited to the NATO project in command of the *Pendleton*. The Military Sea Transportation Service was involved in the provisioning of the construction of a string of radar outposts along the Arctic rim in Alaska and northern Canada, the Distant Early Warning (DEW)

Line designed to detect Soviet bombers in an eventual nuclear assault on the States from over the North Pole. It was a huge, billion-dollar operation that had begun in the summer of 1955, the DEW becoming fully operational in late summer 1957, stretching 4,000 miles along the 70th parallel from Cape Dyer on Baffin Island to the Alaskan border near Komakuk Beach. The US Air Force had initiated a study of air defences in 1952, as it was concerned that the then current early warning systems, known as the Pine Tree Line across Southern Canada, did not give sufficient warning time of a Soviet attack. The Lincoln summer study (named after the MIT Lincoln Laboratory, centre of radar development during the war) had recommended the construction of the DEW Line across Alaska and northern Canada. Despite the huge cost, Western Electric was commissioned to build the Line, and Canada persuaded to cooperate with the US military (Eisenhower's mind was concentrated on the issue after the Soviet's first thermonuclear test in August 1953). Before the era of Soviet intercontinental ballistic missiles (ICBMs), the DEW Line was the central plank in the American's continental defence systems against manned bomber nuclear attack. It accompanied a more general militarization of the Arctic by NATO in direct response to the huge Soviet naval and air forces on the Kola peninsular; both military machines pouring enormous resources into the Arctic Circle.[5]

In many ways, the Arctic came to symbolize the Cold War, secret, inaccessible, bitterly cold, hiding within its wastes enormous bases such as Thule in Greenland, incredible surveillance systems and mind-numbingly powerful weaponry. The region defined nuclear strategies when it came to envisioning direct Soviet–US nuclear war, both military complexes planning on the basis of first and second strikes over the pole. The zone changed the nature of Cold War technological development, as later with the stationing of nuclear-powered attack submarines beneath the polar icecap. The idea of a Cold War theatre was shaped by the polar confrontation, a zone where bombers, missiles, radar stations, armies and navies mimicked each other in frozen attitudes of combat preparedness, locked into endless icily deadly manoeuvres.[6]

Ginsberg's ship offloaded its provisions and equipment at Fort Wainwright and Point Barrow and, on 20 August 1956, the *Pendleton* renegotiated the Bering Strait:

> Sunsets at Point Barrow – its appearance of Moscow, the two Kremlin Towers way off on the landspit. The Indian totem-pole painted-zigzag-red radar tower, rows of boxes on beach, houses, and fields of oil drums.
>
> Sun molten at ocean edge.
>
> I took a ride on the LCM, the larger ships appeared huge hulls like castles on the water. Instead of treading familiar decks, I looked up on moats and castles isolated a mile apart.

> On the prow today passing back south by Diomede Island and Bering
> Strait, still invisible in rainy rolling water, thin drizzle, for half an hour,
> the waves wilder than usual, orange footed birds suddenly appeared up
> out of combers at crests rising into the air or dived right down in front of
> the ship just before prow foam reached it.
>
> I sang fragments of Messiah looking at the waters, pieces of Isaiah I
> read yesterday. Eli Eli Lama sabacthani. Thunder in the mist. Adonai
> Elohenu Adonai Echad. Tears in my eyes. The waters are still strange.
> For a moment they seemed at the mercy of the Lamb. A continual rolling
> as of a million sheep backs. Birds in and out of great waves, at home.
> Looking back, the iron ship, welded gun turret raised up its grey (milky)
> maw immediately before me. I am afraid of the ship, and the ocean shows
> no mercy. Only my own voice singing pitiful in the wilderness and rain.
> (*Journals Mid-Fifties*, p. 306)

The resemblances between the DEW Line site and the Soviet capital its technology was designed to outwit repeat earlier intuitions by Ginsberg, specifically in his tally-card dream, of the processes by which Cold War surveillance
tends to nurture a deep internalization of the enemy within the very structures
of American defence systems. The discovery of this secret resemblance only
serves, however, to shroud (or generate) a further mystery: the totemic significance of the radar towers that constitute the Line, mixed in with peculiar
bafflement at the strangely feudal military machine the Line protects. Totems
summon taboos and Freud's association of totem with ancestry, tribal names,
father metonyms: what tempts is a family explanation of the strangeness of the
scene, a psychoanalytic anxiety as familiar as the decks he treads upon. The
radar tower as totem stands in for the patriarch defending the psychic coasts
from invasion by the alien Russian ghost-mother, who has nevertheless shaped
the defended homeland in her secret image. The psychoanalytic is troubled,
however, by the alien shapes of the Moloch upon the waters, isolated castles of
a defamiliarizing system Ginsberg hardly understands.

The struggle between familial and superpolitical readings is played out in the
rerun of the Bering Strait experience. Once again, Ginsberg accepts the mystifying invisibility of the Cold War as a pastoralizing dream of peace, despite the
nightmare birds, the wild sea, and the emotional difficulties of the attempts to
articulate Kaddish. The strange birds are read, against the evidence of their suicidal dives, as at home in this interzone. The intimations of anxiety in the wild-
ness of the waves are pacified by the invocation of sheep and lamb. Yet the Cold
War will not be put to bed, but rises in the fetish form of the gun turret. This
totem has both genders: it is father's gun and mother's mouth ('(milky) maw'
recalling milky mother), in mocking appropriation of the comfortably private
Oedipal anxieties. The ship has militarized the army and navy's secret enemy,

the homosexual recruit, within the dream-structure of its weapons – the gun a womanly man – a dream weapon aimed, not at the Communists invisible behind the mist, but directly at Ginsberg, treacherous subversive on Moloch's decks, on Cold War seas. In the Bering Strait, interzone between East and West, along the dateline, so outside time, liminal to the untranscendable horizon of both powers, yet saturated, as ground, by the totemic forces of their radar sweeps, under the alienating surveillance of their feudal secrecies, it is the citizen-recruit who is revealed as the true target of military-familial history. Moloch has recruited the ghost of Naomi Ginsberg, acts the Oedipal father to the pervert-invert, refuses his deepest desire to say Kaddish, tempts the novice dissenter with false dreams of peace, shrivels the resisting imagination to a lonely voice that modulates to the rhythms of its seas and war machines. Is it any wonder that Ginsberg used the money earned on this nightmare trip within Moloch to escape? And he would escape to the other interzone between East and West, the hot zone favoured by Burroughs, Mexico and Tangiers, places most unlike the polar icescapes and mindscapes governed by Cold War history.

Another visitor to the Arctic zone, similarly caught up in the meshes of sexual and military affairs, is Nabokov's Humbert Humbert. If the Arctic provided Ginsberg with the ambiguous rites of passage necessary to leave the United States, it serves as a preparatory zone for Humbert Humbert's assimilation of, immigration and dissimulation of himself into, North America. Arriving in the US in 1940, he spends two years as academic researcher and ad-man in New York, and roughly a further two years in sanatoria for breakdown, a result, he writes, of the 'excruciating desires and insomnias' brought on by his unfulfilled paedophilia.[7] He is encouraged to join a twenty-month research trip to Arctic Canada by a sanatorium doctor, an expedition he joins some time in 1944. He travels north nominally as a recorder of the fieldworkers' 'psychic reactions', but is puzzled by the whole operation. He had, he writes, 'little notion of what object the expedition was pursuing', suspecting from the number of meteorologists engaged in the expedition that it must have something to do with tracking 'the wandering and wobbly north magnetic pole' (*Lolita*, p. 33). But the projects of the various groups of the expedition are mystifying:

> One group, jointly with the Canadians, established a weather station on Pierre Point in Melville Sound. Another group, equally misguided, collected plankton. A third studied tuberculosis in the tundra. Bert, a film photographer – an insecure fellow with whom at one time I was made to partake in a good deal of menial work (he, too, had some psychic troubles) – maintained that the big men in our team, the real leaders we never saw, were mainly engaged in checking the influence of climatic amelioration on the coats of the arctic fox. (*Lolita*, p. 33)

Despite the ludicrousness of these nominal projects, the suspicion that psychological misfits like himself are being used as a front for the secret project of the invisible 'real leaders' is pacified by the odd ways the Arctic does in fact seem to have a healing effect on Humbert Humbert's sexual mania. For the Arctic is a zone beyond desire, its 'fantastic blankness and boredom' accompanied by the absence of paedophile temptations: 'I felt curiously aloof from my own self. No temptations maddened me': the 'little Eskimo girls' are repulsive to him (p. 33). 'Nymphets', he writes, 'do not occur in polar regions' (p. 34).

The blankness of his libido is shadowed by incuriosity concerning the veiled purposes of the expedition, though threaded through the wearisome jocularity of Humbert's prose are intimations of war and Cold War. The Kremlin is alluded to, recalling Ginsberg's vision of the towers at Point Barrow: 'I left my betters the task of analysing glacial drifts, drumlins, and gremlins, and kremlins' (p. 34). The Cold War is sketchily referred to: his work as psychophysician is jokingly called 'cold labour' by his scientist colleagues (p. 34), in allusion to the uses of experimental psychology in the 1940s and 1950s to develop what were called human–machine systems, particularly with a view to maximizing the efficiency of radar operators. Humbert's report on the expedition is published, he writes, in the *Annals of Adult Psychophysics*, and included 'perfectly spurious' data on the fieldworkers' reactions, as well as several bogus psychometric tests, and it is clear that both narrator and author are parodying experimental psychology. Nevertheless, it is also clear that Humbert is knowingly aware of the relations between the psychophysics he was asked to do and the secret military project:

> that particular expedition [. . .] was not really concerned with Victoria Island copper or anything like that, as I learned later from my genial doctor; for the nature of its real purpose was what is termed 'hush-hush', and so let me add that, whatever it was, that purpose was admirably achieved. (*Lolita*, p. 34)

Humbert's coyness here is a signal of his playfully arch complicity in the mechanics and economy of wartime and Cold War secrecies, for they match his own secret sexual project. The choice of Canada's Northwest Territories for the Arctic interlude is not random: the area was not only the bedrock of the radar DEW Line, but in the years Humbert is sent there the focus of intense exploration, for uranium.

The US government, as part of the Manhattan Project, requested the reopening of Eldorado Gold Mining Company's uranium mine at Port Radium, Northwest Territories, situated at Great Bear Lake in the Arctic Circle. Uranium from the area ended up in the bomb that fell on Hiroshima. The Canadian government nationalized Eldorado in 1944, and soon after the war, through its Atomic Energy Control Board, lifted the private prospecting ban and offered incentives to private prospectors in 1946. This ushered in the 'uranium rush', leading to over 10,000 radioactive ore discoveries, most surreally at Uranium City on Saskatchewan's Lake Athabasca. What wartime uranium prospectors would have been looking for in the secret expeditions before the uranium rush would have been the telltale pitchblende seam deposits, most commonly found in Pre-Cambrian granite, source of uranium. Nabokov hints that this is what the 'big men' on Humbert's expedition were really looking for in the juxtaposition, mock-innocently separated by a paragraph break, of these two sentences:

> the big men in our team, the real leaders we never saw, were mainly engaged in checking the influence of climatic amelioration on the coats of the arctic fox.
>
> We lived in prefabricated timber cabins amid a Pre-Cambrian world of granite. (*Lolita*, p. 33)

It is Arctic *rocks* the leaders are interested in, not the arctic *fox*, a rhyming act of camouflage that Humbert learns to exploit for his own purposes in his complex cryptogrammatic games. It was particularly the pitchblende colouration of Arctic Pre-Cambrian granite that prospectors would have been 'mainly engaged in checking', though the whole expedition aims to camouflage its geophysics under the guise of other, purer disciplines (it is striking that the list of scientists Humbert tells us are on the expedition include botanists, meteorologists, nutritionists, psychophysicians, but no mineralogists, and yet 'Victoria Island copper' is suggested as the front).

The development of the atom bomb is intimately related to the Northwest Territories, as were the consequences of its development, the paranoid human–machine systems of the DEW Line. Nabokov is implying, cryptically, that the secret operations of the Second World War trained a whole generation of intellectuals, recruited into the war's scientific projects, in the arts of secrecy and hush-hush camouflage. The training involved the development of ways of co-opting the human body, at the most basic levels of perception, to the human–machine technology of the Manhattan Project and the DEW Line: secretly looking for pitchblende modulates effortlessly into secretly looking for 'kremlins' through the radar analysis of new kinds of visual signal. But more importantly for Humbert's 'real purpose' is the training in a new kind of secrecy, the hush-hush techniques of camouflage learned on 'that particular expedition'. The camouflage takes the form, specifically, of psychological/psychiatric deception, a private counterintelligence technique to mislead Freudian interpretation, later refined into the methods used to control Lolita. Returning to the States, he suffers a further 'bout with insanity', but discovers that now, after his trip to the Arctic zone, he can deploy serious fictional techniques of image management:

> I discovered there was an endless source of robust enjoyment in trifling with psychiatrists: cunningly leading them on; never letting them see that you know all the tricks of the trade; inventing for them elaborate dreams, pure classics in style (which make *them*, the dream-extortionists, dream and wake up shrieking); teasing them with fake 'primal scenes'; and never allowing them the slightest glimpse of one's real sexual predicament. By bribing a nurse I won access to some files and discovered, with glee, cards calling me 'potentially homosexual' and 'totally impotent'. (*Lolita*, pp. 34–5)

What seems here a mere lame parody of psychiatry actually describes a set of displaced and deranged camouflage techniques soon to be unleashed on his victim, Lolita. He will impose fake primal scenes on her with his 'parody of incest' (p. 286). He will invent nightmarish dreams for her, extort her imagination, cunningly lead her on into a web of camouflaged identities, make her, his 'patient', believe she has witnessed her own conception as nymphet, consuming her, the schoolgirl, all the while sleeping admirably in the safe disguise of father and guardian. It is not only the pseudo-knowledge of Freudian techniques that enables him to control her, though this is certainly at the root of one of his impersonations of himself: 'The child therapist in me (a fake, as most of them are – but no matter) regurgitated neo-Freudian hash and conjured up a dreaming and exaggerating Dolly in the "latency" period of girlhood' (p. 124). It is also the robust enjoyment involved in the act of mimicking the power games of wartime and Cold Wartime – the camouflage, the surveillance, the brainwashing, the paranoia, the Hooverite victimization, the spy shape-shifting, the propaganda, the play with secrets, code names, fake fronts, the nuclear terrorizing of children, the infiltrations and demonizations – these are some of Humbert Humbert's favourite things.

If the polar regions educated him in the art of camouflage, what is being concealed most carefully is the analogy between 'the nature of [that particular expedition's] real purpose' and Humbert's 'real sexual predicament' (p. 34). The connection nevertheless seeps through the confession: in his 1947 diary, he specifically uses the story of his 'arctic adventures' as a cover for 'ethereal caresses' of Lolita under Charlotte's very nose, though the adventures are trivialized into a fiction about shooting a polar bear (p. 45).[8] Planning to rape Lolita on a trip to Hourglass Lake, he dreams of himself as a 'pockmarked Eskimo' desperately trying to break through the ice, acknowledging that the dream is an Arctic parody of his attempts to gain sexual access to his stepdaughter (p. 53). The parallel between his deployment of his sexual mania and the secrecy of the mining operations is hinted at here, but for most of the novel remains muted, censored, just as he censors any reference to his psychiatric history.

But the Arctic episode returns to haunt the confession late in the fiction he does write, once he knows that he has lost Lolita. Dick Schiller, her husband

and veteran of the war, has been offered a job, Lolita tells him in her letter, 'in Alaska in his very specialized corner of the mechanical field, that's all I know about it' (p. 264). When he meets him, he discovers he has 'Arctic blue eyes' (p. 271). Odd and unsettling questions of patriotism are raised by Dick's deafness, a disability resulting from his service, as Humbert confuses the Schillers' move north with his own trip to the Northwest Territories, and Dick mishears the question as about his one-armed neighbour, Bill:

> 'And so,' I shouted, 'you are going to Canada? Not Canada' – I re-shouted – 'I mean Alaska, of course.'
>
> He nursed his glass and, nodding sagely, replied: 'Well, he cut it on a jagger, I guess. Lost his right arm in Italy.' (*Lolita*, p. 273)

In context, the exchange ignites a whole series of anxieties about Humbert's un-American status – he is in his own description 'a brand-new American citizen of obscure European origin' (p. 105), a shabby émigré (p. 194) from 'sweet, mellow, rotting Europe' (p. 280) treated like one of those suspicious 'foreigners – or at least naturalized Americans' by the public (p. 194), whose citizenship and nationality is dubious ('Mrs Hays [. . .] asked me if I were Swiss perchance' (p. 237)). His confusion over Canadian Arctic and Alaska signals how insufficiently American his knowledge might be – as when, earlier in his jaunt around the States with Lolita, he seems not to know about Independence Day (p. 243). At the time of the exchange, September 1952, Alaska would have still been a US colonial territory, bought from the Russians in 1867,[9] awaiting its star – it would become the 49th American state on 3 January 1959, the year *Lolita* was published.

The clumsy ignorance of the distinction between a European ex-colonial dominion, Canada, and US-controlled territory is damned by Dick's allusion to the American role in liberating old Europe – Dick's war-wound deafness, in the innocence and simplicity of the mistake, and in adding ordinary, heroic soldier-citizenship to the mix, makes the indictment even more damning. Nabokov is suggesting, with light comic timing, how deviously Humbert's own sense of his slippery allegiances is deliberately inviting, and outrageously satirizing, traditional US patriotism and the Americanism of the solid-citizen warrior ethic.

The episode fits in with the whole final movement of the book, in which Humbert Humbert turns upon himself in bitter-seeming judgement on his own betrayal of Lolita, and of the country which so foolishly let him in with his subversive secret freedoms. And again, the connection between girl-child and nation is developed round the trope of uranium. If we ask where else in the novel we find Humbert sitting on granite, meditating upon his own desire from beyond that desire, and in hush-hush proximity to uranium, then it is after the murder of Quilty, as he awaits the police. He remembers, on a day soon after Lolita's disappearance, being forced by 'an attack of abominable nausea' up the 'ghost of an old mountain road' (p. 305). He walks to a low stone parapet on 'the precipice side of the highway', and hears 'a melodious unity of sounds rising like vapour from a small mining town that lay at my feet, in a fold in the valley' (p. 306):

> One could make out the geometry of the streets between blocks of red and gray roofs, and green puffs of trees, and a serpentine stream, and the rich, ore-like glitter of the city dump, and beyond the town, roads criss-crossing the crazy quilt of dark and pale fields, and behind it all, great timbered mountains. But even brighter than those quietly rejoicing colors – for there are colors and shades that seem to enjoy themselves in good company – both brighter and dreamier to the ear than they were to the eye, was that vapory vibration of accumulated sounds that never ceased for a moment, as it rose to the lip of granite where I stood wiping my foul mouth. And soon I realized that all these sounds were of one nature, that no other sounds but these came from the streets of the transparent town, with the women at home and the men away. Reader! What I heard was but the melody of children at play, nothing but that, and so limpid was the air that within this vapor of blended voices, majestic and minute, remote and magically near, frank and divinely enigmatic – one could hear now and then, as if released, an almost articulate spurt of vivid laughter, or the crack of a bat, or the clatter of a toy wagon, but it was all really too far for the eye to distinguish any movement in the lightly etched streets. I stood listening to that musical vibration from my lofty slope, to those flashes of separate cries with a kind of demure murmur for background, and then I knew that the hopelessly poignant thing was not Lolita's absence from my side, but the absence of her voice from that concord. (*Lolita*, p. 306)

It is a moving moment, and almost succeeds in winning readers over to his side. The 'abominable nausea' is a sickness at the evil he has done in robbing Lolita of her childhood, and the all-American town, laid out at his feet like a Biblical temptation, sings its heavenly song damning him for ever as sick pervert Satan on the mount.

But it is a mining town, like the mining town Dick and Lolita will be escaping to in Alaska. What rich ore is mined in the great timbered mountains around? Humbert does not say; but Nabokov does. Several times, during the composition of *Lolita*, Nabokov made sure in letters to friends (most importantly Edmund Wilson) that the town would have a name and location. He made doubly sure again afterwards, in his butterfly-hunting publications and in the 1956 Afterword, that the name be there as identifiable, locatable, researchable. It is the most sustained act of relevance footnoting done by Nabokov with one of his own texts, as though to underline, and underline again, the importance of mapping his (and Humbert's) invented America onto the real sociopolitical United States. Clearly the auditory epiphany is at the heart of how we interpret

Lolita, and the interpretation lies in the identity of the mining town – this is what the extratextual network of writings insists upon.

The Afterword is most immediately germane, since it was designed to serve as the Author's Last Word and be published at the end of the novel:

> Every summer my wife and I go butterfly hunting. The specimens are deposited at scientific institutions, such as the Museum of Comparative Zoology at Harvard or the Cornell University collection. The locality labels pinned under these butterflies will be a boon for some twenty-first century scholar with a taste for recondite biography. It was at such of our headquarters as Telluride, Colorado; Afton, Wyoming; Portal, Arizona; and Ashland, Oregon, that Lolita was energetically resumed in the evenings or on cloudy days. (*Lolita*, p. 311)

This twenty-first-century scholar followed the hint of the first location label on the list, Telluride, and consulted that extraordinary volume *Nabokov's Butterflies*, which tells us that it was here in the summer of 1951 that Nabokov discovered 'the first known female of *Lycaeides sublivens*', which 'led him to commemorate the locale in the celebrated "final" scene in the novel, Humbert's vision from a mountain road of the mining town below, its tranquillity broken by the sounds of children at play'.[10] The experience is based on one of his own at Telluride in July 1951, as he made sure of detailing to Edmund Wilson in a letter written in early September 1951:

> I do not recall if I told [you] of some of my experiences in the San Miguel Mts. (Southwestern Colo., Telluride and vicinity) and near or in Yellowstone Park. I went to Telluride (*awful* roads, but then – endless charm, an old-fashioned, absolutely touristless mining town full of most helpful, charming people – and when you hike from there, which is 9000', to 10000', with the town and its tin roofs and self-conscious poplars lying toylike at the flat bottom of a *cul-de-sac* valley running into giant granite mountains, all you hear are the voices of children playing in the streets – delightful!) for the sole purpose, which my heroic wife who drove me through the floods and storms of Kansas did not oppose, of obtaining more specimens of a butterfly I had described from eight males, and of discovering its female. I was wholly successful in that quest, finding all I wanted on a steep slope high above Telluride – quite an enchanted slope, in fact, with hummingbirds and humming moths visiting the tall green gentians that grew among the clumps of a blue lupine, *Lupinus parviflorus*, which proved to be the food plant of my butterfly. (Boyd and Pye, *Nabokov's Butterflies*, pp. 478–9)

He spoke of the discovery again in a letter to Elena Sikorski of 6 September 1951, where the butterfly was described as 'my exceedingly rare god-daughter' (Boyd and Pye, *Nabokov's Butterflies*, p. 479), and published a paper on the find in *Lepidopterists' News* in August 1952, remarking that the creature had 'a curiously arctic appearance [. . .] somewhat resembling [. . .] forms from northwestern Canada and Alaska' (Boyd and Pye, *Nabokov's Butterflies*, pp. 481–2). He recalled the trip to an interviewer in June 1959: '"The Southwest is a wonderful place to collect," he said over his soft-boiled eggs. "There's a mixture of arctic and subtropical fauna. A wonderful place to collect"' (Boyd and Pye, *Nabokov's Butterflies*, p. 530).

It is clear from these letters, notes and butterfly writings that Nabokov wished to leave a textual trace of the relations between his daytime hunting of the female *sublivens* (his god-daughter) and the evening compositional quest for stepdaughter Lolita's body and soul. Humbert is a predator seeking Lolita as prey, as he several times admits. His lust for her is a killing act of pseudo-scientific collection ('Nowadays you have to be a scientist if you want to be a killer' (*Lolita*, p. 87)). More specifically, the names Humbert and Dolores are signalled as issuing from the locality: Telluride is a ridge away from Dolores County and the Dolores River. Humbert is likened to a hummingbird in some of the wordplay, as when at Conception Park, he and Lolita see 'hundreds of grey hummingbirds in the dusk, probing the throats of dim flowers' (p. 155); though he shoots one when practising for the Quilty murder (p. 214), further proof, as if we needed it, of the alter-identity of the two men. Indeed, the abduction, abuse and indoctrination of Lolita by the two men, Quilty and Humbert, is a particularly trenchant thematizing of the sacrificial trope investigated by this study, the doubling of the victimizer foregrounding the double agency of Cold War power on the subject as fake-paternal and covertly destructive.

The find and locale are also demonstrated as the origin of the Arctic motif, with the character of the local fauna, and the Canadian and Alaskan resemblances of the female *sublivens*, the Wilson parenthesis making sure that the motif is woven into connection with the attention to children at play. What Nabokov does not tell us, but which would have been clearer to his contemporaries, notoriously so, is the connection between 'Southwestern Colo., Telluride and vicinity' and uranium.

The Four Corners region, where the states of Colorado, Utah, New Mexico and Arizona meet, was the site of the biggest uranium rush and boom of the century. It became a public phenomenon in 1952, when Charlie Steen, an unemployed geologist, discovered an enormous uranium deposit in the Lisbon area, south of Moab, Colorado, in 1952. Before that, as Raye C. Ringholz has shown in her study, *Uranium Frenzy*, the Manhattan Project had ordered hundreds of secret Army Corps of Engineers geologists to seek for uranium in the States.[11] Stocks of uranium from Canada and the Congo were expensive and insufficient, and the US desperately needed domestic sources. The Four Corners was the most likely area, as it had already been the scene of the radium and vanadium booms of the 1910s and 1930s.[12] The Manhattan geologists, with the help of local legends, like Fendell Sitton, vanadium miner dubbed 'Uranium King' (Ringholz, *Uranium Frenzy*, p. 17), converted the vanadium mills in the Colorado towns of Durango, Rifle, Naturita and Uvaran into uranium mills (p. 15), and scoured the canyons for ore with Geiger counters. 'They were the ones', writes Ringholz, 'who pioneered the method for seeking the elusive ore. Carrying out their hugely classified wartime mission, they ushered in a brand new field of mineralology' (p. 16).

With the end of the Second World War, the AEC replaced the Manhattan Project and launched, in 1948, 'the first federally-controlled, federally-promoted and federally-supported mineral rush in the nation's history' (Ringholz, *Uranium Frenzy*, p. 16). The AEC promised to maintain artificially high prices for uranium ore, further agreeing to pay prospectors a $10,000 bonus for each separate discovery. This was backed up by sensational accounts of easy riches in newspapers and magazines; Charlie Steen was galvanized into action by an article in the December 1949 issue of the *Engineering and Mining Journal*, entitled 'Can Uranium Mining Pay?', which urged prospectors to look to Colorado (Ringholz, *Uranium Frenzy*, p. 12). He also recalled reading racy accounts of the secret Geiger counter searches of the Army Corps of Engineers (Ringholz, *Uranium Frenzy*, pp. 15–16) – the wartime secrecy and the connection with the Manhattan Project made the prospect of following in their footsteps all the more attractive. The announcement led to a rush to the region, with Charlie Steen competing with hundreds of amateurs with store-bought Geiger counters.

So whilst Nabokov was hunting for his butterflies in 1951, other collectors were scouring the same landscape for uranium to boost the nuclear programme. The south-west was indeed a wonderful place to collect. Before 1952 and Steen's discovery, the uranium rush had not yet turned into a boom, but retained the mystique and kudos of the Manhattan Project. After 1952, the boom got seriously under way, with massive investment in mines, terrible ecological consequences from the radioactive tailings, and an ethnocidal death rate for the Native American tribes on whose land the uranium mines were mostly sited and who provided the cheap, expendable labour. The boom was satirized by Hollywood in films like *Uranium Boom* (1956) (billed as the 'inside-story of the atom-age boomtowns') and the Bowery brothers' *Dig That Uranium* (1956) ('They're huntin' for the HOT ROCKS in the uranium search that panicked the west!').

When Nabokov signals to his readers in 1959, two or three years after the height of that boom, that Humbert is remembering looking down at Telluride,[13] a town at the heart of the Four Corners, in late 1952, smack in the middle of the Charlie Steen years of private uranium prospecting, and has his perverse scientist recall his wonder at the 'rich, ore-like glitter of the city dump', how he listened keenly for a 'vapory vibration of accumulated sounds' alerting him to something 'majestic and minute, remote and magically near, frank and divinely enigmatic', he is deftly and deliberately associating Lolita with the elusive ore, and Humbert's quest with Manhattan Project Geiger-counter prospecting. It works something like an analogy which super-breeds comparisons: children are America's real source of power and energy and wealth, not the greedy radioactivity of nuclear power. The uranium boom and the baby boom are interlocked forces defining the heartlands of the Cold War US, meshing domestic and international policies and ideologies. The uranium mined to protect our children may be used by the enemy to destroy them, the energy both sustaining the safe breeding grounds of middle America and threatening them with holocaust. Lust for nuclear fuel is like lust for the child, nucleus of the nuclear family.[14]

If Lolita is like uranium for Humbert, it is because she is a precious metal he can rip from her environment. Looking down on Telluride from uranium-rich mountains upon memories of her summons the ghost of previous orgasmic desires ('the brink of that voluptuous abyss'), but what seems the deep solipsism of the paedophile turns out to be something triggered by internalized nuclear culture: 'Lolita had been safely solipsized [. . .] we were fantastically and divinely alone; I watched her, rosy-gold-dusted, beyond the veil of my controlled delight, unaware of it, alien to it [. . .] Suspended on the brink of that voluptuous abyss' (pp. 59–60). The lust for her 'rosy-gold-dusted' body replays the ways the uranium rush borrowed its tropes from the gold rush. That 'controlled delight' is a vicious sexualization of the atom bomb's and H-bomb's controlled explosions, consuming what fuels their destructive cores. Like a thermonuclear blast, Humbert feeds off the child's energy, profiting from the terrible forces released by its transformation into sexual forces. He imagines himself as exploding off her heat, with her as the innocent observer 'beyond the veil', as though she were one of the safe scientists watching the blast behind their smoked glasses. But she is expendable fuel, solipsized and annihilated within the sexual machine which is Humbert Humbert.

He dies on 16 November 1952, the month of the world's first thermonuclear controlled explosion, based on radiation implosion, code-named 'Ivy Mike' ('m' for 'megaton'), on Elugelab island in the Eniwetok Atoll of the Marshall Islands, and on the very day of the Ivy King test ('k' for 'kiloton'), dropped by bomber on Runit Island, Eneweta – more appropriate to bomber-height Humbert at Telluride since its core was pure uranium (highly enriched uranium, oralloy).[15] The bomb, called a Super Oralloy Bomb, was the most powerful fission device ever built to be dropped on a town or city, and had the evil acronym SOB – 'her sobs in the night – every night, every night' (p. 173). The mushroom cloud produced by such bombs haunts Lolita as a figure for the threat posed by paedophile 'fathers' to innocent children: Quilty writes a play titled The Strange Mushroom significantly before his next, Fatherly Love (p. 31), and Lolita's classroom at Beardsley is 'Mushroom', in which hangs a print of Reynolds' 'Age of Innocence' (p. 195).

The sexualization of nuclear technology is the most important of what Nabokov in the Afterword called 'the secret points, the subliminal co-ordinates' of the novel (pp. 314–15). The process of sexualization is a perverse act of solipsism which internalizes the mining, processing and deployment of uranium-sourced energy, and succeeds because the technological process is itself already sexualized. We can see this in the ways the pulp Hollywood films about the uranium boom paralleled the mining of the hot rocks with sleazy plots about dangerously 'hot' women. *Uranium Boom* has two men discover uranium but fight over a woman; *Dig That Uranium* pitches the sultry Mary Beth Hughes as *femme fatale*. The naming of the uranium mines reveals a similar troping: one of the mines in the Colorado area is called 'Uranium Girl'; Charlie Steen's mines all had Spanish names like 'Mujer Sin Verguenza', 'Mi Corazon', 'Te Quiero', 'Linda Mujer' and 'Mi Amorcita' (Ringholz, *Uranium Frenzy*, p. 22). As Sanders argues, the confidentiality of the uranium mining was part of the lure: 'This secrecy which the landscape seemed to manifest was also a seductive ploy – hard-to-get, but promising an assignation with the prospector or miner, the infertile land was finally to offer itself to engenderment' (Sanders, 'The Hot Rock in the Cold War', p. 164).

The trope repeats the Gold Rush convention of identifying precious metal with the sexual object of desire, most notoriously with *The Gold Rush*, Chaplin's 1924 film. Chaplin's child-wife Lillita McMurray (of Spanish-Scottish-Mexican background), professional name Lita Grey, was initially given the part of the girl the Tramp dreams about in his Gold Rush cabin in the snows. The dream girl is a sexual sublimation of the desired mineral: Lita Grey was fifteen during the shooting, but was replaced once she became pregnant and Chaplin secretly married her.[16] There is no doubt that she was one of the secret sources of the name Lolita, the Gold Rush precursor to atomic-age Dolores.

The name Dolores, taken from the river that runs through the uranium mines and mills of the Four Corners, contains the word 'ore' within itself, a pun the early miners doubtless appreciated. Uranium ore-processing facilities operated along the Dolores river valley in the 1940s and 1950s, leaving a million tons of radioactive tailings with considerable risk of groundwater contamination. Nabokov/Humbert covertly alludes to this controversial issue in the manner of Lolita's death – she 'died in childbed, giving birth to a stillborn girl' (p. 6). The relationship between radioactivity and the rate of stillbirths and cancer in children was a highly emotive and 'hush-hush' issue in the years of the main composition of *Lolita*, up to December 1953. Scientific studies of the survivors of Hiroshima and Nagasaki between 1947 and 1952 looked at genetic damage, incidence of leukaemia and stillbirth rates.[17] A great deal of information was also available in the annual reports of the Atomic Bomb Casualty Commission. Its 1950 report, *The Effects of Atomic Weapons*, for example, notes coldly that one of the symptoms in the pathology of radiation sickness is 'an increased incidence of miscarriages and premature births, and an increased death rate among expect-ant mothers'.[18] The facts were chilling, as Jim Garrison observed: 'All recorded cases of pregnant women within 3,000 metres of Ground Zero resulted in mis-carriages or premature births at which time the infants died. Pregnant women beyond 3,000 metres suffered a 66% miscarriage and stillbirth rate.'[19]

J.V. Neel and W.J. Schull, in their 1956 work[20] on behalf of the Atomic Bomb Casualty Commission, summed up much of the research since the war. It is an ugly document, attempting to downplay most of the evidence of genetic malformation on the children even of men and women who suffered direct irradiation. But it does give an indication of the abiding fear since 1945 that irradiation led directly to stillbirth. In the hideous language of the Commission, the report provides statistics on the effects of 'genetic and somatic damage' and 'maternal exposure' on stillbirth rates (Neel and Schull, *Effect of Expoure*, p. 124), notes a distinct rise in frequency in what it calls 'category 1 mothers' (those in the two cities when the bombs fell), and a correlation between high rates, 'very young mothers' and their 'maternal radiation history' (p. 196).

There was also considerable hush-hush research in 1949 and 1950 into the carcinogenic effects of radon and radon-daughter contamination at uranium mines in the Colorado Plateau. William F. Bale's Memorandum in July 1951 was the first substantial statement of the likely dangers associated with radon daughters, the decay products of radon, on uranium miners in Colorado. It formed part of a series of health reports and investigations by the AEC, the Public Health Service and the Bureau of Mines, which culminated in an AEC conference in December 1950 where 'Dr. William Bale pointed out that the immediate daughters of radon (RaA, RaB, and RaC) were more important sources of radiation to lung tissue than was radon itself.' A medical survey of miners at the main uranium mills in Colorado was undertaken in the summer of 1951, just as Nabokov was hunting his butterflies at Telluride. The survey was accompanied by Occupational Health meetings which informed official agencies and mining companies of 'the health hazards connected with uranium mining and [. . .] methods of measuring radon daughters'.[21]

Lolita, then, was composed in a country on the cusp of the uranium boom, at a time when the AEC was establishing domestic sources of uranium in Colorado to replace the Canadian Arctic supply and issuing heavy propaganda to prospectors about the gold-rush riches in the Four Corners. At the same time, the US was still absorbing the terrible research into the Hiroshima and Nagasaki bombings and very scared indeed about the radiation effects of radon daughters in those same uranium mines.[22] The double nature of uranium – at once source of wealth, destructive power and energy, and agent of lethal radioactivity – secretly structures the encounter between Humbert and Lolita. Though for Humbert, she represents the forbidden and secret precious metal, radiating nymphet energy, it is he who is the lethal, sterilizing force, causing her deep somatic damage, sealing her fate as a very young mother, condemning her and her girl-child to death after the 'radiation history' he has exposed her to. Though she is the 'daughter', it is his obsession with daughters which creates the invisible but killing atmosphere, a radon-daughter effect.

Radon's decay and degradation are hinted at: 'it was still a nymphet's scent that in despair I tried to pick up, as I bayed through the undergrowth of dark decaying forests' (*Lolita*, p. 76); 'my degrading and dangerous desires' (p. 25). The dangerous dust of radioactive waste, lodged in bone tissue, is insisted on in the first vision of Lolita's body: 'the little bone twitching at the side of her dust-powdered ankle' (p. 41). It is continued in an extended dust motif: 'the sun-dusted air' (p. 57), 'rosy-gold-dusted' (p. 59). It becomes threatening when associated with Charlotte's death: 'dust was running and writhing over the exact slab of stone where Charlotte, when they lifted the laprobe for me, had been revealed, curled up, her eyes intact, their black lashes still wet, matted, like yours, Lolita' (p. 104). And it is finally directly aimed at Lolita herself, in the form of the amethyst phials of sleeping draught used in the rape plan: each of the phials from his 'boxful of magic ammunition' is described as a 'microscopic planetarium with its live stardust' (p. 109). The dangerous emanation from the 'ore-like glitter of the city dump' is not the rare nymphet, but Humbert himself, the decaying, corrupt set of desires: 'And I shall be dumped where the weed decays, / And the rest is rust and stardust' (p. 255).

Humbert believes Lolita to be the source of radiation, in the ways he associates her with Annabel the moment he first sees her in Ramsdale. It is a vision he remembers throughout the book, and it returns to him on the last day he sees Lolita: 'For some reason, I kept seeing – it trembled and silkily glowed on my damn retina – a radiant child of twelve, sitting on a threshold, "pinging" pebbles at an empty can' (p. 277). But as the 'retina'–'radiant' chiming confirms, it is something in his own projective radiating gaze which is the real radioactive force, creating a lethal nuclear threshold for Lolita. The chiming recalls the Annabel tryst because it was that defining inaugural moment of unfulfilled desire which had already been infected and inflected by the *Waste Land* context of uranium hot rocks, the 'violet shadow of some red rocks' (p. 13) associated with the 'faint radiance' imagined as emitted by Annabel's 'face in the sky' (p. 14). The radiation goes deep, deep into Humbert's somatic machinery, 'my heart, my throat, my entrails' (p. 15). The nuclear force of this transgressive desire is 'mined' in the Arctic episode as secret technology and unleashed on Lolita in the form of an ogre's hunger for her somatic interiority: 'My only grudge against nature was that I could not turn my Lolita inside out and apply voracious lips to her young matrix, her unknown heart, her nacreous liver, the sea-grapes of her lungs, her comely twin kidneys' (pp. 162–3).

This is X-ray cannibalism as atomic death-ray, discreetly linked in Nabokov's Cold War-secretive prose to radios and radioactivity: 'Ray-like, I glide in through to the parlor and find the radio silent' (p. 49). Humbert uses radio to mask the sounds of his repeated rapes, and rays of sinister X-ray light ('skeleton glow', 'intercrossed rays') to reveal Lolita's body to his night-time gaze: 'The door of the lighted bathroom stood ajar; in addition to that, a skeleton glow came though the Venetian blind from the outside arclights; these intercrossed rays penetrated the darkness of the bedroom and revealed the following situation' (p. 127). The 'situation' is Lolita's sleeping form, 'lightly veiled body and bare limbs' revealed and penetrated down to her bone structure: 'a band of pale light crossed her top vertebrae' (p. 127). The ray is his sexual gaze in the form of a blazing, radioactive blast of energy which aims to penetrate her body, like a dildo (the meaning of 'olisbos'): 'I had put the radio at full blast. I had blazed in her face an olisbos-like flashlight' (p. 94).

The ray is a concentration of his *'grand péché radieux'*, a radiating transgression which has at its heart 'sterile and selfish vice' (p. 276). His attitude to Charlotte's body collocates imagination of pregnancy, Lolita as foetus, bedtime light rays and a sterile touch:

> This was the white stomach within which my nymphet had been a little curved fish in 1934. This carefully dyed hair, so sterile to my sense of smell and touch, acquired at certain lamplit moments in the poster bed the tinge, if not the texture, of Lolita's curls. (*Lolita*, pp. 75–6)

The neutralizing sterility is secretly to do with uranium: 1934 was the crucial year of the discovery of artificial radioactivity and fission by Enrico Fermi when he irradiated uranium with neutrons. And that sterilizing radiation is aimed at Lolita's womb, her powers of conception; the numbing perversion of it all is the analogy deep in Humbert's textual credences between that creative space and the murderous unconscious within his own body:

> 'Mr Uterus [I quote from a girls' magazine] starts to build a thick soft wall on the chance a possible baby may have to be bedded down there.' The tiny madman in his padded cell.
>
> Incidentally: if I ever commit a serious murder . . . (*Lolita*, p. 47)

The walls of her uterus form the cell he wishes to occupy, as though she must bear the burden of providing his radiating madness with a new habitat, a new killing ground for his sterilizing processes.

It is the first rape that seals her fate – she is killed inside: 'More and more uncomfortable did Humbert feel. It was something quite special, that feeling: an oppressive, hideous constraint as if I were sitting with the small ghost of somebody I had just killed' (p. 139). The act of incest causes lethal inner somatic damage, she a Dolores of pains deep within: 'Presently, making a sizzling sound with her lips, she started complaining of pains, said she could not sit, said I had torn something inside her' (p. 140). Humbert is a death-ray, lethally dosing

Lolita with killer gamma rays, with sustained exposure to the 'radon daughters' of his paedophilia: '" . . . If you really wish to triumph in your mind over the idea of death —" "Ray," said Lo for hurrah, and languidly left the room, and for a long while I stared with smarting eyes into the fire' (p. 285).[23] He thinks she says 'hurrah', but Lolita knows his dirty little nuclear secret and says the secret word: his radioactive eyes smart at this, her triumph over the idea of Humbert Humbert.

Lolita's death-ray is a compound of science fiction and a memory of the New Yorker-Yugoslav inventor Nikola Tesla's design for a charged-particle beam weapon; it hit the headlines in 1940 as Tesla's death-ray:

> Nikola Tesla, one of the truly great inventors who celebrated his eighty-fourth birthday on July 10, tells the writer that he stands ready to divulge to the United States Government the secret of his 'teleforce,' with which, he said, 'airplane motors would be melted at a distance of 250 miles, so that an invisible Chinese Wall of Defense would be built around the country against any attempted attack by an enemy air force, no matter how large.' [. . .] This 'teleforce' [. . .] would operate through a beam one-hundred-millionth of a square centimetre in diameter, and could be generated from a special plant [. . .] A dozen such plants, located at strategic points along the coast, according to Mr. Tesla, would be enough to defend the country against all possible aerial attack. The beam would melt any engine, whether Diesel or gasoline-driven, and would also ignite the explosives aboard any bomber.[24]

The Chinese Wall of Defense created by Humbert's radiating and irradiating gaze is there both defending the mapped space of North America, and deep within his victim Lolita's body, invading and contaminating its 'thick soft wall', his 'padded cell'. Research into beam weapons was being undertaken in both the Soviet Union and the US during the 1950s, based on Tesla's wartime invention, in the quest for an ultimate anti-aircraft and anti-missile defence system. The covert reference to science-factional Cold War defence systems firms up the secret impression throughout *Lolita* that what is being beamed upon Lolita is as much a lethal projection of Cold Warrior paranoid aggression as it is a sexually voracious invasion of her mind and body. It is clear that the late 1952 hush-hush project in Alaska, which Dick Schiller is invited to join as a brilliant young mining engineer, must be the DEW Line – mining engineers were used to construct the stations in 1952–3. The DEW Line, as a warning system designed to protect the body of the United States against nuclear attack, is an apt figure for the new measures of security Lolita must align herself with to protect her own body from invasion by Humbert's gamma-ray gaze and desire. Yet Alaska is not quite US territory – it is still in 1952 a landscape bought from the contemporary enemy. The DEW Line is not sufficiently distinguishable from the paranoid machinery invented by Tesla, a death-ray aimed at incoming aircraft being investigated as line of defence against nuclear bombers. If Humbert, as somatic machine, has internalized Tesla's rays, the DEW Line is also a projection of his Cold War sexualized technology. Going north to Alaska, as a form of escape from a United States corrupted by Humbert's *On the Road* tour and survey, is not only not going far enough: it may very well, according to the secret coordinates of the novel's geography, be entering the very Arctic zone which fostered Humbert's incorporation of Cold War intelligence techniques. The DEW Line hoped to master the forces unleashed by the history connecting Manhattan Project uranium mining in the Northwest Territories to the traumatized culture generated by Hiroshima, including the uranium frenzy in the Four Corners. Yet the Line is just as much a creature of that history as Tesla's death-ray had been a proleptic anticipation of it.

Dolores Haze dies a month after Humbert, in Gray Star, 'a settlement in the remotest northwest' (p. 6). The secret uranium text has come full circle, to the Arctic Circle where Humbert first learned his techniques of stealth, controlled delight and 'polar' camouflaging of his nuclear secret purposes. She dies at Gray Star not only because a grey man has extinguished her star, but because Alaska is an intermediate zone: bidding for a star which it would receive only in 1959, still in the grey zone between a fully fledged American State and dubious ex-Russian territory. The Arctic zone is also dusty with the history of nuclear weapons, the future US state grey with the idea of radioactive dust lying behind Humbert's cant-romantic uses of 'stardust'. The Arctic is a zone that ends a life poisoned by Humbert's incorporated systems of predatory nuclear paranoia. Just as Humbert identifies the car that tails them during the tour of the States with 'a sickness, a cancer', 'a pain in a fatal disease' which creates (or is generated by) the contagious 'interspace' between the two vehicles, 'a zone of evil mirth and magic' (pp. 216–17), so too is Alaska fraught with the radiation sickness emanating from the interspace separating the two superpowers, the interzone Ginsberg experienced at the Bering Strait. It is a zone beyond coordinates, beyond desire, yet also a place beyond possible decontamination, fallout zone for the secret nuclear energies which have defiled the dreamy country of the States (p. 73).

Like a latterday Abbott Handerson Thayer (Humbert and Lolita live on Thayer Street in Beardsley), Humbert combines an 'artistic' paedophiliac-incestuous-sentimental gaze on his angelic 'daughter' with the indulgence of secret wartime fantasies of predatory camouflage.[25] The subjugation of the child-victim is made heroic in the abuser's eye by the very act of inflation of the child into trope and figure for America's nuclear secret. The transgressive obscene secret – sex with a minor on a mock-epic journey that circumscribes the States within a boxlike line – is fuelled and overblown by the insane fantasy translation of Lolita into a literal national treasure, of a metal so precious that its power not only constitutes the superpower status of the nation, but can be deployed to destroy that same nation.

Humbert argues that 'the old link between the adult world and the child world has been completely severed nowadays by new customs and new laws' (p. 124). What he fails to say outright, but betrays in every rhetorical move of his confession, is that the new customs and laws he exploits are precisely the American-Freudian practices and credences which he pretends blinded him to the nature of the real child Lolita. If it is American Freudianism, preaching the already-sexualized nature of the latent child, which is abused to succour his fantasy of the 'fey child I had prepared for my secret delectation' (p. 124), it is the Cold War which identifies this secret victim with the natural resources needed to fuel the machinery of power. The child is what nuclear weapons are designed to defend, yet the radiating effects of uranium target young women and their unborn children. Lolita is the secret sacrificial victim generated by this terrible contradiction, the child desired and destroyed by the same set of unconscious forces.

Victim and uranium come together in Humbert's controlled fantasies, which exploit nuclear culture's dirtiest secrets and psychoanalytic structures. Humbert identifies the topography of America with Freud's topics: the map of the US is made the arena of primal scenes enacted in motels separated by drives both mechanical and unconscious. The ego-defences which might save Lolita from these drives are identified with the compromised DEW Line in the Arctic zone where he learnt how to deploy his predatory techniques. The physical unconscious, source of dangerous energies and lethal motivations, is conceived geophysically within the innocent-seeming American landscape, in the form of immeasurably powerful and destructive matter: the uranium fuelling the arms race. Solipsizing Lolita is identical with solipsizing Cold War America – both girl and state are under threat from the means of their defence, the fake-paternal predatory power of the treacherous guardian on the one hand, and on the other the paranoid-aggressive power of nuclear technology. Humbert, as lethal ray, as paranoid predator, is a criminal psychiatrist radiating, exploiting and exposing the nuclear symptoms of Cold War sexuality, writ large across the map of the United States and deep within its mineral core, printed on 'every pore and follicle' of Lolita's body (p. 270), and deep within, in matrix, heart, liver, lungs and kidneys.[26]

Ginsberg was hardly to allude to his Arctic experiences in later life. But that the experience hurt and went deep is clear from the few references he does make. In 'Death to Van Gogh's Ear', written in Paris in 1958, he is driven to morphine-fuelled near-hysterical condemnation of the US government and its Cold War machine, and suddenly turns against himself:

fiends in our government have invented a cold-turkey cure for addiction
    as obsolete as the Defense Early Warning Radar System.
I am the defense early warning radar system
I see nothing but bombs.[27]

ICBMs had rendered the system obsolete, along with the Kaddish-broken guilt
of his complicity on the *Pendleton* ship supplying the Line. In a 1978 interview,
Ginsberg reflected on the idea of complicity:

> From 1955–65 I made it a business of reading for free and supporting
> myself by sailing in merchant ships up under the DEW line. Cause I didn't
> think poetry and gold should mix. Particularly in that kind of America,
> where everybody was competing for gold, things would get too mixed up,
> I thought poetry should be something outside the system.[28]

But, as the Van Gogh poem demonstrates, poetry and uranium do mix, the Line
of the defence system fusing and fissioning with the poet's own poetic lines,
compounding private paranoia and national nuclear anxiety.[29] Ginsberg's long
line mimics the long DEW Line, his poetry sacrificed to the gods of uranium
and plutonium at the most intense moments of defence and resistance: 'I am the
defense early warning radar system / I see nothing but bombs.'[30]

When Ginsberg finally managed to write *Kaddish* in those feverish forty
hours in Paris in 1958, eking out the money earned serving the DEW Line, it
was bravely to confront the minute particulars of the history of Naomi's paranoia, absorbing it deep into his body as radical early warning system against the
forces of Moloch he had glimpsed in the shrouded shapes in the Bering Strait.
During a breakdown in 1938, terrified of 'side-street spies', 'Hitlerian invisible
gas' and poison germs, convinced she'd had '3 big sticks' inserted into her back
by evil hospital staff, mistaking her loved ones for assassins, Naomi forced
her twelve-year-old son to accompany her on a terrible journey from Paterson
to Lakewood, New Jersey, 'near where Graf Zeppelin had crashed before, all
Hitler in Explosion' (*Kaddish*, pp. 14–15). Like Humbert Humbert in his paranoid drive across the States with his captive 'daughter', Naomi forced her son
to accompany her on a trip across the country, transforming its landscape into
the sinister geography of her persecution mania:

> and you covered your nose with motheaten fur collar, gas mask
> against poison sneaked into downtown atmosphere, sprayed by
> Grandma –
> And was the driver of the cheesebox Public Service bus a member of
> the gang? You shuddered at his face, I could hardly get you on – to
> New York, very Times Square, to grab another Greyhound –
> where we hung around 2 hours fighting invisible bugs and jewish
> sickness – breeze poisoned by Roosevelt –

out to get you – and me tagging along, hoping it would end in a quiet room in a victorian house by a lake.

Ride 3 hours thru tunnels past all American industry, Bayonne preparing for World War II, tanks, gas fields, soda factories, diners, locomotive roundhouse fortress – into piney woods New Jersey Indians – calm towns – long roads thru sandy tree fields –

Bridges by deerless creeks, old wampum loading the streambed – down there a tomohawk or Pocahontas bone – and a million old ladies voting for Roosevelt in brown small houses, roads off the Madness highway.

(*Kaddish*, pp. 13–14)

This is a landscape made nightmarish by the history of persecution, from the history of the ethnic cleansing of native American culture from the Eastern seaboard, through the poisoning of the country by the industries of warfare, proleptically forward to the holocaust haunting the American air. The family is turned into a treacherous network of enemies – underscored by Ginsberg's prose alliteration sequence 'gas mask', 'Grandma', 'gang' – a network written into the industrial structure of modern America ('gas fields'). Jewish, Communist and immigrant, the Ginsbergs experience ethnic sympathy with the destroyed Algonquian culture, which modulates into a paranoid intuition of the hostility of white settler Americans to their new foreign bodies. If the journey from Paterson to Lakewood is a trip into a paranoia that feeds off foreboding about nascent fascist anti-semitism in 1930s and 1940s America, it is also a frightening warping of a boy's imagination by a mother forcing him to hate and fear his own country, initiating him too early into a vision of a lethal landscape, militarized by fascist history, toxic with genocidal violence. Naomi's decision to flee to Lakewood, where the Rockefellers used to retire on vacation, seems like a quest for refuge from the urban-industrial States poisoned by history – yet the town is imaginatively at the heart of the psychogeography most feared, scarred as it is by the Hindenburg disaster and its fascist aftermath, the enemy war machine.

The most disturbing feature of Naomi Ginsberg's paranoia was its obsession with the toxicity of the air in all its forms, in particular her fear of radio as a means of mind control and murder. 'Hitlerian invisible gas' seeping through keyholes merges with terror at radio voices insinuating themselves 'thru the wires in her head, controlled by 3 sticks left in her back by gangsters in amnesia, thru the hospital' (*Kaddish*, pp. 15, 21). Medical intervention, which would eventually lobotomize her, has accustomed her to imagining her body as colonized by technology. The paranoia locks into the 'jewish sickness' of internalized fascist terror and transforms her dream body into a piece of military hardware, her head a radio, her back a cockpit control stick assembly in some chemical weapon bomber of the mind. She is being 'flown' by sinister air-traffic control. And part of their mission is to turn her against her own allegiances (Zhdanov and Trotsky are out to get her too), against her own family (Aunt Rose, Uncle Ephraim, her sister Elanor, Louis and Allen himself), against America and America against her; to turn even her own body against her (the convulsions, vomiting, the 'croaking up her soul' (p. 22)), and the doctors against her body, with their electric shocks, lobotomies and mind-killing drugs.

For Ginsberg after the Bering Strait visions, this terrible self-destruction and the hideous initiation into paranoid States provides the key (as in the key in the window in Naomi Ginsberg's vision in *Kaddish*) for the interpretation of Cold War America, and this against the grain of his natural optimism, his breezy ecstasies and improvised happy creeds. Like Lolita moving beyond Humbert to Alaska, Ginsberg is both abused and disabused. The drug trips he took that formed the basis for the 1959 poems 'Laughing Gas', 'Mescaline' and 'Lycergic Acid' reprise the Greyhound journey of 1938 through Naomi's United States and the USNS *Sgt. Jack J. Pendleton* voyage in 1956 to the interzone. 'The pain of gas flowing into the eye' of 'Laughing Gas' recalls his mother's 'gas mask against poison' and the gas fields beyond Bayonne, summoning a dream bus run by 'TRACKLESS TRANSIT CORPORATION' (*Kaddish*, p. 80), destination Buchenwald and the universe 'smashed / to smithereens by the oncoming / atomic explosions with / Eisenhower as once President / of a place called U.S.' (*Kaddish*, p. 76). The 'smell of Naomi' robs him of sexual desire for both men and women in 'Mescaline', a poem haunted by a path towards death and her paranoia: 'and I am too conscious of a million ears / at present creepy ears, making commerce' (*Kaddish*, p. 85). The million-eared creature turns into 'a multiple million eyed monster' humming in his typewriter in 'Lycergic Acid', 'electricity connected to itself, if it hath wires / it is a vast Spiderweb / and I am on the last millionth infinite tentacle of the spiderweb' (*Kaddish*, p. 86). Its name is God, but God as Moloch, the Moloch of the Cold War, a radio noise in the head, a creature deep in the belly and out there in the dark sea of the interzone Strait: 'it wants another form another victim / it wants me' (p. 90). In this Cold War that singles out each citizen as its next victim, the war that killed Lolita and haunted Naomi to her death, there is no flight except to the nuclear-polar terminal zone: 'No refuge in myself, which is on fire / or in the World which is His also to bomb and Devour!'[31]

It took a real war, the hot Cold War of Vietnam, to bring Ginsberg to his senses, to cure him of the paranoid sickness caught on the *Pendleton* which had brought on the internalization of the toxic landscape seen from the outlandish bus journey of 1938. In the great poems of *The Fall of America*, Ginsberg undertook a set of personal re-enactments of that journey in Greyhound, automobile and plane to re-chart the paranoid territory of Naomi's US in the light of the new conflict.

A reaction against the aggression against himself and against the memory of his mother began to thaw the internal Cold War in the *King of May* poems, particularly in the injunctions towards a more forgiving, radically sentimental attitude in 'Who Be Kind To'. There Ginsberg urges his self-consciousness to basic human kindness towards his own mortal body ('Be kind to your self, it is only one / and perishable'), and also, importantly, towards his mother ('Be kind to your disappearing mother') and towards the United States, despite its transformation by the military–industrial complex seen on the trips to Lakewood and Point Barrow:

> Be kind to this place, which is your present
>   habitation, with derrick and radar tower.

(Collected Poems, p. 359)

The kindness may be flaky and provisional, vulnerable to the charge of the naive pastoralism which had marred many of the diary entries in 1956, yet it marks a determination to make space for affirmations that a thorough-going paranoid interpretation could still irradiate and wither; a determination, in other words, to move beyond the Cold War as crippling symptom, a determination 'to end the cold war he has borne / against his own kind flesh' (*Collected Poems*, p. 362).

It was on the 1965–6 journeys across the States undertaken for *The Fall of America* that Ginsberg, freed up to write in the detailed and sensitive testimonial style of his diaries by the Uher tape-recorder bought with Bob Dylan's gift of $600, managed to exorcise the false Cold War symptoms and properly represent the realities of the Cold War America revealed by Vietnam. 'Wichita Vortex Sutra' took Ginsberg by car to Wichita, Kansas, site of the Boeing facilities which had built the B-52s. 'Kansas City to Saint Louis' took him through Fulton, Missouri, location of Churchill's Iron Curtain speech. 'Iron Horse' sees Ginsberg on a train picking up soldiers, heading for the war, at Amarillo, Texas, site of the Pantex Plant, the Department of Energy's facility for the assembly of nuclear weapons; then by Greyhound from Chicago to New York, revisiting the phantom war landscapes glimpsed from the Greyhound in 1938. The political naivety of Ginsberg's unilateral declaration of the end of the war in the Wichita poem is belied if one understands that the auto-poesy really did end the Cold War Ginsberg had borne against his own kind flesh. These journeys across the heartlands of America revealed the real face of America's war economy, enabling a transformation of the hysterically visionary paranoia inherited from Naomi and the Bering Strait into a more controlled and detailed denunciation of the secret war machine running America. Seeing Wichita, reading his poems to Wichita, registering the minute particulars of Wichita enabled Ginsberg to record in detail the precise lineaments of the indoctrination of mainstream America by the war administration down at the level of its local geography, its daily language and everyday economy. These proximities and acts of ordinary witness cure Ginsberg of his guilt over the death of his mother, and establish a new vision of the links between the war culture and his mother's fate:

> [Wichita that] murdered my mother
> who died of the communist anticommunist psychosis
> in the madhouse one decade long ago
> complaining about wires of mass communication in her head
> and phantom political voices in the air
> besmirching her girlish character.
>
> (*Collected Poems*, p. 410)

The link between Wichita and Naomi is no longer a DEW Line of spectral coincidences, but a real set of circumstances. These circumstances reveal the minute particulars of the relations between American-Freudian surveillance of Russian Americans like Naomi and the Cold War: its ideology ('communist anticommunist psychosis'), its technology (the radio-radar complex of the 'wires of mass communication'), its propaganda ('phantom political voices in the air'), all culminating in the government's deployment of its Wichita-constructed bombers in Vietnam.

Yet these auto-poems are not stricken and self-destructive in the articulation of these complex interconnections, but practise a special form of kindness, even or especially to the people of Wichita, even or especially to the soldiers on the iron horse to war:

> Through the highway's straight,
> dipping downward through low hills,
> rising narrow on the far horizon
> black cows browse in caked fields
> ponds in the hollows lie frozen,
> quietness.
> Is this the land that started war on China?
> This be the soil that thought Cold War for decades?
> Are these nervous naked trees & farmhouses
> the vortex
> or oriental anxiety molecules
> that've imagined American Foreign Policy
> and magick'd up paranoia in Peking
> and curtains of living blood
> surrounding far Saigon?
>
> (*Collected Poems*, p. 403)

The attention to detail is so tender, like Dylan singing ('His tenderness penetrating aether, / soft prayer on the airwaves' (p. 409)), that Wichita retains its Whitmanesque pastoral sublimities at the same time as being prey to and source of the more sinister uniformities of the Cold War. The delicate balance between commination of the nation and imagination of the nation's quietness performs an exorcising of his own paranoia, seeing its symptoms writ large on the international political scene, simultaneously tracking the enemy to its lair in the Kansas heartlands and redeeming the US landscape of its monstrous complicities by way of a vision, a vision of its true peace.

NOTES

1. Schumacher, *Dharma Lion*, pp. 232–3.
2. Ginsberg, *Journals Mid-Fifties: 1954–1958*, p. 260. On Ginsberg and the Cold War, I am grateful to the following critical works: Tytell, *Naked Angels*; Harris, 'Cold War Correspondents'; Jarraway, '"Standing by His Word"'; Trigilio, *'Strange Prophecies Anew'*; and Davidson, 'From Margin to Mainstream'. Other works that have informed my thinking about Ginsberg include Prothero, 'On the Holy Road'; Snyder, 'Crises of Masculinity'; Hyde, *On the Poetry of Allen Ginsberg*; Jeffs, *Feminism, Manhood, and Homosexuality*; and Herring, '"Her Brothers Dead in Riverside or Russia"'.
3. Cf. Butler, *Bodies that Matter*.
4. For the importance of the policing of sexual deviance in Cold War America, cf. Corber's *Homosexuality in Cold War America*.
5. Cf. Sutherland, 'The Strategic Significance of the Canadian Arctic'; Purver, *Arms Control in the North*, pp. 21–2; Mercogliano, 'To Boldly Go Where No Fleet has Gone Before', at www.usmm.org/msts/arctic.html, accessed 9 December 2008; and Bouchard, 'Guarding the Cold War Ramparts: The U.S. Navy's Role in Continental Air Defence', pp. 111–35. The DEW line became obsolete during the 1970s but was renovated in the late 1980s as the North Warning System.
6. The pole as ultimate theatre of the Cold War is staged in the 1951 science fiction film *The Thing*, where an alien feeds off human blood whilst the military track it with Geiger counters, eventually killing it with radioactive isotopes. Cf. Henriksen, *Dr. Strangelove's America*, pp. 54–8. Also discussed by Biskind, *Seeing is Believing*, pp. 126–36.
7. Nabokov, *Lolita*, p. 32. Political readings of Nabokov are rare and there is precious little on his work in Cold War contexts. I am grateful for the following interpretations in my reading of *Lolita* for their political angle and their perspicacity about the sexual victimization of Lolita: Anderson, ' Nabokov's Genocidal and Nuclear Holocausts in *Lolita*'; Wood, '*Lolita* Revisited' and his indispensable *The Magician's Doubts*; Centerwall, 'Hiding in Plain Sight: Nabokov and Pedophilia'; Green, *Freud and Nabokov*; Maddox, *Nabokov's Novels in English*; and Levine, '"My Ultraviolet Darling": The Loss of Lolita's Childhood'. For the background, I acknowledge the equally necessary work of Boyd, both the biography (*Vladimir Nabokov: The American Years*) and the book on *Pale Fire*; Lyons, 'Nabokov in America'; Alexandrov, *The Garland Companion to Vladimir Nabokov*; and Johnson, 'The Labyrinth of Incest in Nabokov's *Ada*'.
8. This childish fiction gains a sinister edge later when he prepares an iced whiskey and soda for Charlotte at the precise moment of her death: the ice blocks for the drink look like little pillows, 'pillows for polar teddy bear, Lo' (p. 96). The death of the mother coincides with an icy resolve to put Lolita to sleep too. The killing of Lolita's childhood is hinted at also in one eerie comic detail from the description of Quilty's house – it contains a polar bear skin (p. 293).
9. The US bought Alaska from Russia in a treaty on 30 March 1867, for $7,200,000.

10. Boyd, 'Nabokov, Literature, Lepidoptera', in Boyd and Pye, *Nabokov's Butterflies*, p. 12.
11. 'Atom General' Leslie Groves, in charge of the Manhattan Project during the war, had wanted monopoly over uranium and, later, thorium stocks in the world, through the clandestine programme code-named Murray Hill Area. Cf. Herken. *The Winning Weapon*, pp. 100–7. For the comparable uranium boom in Australia, cf. Sanders, 'The Hot Rock in the Cold War'.
12. The Curies had thought radium could cure cancer, and radium could be extracted from the pitchblende and carnotite waste products of the mineral mining of the south-west. Vanadium strengthens steel, so was necessary for the rearmament programmes of the prewar years (Ringholz, *Uranium Frenzy*, p. 12).
13. Named in 1881 after the rare element found in gold and silver ores.
14. The association of nuclear threat, the 'deadly shower' of radiation and schoolchildren became central to the civil defence measures of the late 1950s, an association even or especially effecting isolated rural towns like Telluride. The *Safety Education* journal in 1959 warned: 'Even isolated rural schools must be alerted to the fact that their isolation is no defense against such a deadly shower, and, like schools in the primary target area, they must be prepared to set up a shelter program to safeguard their children against contamination' (quoted in Henriksen, *Dr. Strangelove's America*, p. 109).
15. Oralloy, named after Oak Ridge alloy, was the wartime code name for uranium-235.
16. Robinson, *Chaplin*, pp. 366–8. Chaplin had first met Lita when she was twelve, using her as the devil's temptation in *The Kid* (pp. 261–2).
17. For instance: Genetics Conference, 'Genetic Effects of the Atomic Bombs in Hiroshima and Nagasaki' (1947); Folley, Borges and Yamawaki, 'Incidence of Leukemia in Survivors of the Atom Bomb' (1952); Neel et al., 'The Effect of Exposure to the Atomic Bombs on Pregnancy Terminations in Hiroshima and Nagasaki: A Preliminary Report' (1953). The Atomic Bomb Casualty Commission (ABCC, formerly the Joint Commission) studying the effects of the atomic bomb in Japan issued a five-volume report in 1951 (Oughterson et al., *Report of the Joint Commission*). A report by R. R. Wilson was submitted to the ABCC in 1951 on nuclear radiation at Hiroshima and Nagasaki, and eventually published in 1956 (Wilson, 'Nuclear Radiation').
18. Los Alamos Scientific Laboratory for AEC, *The Effects of Atomic Weapons*, p. 353.
19. Garrison, *From Hiroshima to Harrisburg*, p. 30.
20. Neel and Schull, *The Effect of Exposure to the Atomic Bombs on Pregnancy Termination in Hiroshima and Nagasaki*.
21. Information from the archive website of the Advisory Committee on Human Radiation Experiments, www.gwu.edu/~nsarchiv/radiation/dir/mstreet/commeet/meet14/brief14/tab_e/br14e1.txt. William F. Bale's memo, 'Measurements of Air-Borne Radioactivity in a Colorado Plateau Uranium Mine', is available at the same address, with final branch <br14e1c.txt>. Duncan Holaday's chronology of events is at: www.gwu.edu/~nsarchiv/radiation/dir/mstreet/commeet/pm03/pm3brf/tab_c/pm03c2a.tx
22. The connection between radiation and young women became stark in 1955, as Henriksen has shown, when peace activist Norman Cousins and Hiroshima minister Kiyoshi Tanimoto, bomb survivor, 'cooperated to organize the transportation of twenty-five young women from Hiroshima to the United States in 1955; these young Japanese were all disfigured as a result of the atomic bombing of Hiroshima and they came to America for corrective plastic surgery'. The women were called the Hiroshima Maidens (Henriksen, *Dr. Strangelove's America*, p. 45).
23. One of the reasons, presumably, that Nabokov chose John Ray, Jr., as the receiver and publisher of Humbert's text. Another example of Lolita's riposte against

Humbert's uranium tastes lies in the screenplay sent by Nabokov to Kubrick in 1960: 'HUMBERT Tell me, what did you like best of all? I think yesterday's canyon, eh? I think, I've never seen such iridescent rocks. LOLITA I think, iridescent rocks stink' (typescript of Lolita: A Screenplay – Short version of 1960, Nabokov archive, Berg collection, p. 95).

24. *New York Times*, 22 September 1940. The project lies behind the Star Wars project to create a space-based laser anti-missile system during Reagan's presidency.

25. Abbott Handerson Thayer was an American artist painting in the *fin de siècle* and early twentieth century who specialized in paintings of angels: he used his own daughters as models for these sickly sweet visions of angelic girlhood. He was also obsessively interested in matters of camouflage, painting exquisite natural landscapes within which were concealed camouflaged animals and birds. His most celebrated camouflage was a snake concealed in autumn leaves. With his son Gerald he published his theories of camouflage, *Concealing-Coloration in the Animal Kingdom*, a text Nabokov certainly knew. Thayer was very anxious that the Army use his camouflage theories in the First World War. *Lolita* is full of a net of allusions to Thayer, not only with Thayer Street, but also in the keyword status of the terms 'camouflage', 'angel' and 'prey': for example, 'the angelic line of conduct was erased, and I overtook my prey (time moves ahead of our fancies!), and she was my Lolita again' (p. 111); 'the real child Lolita or some haggard angel behind her back' (p. 124); 'I am thinking of aurochs and angels' (p. 307); 'the peacocked shade of trees [. . .] [Quilty] stood, in the camouflage of sun and shade' (p. 235).

26. Joseph McCarthy's paranoia also associated subversive terrorism, an allegorized United States and the individual's defenceless body in one of his more hysterical images: 'One Communist with a razor blade poised over the jugular vein of this nation or in an atomic energy plant can mean the death of America' (quoted in Henriksen, *Dr. Strangelove's America*, p. 47).

27. Ginsberg, *Kaddish*, p. 62.

28. *Gargoyle* 10 (1978) — interview with Eric Baizier, Reywas Divad and Richard Peabody. Available online at www.gargoylemagazine.com/gargoyle/Issues/scanned/issue10/ginsberg.htm, accessed 12 August 2008.

29. Cf. 'Plutonium Ode', in Ginsberg, *Collected Poems*, p. 704.

30. For nuclear poetics, cf. William Carlos Williams, *Paterson*, p. 178.

31. From the 1960 poem 'The Reply', *Kaddish*, p. 97.

4

COLD WAR SEX WAR, OR THE OTHER BEING INSIDE: BURROUGHS, PALEY, PLATH, HUGHES

In a 1979 interview, Grace Paley outlined the relations she saw between 'the politics of the ordinary life of women and men, and the organizational or activist politics' of the nuclear disarmament movement, 'which brings together our own personal flesh, our bodies, as women':

> For a long time I thought about ourselves as women, and what places like Three Mile Island or Love Canal meant to us and to the children we bore and to our own flesh. Then I saw that this also involves men in a way I hadn't thought about before, not just in terms of their being affected but also in a sexual way. This unseeable, unsmellable radiation attacks particularly the foetus, the small growing child, and particularly the egg. [. . .] if [men] would think what was happening to them was the violent if invisible entrance into their sexual bodies, and the attack upon the innocent sperm, if you want to call it that, as well as the pure egg, [then] men would begin to understand what rape was all about.[1]

The Cold War nuclear programme drew minds into its strange, subatomic world at dimensions the body's senses could not record,[2] a world of radiating particles lethal to the innocence of the body's own cells, beamed in waves as if from some evil communications system, insidious, electron-microscopic, a man-made viral epidemic. The spectre of nuclear accident haunts the texts of the period, taking the form within the dissident imagination of a mental imaging of the visceral body suffering blasts of nuclear radiation, mutant

symptoms developing within the living tissues of the equally mysterious ana-
tomical world.

It is this subatomic, cellular and somatic anxiety which drove so many
women into the peace movement. As peace activist Jeannette Buirski put it:

> We cannot see, hear or feel this radiation – the X-rays, alpha, beta and
> gamma rays – we can only see the symptoms. [. . .] The basic building
> blocks of living things are the cells: millions of bone cells, blood, nerve,
> skin, gut cells unite to form that complicated system, the body. As old cells
> die, or children grow, the division of 'parent' cells produces new cells. At
> this stage the cell is most vulnerable to the effects of radiation. When the
> foetus is developing within the womb the fertilised egg cell has to begin
> the long process of repeated cell division to produce the end-product, the
> baby. Cells and babies are part of the material world, so bombard their
> atoms with neutrons, X-rays, gamma, beta rays and the delicate atomic
> structure, and hence function, of the cell will be destroyed. We don't
> *know* this is happening, not until the symptoms of radiation sickness
> appear, or the number of deaths from cancer increases or genetic deformi-
> ties appear in greater numbers in future generations.[3]

Peace activist women took action against nuclear technology partly as defend-
ers of the cellular systems of their bodies, especially within the reproductive
zones the man-made pathogen seemed designed to destroy. Motherhood is here
redefined as a defence of the 'parenting' power of cell division, at the electron-
microscopic level of the cells' delicate atomic structure, against the lethal,
deforming and sterilizing symptoms of an imperceptible raping technology.

Grace Paley recalled joining the Greenwich Village Peace Center in 1961, and
remembers how peace movement numbers swelled with the influx of anxious
mothers: 'Many of us had children and were worried about the nuclear tests
that were sending radioactivity into the air – particularly strontium 90, which
travelled through air, to grass, to cows, to our children's milk.'[4] Nurturing
care for the developing bodies of their children is zoomed down to the invisible
subatomic level, defending milk cells against radioactive air, the death cycle of
contamination a vicious dark parody, at this infinitesimally small dimension,
of the life cycle of sun–grass–cow–milk–child.

The imperceptibility of the radioactivity matches the invisible, unfeelable
nature of the organs under threat, almost as though ionizing radiation were the
body's dark star, a designed enemy and technological pathogen whose point
and purpose are visceralization within the bodies of mothering women.[5] Its
mode of invasion, its silence and undetectability, its infection of nurturing processes, its nuclear power, its status as radiation make fallout the evil twin to the
sun's benign rays. This negative replication of good energy is also characteristic
of the radioactive metals feared by the women activists – strontium 90, emitting

its deadly beta ray, behaves chemically like calcium, concentrating in the bones and teeth like mother's milk.

In 'Living', one of Paley's short stories from the 1960 collection *Enormous Changes at the Last Minute*, peace activist mothers Ellen and Faith discover they are both dying from mysterious ailments. Faith is uncontrollably bleeding, blood 'rising from my cold toes to find the quickest way out'; Ellen has terminal depression created by fear. Faith survives, though she is by far the more cynical of the two: "'Life isn't that great Ellen [. . .] What's the big loss? Live a couple more years. See the kids and the whole cruddy thing, every cheese hole in the world go up in heat blast firewaves."' Both single women abandoned by feckless husbands, they have protested against the Cold War, 'past[ing] white doves on blue posters and pray[ing] on Eighth Street for peace'.[6] Both are Jewish, living in the unnatural seasonal rhythms of this outwardly Christian nation – they both contract their diseases over Christmas and Ellen dies the following Christmas.

The tale is brief, narrated in disjointed, derangedly childlike, mock-comic tones, as though Faith were parodying the double ghettoization of her mind as single Jewish mother in New York, the comedy of the stock *shtetl* prankster merged with the infantilized self-trivializing of the 1950s housewife, held together, only just, as angry satire against such a reading of her. Together the two registers generate a strangely muted, depressed panic and hysteria, a process of disintegration there in the broken syntax and semantic discontinuities, as though language itself were under enormous pressure, under terminal threat.

Faith as survivor cannot even face her own anti-nuclear anxiety – it is displaced onto the neo-Christian environment of her neighbours:

> I drank a little California Mountain Red at home and thought – why not – wherever you turn someone is shouting give me liberty or I give you death. Perfectly sensible, thing-owning, Church-fearing neighbors flop their hands over their ears at the sound of a siren to keep fallout from taking hold of their internal organs. You have to be cockeyed to love, and blind in order to look out the window at your own ice-cold street. (Paley, *Collected Stories*, p. 165)

The cold of the street finds its symptom in the cold in her body, both constituting the icy environment of the Cold War. The sense of alienation from the Christian nation is registered symptomatically too in the contempt at the stupidity of the church-fearing neighbours, yet as a true symptom it signals the deep disturbance that nearly kills Faith, destroying Ellen. For fear of fallout *does* come through the ear for Ellen and Faith, textually, as alarmist language, a distorting, deforming and disfiguring invisible force you can sense but cannot see. It seeks out mothers, women alone, activists for peace in defence of their children, inhabiting the womb as paranoid fear and causing the mock-menstrual blood to flow as life-aborting power.

The male doctors tell Ellen and Faith their sickness is self-induced, silly hysteria: Ellen's doctor tells her 'he never saw anyone with so little will to live'; Faith's tells her, like a child, 'Noone bleeds for ever.' Both mothers are rearing boys, bringing them up to fight in the Koreas and Vietnams, or as fodder in a hopeless nuclear exchange, little soldiers with brittle bones. Only without the boys can Faith heal up: 'My sister took the kids for a while so I could stay home quietly making hemoglobin, red corpuscles, etc.' (Paley, *Collected Stories*, p. 166). Paley's tale is an unstable mix of dark gallows humour, testy deranged allegory, an infection-inflected prose fantasy, sad dialogue and exercise in controlled paranoia, and works because its target – Cold War nuclear culture – is also a matter of deep morbidity, a national hysteria, a fantastic paranoia of insane tests and contained contamination of the world. And filtering through the broken lines of comic syntax is fear that nuclear arms are a *male* weapons system deployed silently and lethally against mother-women, recruiting all men, down to doctors and sons, a killing military 'defence' system aimed at maternal body systems of nurture, growth and love. There is terrible intertwining mimicry in this imagining of a potential Cold War between the genders: the male technology virally, negatively replicating the reproductive system; the comic backchat of Faith's prose reproducing the virus by imitating its modes of infiltration and disintegrating irradiation, turning them back as satire upon the master discourses of the viral Cold War.

For Faith, the 1950s Cold War had been a time of beleaguered victimization within the domestic sphere: 'these scary, private years' (Paley, *Collected Stories*, p. 167); scary because of the rise of nuclear threats to the world at the level of the nuclei of women's stem cells; private because domestic ideology in its Cold War form had once again atomized women into single, privatized units within separate households, policing them within those spaces with infantilizing mockery and secret destructive energies. Only by showing other women that such destructive energies are aimed at the whole gender and not just at the deviant activist single mothers, and only by showing men that such energies are species-suicidal, a form of insane killing of sons on battlefields and within the male germ cells too, could the scary, private years be converted into a real movement for peace.

The gendered viral properties of nuclear paranoia feature in very different form on the male side of the divide, specifically in the lugubrious, apocalyptic fictions of William Burroughs. In his word-virus theory of (de)composition, Burroughs splices together codes from information technology, artificial intelligence and virology to conjure up a new, subversive, writerly praxis. One of the sinister biotechnicians in *The Third Mind* introduces the new 'science' to his audience: the scientists' 'image' is encoded at molecular level, developing into an information virus infecting the population of the world with replicas of itself within their chromosomes. To ensure that 'the last groups to go replica' would not notice the viral effects, a rapidly mutating information virus is engineered. And it is here that Burroughs reveals the real source of his 'viral' textual terrorism:

> Information speeded up, slowed down, permutated, changed at random by radiating the virus material with high-energy rays from cyclotrons, in short we created an infinity of variety at the information level, sufficient to keep the so-called scientists busy forever exploring the 'richness of nature'.[7]

At the root of the comically exaggerated anxiety is a nightmare of DNA-mutation by radiation: the viral effects are consciously modelled on the traumatizing data gathered by 1950s and 1960s scientific investigation into the effects of ionizing radiation on the chromosomes of living tissue.

Burroughs' cut-ups are a viral method of replicating text, imitating the ways viruses transcript and translate a host cell's genetic DNA. As he argued, facetiously and grimly, in *The Ticket that Exploded*, the word in the Cold War is now a virus, a 'parasitic organism that invades and damages the central nervous system',[8] tricking the mind and body of the host into believing the infected neural cell is its own. Burroughs is here forging an analogy between the insidious processes of state propaganda, ordinary reading habits and the ways a viral epidemic spreads in a population: books, texts and ideology invade the minds and occupy neural space by replicating their sequences within the individual's grey matter. The cut-up technique is thus a viral replication (satirical mimicry) of nuclear culture's own viral methods of mind control.

What the word virus does more specifically is creepy and telling: it convinces the host to accept an alien body system into itself, or rather it translates the body's own cells into an enemy other's. Queering of the Cold War body occurs as the virus secretly turns the male cells into their opposite, the 'Other Half', to create within male corporeality a new viral reality mimicking the 'alien and hostile' ontological status of the automatic somatic systems, thus generating a sex Cold War within the host system of the private body:

> The realization that something as familiar to you as the movement of your intestines the sound of your breathing the beating of your heart is also alien and hostile does not make one feel a bit insecure at first. Remember that you can separate yourself from the 'Other Half' from the word. The word is spliced in with the sound of your intestines and breathing with the beating of your heart. The first step is to record the sounds of your body and start splicing them in yourself. Splice in your body sounds with the body sounds of your best friend and see how familiar he gets. (Burroughs, *The Ticket that Exploded*, p. 50)

For Burroughs, we all carry an alien around with us all the time: it is the automatic body systems that accompany consciousness, the silent and unconscious processes and organs of the body 'below'. Our relationship with this alien presence is neutral, routine, until fear of invasion by viral or nuclear infections and mutations triggers hypochondriacal hysteria, a body paranoia that senses the somatic body as potentially alien, aberrant, hostile. New technologies that accompany nuclear modernity, molecular biology, information theory, genetic engineering, are all modelled, Burroughs' wild comedy suggests, on replicating this Cold War body paranoia in viral, textual forms somewhere at the back of the Cold War citizen's newly besieged mind. They breed new weird fears of viral radiation invading the nuclear sanctities of the body's secret cells, taking them over, splicing in sections of enemy DNA within defenceless chromosomes, turning our hostile bodies into the bodies of the spectral enemy.

At the root of the paranoia is nuclear radiation effecting irreversible mutations of the Cold War subject's sexual identity at the level of the chromosome. In Burroughs' fantasy, the alien invaders are gay, the Venusian boy-girls led by Johnny Yen in control now of the Other Half, who impose 'a sexual blockade on the planet' (Burroughs, *The Ticket that Exploded*, p. 209). They do so in reaction to the sexual Cold War that has ravaged the planet:

> The human organism is literally consisting of two halves from the beginning word and all human sex is this unsanitary arrangement whereby two entities attempt to occupy the same three-dimensional coordinate points giving rise to the solid latrine brawls which have characterized a planet based on 'the Word', that is, on separate flesh engaged in endless sexual conflict. (Burroughs, *The Ticket that Exploded*, p. 52)

Sexual identity is scripted into the cell's nucleus with the two chromosome sets and the XX/XY chromatids. The word virus breeds a body paranoia which polarizes the genders at this subatomic dimension, turning the males against the female aliens within, Cold War Sex War, X against the Y within. The parodic Nova police copy the tactics of the Venusian boy-girls and act as subversive counter-virus, manipulating the gender-dividing textual-viral techniques of the power elites to create a new post-human gender, male spliced into female DNA, the body's 'other half' now irradiated, functioning as a mutant field of queer life forms and meanings.

That Burroughs was thinking of Cold War geopolitical polarization as the root model for his sex-war, chromosomic-viral fantasy is clear not only from the register ('two entities . . . occupy[ing] . . . the same planet . . . in endless . . . conflict') but also from the play with the Cold War invasion-of-the-body-snatchers clichés of 1950s SF, the space race jokes, the biological weapons paranoia, and the Cold War territory of the novel's settings: Africa, for instance, signifying both countercultural junky playground and site of terrorist Third World resistance to superpower.

But it is significant that, as with Paley, the Cold War issues zoom down to the ultramicroscopic dimension of the sex chromosomes, 'viral' irradiation of the cellular structures of the reproductive system. As with Paley, the nuclear war at the level of the nucleus is being fought as a secret war of the sexes. And like Paley, Burroughs senses continuities between his own comic prose (disintegrative syntax, satirical mimicry, collage/cut-up techniques) and the ways and means of Cold War nuclear culture, technology and propaganda. For both writers, comic dissident prose is the mutated by-product of deep-seated anxieties about radiation's effects on living tissue.

For all their similarities, however, Paley and Burroughs are divided. For Paley, nuclear culture is a man-made destructive force aimed principally at the mother's womb, a form of rape to be resisted by solidarity between men and women as ecological respecters of the environment, global and somatic. For Burroughs, the quasi-viral mutations of radiation are to be welcomed at some extreme level, as models for the fabrication of a world without women, a world with a new mutated gender that will leapfrog over the Cold War's nuclear genders, beyond homosexual or 'composite' identities forged as straight resistance to heterosexuality. Despite the radical nature of his comic verve, Burroughs sides with a mutated form of Cold War machismo in which technology challenges women's 'flesh monopoly of birth and death' (*The Ticket that Exploded*, p. 8). Burroughs plays with desire as a viral form of energy in which 'the desire to dominate, to kill, to take over and eat the partner' is secretly harnessed and released by disabling 'the *regulatory centers in the nervous system*' (p. 20), the true target being a lurid, monstrous female within the body.

This is visualized, in its junk form, as a swamp monster, the 'transparent green shape [. . .] glinting with slow fish lust of the swamp mud' (*The Ticket that Exploded*, p. 89), parasitically occupying the dividing line down the centre of any male body. The monster lives virally as virtual killer-mother between the two halves of the male psychic body, Oedipally seducing its host-son into heterosexual forms of gay sex by titillating the internal organs from within:

> Long tendril hands penetrated Bradly's broken body caressing the other being inside through the soft intestines into the pearly genitals rubbing centers of orgasm along his spine to the neck – Exquisite toothache pain shot through his nerves and his body split down the middle. (Burroughs, *The Ticket that Exploded*, p. 89)

Its viral caress is obscenely verbal – 'Sex words exploded to a poisonous color vapor that cut off his breath' (p. 89) – because its words fabricate a sexual guilty inwardness out of the host body's 'sub-vocal speech' (p. 160). The inwardness is mimed in the replication of sound-effects internal to the novel's

speech-lines: the 'b' run in 'Bradly's broken body . . . being', the 'inside' asso-
nances along 'inside', 'intestines into', 'genitals', 'spine', 'Exquisite'. Its success
depends on the host subject's fantasmatic identification of her with the alien,
hostile 'other being within', the visceral body. Inward sub-vocal speech is hers
but made to feel 'mine' by this subversive, viral seduction of the other being
of the internal organs.

The swamp monster returns as 'a phantom woman with red hair and green
flesh', her mouth filled with tendrils 'covered by stinging red hairs [. . .]
penetrating my mouth and throat, feeling into my rectum and penis, twisting
around the spine touching electric centers of orgasm in the neck that popped
silver light in my eyes' (p. 99). The green flesh of the 1950s SF Martian other
is fused with the red hair and tendrils of the Communist radioactive invader, a
creature inhabiting the unknown erogenous-electrical zones and systems of the
political body of the Cold War subject.

Burroughs is modernizing the ancient myth jokingly told by Aristophanes
in Plato's *Symposium*: Zeus split primitive humans in two, 'like a sorb apple
which is halved for pickling'. We are all split apples, yearning for our lost other
halves. The other half is there, spectrally, virally, within the male body as lost
phantom Eve (she who first split the forbidden apple) attached to the absent
spare rib. Burroughs takes the myth and translates it into Cold War Freudian
terms, as we learn from the Fluoroscopic Kid's lecture on the subject in the '*in
that game?*' section:

> The body is two halves stuck together like a mold – That is, it consists
> of *two* organisms – See 'the Other Half' invisible – (to eyes that haven't
> learned to watch) – Like a Siamese twin ten thousand years in show
> business engaged by a silver cord to all erogenous zones – lives along the
> divide line – is an amphibious two-sexed actor half-man half-woman –
> double-gated either sex can breathe air or the underwater medium up
> your mother's snatch – 'the Other Half' is 'You' next time around – born
> when you die – that is when 'the Other Half' kills you and takes over. [. . .
>] Sub-vocal speech *is* the word organism the 'Other Half' spliced in with
> your body sounds. [. . .] Why not take over both halves of your body so
> you don't need any mooching 'Other Half' – Why not rewrite the message
> on 'the soft typewriter'? – Why not take the board books and rewrite all
> messages? – Why not take over the human body right down the middle
> line? (Burroughs, *The Ticket that Exploded*, p. 160)

The whole body is a gigantic form of stem cell, containing classified genetic
code sequences typed out by some sinister DNA-bureaucrat. Two male-female
X-Y chromosome sets, twin systems doubled up by DNA's double helix
copying system, are ready to copulate and separate when reproduction is necessary at point of death, a planned coup by the fifth column. In viral terms, a

shadowy phantom female virus is busy within the massive cellular structure of the whole male body, replicating and translating genomic RNA (sub-vocal speech messages) in the cytoplasmic zone of the internal organs (the other being within) before seducing the male nucleus into believing her proviral DNA to be his own, thus helping her create her daughter progeny virions. She is a radioactive virus, splitting the cellular body as the atom was split, splicing into DNA codes like a nuclear spy saboteur, breaking the X-potential of the male chromosome with her killer rays. In aligning genetic with secret service codes, secret informational commands with the sub-vocal speech of the somatic unconscious,[9] chromosomic reproduction with brainwashing identity programming, Burroughs is replicating nuclear culture's military paranoia as sub-Freudian biotechnology within the political-cellular structures of the male Cold War citizen's body and text.

The enemy is woman, seducing the progressive male into counter-evolutionary recession to primitive sexual identities calqued on heterosexual forms of identity, swamp sex with the swamp mother inside his insides. If the male cell-body is under such threat it is because radioactivity is female, sterilizing male self-creative energy and disabling evolutionary moves to the post-female with two-sex replications and (sound-)repetitions: 'the past is radioactive. Time is radioactive. Virus is radioactive. The nova formula is simple repetition down a long lane of flash bulbs' (*The Ticket that Exploded*, pp. 193–4). Flash bulbs are the orgasms which seduce the subject into believing in his own sexual choices, thus fixing him, as in a flash photograph, as reproduceable item in a long matrilineal 'lane' through radioactivated time. Writing with the cut-up method, backed up by Brion Gysin's tape-recorder feedback techniques, is a way of recolonizing the divide line, exorcising the killer mother to free up somatic space for the post-nuclear self-cloning male and his new textual body. Free of the Cold War sex war in his genes, male mind has banished Y from his chromosomes, at last free from the alien female sub-vocal speech feeling up his body sounds.

The Cold War is a sex war, then, the confrontation of Soviet and US military machines masking the warring genders: 'The war between the sexes split the planet into armed camps right down the middle line divides one thing from another.'[10] The cut-up technique's use of the fold-in mimics this confrontation, as do Gysin's two tape-recorders, scrambling and splicing off each other in self-cancelling antiphonal argument. The introduction of a third recorder and the textual reconstitution of the fold-ins as tertiary cut-up aim to perform the act of rewriting the middle line which divides men and women, acting something like a non-aligned resistance cell 'between' superpower propagandas. In essence and effect, however, the methods are childish and amateurish, a boy's origami game, archly Dada-laddish exercise in ludic tape-recording, makeshift chemistry-set antics, inadequate after the massive build-up. Cut-up and double tape-recording must be some kind of joke resolution of the deep misogynistic conflicts being trawled in the compositional process. If they are not, then they are comic symptom of those conflicts, replicating the neurotic Cold 'war between the sexes' written in to every cell of Burroughs' prose.

An alternative view would be to see the combination of cut-up, triple recording and sex war-Cold War tropes of viral replication and division as a metaphorical substantiation of the Cold War links between nuclear energy and genetic research, involving a pseudo-genetic crossing over of literary and science-cultural codes. A similar crossing over will be attempted here, alternating between critique of chromosome genetics and molecular biology in nuclear culture and a reading of the textual relations between Ted Hughes and Sylvia Plath as exemplary Cold War-literary couple.

The 1940s, 1950s and early 1960s had seen the triumph of Anglo-American genetic research, beginning with confirmation of the mutagenic effects of X-ray and atomic radiation within the chromosome – Hermann Muller was awarded the Nobel prize in 1946 for his work in this area. In 1944, the Rockefeller Avery group had found that the transforming principle within the nucleus was nucleic acid, DNA; with the invention of the scanning electron microscope and more sophisticated staining and X-ray techniques, the discovery would lead to the Watson–Crick double-helix model in 1953, and the cracking of the genetic code by Nirenberg and Matthaei between 1961 and 1965. The electron microscope revealed the extraordinary complexity of the cell,[11] encouraging fantastically involved research into nucleo-cytoplasmic interactions. Coupled with equally rich discoveries in the viral field where work on bacteria and bacteriophage viruses unlocked the links between gene and protein structures, this would eventually lead to the discovery of the mechanism of protein synthesis in 1961 following biochemists François Jacob and Jacques Monod's work on the function of messenger RNA – mRNA replicates nuclear DNA, moving from the nucleus into the cytoplasm ribosomal sites where the protein is synthesized.

These extraordinary discoveries in cytology took place at the same time as the equally momentous developments in nuclear science, from the Manhattan Project through the H-bomb tests to the dissemination of the facts about the long-term genetic damage wreaked by fallout and radiation. It was more than a fluke that the two sciences of genetics and nuclear bomb development were to come together in ordinary people's minds. That they both concentrated on the nucleus was more than a folk emphasis, in other words. Muller had been the first to use radiation and X-rays to induce mutations in *Drosophila* (fruit-fly) chromosomes and had been arguing since 1926 that radiologists should protect themselves and their patients from the X-rays they were routinely beaming into bodies. After the war and with the public platform afforded him by his Nobel, he warned the world and the scientific community about the lasting mutagenic effects of fallout radiation, in particular arguing that the scare stories about mutant monstrosities were designed to fool the world about the dangers since they could be so easily disproved. For him and for a growing number of fellow geneticists, the combination of the recessive and lethal dominants caused by fallout-induced chromosome breaks in dividing cells would not necessarily affect the phenotype (the visible body). The effects would mostly be invisible and somatic, working at the nucleotide level and remaining within the reproductive body for as many as twenty generations, a Mendelian nightmare dormant within the germ cells which could be activated as lethal 'radioactive' process decades or generations down the line.

Barbara McClintock had found that the breakages in the chromosome induced by even tiny doses of X-ray had lasting genetic effects, breakage leading to fusion of the broken 'centric' fragment (meaning 'containing the centromere', the central zone of the chromosome) once the cell begins to divide and self-reproduce, leading to bridge formation, with permanent loss of the acentric fragment within the cytoplasm and consequent lethal aborting of the cell. Muller speculated in 1957 that the victims of Hiroshima and Nagasaki who died of radiation sickness were killed by this breakage–fusion–bridge (or bfb) cycle, which, in Elof Axel Carlson's words, 'prevented rapidly dividing cells in the blood and in the lining of the capillaries and intestines from replenishing the cells lost by chromosome breaks':[12] this explained the localization of all the symptoms of radiation sickness within actively dividing tissue. It also explained, for Muller, the 'radiation-induced sterility and high susceptibility to radiation damage of fetuses in early pregnancy' (Carlson, *Genes, Radiation, and Society*, p. 349).

In 1962, Sylvia Plath was asked by the *London Magazine* to define her position within Cold War culture:

> The issues of our time which preoccupy me at the moment are the incalculable genetic effects of fallout and a documentary article on the terrifying, mad, omnipotent marriage of big business and the military in America – 'Juggernaut, The Warfare State', by Fred J. Cook in a recent *Nation*. Does this influence the kind of poetry I write? Yes, but in a sidelong fashion. I am not gifted with the tongue of Jeremiah, though I may be sleepless enough before my vision of the apocalypse. My poems do not turn out to be about Hiroshima, but about a child forming itself finger by finger in the dark.[13]

Plath's move from genetic effects through marriage to foetal development ponders the relation of gender, poetry and nuclear culture in ways that seem to opt for the private figure of the maker, both mother and poet, set 'sidelong' to the 'fallout' effects of the military–industrial complex. Yet the choice of the private zone of motherhood may be a political act in itself, in so far as the relation of mother to child in the womb has become a target in the warfare state. 'Sidelong' may be Keatsian-coy or it may be Woolfian-feminist, as in *Orlando*: 'The man looks the world full in the face, as if it were made for his uses and fashioned to his liking. The woman takes a sidelong glance at it, full of subtlety, even of suspicion.'[14] But here it is the fallout and the warfare state which have sidelong influences: their very insidiousness and ubiquity, at both genetic and supercultural levels, breed viral subtlety and suspicion in the most innocent acts of female making. Plath leaves open the question whether her choice of (confessional) female zones in her poetry, figured in the 'child forming itself finger by finger in the dark', is a naive act of self-censorship – a possibility half-confessed to in the *London Magazine* questionnaire when she describes her poems as 'deflections' – or a crafted and crafty mobilizing of symptomatic material knowingly contextualized in the fallout–warfare state of Cold War culture.

The allusion to Fred Cook's Juggernaut piece for the *Nation* would suggest the latter.[15] Cook's article and subsequent book, *The Warfare State*, are one of the first detailed testings of Eisenhower's warning, in his farewell address of 17 January 1961, of the threat to democracy posed by the 'military–industrial complex' spawned by the Cold War. Cook argues that the Cold War gave the US radical right the perfect opportunity to sustain the gargantuan military spending of the Second World War into the postwar. The alliance between big business and the armed forces could then steer domestic spending away from creeping-socialist New Deal welfare towards the permanent war economy of the warfare state, boosted by nuclear paranoia through strategic Cold War propaganda. Cook's principal theme is that the 'postwar wedding of the Military and Big Business' established a state of affairs whereby 'the welfare of the nation has become dependent on the arms race and the federal expenditures that keep it going': 'all of this is completely preferable to the only other visible alternative – the funnelling of comparably fantastic billions into "socialistic" programs for better housing, better highways, better schools, better medical care'.[16] The all-male 'wedding of the Military and Big Business' with their weaponry and missiles excludes the 'feminine' New Deal zones of house, school and hospital. Cook's analogy is sustained throughout *The Warfare State*:

> The Military was the vital half of this new partnership, for without it, without its prestige and its solemn and expert warnings of ever-present danger, the combine would be robbed of its excuse for existing. But Business brought to the wedding no inconsiderable dowry, its billions, its control of industry, its enormous power over all the large media of information, either through outright investment or life-and-death advertising, made it a worthy bride of the admirals and generals. (Cook, *Warfare State*, p. 64)

Cook's marriage conceit figures the groom as the soldier, the businessman as the bride, cross-dressed oligarch. The peaceable territory of the domestic sphere, the zone of the civilian-citizen, has been bought out by the masculinist forces, locked into a billion-dollar war economy built on the threat of Communist–New Deal invasion and nuclear devastation. In gender terms, woman signifies the New Deal citizen robbed of her possessions by the two males wedded to their nuclear complex. The two men together form the warfare state, 'the military–industrial colossus' (*Warfare State*, p. 21) – this is Cook's term and his colossus is just as pithy and historical as the Colossus Father ruling Plath's unconscious.[17]

The split between domestic and foreign spending policies is reproduced for Cook in the schizophrenic Kennedy administration, determined to curb the military–industrial complex by reining in power to a civilian White House, and yet committed to the arms race in the light of the Berlin crisis and Soviet breaches of test-ban treaties. The immense power of the Pentagon, employing a tenth of the nation's entire work force, owning 32 million acres of the United States, consuming 63 per cent of Kennedy's budget, is funnelled as cash into the big corporations, both committed, as a 'married' couple, to this huge investment in the garrison mentality of Fortress America. Kennedy and Robert McNamara, the secretary of state for defence, were powerless to curb the colossus' influence over policy, and with the breakdown of the Geneva test-ban talks and the Berlin crisis, the oligarchy had it all its own way. For Cook, the Geneva talks were programmed to fail by the Complex, just as they had failed in 1955 when the Russians had made the astonishing 10 May offer promising to abolish nuclear weapons. The Americans had answered with the 'Open Skies' proposal, which was little more than a surveillance programme, and then performed a sudden volte-face backtracking from disarmament, arguing instead for the retention, in Donald Quarles' words, of 'overwhelming air-atomic power', of the 'capacity to retaliate', of atomic bombs 'in such quantities that no nation could hope to start a major war without being destroyed' (*Warfare State*, p. 220). The test-ban negotiations in Geneva, 1959, had been similarly scuttled, according to Cook, by the Pentagon colossus. The American delegation had suddenly insisted that there was no way of registering underground nuclear tests, using the 'big hole' theories of the increasingly rabid Edward Teller, the director of the H-Bomb programme at Los Alamos. This forced the Russians to protest, the perfidy of which was then used to break the negotiations.

Plath's article and Cook's *The Warfare State* were both written in the aftermath of the failure of the Kennedy administration's 1961 test-ban negotiations with the posturing and belligerent Soviet premier Khrushchev. The Russians went on to break the three-year moratorium, going ahead with fifty rapid, extremely radioactive tests in the high atmosphere. Cook's thesis is that the

Russians hardened their tactics, became belligerently Cold Warlike in reaction to American duplicities in the previous test-ban negotiations. On 5 September 1961, Kennedy announced that the US would resume tests in the lab and underground. Despite numerous United Nations offers, repeated pleas for test bans from the administration and from around the world, 'Khrushchev's multimegaton monsters had poisoned the fabric of the world and the minds of men, and the only reality resided in the grim determination of the warriors to match megaton with megaton, power with power to the final and inevitable conclusion' (Cook, *Warfare State*, p. 251).

The effect in America was profound. For the first time, Cook wrote, world alarm had led to world protest. Massive peace rallies were organized by CND in London. In America, 'for virtually the first time, the words of the warriors no longer were taken as the final and unanswerable verdict':

> University professors drafted open letters to President Kennedy urging that we refrain from the final round of madness; psychologists and mothers and college students organized protest meetings and picketed in ban-the-bomb demonstrations. Marchers paraded in orderly fashion before the White House in Washington; sit-downers clogged the sidewalks in front of the Atomic Energy Commission in New York; there was even a miniature riot in which police flailed the advocates of peace in Times Square. For almost the first time since the witch-hunt hysteria began in 1948, the voice of dissent was being heard in the land; conscience found the courage to speak. (Cook, *Warfare State*, p. 251)

Yet with equally unprecedented pressure from the Pentagon, from the Teller cabal of nuclear scientists and from the CIA militarists, Kennedy was forced to announce, on 2 March 1962, that America would resume testing in the atmosphere.

That same month Plath wrote the verse radio play 'Three Women: A Poem for Three Voices', set in a maternity ward. The second voice is that of a secretary, who is convalescing after a miscarriage, suffering from suicidal depression. But it is not a depression that is hers alone; it is a species depression, a nuclear nightmare: 'I saw death in the bare trees, a deprivation.' She fears the death she carries home is some lethal airborne toxin: 'Is it the air, / The particles of destruction I suck up?' This suicidal menace in the air, in the miscarrying body she bears, has something to do with the typing she does for 'the man I work for', who laughs at her pale terror:

> The letters proceed from these black keys, and these black keys proceed
> From my alphabetical fingers, ordering parts,
>
> Parts, bits, cogs, the shining multiples.
> I am dying as I sit.[18]

The chain of command, from 'man I work for' through keys to characters on page to parts ordered, is an eerie mechanical replica of the genetic chain of command, here geared to the military–industrial complex which has poisoned the air with radioactive fallout, aborting her child at the molecular chromo-somal level with its 'particles of destruction'.[19] Her own body parts, there as alphabetical fingers at the keys, are in service to the desiring machine of the Cold War with its 'parts, bits, cogs': the fingers are made to countersign the process that kills the mothering force harbouring the 'child forming itself finger by finger in the dark'. The child is disassembled, becoming 'parts, bits, cogs' under the sidelong influence of the breakage–fusion–bridge cycle of fallout radiation.

The mother's work in service to the Cold War's genetic script and code, fab-ricating 'shining multiples' (magic numbers on the page, shining metal shapes of (war-)machines on the assembly line) is sterilizing her *as she sits*, within the lap of the body that writes. For the colossus has access to the world of her organs, like the surgeon in the September 1961 poem 'The Surgeon at 2 a.m.'. The colossus is a shining multiple, a congeries made up of the 'faceless faces of important men', 'jealous gods' who seek to colonize the woman's body and make it 'flat' as theirs (Plath, *Collected Poems*, p. 179) in the name of the arms race, deathly genetic parody of the conceiving, loving power of that body: 'And now the world conceives / Its end and runs toward it, arms held out in love' (p. 181). Conception and apocalypse, loving body and arms race fuse as the warfare state is internalized within the Cold War creative imagination. The mother must learn to hate herself in the process ('Hating myself, hating and fearing' (p. 181)), must learn to censor her knowledge of the Cold War face-less men of the Complex, learn to name the enemy as herself ('I am accused' (p. 180)), substituting for those faces the deep Cold War male fiction of the vampire mother within: 'She is the vampire of us all. So she supports us, / Fattens us, is kind' (p. 181).

Muller had suffered censorship in 1955 when his paper for the UN conference on the peaceful uses of atomic energy in Geneva was muzzled by the Cold Warrior AEC commissioner Willard F. Libby. Libby had learned that Muller was a suspect radical before the war – a thick FBI file itemized Muller's activities as a Communist sympathizer, especially his four-year spell in the USSR in the 1930s (when he had worked with the Soviet geneticist Vavilov), his socialist-eugenic arguments in his *Out of the Night*, and his participation in the Spanish Civil War. The fact that he had worked in Spain with Norman Bethune, who had died in China as a blood doctor in Mao Tse-tung's army, and with nuclear spy Bruno Pontecorvo in Edinburgh made it inconceivable that his voice be heard at Geneva. This was especially the case given the fact that his long and detailed paper on the changes wrought to the genetic system by radiation dared to raise Hiroshima and Nagasaki, which the AEC considered 'out of bounds'. The censorship did not work, happily enough – the press and fellow scientists kicked up an enormous fuss about the crude attack on freedom of speech, and the paper was published in the *Bulletin of Atomic Scientists*.

Muller was familiar with US censorship – his 1926 warnings about medicinal use of X-rays had been similarly shut down by an angry radiologist cabal. He had also been forced to leave the States after discrimination within the universities levelled against his socialist sympathies and half-Jewish ethnicity. He was similarly familiar with governmental ways of curtailing difficult science – he had seen many of his friends in the Soviet Union go to the wall once Stalin had decided that the neo-Lamarckian Lysenko was right to consider Mendelian genetics subversive bourgeois idealism. For Lysenko, the stable mathematics of genetic crossing-over smacked of biological determinism, and he had conjured up an absurd theory of environmental control of genetic changes, claiming the ability to change winter wheat into spring wheat miraculously by soaking in water. With Stalin's approval, Lysenko gained a power base in the Soviet academy which led to purges of 'Morganist' geneticists (after Morgan and his famous fly lab at Columbia, where Muller cut his teeth), including the death of Vavilov in a labour camp in 1942. Lysenko's ascendancy continued right to the end of Khrushchev's period in power and encouraged a Cold War polarization of genetics between Mendelian chromosome genetics and molecular biology, now associated with US capitalist systems, and the rival neo-Lamarckian view of the instantaneous Darwinian adaptation of life forms under environmental pressures, considered by Lysenko and Stalin to be more orthodox, revolutionary and materialist.

If this war between the microbiologists split the planet into armed camps right down the middle line, this was appropriate, since the science itself was about splitting, the Mendelian crossing-over processes depending on replication through the exquisite mitosis/meiosis division of the chromosomes into separate cells. The splitting of the cell was under enormous threat, though, from its dark mimetic twin: the effects of the splitting of the atom, making chromosomal genetics a Cold War issue deep within the sexual reproductive processes. Cytogenetics had become a Cold War-inflected study of gender conflict: the use of radiation artificially to induce genetic change was principally applied to sex-linked mutant genes. Muller in the late 1920s had begun by irradiating *Drosophila* sperm cells to generate true gene mutations: the X chromosome was the key to radiation genetics. The X-chromosome studies were complemented by treatment of unfertilized females, with particular attention to lethal mutant genes in subsequent crops of eggs.[20] The genetic study of survivors of the Hiroshima and Nagasaki bombs called for by the Atomic Bomb Casualty Commission's Committee on Atomic Casualties in 1947 equally focused on the abnormal foetal developments in survivors as a marker of dominant lethals (genetic abnormalities leading to the death of the organism) which might suggest heritable mutations.[21]

By the mid-1950s, with resistance to H-bomb testing an election issue, especially during the Eisenhower–Stevenson presidential campaign, the genetics committee of the Committee on Biological Effects of Atomic Radiation (BEAR) also examined Jim Neel's work on the bomb survivors, with Muller playing a key role in their report, published June 1956. The report took on board what became known as the Muller–Haldane principle, by which, in James Crow's words, 'each mutation, however mild, has the same average effect on the fitness of the population'; indeed, the more subtle the mutation, the longer it would be likely to persist in the population as a whole, leading to what Muller referred to as 'genetic death', or single gene extinctions.[22] As a result, the report strongly recommended that the standard of acceptable man-made radiation levels be set as low as possible, close to levels of natural background radiation. The report attracted huge publicity in the press, its major innovation being, as Crow remarks, 'to regard the population average as the controlling consideration. Previously, all radiation protection standards had been based on observed somatic harm to the individual, and therefore involved much higher doses' (Crow, 'Quarreling Geneticists and a Diplomat', p. 462). The report had the effect of alarming the population of the world concerning the invisible, long-term, mutagenic effects of man-made radiation particularly on reproductive systems.

The report identified, powerfully and shockingly, the mutagenic effects of nuclear weapons systems on the nuclear-cytoplasm structure of the reproductive system of the human species as a whole: witness the report's stress on *man*-made radiation, its recommendations for low roentgen standards in terms of 'accumulated gonadal dose', on the 'genetic damage' concealed in partially dominant recessive mutations among children in Hiroshima and Nagasaki, and its concern for the minute effects of weapons testing, despite the tiny 0.1 roentgen level detected, due to its global spread across the world.

Ted Hughes identified his early vocation as a poet in a Wordsworthian moment on the Yorkshire moors, a desolate place of ultimate exposure: 'the light, at once both gloomily purplish and incredibly clear, unnaturally clear, as if objects there had less protection than elsewhere, were more exposed to the radioactive dangers of space'.[23] If the object world of his poetry is radioactive in this way, then the animals which are encountered in its light and space are predatory machines of nuclear warfare.

'Pike' is about an encounter with an ancient warrior identity, a killer from the egg, as in some recessive murderous energy retained in the human species despite civilization ('Killers from the egg: the malevolent aged grin'). Its force is an energy which is capable of murder, of destruction of others, of its own species, in this comparable to the human species it haunts within the pond of the poet's national unconscious ('as deep as England'). Its true identity is nuclear submarine, iron in its eye: 'Of submarine delicacy and horror. / A hundred feet long in their world'.[24]

The killer birds in 'Thrushes' are equally machinic, 'weaponized', ruthless, predatory energies:

> Terrifying are the attent sleek thrushes on the lawn,
> More coiled steel than living – a poised
> Dark deadly eye, those delicate legs
> Triggered to stirrings beyond sense.[25]

The thrushes are like nuclear bombers, their coil of DNA a trigger mechanism, ready to release 'dark deadly' energy into the environment.[26] If humanity has lost touch with its religious fears, the poem argues, then there is nothing to stop us becoming like the thrushes: there is no obstruction left to deflect this terrifying force within the species. Under the auspices of the Cold War, the force lies dormant in the form of thousands of nuclear missiles aimed with their dark deadly eyes, like killer animals released by ancient warrior instincts. For Hughes, the thrushes obey a murderous instinct coterminous with the 'divine' hereditary law: the same 'bullet and automatic / Purpose' governs the feeding of the shark on its prey and the compositional drive of male art ('Mozart's brain had it, and the shark's mouth / That hungers down the blood-smell'). This is a poetry of the unconscious as nuclear silo, correlating Jungian archetypal drives, Mendelian DNA mutation and the destructive potential of concealed nuclear weapon systems.

The predatory creatures encountered in Hughes' poems are mutants of the imagination, dark and deadly recessive forces triggered in the genes by the radioactive dangers of space. These radioactive dangers had become spectrally systemic to the imagination of the human species at least since the disastrous Castle/BRAVO atmospheric tests of 1953, and the fears were reactivated during the Russian multi-megaton tests of 1960–1 – the fallout from the tests had been carefully tracked by NATO monitoring stations as it drifted west. The radiation mutants are cybernetically identified with the nuclear weapons systems at the root of the radiation paranoia, the submarines, ICBMs and nuclear bombers policing the world. The cyborg mutations are the stuff of SF fantasy, yet they retain their power, for Hughes, because they can be made to stand for the male technological-aesthetic energy he equated with the making of poetry.

They can be made to do so because of an obscure identification of genetic biological determinism with the creative unconscious, as with Lipot Szondi's psychogenetics in his *Experimental Diagnostics of Drives* (1952).[27] The genetic unconscious, at the crossroads between the Freudian Oedipal unconscious and Jungian race consciousness, is a DNA complex of hereditary drives going right back through generations, thousands and thousands of human beings, back to the recessive secrets of the animal world, red in tooth and claw, still locked into the acres of information along the coils of DNA. The genome, for Szondi, contains ancestral drives, 'genes of family, kinship, stock and tribe, all the way back beyond Cain and Abel to Adam and Eve', including the genes 'of the zoological group of ancestral animals preceding our human ancestors' (Szondi, *Experimental Diagnostics of Drives*, p. 107). The drives are structured according to a dominant-recessive struggle for mastery between paternally and maternally inherited drives, a struggle between aggressive and passive tendencies which will determine the individual's pathology. 'The two tendencies operate in opposite directions: for instance, sadism-aggression-activity versus masochism-autoaggression-passivity' (Szondi, *Experimental Diagnostics of Drives*, p. 50). Szondi bases his psychogenetics on Freud's dualistic cellular theory of primitive Eros and Thanatos drives; Szondi argues that Freud's theory is indeed a step towards a genetic theory. If the sexual drives have evolved 'from that immortal faculty of the sex cells which draws together elements of living substances', and the ego drives 'from the libidinal charge of the mortal soma cells', then it follows that 'the source of all drives lies in the genes', chromosomes containing sequences of so-called drive genes (pp. 3, 6). These drive genes combine paternal and maternal strains, and thus perpetuate 'a polarization of needs and tendencies', in particular between 'feminine affection' and 'masculine aggression' (pp. 7–8).[28]

The Cold War, in psychogenetic terms, is a war waged by the ancient warriors unleashed by radioactivity from their hideouts among dormant genes, 'heterozygotic lethal mutations' (Szondi, *Experimental Diagnostics of Drives*, p. 11) made up of male-animal-aggressive drives free of Eve's passive tendencies. For the nuclear male Hughes, the coiled steel of DNA is the architect both of the nuclear weaponry whose mutational energy had unleashed the dark creatures in the first place, and of the killing, automatic purposes of those weapons systems, purposes encoded deep in the genetic unconscious of the male body.

The second consideration which saw cytogenetics develop into a field for the waging of the Cold War as sex war turns on the relations between the nucleus and the cytoplasm, particularly as Mendelian genetics modulated into molecular biology. Despite the obvious fact that nuclear DNA is a product of both maternal and paternal genes coming together during meiosis, it was still the case that the chromosomes in the nucleus were regarded as 'male' and the cytoplasm as 'female'. This was partly to do with the remaining traces of the belief system which had identified the nucleus with the sperm-head and the cytoplasm with the egg. These traces were bolstered by the sensational news of successful nuclear transplantation (particularly after 1952 with the Briggs and King experiments with amphibia) whereby donor nuclei were injected into egg cells from which the nucleus had been removed.[29] Equally, fruit-fly geneticists

were finding significant signs that the cytoplasm of the egg cell might prede-
termine the pattern of morphogenesis of sex organs, a process they christened
the maternal effect (Wilkie, *Cytoplasm in Heredity*, p. 94), seeming to confirm
the common view that cytoplasmic inheritance indicated the predominance
of the maternal influence in heredity. Progeny of divisions and replications of
cells (whether through the self-cloning reproduction of mitosis or the divisions
initiated after fusion of egg and sperm) are called daughter cells, as significantly
are viral progeny and radioactive products of material like radon. This seemed
again to confirm cytoplasm as enucleate ooplasm or egg waiting for a male
nucleus to supply it with a DNA command centre, whilst also eerily linking
viral, radioactive and reproductive replicatory processes. The christening of the
pairs of chromatids that come together in genetic interactions as 'sisters' goes
along with this gendering of somatic cell division.

This weird sexual myth may also have been encouraged by the fact that
so much of the genetic information had come from the choice of *Drosophila*
as perfect species for genetic research – with the fruit fly as with the human
genome, XX produces females, and XY males. The fascination of geneticists
with male sterility as a result of 'female' cytoplasmic influences may be telling.
As Darlington put it in his 1958 *Evolution of Genetic Systems*:

> Floating in several populations of *Drosophila bifasciata* is a plasmagene
> [which] kills nearly all the XY embryos, that is the males, in the progeny,
> before hatching. This reaction of nucleus and cytoplasm thus produces
> much the same effect on the population and on its breeding system as the
> sex-ratio gene complex in other *Drosophila* species: it raises the propor-
> tion of females in the whole population. In its effect on the individual,
> that is physiologically, the reaction is much the same as those producing
> male-sterility in plants.[30]

The knock-on effects of the fruit-fly work were to encourage a gender paranoia
about mutagenic and cytoplasmic forces in nuclear culture, as though radioactivity in the air would at once destroy the species through its assault on the
chromosome, but also favour, in irrational ways, the female of the species in
an evolutionary 'decision' to wipe out the male through sterilizing mutagens,
with a dominant proportion of feminist-Amazonian self-reproducing females
in the population.[31]

In a 1971 interview on 'Poetry and Violence', Hughes explored the positive and
negative implications in given key words. The implications, he argued, could
be laid out on a graph in a symmetrical pattern, 'like the chromosomes on the
genetic nucleus of the word'.[32] Mawkish media culture is appalled by the 'positive' predatory senses of the word 'violence', yet they nevertheless remain there
on the chromosomal graph as 'secondary, recessive' meanings (*Winter Pollen*,

p. 255). The negative sense of the word is dominant, as in a dominant genetic strain, and has to do with 'the idea of *violation* [...] a rape of some kind, the destruction of a sacred trust, the breaking of a sacred law' (p. 254). This dominant chromosomal meaning has obscured the potential within the word for 'strong, positive violence' (p. 254), instanced in Hughes' own 'poetry of positive violence, poetry about the working of divine law in created things' (p. 259). This is the violence meditated on in 'Thrushes': 'there is a clear and strong sense in which both Thrush and Shark are obeying – in selfless, inspired (i.e. lucid) obedience, like Mozart's brain – the creator's law which shaped their being and their inborn activity' (p. 258).

Discovering this obedience to the creator's law in the recessive meanings of the word 'violence' is a little like a self-fulfilling prophecy, since Hughes would only be looking out for such biological determinism in the word's connotative field if he were starting off with *a priori* assumptions associated with the determinisms written into the masculinist theory of the chromosome. The primitive forces intuited in the shark and the thrush are, in Dennis Walder's words, 'genetic, rather than divine, or historical'.[33] Yet they are historical too, to the extent that Hughes senses the stirrings of primeval energies in the apocalyptic posturings and endgame technologies of the Cold War. The two enemies that hate each other in 'Law in the Country of the Cats' are thinly disguised figures for Cold Warriors. Hughes approves of their dismissing soppy liberal hopes for 'perpetual peace', and imagines them forced to obey the warrior instincts encoded in their animal blood: they hate each other as 'dog and wolf because their blood before / They are aware has bristled into their hackles' (Hughes, *Collected Poems*, p. 41).[34] The meanings in the words we use, the moves the military–industrial complex makes, the destructive-reproductive energies of sex and love, the making and breaking of poems and children, the relation of the West to the cultures it controls, the dreamwork of individuals and cultures at war: all are driven and shaped and determined by the genetic power relations encoded into the genome.

And all these are obeying the divine genetic law which entwines prandial and sexual energies – we must eat as we must mate. As Hughes harshly put it in the 'Lovesong' of *Crow*: 'He loved her and she loved him / His kisses sucked out her whole past and future or tried to / He had no other appetite / She bit him she gnawed him she sucked / She wanted him complete inside her' (*Collected Poems*, p. 255).[35] At the chromosomal root of all encounters between positive and negative energies are the encounters between man and woman, between predator and prey: in the Jungian recesses of the chromosome, man/woman is crossed over with predator/prey, tangled up together as twin drives, a double helix of animal and sexual energies. Sex is genetic exchange, a crossing-over of these dual energies, which in terms of unconscious dreamwork pans out as a quite literal exchange of limbs and brains: 'Their heads fell apart into sleep like the two halves / Of a lopped melon, but love is hard to stop / In their entwined sleep they exchanged arms and legs / In their dreams their brains took each other hostage' (*Collected Poems*, p. 256).

The entwining of each gender around its opposite sex – at the level both of the chromosome and of the chromosomal meanings of the words they say to each other – happens along (and establishes) a stark dividing line too. As Hughes puts it in the poem 'Incompatibilities', desire is 'a vicious separator' in spite of 'its twisting women round men' (*Collected Poems*, p. 28).[36]

But the real culprit is not desire, but male desire and its trumped-up DNA-ideological machinery. It is male desire under the Cold War which motivates the twisted combination of the dream of woman as at once sexual subaltern (coiling round her man) and predatory white goddess. Women as objects of desire are suspended, as the lily is suspended in 'To Paint a Water Lily', between two fantasies of violence: the violence of Cold War technology occupying airspace (the bullet-like dragonflies and their molten metal) and the violence of primeval recessive drives in the male warrior psyche (the prehistoric monsters of the pond; *Collected Poems*, pp. 70–1).[37] It only takes a slight turn of the screw to tighten old-style misogyny to suit Cold War male dreamwork, to make the lily the target of the warfare state both airborne and submarine. If Hughes adopted Graves' white goddess myth, it was to do precisely that. Ekbert Faas has shown how Hughes borrowed Plath's figure of the desecrated patchwork woman, the woman subjected to the dark experimentation of the hospital in texts like *The Bell Jar*, 'Tulips' and 'The Applicant', and patched it into the Graves theme of the return of the goddess after hundreds of years of Christian patriarchy.[38]

The result is a grotesque amalgam, as we can see in the 1970s fantasy *Gaudete*, which had begun life in 1962 as a film script: the male hero, consecrated by bull blood and sperm, conjures a harem of sexually submissive women out of the village, and in his oneiric imagination, dreams of the patchwork goddess rising from the mud swamp of his desire:

> It is a woman's face,
> A face as if sewn together from several faces.
> A baboon beauty face,
> A crudely stitched patchwork of faces.[39]

Clearly she is a patchwork of the 'demortalized organs' (*Gaudete*, p. 130) of the bodies of all the women being desired as much as she is the recessive swamp-mother matriarch of the genes, and what is being desired is not sexual satisfaction but appropriation of the female power to give birth. The white goddess figure is imagined as being *given birth to* from the newly mutant male dream body:

> He sees himself being delivered of the woman from the pit,
> The baboon woman,
> Flood-sudden, like the disembowelling of a cow

> She gushes from between his legs, a hot splendour
> In a glistening of oils,
> In a radiance like phosphorus he sees her crawl and tremble.
>
> (*Gaudete*, p. 105)

The fear of female genetic self-sufficiency and creative agency is countered by this new evolutionary dream in which the male assumes the power of birth. As a necessary corollary to this, Lumb splits into two: dark, primitive, killer self and preacherman self, and a woman must be sacrificed. The doubling and the dream of birth-power underwrite Lumb's ritual rape and murder of Felicity, a murder re-enacting ancient, murderous misogyny. Hughes' reading of Shakespeare turns on the belief that the sixteenth and seventeenth centuries were the times of struggle 'between Calvinistic witch-hunt misogyny and the Celtic pre-Christian Mother worship surviving in the cult of the Queen',[40] a struggle which eventually results in the upheaval of the Civil War and what Hughes called 'an epidemic of murders of women' (Faas, 'Chapters of a Shared Mythology', p. 118).

In the new civil war of the Cold War, a similar struggle between misogyny and mother worship is being enacted. The misogyny takes on the contours of Cold War technology, 'weaponizing' the predatory animals at the back of the male mind. The mother worship is Cold Warlike too, taking the form of a mutational appropriation of female splitting and reproductive powers by the genetically modified male. Bringing misogyny and mother worship together is the 'fungus of jealousy'[41] of women's bodies, in particular their alien goddess-like power during pregnancy:

> The glistening tissues, the sweating gasping life of division and multiplica-tion, the shoving baby urgency of cells. All her pores want to weep. She is gripped by the weird pathos of biochemistry, the hot silken frailties, the giant, gristled power, the archaic sea-fruit inside her. (*Gaudete*, p. 39)

Something about nuclear culture has spawned this new resurgence of the seventeenth-century civil war of the sexes and its epidemic of murders of women, and it must have something to do with the dangerous slippages in sexual identity generated by the discoveries in genetics, allied to the apocalyptic imagining of the fallout mutations that nuclear warfare would bring about. Hughes' principal pre-occupation in the last three years of Plath's life was with species survival: 'in our time,' he wrote in 1962, 'the heroic struggle is not to become a hero but to remain a living creature simply'.[42] That survival might depend on the mutational ability of the human body to engender itself through encounter with another body *of what-ever gender* in a post-nuclear state. In one of the *Crow* poems, 'Notes for a Little Play', two bodies come together after nuclear war, ungendered horrors, 'hairy and slobbery, glossy and raw' (*Collected Poems*, p. 212).[43] They enact the 'strange dance' of sex, typically a mix of animal, sexual and prandial energies ('They sniff towards each other [...] / They fasten together. They seem to be eating each other'). They are mutant survivors, new nuclear creatures which do not need the old genders, for they are 'Mutations – at home in the nuclear glare'.

All this would be merely disheartening if it were not so clear that Hughes is feeding off the anti-nuclear anxieties about mothering and mutation which contributed to Plath's suicide in 1963. It is as though her death must be made instrumental to the revelation of the new genetic forces being released by the mutational nuclear culture within the germ cells, just as Janet's suicide and Felicity's murder are instrumental to the revelation of Lumb's oneiric fantasy of self-germination in *Gaudete*. In his article 'Sylvia Plath and Her Journals' Hughes had noted Plath's 'instinct for nursing' and her fragility at the atomic level of ontology, and related both to the recurrent delivery motif:

> Maybe her singularity derives from a feminine bee-line instinct for the real priority, for what truly matters – an instinct for nursing and repairing the damaged and threatened nucleus of the self and for starving every other aspect of her life in order to feed and strengthen that, and bring that to a safe delivery.[44]

The nucleus of the self demands feeding like a child, demanding maternal servility and self-sacrifice from the mother-drone poet. The DNA must have its way and the cytoplasmic servant as mother-wife must dedicate herself to the nurturing of the god in the coil of chromosomes.

Anxieties existed for women in the sociobiological arrogance of geneticists and their 'male' DNA with its domineering patriarchal control over the subservient cytoplasm and its inferior version of the genetic transforming principle, RNA. Even the double helix was coded by Crick as a sexual partnership of a traditional kind: commenting on the fact that DNA chains were always found in pairs, never singly, he quipped: 'Nucleic acid, in fact, seems capable of behaving in a regular manner only in the married state.'[45] If DNA was tough husband, then RNA was weak wife. According to what was called the Central Dogma (Crick's own formulation), DNA told RNA what to do, and RNA dutifully made proteins. Before messenger RNA was theorized, geneticists tended to read 'her' this way, in order to deal with the troubling fact that viruses and phages carry RNA as well as DNA. Rollin Hotchkiss, for example, discussing Crick's 1957 paper amongst others in the same publication, is willing to accept that both DNA and RNA are 'bearers of biological specificity', but only if DNA is understood as centrally dogmatic chief of the cellular home:

> Within the cells themselves we are accustomed to thinking of the DNAs as exerting some degree of supremacy over the RNAs. This is partly because the sperm, for example, contributing DNA and little or no RNA, seems

to furnish a genetic heritage approximately equal [. . .] to that of the egg, which also contributes RNA and cytoplasm. It is now usual, in some degree [. . .] to picture protein synthesis as lower in the hierarchy and dependent upon the nucleic acids.

Perhaps the confusing relations between RNA and DNA may be illuminated by the speculation that, as a genetic determinant, RNA was replaced during biochemical evolution by the more molecularly and metabolically stable DNA. Cell lines have preserved the RNA entities which, evolutionwise, were primary to DNA and may have allowed them to store their information in DNA and thereby become subservient to it metabolically. This secondary position would in a sense have been forced on RNA because of its lower stability and, perhaps, because of its failure to become organized in such an elegant apparatus as the chromosomes. Viruses, as products of retrograde evolution by loss of function, may have had a choice of either RNA or DNA when specializing to get themselves made in the ample environment of the host cell.[46]

Note how Hotchkiss is perfectly aware of the constructed nature of the myth with his 'we are accustomed to thinking' and 'it is now usual [. . .] to picture'. The supremacy and subservience are explicitly gendered as male and female with the sperm–egg argument, the male conservatism of the chromosomes hailed in the assumption that elegant and stable biochemistry is, in evolution terms, a wise move. The female cytoplasmic RNA is a willing slave to DNA's power over information within the family home, the 'ample environment' of the cell, a space dominated by the central dogmatic presence of the elegant and stable apparatus of Codemaster Daddy DNA.

Though the cell is under threat from cunning viral interlopers, adulterous mimics or sneaky lovers, the very fact they choose to choose between DNA and RNA is proof that they are lesser beings, mutant recessives, floating primitives as debased and 'primary' as swamp-monster woman-as-RNA. If the virus chooses *her* to get himself made, then perhaps they deserve each other. Perhaps RNA viruses are female in this retrograde way, their interactions a kind of same-sex sex which, though disgusting, is sterilizing in unthreatening ways. Though, on the other hand, it might prove that RNA is something of a virus herself in the secure family home. Viruses mimic RNA's subservience, which is viral in its potential for resentful and wrecking imitation of DNA's exclusive power over codes and information processing.

Love is a virus, for Hughes, especially if there's guilt involved: 'Jennifer's insinuatingly amorous lamenting tones seem to have entered his blood, like a virus, with flushes of fever and shivers, and light, snatching terrors' (*Gaudete*, p. 71). For Hughes, as we have seen, sexual desire is a parody of the entwining, coiling, reproductive relation of RNA to DNA, itself calqued on DNA's double helix. Sexual guilt imitates the flushes and shivers of desire but mutated into symptoms of sickness, like influenza in the blood . Dr Westlake is sexually attracted to Jennifer because her sister Janet killed herself over Lumb: Jennifer's grief summons the ghastly kick he gets out of remembering 'that dead girl's grey-pink parched-looking lips' (p. 71). The guilty attraction to Jennifer disguises and sustains the dark necrophilia, with something of an incestuous charge. The flu virus, with its self-replicating viral RNA, matrix protein and budding progeny, is an apt image for Westlake's guilt since it is all about mothers and sisters and illegal transgressive imitations of maternal-cytoplasmic reproduction. At the heart of the viral fiction of male desire is the dead girl suicide, melodramatized as supertragic support to the Lumb agonist. Westlake is a poor cover for the guilt Lumb should be feeling for stage-managing Janet's suffering. The replications of desire, guilt and erotic death are viral and out of control, symptoms of a sickness caught at the height of the Cold War, 1958–63.

Before Plath died, in a very strange poem published in 1959, 'A Woman Unconscious', Hughes tracked down his necrophiliac attraction to dead women's faces, and found his attraction imitating, as a virus imitates, Plath's hospital poetry:

> Onto the white hospital bed
> Where one, numb beyond her last of sense,
> Closed her eyes on the world's evidence
> And into pillows sunk her head.
>
> (*Collected Poems*, p. 63)[47]

This obscure death is related somehow to the worldwide threat of nuclear holocaust posed by the Cold War, and it is a threat aimed specifically, Hughes knows, at mothers and their children:

> Russia and America circle each other;
> Threats nudge an act that were without doubt
> A melting of the mould in the mother,
> Stones melting about the root.
>
> (*Collected Poems*, p. 62)

The nuclear conflict nudged into action by the circling superpowers has the maternal womb as its main target, yet the poem's own target is the vision of the woman unconscious on the hospital bed. The link between the Cold War's assault on the mother's mould and the hospital vision is obscure, tangled up in awkward syntax:

> And though bomb be matched against bomb,
> Though all mankind wince out and nothing endure —

> Earth gone in an instant flare —
> Did a lesser death come
>
> Onto the white hospital bed.

Either this means the imagining of nuclear species death is a mere fable compared to the real grief we feel at the dying of a single human being, or it means that somehow the 'lesser death' of a woman might miraculously avert the eclipse of 'all mankind', as with some necessary sacrifice. The syntax is so depleted and in-turned here presumably because the sacrifice cannot be articulated without a 'wince' of embarrassment so deep it mimics the flare of absolute destruction. The Cold War spectacle of male reproduction of enemy male behaviour, Russia and America circling each other as viral facsimiles, bombs matching bombs against the womb, is founded on the unspeakable sacrifice of the last mother-woman on ravaged earth, trapped in lethal coma on Plath's hospital death-bed.

The two males in the fiction, by threatening destruction of the mother's mould, trigger a suicidal withdrawal in the unconscious of the woman, who should accept the law of their dominance as though genetically obedient to this new mutation in the genome. For Hughes, these mutations, at home in the nuclear glare, signify the triumph of twin male energies over the only temporarily resurgent white goddess mother-poet, as though DNA could mutate to generate a male cytoplasmic environment with no need for the 'unconscious' intermediary of the female RNA. The woman must, like Little Miss, accept the 'dream where the warrior comes' (*Collected Poems*, p. 20),[48] bow out of the reproductive system before the new male energies, the pikes, thrushes and killer crabs of the nuclear arsenal. She must lie *still* and let the male superpowers do their mutant work. For Hughes the violent creature under the law of sacred DNA has an 'agile velocity' which is 'a kind of stillness'.[49] It is this stillness which is imitated by the mother-woman poet in her dying coma.

In the last draft of 'Sheep in Fog', Plath had introduced the line 'My bones hold a stillness'.[50] In his 1988 analysis of the drafts of the poem, Hughes had commented that the new line represented Plath's obedience to the 'inexorable inner laws of the poem', a true vision of necessity when compared to the previous drafts' wishful belief in some 'hopeful outcome'.[51] That 'makeshift and inadequate' optimism had turned round the 'sacred image of sheep that are both Patriarchs and cherub-faced babies, her Husband and her Children'. It had to be dealt a death blow and the stillness accepted deep into the structure of her body, in passive mimicry of the new male gods of this world and their stillness (as lethal velocity) under the inexorable inner laws of positively violent DNA.

The final draft, written in December 1962, was for Hughes a self-protective compromise, Plath unwilling fully to accept the suicidal myth implied by the

Icarus narrative of intermediary drafts. The compromise is described as a Cold War treaty: 'a Treaty – a formal truce maintained under tension between opposed and mutually hostile interests' (*Winter Pollen*, p. 211). Those interests are the male gods of violence, which together form a compact 'intruder' into the poem for Hughes, tempting Plath to take her own life: the two-headed intruder must be banished into the depths, Hughes writes, 'where it remains, peering obliquely from "rust", through the train's breath, the blackening flower, and the "stillness" held in her bones' (p. 210). Plath must compose according to the inexorable laws of the intruder's DNA, writing mere 'inner dictation' (p. 210), her letters proceeding from the violent black keys and codes of the mutually hostile interests of the male Cold War ranged against her power to create.

Resistance to the typecasting of DNA–RNA interactions is demonstrable in the work of Barbara McClintock. Developing her work on the bfb cycle using radiation-induced chromosome breaks, she discovered that mutable genes appeared to be transferred from cell to cell during development of the maize kernel by what she called an activator gene. She suggested that the gene-jumping, occurring as a result of the trauma of the X-rays, might be the work of heterochromatin, the parts of the chromosome where there are few genes, areas of 'junk' DNA. The very idea was troubling, since 'heterochromatin' implies that it is *other to* the nucleus's DNA.[52] Her paper, published in 1950, was met with scorn and derision by many male co-geneticists. Her research was suspected of being neo-Lamarckian, a suspicion confirmed when she went on to work as an ethnobotanist helping Mexican and South American Indians artificially 'evolve' wheat. Her theory of transposition implied not only, as Stadler argued, that 'expression effects may be the actual cause of apparent gene mutations',[53] a finding which Lysenko would have applauded, but also that the sacred DNA might contain secret mutagenic activators, agents of instability and mutability deep within the elegant and stable gene apparatus, capable of initiating, especially under radiation-traumatic circumstances, a chain reaction of 'mutable loci' along the chromosome: 'once such loci arise, other mutable loci arise through transposition of the inhibiting chromatin substances to other loci which in turn become mutable', McClintock claimed, calling the process a 'chain of events'.[54]

As Evelyn Fox Keller has argued, McClintock's paper challenged the Central Dogma in more ways than one. According to the dogma, Keller writes:

> the DNA is posited as the central actor in the cell, the executive government of cellular organization, itself remaining impervious to influence from the subordinate agents to which it dictates [. . .] To McClintock, transposition provided evidence that genetic organization is necessarily more complex, and in fact more globally interdependent, than such a

model assumes. It showed that the DNA itself is subject to rearrangement and, by implication, to reprogramming. Although she did not make this explicit, the hidden heresy of her argument lay in the inference that such reorganization could be induced by signals external to the DNA – from the cell, the organism, even from the environment. [. . .] even though McClintock is not a Lamarckian, she sees in transposition a mechanism enabling genetic structures to respond to the needs of the organism.[55]

McClintock's theory of transposition may seem to challenge the male supremacist Central Dogma, and supports a neo-Lamarckian 'Soviet' view of the heterochromatic, revolutionary potential of induced cell mutability. More importantly, it also suggests that the nuclear chain reactions unleashed by radiation muta-genetics are gendered by nuclear culture in extreme and traumatic ways; gendered in 'viral' forms because of the similarities between transposition and viral transduction, viral-nuclear in the infectious spread and replication of mutable loci. And as she worked against harsh and bitter resistance from her male colleagues, she simultaneously discovered something else: at the heart of the Cold War between the geneticists was a dark and commandeering energy – ordinary misogyny. 'There is something in this,' she told Nancy Hopkins at Cold Spring Harbor at the end of her career, 'something in this that we don't understand; there is something biological, I think, about this relationship between men and women and these men just don't like these women! I'll never understand it to the day I die!'[56]

Plath discovered a method of outwitting the colossus: she would write poems that gave all its secrets away, itemizing the geneticized misogynistic fantasy of the Cold War, with herself playing the various roles of the women victims. 'Waking in Winter', for instance, takes us through the wintry landscape of the Cold War, a zone of 'burnt nerves', metal dawns, industrial death ('assembly-line of cut throats'), and nature infected by lethal toxins: 'the green / Poison of stilled lawns' – 'stilled' like the hospital patients under 'Old Mother Morphia', figures for the citizens of Fortress America (mothers, typically, the convenient scapegoats).[57]

Other poems again would parody the voices of the paradigmatic 'two men' of Cold War encounter,[58] enemy of female creative power (to give birth, to synthesize protein), as though to establish a principle of mutant comedy within the dogmatic structures of their verbal world. In 'Death & Co.', the two men are given their appropriately deadly identities. For them, the female speaker is 'red meat', and they aim to kill off her babies 'in their hospital / icebox'. One is clearly Death, but the other is more insidious – the smiling, masturbating lover who 'wants to be loved' (*Collected Poems*, p. 254). The speaker must lie still as death to escape them ('I do not stir') – and it may be that very act of stillness that kills her off: 'Somebody's done for' (p. 255).

At the same time, other texts would work against the set of fantasies through rapid changes and metamorphoses, with something of the quicksilver force of McClintock's cell mutability. Jacqueline Rose has shown how, with the extraordinary Theodore Roethke pastiche, 'Poem for a Birthday', 'the identity of the speaker [. . .] mutates itself into things which in turn mutate. [. . .] these identities are always fragile, bits and pieces of attributes, fragments of the only partly recognizable creatures they evoke'.[59] Such mutation disperses too easy targets of blame, Rose argues, as though Plath were warning future polemicists of the pitfalls involved in searching for a single enemy. I would argue, however, that 'Poem for a Birthday' does have a multiple target in mind: Cold War misogyny – hence the real anger levelled at the victimization of women in the 'Witch Burning' section, her version of Hughes' sensing of the analogy between seventeenth- century witch-hunts and the Cold War; at the treatment of the mentally disturbed ('A current agitates the wires / Volt upon volt') in 'The Stones'; at the ways the Cold War forced women deep into womb-like attitudes of stillness where they would be tempted into believing it was all their mother's fault, mother as cannibal vampire in 'Who': 'Mother of otherness / Eat me' (*Collected Poems*, pp. 137, 131). The mutations of the speaker are strategies of parody and defence, virally reproducing the male imaginary's radioactive obsession with the 'marrowy tunnels' of the female body's insides, at the same time as they are demonstrations of the 'cell mutability' and sudden identity-transformations of female making: 'This is a dark house, very big. / I made it myself, / Cell by cell from a quiet corner' (*Collected Poems*, p. 132).

The three methods – fantasy-descriptive, self-protectively satirical and cell-mutable – combine like complex protein to provide a devastating critique of the psychosomatic territory and ideology of the masculinist Cold War, whether it be the vision of the relations between nuclear holocaust, radiation, and attack on the mental and physical health of mother-poets, as in 'Fever 103°'; or the intimation in 'The Fearful' that women are being tempted towards abortive hatred of the child as 'Stealer of cells' by the ways Cold War males have put on their warrior–killer DNA-masks (*Collected Poems*, p. 256); or the suspicion in 'Getting There' that the West's obsession with Russia ('It is Russia. I have to get across, it is some war or other') might conceal a real revelling in sheer male violence and bloodletting aimed at the body of women: 'the body of this woman, / Charred skirts and deathmask' (*Collected Poems*, pp. 247–9). Most of all it is in the gathering sense that the mighty colossus against which she has ranged her mutable powers – which counts mothers as its main target – is no Electra fantasy, but a true hydra, a giant, global warfare system which had recruited men, even her own husband, to its Cold War machine.[60]

Plath's bell-jar suicide attempt in 1953 occurred the same year Hughes dreamt his life-changing shamanistic fox dream. Her short story 'A Wishing Box', written the year she met Hughes, plays with this coincidence, with an imaginatively empty woman, Agnes, trying to rival the powerfully rich dream-work of her male partner, who specializes in animal dreams, 'fox dreams [. . .] his dream of the giant pike'.[61] When she confesses her failure to dream, he begins to coach her in patronizing ways. She can only really hope to rival him by returning to the dreams of her girlhood, in particular a tacky dream where she flew over Alabama with Superman: 'We flew over Alabama; I could tell it was Alabama because the land looked like a map, with "Alabama" lettered in script across these big green mountains' (*Johnny Panic*, p. 51). Unfortunately, it is only through suicide that she can make such a return in dreamtime, the still-ness of that ultimate tranquillizer, death, giving her up to the Superman of her callow past: 'Her tranquil features were set in a slight, secret smile of triumph, as if, in some far country unattainable to mortal men, she were, at last, waltzing with the dark, red-caped prince of her early dreams' (p. 55).

Plath is comically aware here of the challenge that would be thrown to her by texts such as 'A Woman Unconscious': the woman must be cheated into believing her useless sacrifice of her own life on the altar of Cold Warrior male violence is an escape from mortal men, when it is clear from the silly dream she dredges from her adolescence that she is only locked all the more into warrior fictions, held still in Superman's arms, suffering the agile velocity of his flight-path, passive witness of the control of this Nietzschean, radiation-mutant machismo over the map of America. And why Alabama? Because in 1956 the state was the focus of the most spectacular extremes of Cold War culture, at once the stage of Martin Luther King's Montgomery bus boycott in defence of Autherine Lucy, and also the location of one of the secret centres of the US ballistic and space programme, Redstone Arsenal at 'Rocket City' Huntsville.

Working at Redstone were key German ballistic missile designers headed by Wernher von Braun – they had been the designers of the Nazi V1 and V2 rockets at Peenemünde and surrendered to the Americans at the end of the war at Oberammergau to be absorbed into the US military complex, through Project Paperclip. In 1956, the arsenal successfully deployed the Redstone missile (named after the arsenal) developed by the von Braun team, as well as the Jupiter rocket which would be so important in satellite and space exploration[62] – in recognition of their work, the German rocket designers had all been made US citizens in 1954–5. Overseeing these developments at Redstone were the Army Ballistic Missile Agency (ABMA), officially operative from February 1956, in charge of coordinating the arsenal's work on the Redstone missile as intermediate-range ballistic missile (IRBM) and as possible satellite launcher. Von Braun had published a thesis in 1954 arguing for Redstone as ideal booster for a four-stage rocket that could launch an artificial satellite – the book had led to Project Orbiter, officially endorsed by Eisenhower in July 1955 in a speech which dreamt of man-made satellites travelling 'at incredible speeds around the earth, 200 or 300 miles above its surface'.[63]

From satellite height, Alabama would indeed look like a map, and concealed in the state's name is the secret ABMA running the missile project. The Nazi prehistory to missile and rocket development is a familiar story. Less familiar might be the suggestion that Plath's obsession with her German Daddy may actually be more political than normally assumed, i.e. that she was pathologizing (or Plathologizing) her nation's own absorption of German wartime technology into its Cold War military–industrial colossus. The wishing-box story is partly about killing envy of the agile velocity of Hughes' animal-genetic militarized imagination, but just as clearly it is about the relation of that imagination to the deadly weapons systems transforming sea, land and space. One of the many missile systems being developed at Redstone Arsenal in 1956 was called Hawk. If Hughes was tempted to obey the inexorable logic of a hawkish DNA, he was only following the post-fascist logic of the missile programme moving at superhuman, superman speeds around the globe – the new god in the sky, the military satellite, eye of the colossus of hawks ruling the military–industrial complex. The systems relation of satellite to rocket is reproduced by Plath in comic-book form as female dreamer in the hands of Superman, looking down on America scripted and named according to the secret codes of the military–industrial complex, the states' old nomenclature (as in 'Alabama') concealing the code of the warfare state (ABMA).[64]

If Agnes succumbs to the Cold War DNA code which licenses male animal-technological violence aiming to still women's creativity, Plath succeeds in trumping the colossus, at least for a while, with her deep parodic knowledge of the secret code, and, more importantly, her sensing of the felt relationship between the domestic commodity-surveillance of the 1950s home, male scripting of woman's cellular interiority and the weapons systems governing political and popular culture. The Superman who takes her up into the Alabama skies and shows her his map is in league with the furniture in her home: 'She felt choked, smothered by these objects whose bulky pragmatic existence somehow threatened the deepest, most secret roots of her own ephemeral being' (*Johnny Panic*, p. 53). The commodities, like the weapons systems, aim to control her right down at the cellular level of her womb-like imagination, just as the shaman-male she is married to, with his psychogenetic fox dreams and pike dreams, would have her simply dream her way into stillness, succumb to the nuclear terms of their special relationship.

The Cold War anxieties involved in the Dogma took on a weird twist once genetics morphed into molecular biology, with a new generation of male geneticists trained in information and systems theories rejecting the woolly Darwinian-Mendelian structural organicism of the Mullers and McClintocks of this world and revelling in the mutagens generated by high-tech viruses and bacteriophages. This meant that potentially liberating discoveries about the cell – the importance of RNA as active agent in protein synthesis, the crucial role played by the genetic material in the cytoplasm's mitochondria, the whole extraordinarily complex and beautiful uncoiling, unzipping and replicating procedures that take place when messenger RNA copies code sequences from DNA – were all recuperated into a forbiddingly technical and ultra-technological DNA preserve of 'male' programming within the cell as information system. The cell was no longer a happy home for the Central Dogma but an information machine within a rigid system in which *both* the male and female were mere feedback items, sexual agents for the survival of the gene-machine itself, organic pathways for the flow and circulation of codes and information. Sex, meiosis and birth are subsidiary reproductive systems that ensure the recombination, transcription, translocation and replication of genetic bytes within the body-as-species computer.

Years before Richard Dawkins' selfish genes, molecular biologists were scripting the DNA genetic code as the selfish core of the whole cellular system. As Wilkie's 1964 summary of the French Jacob and Monod's 1961 work on messenger RNA demonstrates, two genetic systems in each cell (the nucleo-cytoplasmic interactions) are integrated into a systems-theory model of gene regulation, with regulator genes, structural genes, operons and repressors working selectively in a complex feedback system: 'regulation of enzyme formation is by feed-back control' (Wilkie, *Cytoplasm in Heredity*, p. 5). The DNA–RNA interaction is subsumed into an 'extensive control system' involving computer-inflected 'operator-gene codes' (pp. 5–6) whereby even the discovery of the genetically active nature of cytoplasmic RNA is incorporated into a steady-state system of regulation and information-transmission. The systems software controls everything in the cell, even or especially its differentiation and mutagenic behaviour. 'Programmed to function in specific ways in a somatic environment' (*Cytoplasm in Heredity*, p. 102), the cell is a congeries of feedback-regulated subsystems all ultimately reinforcing the greater control of the system by nuclear genes.

One could argue that the systems model was developed partly and importantly to control the alarming fact that the cytoplasm had such a crucial role to play in synthesis. We can get a sense of this from a remark by the French team before the discovery of messenger RNA:

> [The assumption that genes act as templates in synthesis] appears unlikely, however, in the face of a growing body of evidence suggesting that the seat of protein synthesis in many types of cells including bacteria, is not the nucleus but rather certain cytoplasmic constituents (ribosomes). We are therefore left to consider the only other alternative, namely that the transfer of information involves functionally unstable intermediaries, and to ask which cell constituents might be likely candidates for such a function.[65]

The discovery of messenger RNA is therefore also an invention of it as 'functionally unstable' intermediary for the humble transfer of nuclear information. The absorption of RNA into the DNA-dominated system had 'her' operations controlled and technologized within a static-dynamic flowcharted network, systematizing her role down to that of helpmeet messenger Iris to DNA's Zeus.

The systems theory which took over molecular biology at this crucial juncture had become the dominant paradigm for the sciences during the early Cold War. Originating in several fields at once – in particular Claude Shannon's information theory, Ludwig von Bertalanffy and W. Ross Ashby's cybernetic general systems theory, and Norbert Wiener's artificial intelligence and feedback theory – and spreading quickly into the social sciences (especially with Talcott Parsons' functionalist theory of social systems), its true source was the concepts of organizational control and feedback generated by the new weapons systems developed for the Second World War. Armed Forces' control and systems engineering, weapon system human factors engineering and military ergonomics are the hidden core of systems theory. As John Hrones put it in 1968:

> The advent of the Second World War with the development of automatic training of guns, radar-tracking systems and missile-guidance systems concentrated a tremendous effort on the understanding of a wide variety of systems. It was in this connection that some of the first attempts to apply systems theory and analysis to a human being occurred.[66]

As cultural theorist Lillian Kay has shown, Vannenar Bush's Applied Mathematics Panel (AMP) was set up in 1942 to recruit the top mathematicians of the time (including Wiener and John von Neumann) to work on bombing and rocket accuracy, work involving 'statistics, numerical analysis, and computation, the theory of shock waves, command and control systems, and the emerging field of operations research'.[67] To do this military work, the relationship between men and machines had to be retheorized. To service the military machine, servicemen had to be subsumed into a structure of combinatory relations that mimicked the flow of information within the programmed or 'taped' weapons of the war's new technologies, just as those technologies had 'borrowed' features from the human nervous system.[68] Wiener and Julian Bigelow, working on anti-aircraft guidance at MIT during the war, had hit upon feedback as the handiest way of integrating the human into machine systems. As Kay puts it:

> Wiener and Bigelow quickly reached the conclusion that any solution of the self-correcting tracking problem was predicated on the feedback principle, operating not only in the apparatus but in the human operators of the gun and plane [. . .] the concept of cyborg had emerged. The cybernetic organism – a heterogeneous construction, part living and part

> machine – germinated within the wartime academic-military matrix and matured within the national security practices of the Cold War. (Kay, 'Cybernetics, Information, Life', p. 34)

Soldiers were viewed as operator subsystems within an algorithmic chain of command, 'engineered' as feedback items in the weapons system as a whole.

The trace of the military origin of systems theory in its subsequent application in molecular biology is discernible in the ways RNA transcription and protein synthesis are commandeered, neutralized, then 'weaponized' in the new algorithmic models. The agency and creativity of RNA are lost in translation in the grimly efficient language of information-handling control systems. DNA is now 'control gene DNA' initiating 'information flow' within a 'control hierarchy'. The role of RNA and other cytoplasmic organisms is reduced to 'control functions which regulate the cellular system'. They are partly subservient to DNA as variables controlled by repressors and inducers, and partly extrinsically controlled through feedback from environmental disturbances.[69] The information flowing from the control gene DNA may be subject to transformation, but those changes are predictable, just as noise and enemy aircraft could be predicted and accounted for on the flow and block diagram of the wartime engineer. Because the information metaphor derived from military weapons systems, the genetic fields it thrived in became structurally linked to the contemporary weapons systems of the atomic age.[70] It was Jacques Monod who was to compare gene-enzyme systems to the systems regulating missile technology, systems 'compatible to those employed in electronic automation circuitry, where the very slight energy consumed by a relay can trigger a large-scale operation such as, for example, the firing of a ballistic missile'.[71]

The unconscious militarization of the body within the warfare state as system, which was one of the effects of the spread of systems theory to all studies of human behaviour, is traceable across the board in Plath's and Hughes' poetry and prose, from the military tropes governing the psychogenetic animals concealed within ancient DNA structures in Hughes' work (the earth owl as 'living missile', the hawk as fascist militarist, the jaguar on its 'short fierce fuse', the ghost crabs as military-genetic forces with their 'packed trench of helmets')[72] to Plath's morbid interest in dismemberment prosthetics, sci-fi paranoia and fear of deep somatic poisoning by technology: the prosthetic suit in 'The Applicant', proof against bombs; Gulliver caught by the Lilliputian 'spider-men', i.e. radioactive mutants, in 'Gulliver'; the crippling 'mercuric / Atoms' within the barren wombspace of 'Nick and the Candlestick'.[73] Whether the impulse is a drive towards acceptance of the killing machine, as with Hughes' admiration for the stillness at the core of nuclear weapons systems, or Plath's move towards a hysterical miming, parodying and mutational resisting of the colossus, both poets intuit the Cold War's system at the molecular level of word and genetic unconscious. 'Meaning leaks from the molecules', Plath wrote in 'Mystic' (*Collected Poems*, p. 269), and it is a meaning sensed as flow within a signifying system of dangerous energies and dehumanized bearers. For Hughes, any form of 'vehement activity' is integrated into the 'bigger energy, the elemental power circuit of the universe'.[74]

The post-Lawrentian sex war Hughes had deduced from the neo-fascist drives in the psychogenetic unconscious may have been a powerful force in the early 1940s and 1950s when the Cold War was finding its way into the paranoid hearts of men. But by 1963 and Plath's suicide, the Cold War's systems had integrated the sex war energies into their circuits so smoothly that they ceased very nearly to be gendered at all. Or rather the 'master- / Fulcrum of violence'[75] in the system's DNA control centre ceased to need *human* mediation as such, only servo-mechanisms of whatever type to serve its automatic purposes[76] – all this of course within the context of the subject's dreaming of the Cold War. Yet the dream is being generated by the system's inhuman 'bigger energy' on its engineered way.

The development of the control theory at the core of systems analysis responded to two factors, as S. Bennett has shown in his history of control engineering: 'first, the nature of the problem that society saw as important – the launching, manoeuvring, guidance and tracking of missiles and space vehicles; and secondly [. . .] the advent of the digital computer'.[77] Control theory bore the traces of this provenance into the other zones of its application, whether it be cell duplication, the construction of a line of poetry or the narratives structuring sexual encounters. If it was some kind of relief to see the crude anthropomorphism colouring descriptions of organic processes go out of the window, the new model of integrated circuits and control flow diagrams threatened merely to mask out behind engineering jargon the old power relations and their accompanying fictions.

Awareness of this shift from sex war myth to 'weaponized' power circuitry is there in Plath's bee poems of October 1962, where her beekeeper female speaker unhingedly identifies the hive both with her own body and with a creaturely subsystem whose energies she, as technological god, can control. With the hive as body, the queen bee serves as secret selfhood, the female bees as burgeoning processes within cells and organs, brood cells as womb – 'the white hive is snug as a virgin, / Sealing off her brood cells, her honey, and quietly humming'.[78] But the body is under surveillance by the external self-consciousness who keeps watch at the 'grid', as though the body were like Ross Ashby's black box, only knowable through differential tests of decoded outputs ('only a little grid, no exit. // I put my eye to the grid. / It is dark, dark').[79] The body, in other words, has been knowingly integrated into a strangely unsettling system by the collusive mind, subject to dark and dehumanizing protocols, reduced to a set of informational differences. But far from occluding the transformative processes 'inside' the insides of the black box, the system turns paranoid and senses them as 'dark, dark' within the unknown feedback unit; the cellular processes of the somatic unconscious have become mysterious and therefore threatening as a result of their integration into the control system's gridwork: 'I am no source of honey / So why should they turn on me?' (*Collected Poems*, p. 213).

With the hive as set of energies under the control of the gaze, Plath shifts into the more abstract schema of systems theory, in which the issue is the incorporation of the female gender into a sinister technology. The female poet feels that she has obscurely betrayed her gender by accepting the control system that gives her power to represent: 'Will they hate me, / These women [. . .] / I am in control. / Here is my honey-machine.'[80] Though she is in control, she is under the control of a male observer ('A third person is watching' (p. 215)), she his obedient feedback-looped code-carrier. Her bees attempt to attack him, only to discover that their attack turns into a controlled imitation and elaboration of the reproduceable features of the male control system, an act of reproduction which leads to their death: 'The bees found him out, / Molding onto his lips like lies, / Complicating his features' (p. 215). Caught up in the coils of this system, the poet now knows that the cost is the loss of any pretention to 'queen bee' status ('Is she dead? Is she sleeping?'), only suddenly to collapse into final dreamwork, yearning for the return of the queen as avenging killer comet:

> Now she is flying
> More terrible than she ever was, red
> Scar in the sky, red comet
> Over the engine that killed her –
> The mausoleum, the wax house.[81]

The colour red not only is a signal of anger, but activates the code for the Cold War, with avenging queen bee as apocalyptic Soviet missile, red-alert viral killer within the empty Gothic house of American domestic space, of American female body, of the political zones controlled by missile-system technology. Female spaces, zones and bodies have all been recruited as servo-mechanisms within the integrated circuit of Cold War 'bigger energy' – only as belated nuclear fiction, occurring *after* the death of female agency, can the 'engine' be resisted. Nevertheless, the fiction does take on surreal subversive energy once released as fantasy formation 'outside' the surveillance of the male DNA-third person: in the last two poems of the bee sequence, 'The Swarm' and 'Wintering', the bees take on more trenchantly military identities, yet aimed against the control system itself, a civil war as gender conflict.

In 'The Swarm' they figure as Napoleon's army, defeated by the technician as Wellington ('The man with gray hands'), and, under Napoleon's lunatic gaze, sacrificed for the good of history. The pessimism of this vision of useless sacrifice of the gender on the altar of 'two-man' military history is turned on its head in 'Wintering', where the complicit female poet exults in her six jars of honey but fears she has sold out to the enemy ('It is they who own me'). Yet she feeds her bees through the nuclear winter of the Cold War ('The cold sets in' (p. 218)), and secretly admires their new gender-exclusive revolution: 'The bees are all women, / Maids and the long royal lady. / They have got rid of the men' (p. 218). The female body and gender, though exploited and milked of the sweet products of their creative energies, nevertheless survive the killing engine of the Cold War control system. They not only survive, but effect a revolutionary countermove against the enemy gender, redefining the wintry Cold War as *their* exclusive space and zone: 'Winter is for women.'

This may be wishful thinking against the missile technology which is feeding, disguising and radicalizing the sex war at the heart of the Cold War, or it may be taken as a proleptic sensing of the militant feminism which would begin to turn against the control systems of Cold War misogyny. At the very least, there is recognition that unpacking the complex relationship between the female poet's art of making, her somatic processes and the military–industrial colossus with the 'weaponized' circuits of its systems uncovers a new code-book for women which recognizes the guilt of complicity, the burden of potential for gender betrayal, the maddening possibility of a self-destructive body-paranoia at work on the gendered subject, the unacceptable costs of too doom-laden a passivity to the killing engines of the Cold War; and yet which at the same time serves notice of warning to the men with grey hands: the gender is planning a revolution the like of which the world has never seen.

On 6 September 1951 in Mexico City, Burroughs accidentally shot his wife Joan dead in a drunken game of William Tell, a highball glass as apple on her head. He managed to get off with help from friends and was never convicted of the crime; its effect on his writing was incalculable. In the introduction to the novel he had partly written just after the shooting, *Queer* – begun March 1952, left unpublished till 1985 – Burroughs admits he might never have become a writer without the shooting, that his superstitious guilt over her death (he must have been possessed by some evil viral energy which made him do it) would colour his subsequent obsession with viruses, control and sex war.

Oliver Harris has brilliantly unpicked the Cold War neo-fascist *folie de grandeur* which structures Lee's seduction of Allerton in *Queer* in Lee's schizophrenic self-allegorizing routines of power and possession.[82] Lee is being controlled by a bigger energy, in accord with 'the Cold War dream of total control' (Harris, 'Can You See a Virus?', p. 260), a destabilizing mix of MK-ULTRA-style mind-control through *yagé*[83] and pawn-manipulation by way of the computing machines in charge of the Cold War's cybernetic systems. Lee acts these fantasies out during his routines in his various metamorphoses as oilman, vice squad cop, British intelligence officer, colonial sex-slaver, etc. Harris insists that these routines cannot be 'naturalized as parodies or satires', or as merely signifying 'the internalization by a homosexual of a homophobia that necessarily splits the subject and alienates him from his own desires' (p. 263). Rather, Lee is quite literally *possessed*, his speech and body taken over, bleeding symptoms of some 'embodied parasitology' (p. 263).

That the parasite desires the exclusion of women and mothers in particular[84] is made explicit in Lee's struggles to disrupt the game of chess between Allerton and his wife Mary, and Harris very convincingly puts this into relation with the chess machines so important to Wiener's cybernetic age of communication and control. There is a connection, therefore, between Lee's radio-ventriloquial, parasitical routines and Burroughs' guilt over the killing of Joan.

Burroughs is quite specific about the shape and scope of that guilt: the relationship he historically made with the real 'Allerton' (including the trip to Panama and deepest, jungliest Ecuador, in the summer of 1951) had displayed features which seemed to be saying the shooting of Joan was pre-programmed in some way. In other words, the parasitic allegory machine which is scripting Lee is preparing him, through this corrupted 'two-man' routine of duplication and mutation, for an act of murderous violence against the 'Mary' queen figure. Harris argues that Burroughs' confession of this in 1985 is deliberately apoliticizing – but this is to misunderstand the Cold War politics Burroughs was interested in, namely the politics which recruited the cybersexual-genetic systems of gendered desire to the cause. The anti-Communist cause is a front for a new demonizing of women as weak forces in the generation of power, information flow, guided technological violence.

Lee's desire is a caged, predatory animal, Burroughs writes,[85] but it is an animal as viral organism, an 'amoeboid protoplasmic projection' (Burroughs, *Queer*, p. 48) which seeks to enter the loved one's somatic space and colonize it from the inside of his insides: the desire is to enter 'the other's body, to breathe with his lungs, see with his eyes, learn the feel of his viscera and genitals' (p. 48).[86] This viral invasion and occupation of the loved one is compared to the close intimacy and secret yearning structuring the relations between the two superpowers, instanced in the MK-ULTRA drug experiments, including Yagé's powers to induce synthetic schizophrenia and telepathy ('mov[ing] in on someone's psyche and giv[ing] orders' (p. 57)). Allerton's work profile already scripts him as a Cold Warrior: he has worked in counterintelligence in Germany, a world of agents and informants and 'a whole fictitious network of Russian spies' (p. 39), so that when Lee is said to admire his 'combination of *intelligence* and childlike charm' (my emphasis, p. 39), we know that Lee's sexual desire for the man is being shaped by fictions of Cold War secrecy, propaganda and control.

These two men cannot help reproducing the allegory of the superpowers' homosocial relationship with each other. They cannot help it, Burroughs suggests, because the same recessive genes are at work simultaneously on both the geopolitical and psychosexual levels. Lee, to seduce this all-male baby-innocent

Cold Warrior, must virally enter his lover's cellular insides and both 'read off' the codes governing Cold War identities and ideologies from Allerton's DNA, and help the recessive genes to mutate into the new queer formations signifying sexual predation, schizophrenic politics, genetic exchange as telepathic intelligence and counterintelligence. Most of all, the recessive genes must turn their warlike energies away from 'homophobic' resentments separating the 'two men'. The chromosomal engineers must change the programs running cybergenetic systems of information and control and direct more energy against the common enemy, the queen of the chess game. Bypassing her with a feedback loop which terminates her usefulness, the two males can then concentrate on the more testing audacities of the zero-sum games of the Cold War. Mary/Joan must die.

Obscuring and then constituting the drive against women is the more overt aggression against US satellite states in Central America. Panama, site of Lee's search for Yagé and therefore of the primitive killer-drive needed for the job, is a 'mongrel town of pimps and whores and recessive genes, this degraded leech on the Canal' (Burroughs, *Queer*, p. 113). The primitive recessive gene is spoken here, through Lee, in its ugliest form: colonial-racist, imperial-eugenicist, America seething with disgust for the dependency culture it has created, a culture which it is none the less secretly addicted to (in the name of *internal* security). This double attitude, colonial and addicted, *is* the recessive gene being tapped. If the trip to Ecuador is a journey towards synthetic versions of those genes, Mexico is a zone where the attitude can find a friendly technology to bond with. Murder is Mexico's 'national neurosis' (p. 36), after all, and Mexican gun culture is conveniently channelled against the weak and defenceless: it is understood, somehow, that this is so *because* of US tutelage. The corrupt colonial mix fosters the mad energies needed to trigger paranoia into action. Lee enjoys reading of a man who drunkenly shoots his wife and children with his .45 in Mexico City's *Ultimas Notícias*, for instance (p. 36). When drunk he also enjoys threatening Mexicans with guns. When Allerton and Mary leave together, Lee vents his frustration by shooting a mouse's head off with his Colt Frontier (p. 77). Central America as Cold War America's backyard provides the 'genetic' desire and drive, the routine forms of hatred, the lethal technology and the training ground.

At another level, Harris is right – in the end it no longer seems to matter whether the target in Burroughs is *campesino* or wife, whether the host body in which viral desire is working is male, female or machine. What matters is what has been allowed to occur, namely the colonization of the writerly imagination by the bigger energy of violent and paranoid state systems. And yet it is still vitally important that it was women who began to turn the tide in the early 1960s against the assault on their gender, children and genes, in a sustained protest against the nuclear culture fostered by the warfare state.

As Amy Swerdlow has shown, in her detailed study of the Women Strike for Peace (WSP) protest movement, the peace movement triggered by the Russian atmospheric tests which Grace Paley had joined, and for whom her Ellen and Faith had 'pasted white doves on blue posters and prayed on Eighth Street for peace', was crucial in persuading Kennedy to push for a test-ban treaty. The WSP was launched by six women in Washington in 1961, members of the Washington chapter of the Committee for a Sane Nuclear Policy. Their networked call for the strike rippled across America: in New York, there were marches on the Russian embassy, the AEC and the US Mission to the UN. According to Catherine Stimpson, in her foreword to Swerdlow's book:

> By 1963, WSP had amazing successes, beyond all its dreams and proph-
> ecies. Making both dissent against the superpowers and superpower
> cooperation more respectable, WSP had helped to change the discourse
> of the Cold War. Making nuclear war less respectable, WSP had aided
> in the ratification of a treaty that banned atmospheric nuclear testing.
> It had also created a debacle for the House of Un-American Activities
> Committee, that perversion of democracy. Under FBI surveillance since
> the beginning, members of WSP were subpoenaed by the Committee in
> 1962. Their appearance, shrewdly planned and bravely executed, was a
> comic masterpiece. Women jammed the committee room, rose in support
> when witnesses were called, applauded the performance of these wit-
> nesses, wore flowers and gave out bouquets, and dangled babies. 'Peace
> Gals', read one headline, in the rhetoric of the day, 'Make Red Hunters
> Look Silly.'[87]

The mass movement created by WSP was energized by the core fears outlined by Paley in her fiction, and by Plath in her poems against the colossus: women activists, Swerdlow recalls, moved 'to militant political action in the name of motherhood' (Swerdlow, *Women Strike for Peace*, p. 1). Their concerns were the concerns that darkened Plath's last days and led her to lie still as sacrifice to the Complex; and it was their lobbying which secured the necessary White House resolve for the test-ban treaty of 1963. It was the WSP protest which is the cultural force Plath alludes to in her defence of the 'child forming itself finger by finger in the dark' in February 1962. Swerdlow, in March of the same year, carried her fourth child *in utero* to Geneva to the Seventeen-Nation Disarmament Conference, to participate in the WSP lobby for a test ban:

> In Geneva I demanded from Valerian Zorin and Arthur Dean, the Russian
> and US chief negotiators, that they act immediately to protect my unborn
> child from the nuclear contamination of the atmosphere that we in WSP
> already perceived as dangerous to health and life. As I pointed to my
> own abdomen, I was careful to explain that my concern was not private,
> that I was pleading for all the world's children, born and yet unborn.
> (Swerdlow, *Women Strike for Peace*, p. 12)

Plath's death and Paley's activism are intertwined in their common origins in the WSP lobbying against the atmospheric fallout assault on the cells of all present and future children, according to the warnings written into the Muller–Haldane principle. In the edition edited by Frieda Hughes restored to the state of the manuscript on Plath's desk the day she died, *Ariel* was dedicated to her two children, begins with 'Morning Song' on the birth of her son and ends with 'Wintering', with its intimations of the nuclear death of all women. The poems were written as imaginative strikes for peace in their analysis of the military–industrial complex, and in their exploration of the psychopolitical formations taken by the Cold War sex war. Her death might be seen as a failure of that strike, yet, as Frieda Hughes insists in her introduction, Plath survived her suicide through Ted Hughes' scrupulous care after her death, as Frieda Hughes recalled:

> he kept alive the memory of the mother who had left me, so I felt as if she were watching over me, a constant presence in my life. [. . .] For me, as her daughter, everything associated with her was miraculous, but that was because my father made it appear so, even playing me a record of my mother reading her poetry so I could hear her voice again.[88]

Ted Hughes' writing after her death, including *Gaudete*, reflects on the high Cold War's sex war as symptomatic evidence offered up to sustain the constant presence of Plath's departed spirit by illustrating the justice of her reading of the gendered drives implicit in Cold War energies. His work reveals the 'double and schizophrenic nature' of the nuclear threat targeting women and children in the world that Plath had discovered with 'Death & Co.': 'I imagine these two aspects of death as two men, two business friends, who have come to call.'[89] Schizophrenic Death, the Warfare State colossus, seduces and targets women at the genetic level: her suicide, as Ted Hughes' work at its best attests, was an enactment of the sacrificial logic of nuclear culture, and at the same time stands as a broken protest as radical as WSP's, not private-confessional but 'pleading for all the world's children, born and yet unborn'.

NOTES

1. Interview with Alan Burns, in Burns and Sugnet, *Imagination on Trial*, p. 123. Love Canal was a former chemical landfill which became a 15-acre neighbourhood of the City of Niagara Falls, New York. On 7 August 1978, President Carter declared a federal emergency due to the severity of the pollution, and the town was evacuated. The nuclear reactor at Three Mile Island, built on a sandbar in the Susquehanna River near Harrisburg, Pennsylvania, suffered near-meltdown on 28 March 1979. The core was exposed, heating up very close to 'China Syndrome' level.
2. One of the women fleeing Three Mile Island recalled her instinctive reaction to the news of the radiation leak: 'I think the only images I could conjure up of the radiation were, of course, the movies from World War II and the bomb. And one of the odd things that, you know, you can't smell it, you can't see it, you can't taste it. My nephew, I believe, was 11 or 12 at the time. When we were within minutes of

driving away, I remember him looking at his arms and saying, "I don't think we're burned. I don't think we got it." And my thoughts were not yes or no, we weren't. My thoughts were, "How do I talk to this kid all the way to Boston without putting any fear in his heart?"' (transcript of interview with Robin Stuart on PBS website for 1999 film *Meltdown At Three Mile Island*, www.pbs.org/wgbh/amex/three/filmmore/reference/interview/stuart03.html, accessed 9 December 2008.

3. Buirski, 'How I Learnt to Start Worrying and Hate the Bomb', pp. 23–4.
4. Paley, 'The Gulf War' (1991), in *Just As I Thought*, p. 255.
5. 'Visceralization' is the movement of a pathogen towards the viscera.
6. Paley, 'Living', in *Collected Stories*, pp. 166–7.
7. Burroughs, 'Technical Deposition of the Virus Power', in *Word Virus*, p. 275.
8. Burroughs, *The Ticket that Exploded*, p. 50.
9. 'What Freud calls the "super ego" is probably a parasitic occupation of the mid brain where the "rightness" centers may be located and by "rightness" I mean where "you'" and "I" used to live before this "super ego" moved in room on the top floor' (Burroughs, *The Soft Machine*, p. 130).
10. Burroughs, *The Soft Machine*, p. 110.
11. The transmission electron microscope was invented in 1932 by Max Knoll and Ernst Ruska, and was commercially available after 1938; the scanning electron microscope, using a cathode ray tube for imaging, was developed by Charles Oatley in 1952.
12. Elof Axel Carlson, paraphrasing Muller's article 'Potential Hazards of Radiation' in *Excerpta Medica* 11 (1957), in his biography of Muller, *Genes, Radiation, and Society*, p. 349. Most of the information here about Muller is indebted to Carlson's superb biography. For basic background information about genetics contained in this chapter, Max Levitan's fine introductory work, the *Textbook of Human Genetics*, is very useful. The University of Utah has a simple and user-friendly guide at www.learn.genetics.utah.edu.
13. 'Context', first published *London Magazine* (February 1962), reprinted in Plath, *Johnny Panic*, p. 92. Other respondents to the magazine's questionnaire are available online through www.poetrymagazines.org.uk/magazine/issue.asp?id=392.
14. Woolf, *Orlando: A Biography*, p. 132.
15. Cook's 'Juggernaut' article appeared in a supplement issue of the *Nation*, 28 October 1961, pp. 277–337.
16. Cook, *Warfare State*, p. 170. Cook quotes a Harvard economist, Sumner Slichter, addressing a bankers' convention in 1949: '[the Cold War] increases the demand for goods, helps sustain a high level of employment, accelerates technological progress and thus helps the country to raise its standard of living [. . .] So we may thank the Russians for helping capitalism in the United States better than ever' (quoted in Cook, *Warfare State*, p. 171).
17. 'O father, all by yourself / You are pithy and historical as the Roman Forum' (Plath, 'The Colossus' (1959), in *Collected Poems*, p. 129). The political meaning of the term underlies and sustains, I would argue, the more familiar interpretation, entertained by Plath herself, of the Colossus as her 'own father, the buried male muse & god-creator risen to be my mate in Ted' (journal entry for 11 May 1958, in *Journals of Sylvia Plath 1950–1962*, p. 381).
18. 'Three Women: A Poem for Three Voices' (March 1962), in *Collected Poems*, p. 177.
19. In this interpretation, I am indebted to Robin Peel's book on Plath and the Cold War, *Writing Back: Sylvia Plath and Cold War Politics*. Peel suggest that the poems in 'Three Voices' are 'directed at a global system which is poisoning the world and causing women to abort, or be infertile' (Peel, *Writing Back*, p. 200).
20. Cf. Muller's 1927 paper, 'Artificial Transmutation of the Gene'.

21. Muller, 'Genetic Effects of the Atomic Bombs in Hiroshima and Nagasaki', first printed in *Science* 106 (1947). Muller was present at the conference which voted for the paper's programme and for a statement based on the Committee's report written by Jim Neel. 'Genetic Effects' is the conference statement.

22. James F. Crow, 'Quarreling Geneticists and a Diplomat', in Crow and Dove, *Perspectives on Genetics*, pp. 460–1.

23. Ted Hughes, 'The Rock', p. 90.

24. 'Pike', in *Collected Poems*, pp. 84–6. First published in *Encounter*, March 1960. Many submarines were named after fish (e.g. SS-211 *Gudgeon*, SS-389 *Piranha*, SS-393 *Queenfish*). There was a submarine USS-*Pike* (SS-173) which served in the Second World War, scrapped in 1957. It was 300 feet long in its world. There was also a First World War submarine torpedo boat called the *Pike*, 63 feet long – renamed the A-5.

25. 'Thrushes', in *Collected Poems*, pp. 82–3. First published in *Encounter*, March 1958.

26. Between 1952 and 1960, the Air Ministry had an operation called Project Thrush, itemizing details of flying training and operating instructions for nuclear bombers in Britain. Cf. Liddell Hart Centre for Military Archives' Nuclear History Database, www.kcl.ac.uk/lhcma/pro/p-air02a.htm, accessed 9 December 2008.

27. Szondi's text is discussed by Deleuze and Guattari in their *Anti-Oedipus*, pp. 289–90.

28. Szondi developed a test for identifying patients' sets of drives using photographs of sufferers of extreme pathological conditions (which included homosexuality). The photography test is proof, if proof is needed, of the eugenicist bias of genetics. Szondi particularly recommended his test for confirmation of the civilizing effects of electroshock treatment on unruly patients.

29. Wilkie, *The Cytoplasm in Heredity*, pp. 95–6.

30. Darlington, *Evolution of Genetic Systems*, p. 186.

31. This male anxiety is played out in comic inverted form with the timid Nietzschean fantasies of the sexually incompetent though superpowerful mutants Superman and Spider-Man.

32. Ted Hughes, *Winter Pollen*, p. 253.

33. Walder, *Ted Hughes*, p. 39.

34. First published in *The Hawk in the Rain*, September 1957.

35. First published in *Northwest Review*, Fall/Winter 1967–8.

36. From *The Hawk in the Rain*, first published in the *Nation*, July 1957.

37. From *Lupercal*, published March 1960.

38. Faas, 'Chapters of a Shared Mythology'.

39. Ted Hughes, *Gaudete*, p. 104.

40. Faas, 'Chapters of a Shared Mythology', p. 118.

41. In *Gaudete*, one of the women impregnated by Lumb feels the 'child inside her' as a 'growing / Fungus of jealousy' (*Gaudete*, p. 55).

42. 'Leonard Baskin' (from an introduction to an exhibition in London in 1962), quoted in Walder, *Ted Hughes*, p. 61.

43. First published in *A Few Crows* in October 1970.

44. 'Sylvia Plath and Her Journals', first published 1982, in Ted Hughes, *Winter Pollen*, p. 179.

45. Crick, 'The Structure of the Nucleic Acids and Related Substances', p. 177.

46. *Special Publications*, p. 227. Hotchkiss worked at the Rockefeller Institute for Medical Research in New York – the Institute boasted John Northrop and Wendell Stanley, who had been awarded the chemistry Nobel prize in the same year as Muller (1946) for their work on enzymes and virus proteins.

47. From *Lupercal*. First published in *Poetry (Chicago)*, August 1959.

48. 'Macaw and the Little Miss', from *The Hawk in the Rain*; first published September 1957.
49. Revised 1992 version of 1971 interview with Ekbert Faas, 'Poetry and Violence', in *Winter Pollen*, p. 262.
50. Plath, *Collected Poems*, p. 262.
51. 'Sylvia Plath: The Evolution of "Sheep in Fog"', written 1988, in *Winter Pollen*, p. 205.
52. 'McClintock's controlling elements were non-genes, genetic particles outside the framework of one-gene one-enzyme biochemical genetics' (Comfort, 'Two Genes, No Enzymes', p. 472).
53. Stadler, 'The Gene' (1954), p. 258.
54. McClintock, 'The Origin and Behavior of Mutable Loci in Maize', p. 208. First published in *Proceedings of the National Academy of Sciences* 36 (1950).
55. Keller, *Reflections on Gender and Science*, pp. 169, 171.
56. Oral reminiscence by Nancy Hopkins, in the Cold Spring Harbor Oral History collection, accessible through http://nucleus.cshl.edu.
57. 'Waking in Winter', in *Collected Poems*, p. 151.
58. Nuclear missiles were protected by the two-man rule. In James Odom's words: 'It took two people to arm the missile. One person had half of the combination and the second one had the other half. On custodial sites (Greece, Korea, Turkey, etc.), a PAL device (permissive action link) was used, and it took two persons to remove it so the arming device could be installed.' Odom was a Nike crewman and first sergeant from August 1960 to September 1974 in the States (Nike missiles website, http://ed-thelen.org/missiles.html).
59. *The Haunting of Sylvia Plath*, p. 54.
60. Cf. Stan Smith's political reading of the poem in the Plath chapter of his *Inviolable Voice*.
61. Plath, 'The Wishing Box', in *Johnny Panic*, p. 51.
62. These missiles are only the ones being developed in early 1956. The arsenal had been instrumental in the development of a score of other missiles, including Honest John, the first US tactical nuclear weapon, the Nike family, and the Corporate and Lacrosse missiles, as well as the Loki rocket, the Sergeant surface-to-surface guided missile, etc.
63. Information from Redstone Arsenal Complex Chronology – 1950–5, available through www.redstone.army.mil/history, accessed 9 December 2008. Robin Peel discovered that '"Ariel" was also the name of an Anglo-American telecommunications satellite, damaged and silenced by the radiation caused by atmospheric hydrogen bomb tests' (Peel, *Writing Back*, p. 41).
64. Superman is identified with aerial war technology in another Plath short story, 'Superman and Paula Brown's New Snowsuit', written in 1955. In the tale, Plath recalls her Superman dreams and games and connects them with America's entry into war with the leitmotif of the sound of warplanes. The war puts paid to the dreams, signifying the 'real world': 'The silver airplanes and the blue capes all dissolved and vanished, wiped away like the crude drawings of a child in colored chalk from the colossal blackboard of the dark. That was the year the war began, and the real world, and the difference' (*Johnny Panic*, p. 166). In her journal, Plath admired 'The Wishing Box' but feared 'the real world in it isn't real enough. It is too much a fable' (entry for 15 June 1959, in *Journals of Sylvia Plath 1950–1962*, p. 497). The unreality arguably suits the fabulous features of the Cold War ABMA, however.
65. Paper by Riley, Pardee, Jacob and Monod (1960), quoted in Thomas, 'Molecular Genetics under an Embryologist's Microscope', p. 295.
66. John Hrones' foreword to Mesarovic, *Systems Theory and Biology*, p. vii.
67. Kay, 'Cybernetics, Information, Life', p. 33.

68. Wiener later argued that the whole idea of digital technology was based on interpretation of the synaptic processes of the nervous system: 'This view of the nervous system corresponds to the theory of machines that consist in a sequence of switching devices in which the opening of a later switch depends on the action of precise combinations of earlier switches leading into it, which open at the same time. This all-or-none machine is called a *digital* machine' (Wiener, *The Human Use of Human Beings*, p. 64.) 'Taping' was the original term for programming.

69. Waterman, 'Systems Theory and Biology – View of a Biologist', pp. 10–13.

70. As Kay argues: 'the multivalent information metaphor [. . .] linked the biosemiotics of molecular biology to communication technosciences, and through these cultural semiotics it constituted the imaginaries of postwar technoculture of the Missile Age and the Computer Age' (Kay, 'Cybernetics, Information, Life', pp. 30–1).

71. Monod, *Chance and Necessity*, p. 68.

72. Ted Hughes, 'The Earth Owl', in *The Earth-Owl and Other Moon-People*, p. 7; 'Hawk Roosting', in *Collected Poems*, pp. 68–9; 'The Jaguar', in *Collected Poems*, p. 20; 'Ghost Crabs', in *Collected Poems*, p. 149.

73. Plath, *Collected Poems*, pp. 221, 251, 242.

74. From 'The Right Lines', in Conquest, *The Abomination of Moab* (1979), quoted by Sweeting, 'Hughes and Shamanism', in Sagar, *The Achievement of Ted Hughes*, p. 73).

75. Ted Hughes, 'The Hawk in the Rain', *Collected Poems*, p. 19.

76. 'The great mechanization of the second world war brought [these machines] into their own, and the need of handling the extremely dangerous energy of the atom will probably bring them to a still higher point of development. Scarcely a month passes but a new book appears on these so-called control mechanisms or servo-mechanisms, and the present age is as truly the age of servo-mechanisms as the nineteenth century was the age of the steam engine' (Wiener, *Cybernetics*, p. 55).

77. Bennett, *A History of Control Engineering*, p. 202. Modern control theory originated in September 1956 with an international conference setting up the International Federation of Automatic Control.

78. 'The Bee Meeting', in *Collected Poems*, p. 212.

79. 'The Arrival of the Bee Box', in *Collected Poems*, p. 213.

80. 'Stings', in *Collected Poems*, p. 214.

81. The bee sequence was based on Plath's own experiments in apiculture in Devon in 1962, detailed in her journal, especially the 'Charlie Pollard and the Bee Keepers' section (*Journal of Sylvia Plath 1950–1962*, pp. 656–9) – note the portentous arrival of the 'awaited expert, the "government man" from Exeter' (p. 658), the fruitless search for the old queen (p. 658), and the story of a female beekeeper whose bees always stung her 'rather sarcastic' husband on the 'nose & lips' (p. 657).

82. Harris, 'Can You See a Virus?'.

83. Cf . Marks, *The Search for the 'Manchurian Candidate'*.

84. Lee was Burroughs' mother's maiden name.

85. Burroughs, *Queer*, pp. 39–40. Is it also like a predatory pike or shark, maybe? Lee is described as a 'predatory fish' snapping at 'scraps of life', 'cut off from his prey by a glass wall' (*Queer*, p. 92).

86. For Harris, Burroughs 'understands power so well precisely because he has always worked from its deep insides' (Harris, 'Can You See a Virus?', p. 244).

87. Stimpson, 'Foreword', in Swerdlow, *Women Strike for Peace*, p. xi.

88. Frieda Hughes, foreword, in Plath, *Ariel, the Restored Edition*, pp. xiv–xv.

89. Plath's script introduction to 'Death & Co.' for the BBC, published in *Ariel, the Restored Edition*, p. 192. The introduction was written 14 December 1962.

5

THE SACRIFICIAL LOGIC
OF THE ASIAN COLD WAR:
GREENE'S *THE QUIET AMERICAN* AND
MCCARTHY'S *THE SEVENTEENTH DEGREE*

Graham Greene's *The Quiet American* has often been praised for its prescience about American involvement in Indochina, less for its analysis of the British view of the American superpower in imperial mode. The novel cleverly updates the love triangle of *The Third Man* to establish this, underlining Greene's interest in the Cold War as a story about the manner in which the United States opts to take over global responsibilities from the old colonial powers. The shift in scene from war-scarred Europe in *The Third Man* to the Communist-insurgent Third World in *The Quiet American* acknowledges the new fact about the Cold War in the early 1950s: that its true battleground was no longer Europe and the captive city but the old colonial possessions of the European nation states.

For Greene, it is the combination of US 'innocent' propaganda with counterinsurgent dirty tricks which is of interest in helping define the precise terms of American assumption of responsibility for colonial wars, and how far that intervention is indebted to the example of other colonial/anti-Communist police operations, in particular the example of British handling of the Malayan Emergency. American counterinsurgency and propaganda in Vietnam were in many ways fashioned according to the successful formulae developed by the British in Malaya. What Greene's allegory sanctions, however, is the suspicion that France and Britain (according to the dictates of the paranoid conspiratorial fantasy generated by the Cold War) may have cunningly caught the US up into colonial conflicts by preaching the Cold War necessities of counterinsurgency, only to abandon America to its fate in the quagmire of an unwinnable war. It is this twisted fantasy which structures the otherwise melodramatic love-triangle politics of *The Quiet American*.

The Third Man had allegorized US–UK relations in Europe in the triangle Martins–Lime–Anna (in the film as Calloway/Martins–Lime–Anna). This is transposed in *The Quiet American* into the triangle Pyle–Fowler–Phuong, figuring the costs and likely outcome of British and American involvement in the insurgent Third World. Paralleling *The Third Man*, both Pyle and Fowler are technically outsiders to the country, there as neutral observers – until both are sucked into the vortex of the political zone by their secret subversive activity, thematized as the guilty working through of rivalry and naked greed (power as sexual desire for Phuong). The same quizzing of the special relationship pertains: the plot turns on whether the repressed hatred for a friend or ally might tempt one to betray him to a fantasized enemy, an obvious reprise of the Freudian plotting of *The Third Man*.

Greene knew a great deal about psychological warfare and subversion in South East Asia, partly through the information he would have gleaned from his brother Hugh, who was involved in the state security apparatus set up by the British Military Authority in Malaya in the Emergency. On secondment from the BBC, between 1950 and 1951 Hugh Carleton Greene ran the Emergency Information Services (EIS), the organization in charge of counterinsurgency propaganda. He was an acknowledged anti-Communist expert, having headed East European Services broadcasting to the Soviet Union and Baltic states. As such he had been embroiled in the top secret propaganda work sponsored by the Information Research Department (IRD) and MI5 – in particular BBC broadcasts to Albania in 1949, aimed at destabilizing the Communist regime. As a liberal Cold Warrior,[1] his work in Malaya suited the new South East Asian policies spearheaded by the IRD and designed to confront the new threat from China in the region. They had opened up a counter-Communist propaganda Regional Information Office at Phoenix Park in Singapore in late 1949.

Propaganda was a key tool in the war against the Malayan Communist Party (MCP) 'bandits', especially in the ideological war for hearts and minds – the very phrase 'hearts and minds' was coined in Malaya, by General Sir Gerald Templer. This was a war that could not be called that (it had to remain an emergency to enable planters to claim damages on their insurance), waged against an enemy which could not be named (the government feared that saying they were a Communist army might legitimize them within Malaya – they began as 'bandits', turned into 'Chinese terrorists' and were only later promoted to 'Communist terrorists'), fought for reasons that could not be made public – to preserve the tin and rubber profits that were crucial to Britain's economy. As Thomas Kaplan has shown, the British were desperate in their requests to the US to buy Malaysian tin and rubber, for the Emergency occurred when the UK was practically bankrupt, after the fierce winter of 1947, the fuel crisis, the dollar gap, and a staggering war debt.[2] As the chairman of the Defence Research Policy Committee, Sir Henry Tizard, argued: 'Until we succeed [in Malaya] we shall only keep alive through the charity of our overseas friends. If we do not succeed, we shall go down forever as a first-class nation.'[3] The IRD *had* to sell the Emergency as an anti-Communist war to the outside world, to ensure support from the United States, potentially resentful of the colonialist nature of British presence, and later of the low-key contribution of the British to the struggle in Korea.

The IRD had been created in 1947 as a mirror organization to Moscow's Cominform (Communist Information Bureau) – Attlee had actually wanted it to be called the Communist Information Department. Funded by secret vote, situated deep within the Foreign Office, it took over the functions and some of the personnel of the wartime Political Warfare Executive.[4] IRD's mission was to supply unsourced anti-Communist texts and documents to opinion makers around the world, as well as selling the British Empire as a progressive 'Third Force'. Backed forcefully by 'hard liberals' in the Labour party, the IRD made Britain the first country to engage in a counteroffensive against Soviet propaganda. It soon expanded to 400 staff, engaging in the vetting of subversives in key organizations (including the BBC), in book production, in the financing and running of news agencies, in the staffing of front organizations (such as Crozier's Institute for the Study of Conflict), and most importantly in the covert supply of information to hundreds of key figures in unions, governments and the media in Britain and around the world, with particularly close links with Reuters and the World Service.[5] It was to Celia Kirwan at the IRD that Orwell sent his infamous list of crypto-Communists in May 1949, whilst dying in the Cotswolds.[6] It was at the IRD that Robert Conquest spent ten years building up his dossiers on Stalin's purges. Through its discreet presses, Ampersand and the Background Books series, it recruited a variety of writers and intellectuals to the cause of ideological warfare – hardline Cold Warriors such as Douglas Hyde and Brian Crozier, public intellectuals like Bertrand Russell and Bryan Macgee, and politicians and unionists such as Denis Healey and Victor Feather. More anonymously, millions of pamphlets, booklets and flyers were produced for dissemination in the Third World, including propaganda to be airdropped in war zones as part of the war for hearts and minds, in Malaya against the MCP, in Kenya against the Mau Mau. It was a massive marshalling of textual and ideological force, all the more impressive for having been kept so secret for so long – its cover was only blown in 1978, when even the government had grown tired of the crude anti-Communist rhetoric the factory at Riverwalk House in Millbank was churning out.[7]

Hugh Greene's mission in Malaya would have been, in part, to help coordinate propaganda initiatives in the country, keying local political policies into the wider IRD issues of South East Asia. The Emergency had kicked off the Asian Cold War – by the time the Greene brothers were in the zone, three major wars were being fought as part of the containment of China, the new Communist aggressor: in Malaya, Indochina and Korea. And, as both brothers would have been aware, it was because of strong lobbying by the British in particular that the United States had taken such a hard anti-Communist line in South East Asia. Malaysia was the most important colonial prop to Attlee's welfare state – the sale of its commodities was easily the largest contributor to dollar resources within the Sterling Area, as such crucial to the UK's maintenance of its currency.[8] To persuade the US to countenance the preservation of British colonial interests, against the grain of their avowed anti-colonial policies, the British needed to convince them that the Emergency was an absolutely necessary anti-Communist war of containment. The French did likewise in their presentation of the war in Indochina. Both countries invited American aid and support in order to keep a hold on colonial possessions, and to generate dollars to substitute for the cash flow that would soon run dry when the Marshall Plan was scheduled to end in 1952.[9]

Just as the UK had been instrumental in persuading the Americans into Europe, so it was through the example of Malayan counterinsurgency and anti-Communist containment that the US was asked to shoulder its economic and military responsibilities in the Asian Cold War. Washington had decided not to intervene to support Chiang Kai-shek in 1949, and the British feared the consequences of this retreat to the 'defensive perimeter' of the Pacific islands. As historian Joseph Smith puts it:

> Since China could not conceivably be considered a military threat to the United States, the Far East was downgraded in strategic importance. American officials directed their attention to what they considered to be the much more pressing threat of communism in Europe.[10]

Dean Acheson's August 1949 white paper explaining American policy with regard to Mao's Red China had caused a huge furore by its do-nothing policy – he had argued that the 'civil war in China was beyond the control of the government' and that the revolution was strictly 'the product of internal Chinese forces' (Smith, *The Cold War*, pp. 55–6). The white paper not only enraged the powerful pro-Chiang China lobby in Washington, sowing the seeds of McCarthyism, but also alarmed the British Foreign Office. To protect British interests in Asia, as well as to secure American investment, the IRD had to work overtime to disseminate information connecting European containment of the Soviet Union with Asian containment of Chinese Communism.

The IRD had lobbied up till then for a 'Third Force' policy, imagining an alliance between India, Britain and the Commonwealth as new power base in Asia. The IRD's chief Asian academic, Guy Wint, had attracted their interest with his eccentric book *The British in Asia*, which had backed this India–UK-led alliance in the region: 'the conversion of the former British Asiatic Empire into a free confederacy of South Asia, which would form a regional unit of the United Nations Organization'.[11] The new drive post-Mao was more resolutely Cold War. Only an Anglo-American anti-Communist policing operation would save South East Asia from the Sino-Soviet threat. By September 1949, the cabinet was being told by its IRD-informed policy advisers that '[it] should be stressed that Malaya is in the front line of the Cold War and that its stability is essential for all of us, including the United States'.[12] To the Americans, Malaya and other British outposts were to be presented as direct analogues of the captive European cities. Bevin described Hong Kong as 'the Berlin of the East', telling Acheson that it ought to be considered the 'right wing bastion of the Southeast Asian front' (Lee, *Outposts of Empire*, p. 18).

Britain not only positioned Malaya as the linchpin in the Cold War front line, but also saw the advantage of making common cause with the French, sturdily supporting their anti-Communist propaganda by stressing the link between Indochina and Malaya. In December 1949, Malcolm MacDonald, British commissioner general in South East Asia, was warning the world: 'If Indo-China is lost, then Siam and Burma will probably go the same way shortly afterwards. That will bring the power of international Communism to the border of Malaya' (Lee, *Outposts of Empire*, p. 43). So successful was this warning, repeated in other IRD-sourced material in this hectic lobbying phase in the run-up to the Korean War, that it is arguable that it is the origin of the domino theory, first expounded by Eisenhower in 1954 during the siege of Dien Bien Phu. The collocation of the Vietnam–Malaya link with Cold War domino theory had a very long shelf-life – it popped out of Kennedy's mouth when he was asked if he believed in the theory in a TV interview in 1963, while defending his counterinsurgency policy:

> I believe it. I think that the struggle is close enough. China is so large, looms so high just beyond the frontiers, that if South Vietnam went, it would not only give them an improved geographic position for a guerrilla assault on Malaya but would also give the impression that the wave of the future in Southeast Asia was China and the Communists. So I believe it.[13]

Furthermore, as Lee has argued, what sealed the Anglo-American special relationship in Asia was the ability of the UK government to paint its objectives in the region not only in anti-Communist Kennan-containment terms, but also as welfare-liberal experiments in devolutionary nation-building. It was the British example of counterinsurgency as social engineering in Malaya which most impressed the Americans. The social experiments could be presented to the world as liberal, decolonizing and democratic, at the same time as they were clearly also designed to preserve colonial-style economic dependency post-independence. To see anti-Communism working both as anti-colonial in the short term and as forging economic neo-colonial interests in the long term chimed in cleverly with American dreams of informal empire in Asia.

When Hugh Greene arrived in Malaya, the biggest job was to ensure the smooth operation, informationally speaking, of the Briggs Plan, that extraordinary experiment in pacification. The new British military commander, Lt.-General Harold Briggs, had ordered the massive resettlement of the thousands of Chinese 'squatters' who provided the MCP with the majority of its members, infrastructure and support. The squatters were Malaysian Chinese seasonal farmers working illegally on land they would clear; the rest of the year they spent as industrial workers – they were therefore potentially Communist proletariat as well as rural terrorists. The British had backed the MCP during the war against the Japanese, but then postwar had decided to side with the sultans and the Malay majority, instituting several fruitless police operations against the squatters, a repression which partly sparked off the Emergency. By resettling the squatters in barbed-wire Resettlement Areas (later called New Villages by Templer), Briggs hoped to drive a wedge between the Malayan Races Liberation Army (MRLA, the military wing of the MCP) and its constituency, a wedge backed up both by starvation operations to destroy rice paddies which might feed the insurgents, and by re-educating the captive squatters within the camps with anti-Communist propaganda, fully urbanizing them by strategically placing the New Villages near towns. By 1954, over half a million people – a seventh of the entire population – had been resettled into over 500 New Villages, three-quarters of them Chinese squatters, 80 per cent Chinese.[14]

The resettlement was accompanied by welfare programmes, many run by evangelical missionaries, with anti-Communist objectives. Anti-Communism forged the essential link between Emergency resettlement and community development. As one 1949 report put it, resettlement welfare worked 'as an inoculation against the disease of Communism',[15] much of the propaganda for which was overseen by Hugh Greene's EIS, who would tour the New Villages in mobile unit field teams, frontline troops in the war for hearts and minds.

Hugh Greene, working as a BBC/IRD co-operative with propaganda and psychological warfare strategies overseen by Phoenix Park, set out his three Cold War objectives in a secret 1951 report to the Colonial Office:

> 1. To raise the morale of the civil population and to encourage confidence in Government and resistance to the Communists with a view to increasing the flow of information reaching the Police.

This, roughly translated, boiled down to pumping propaganda talks, texts, films and radio broadcasts into the New Villages, whilst offering huge bribes to informants.

2. To attack the morale of members of the MRLA, the Min Yuen [the MCP's People's Organization] and their supporters and to drive a wedge between the leaders and the rank and file with a view to encouraging defection and undermining the determination of the Communists to continue the struggle.

This entailed extensive use of defecting 'surrendered enemy personnel' (SEPs) as propagandists to encourage disaffection in enemy ranks – Hugh Greene used the defector Lam Swee, MCP leader, as scribe to persuade the rank and file to surrender, with waterproof pamphlets carrying the tabloid-style byline 'I surrendered after my commanding officer had stolen my girlfriend.'[16] Other IRD material included the printing of surrender leaflets showing the dead faces of MRLA comrades: 'Would you rather be dead like these?' The wedge between leaders and rank and file also consisted in significantly increased bounties paid out for the heads of leading bandits.

3. To create an awareness of the values of the democratic way of life which is threatened by International Communism.[17]

Basically, this meant disseminating IRD material, within the New Villages through public relations and missionary welfare, and directly to the MRLA in the hills by way of massive RAF propaganda-leaflet drops promising bribes to those who surrendered. It was not only leaflets – Hugh Greene had been hired as a radio man, and his expertise in broadcast and film propaganda began a transformation of the communications methods used. He increased the mobile broadcasting units and combined them with tours of SEPs, and began the practice of using jeeps and boats. The success of these measures was such that they eventually led to use of planes, the so called 'voice aircraft', Austers and Dakotas flying low over insurgent jungle broadcasting messages through loudspeakers specifically targeting individuals ground intelligence had identified in the MRLA.[18] For Hugh Greene, such psy-war techniques worked because they were being deployed upon a population already terrorized by being subject to both MCP terrorist attack and New Village ethnic resettlement: 'the only human emotion which can be expected to be stronger than fear among a terrorised population with very little civic consciousness', he informed the Colonial Office in his report, 'is greed'.[19]

When Graham Greene visited Malaya in November 1950 as a *Life* reporter, his brother had been working at the EIS a month. Greene stayed with Hugh very briefly on arrival, but did spend Christmas with him at Malacca in between his busy tours of the country, before flying on to Vietnam in January 1951. The real core of his trip there was the meetings with the beleaguered planters and a dangerous patrol with the Gurkhas, but the image that lasted, turning up in the pages of *The Quiet American*, was the sight of a murdered Malay constable, stripped naked, beaten about the mouth and stabbed through the heart by the MRLA, carried into a tin mine by a Gurkha patrol strung on a pole, 'like a new joint at the butcher's', as Greene recorded in his diary (Sherry, *The Life of Graham Greene*, p. 357). Though shocked by the sight, and moved by the tender offices of a brother Malay who 'put a cushion under the dead head',[20] Greene was not so shocked as not to wish to take a photograph of the dead head – in a letter to his mother he wrote: 'I had to nerve myself to take a close-up photo of him' (Sherry, *The Life of Graham Greene*, p. 357). It is the kind of nerve that Hugh Greene would need to paste the close-up photos of the dead onto his propaganda leaflets.

Greene's copy for *Life* magazine was sympathetic to the plight of the planters, admiring of the toughness of the Gurkhas, and shocked by the terror tactics and atrocities committed by the MRLA. The article is showily anti-Communist and patriotic:

> Our British consciences could be clear – we were not holding the Malays against their will; we were fighting with them against Communism and its Chinese adherents. [. . .] [These bandits] were the commandos of Communism, organised like a Russian division.[21]

It uses material obviously supplied to him by Hugh, captured documents of the MRLA troops in the jungle, to parody their fanaticism. In language clearly also supplied to him by his IRD-informed brother, this war was a psychological war where 'defeat was in the minds of men', especially when the real strength of the MCP lay not in the terrorist attacks but in the 'unarmed combatants of the ground organisation known as the Min Yuen', experts in 'intelligence, propaganda and liaison work' (*Ways of Escape*, p. 152). In the war against the Min Yuen, resettlement was the key strategy – Greene is full of hard-nosed, clear-sighted praise for the Briggs Plan and its starvation policy, the 'other measures' necessary to defeat the enemy in the jungle:

> The squatters were not necessarily Communist sympathisers, though it was hard to see what they could possibly lose by a Communist victory. But who of us would refuse food to a terrorist at the point of a bayonet? These squatters were being brought together into new villages which could be surrounded with wire and properly policed. The old huts were burned. The squatters were provided with building materials or houses, a small sum of money and a legal tenure of their new land. (*Ways of Escape*, p. 153)

All in all, the writing on Malaya is pure IRD, produced to please his brother, especially when addressing an American audience at this crucial horse-trading moment in the special relationship. Its tone, content and purpose are indistinguishable from the propaganda being produced by the EIS and Phoenix

Park – strong anti-Communism aimed at convincing the American readers of *Life* magazine that the British in Malaya are at the Cold War front line, defeating Communist commandos not in the jungle, not in the New Villages, but *in the mind*.

Resistance to his own collusion in the secret propaganda war is noticeable as the merest traces in the Malayan copy. The last paragraph of the *Life* article admits that he sometimes feels 'a measure of compassion for these men, struck from the air, hunted however ineffectively by patrols, bled by leeches, with insufficient food and medicines', but only to recuperate the compassion into a further twist of the IRD knife: 'their success measured in a resettlement officer or a planter killed, a bus burned, a patrol ambushed and a Sten gun captured' (*Ways of Escape*, p. 153), i.e. the MRLA are weak and random terrorists. Yet secret resistance persists in the unsettling repetition of 'measure', 'measured', picking up on the euphemism for the Briggs starvation plan, 'other measures'. The writer baulks at the cold calculation of feeling and policy in this very dirty war, a war where even compassion is measured according to the abstract formulae of the bureaucrats running the 'other measures': the burning of the squatters' huts, the brainwashing in the resettlement camps. Resistance is traceable too in that haunting image of the Malay on the pole, the tortured, broken 'dead head' photographed for *Life* magazine. Though the head is photographed as an act of counterinsurgency propaganda – as 'close-up' evidence of the brutality of the MCP – the image has a strange, iconic power for Greene, working to figure the peasant victims of the hot Cold War.

When Greene moved from Malaya to Vietnam, he carried with him this guilt over the way he had twinned his writing talent with his brother's security-state propaganda drive. The guilt comes out in the quite different political stance taken in the *Life* copy produced about Vietnam. As Greene later recalled, the editors:

> did not like the article I wrote [in Vietnam in the autumn of 1951], but they generously allowed me to publish it in *Paris-Match*: I suspect my ambivalent attitude to the war was already perceptible – my admiration for the French army, my admiration for their enemies, and my doubt of any final value in the war. (*Ways of Escape*, p. 157)

This is tantamount to admitting that *Life* wanted Cold War propaganda designed to sue for American aid, a 'Korean' view of Indochina, a repetition, in other words, of the Malayan anti-Communist copy. What Greene did with the Vietnam copy was to support French colonial culture openly in order to betray the fake Cold War being fought in South East Asia.

To write against the Americans in Vietnam was to write against the IRD, for it threatened the precious domino theory which was the key ingredient in the propaganda. In the early material Greene produced for *Life*, but which he had to pass on to *Paris Match*, Greene seems at first to play the game, dutifully reproducing the domino theory line: 'If Indo-China falls, Korea will be isolated, Siam can be invaded in twenty-four hours and Malaya may have to be adandoned.'[22] But the rest of the article works to undermine the clear anti-Communist line necessary for credence in the Asian Cold War. Such clarity smacks, Greene writes, of the 'illusion of simplicity'. The war might appear simple from some unreal ideological height (Greene imagines himself surveying the 'panorama of war' from the bell tower of the cathedral of Phat Diem). But on the ground, the war is a 'confused struggle', with mad militias ('a Catholic Bishop who commands his own army and hates the French more than the Communists') and Third Force lunatics: 'the chief of a Third Force who makes war on everyone and places high-explosive bombs in the very centre of Saigon in order to kill innocent civilians' (*Ways of Escape*, p. 130). The anti-Communism which Greene had supported in Malaya is largely irrelevant: 'Western slogans and all that talk the politicians retail about the necessity of containing Communism seem here to apply only to a very small part of the picture.' Vietnam for Greene is 'a creation of Western powers confronting the thrust of nationalism as much as Communism' (p. 130). The domino theory collapses into a heap of broken images once the polarized simplicity of anti-Communism, with its two-man logic, is forced to admit the intermediary hosts, the Third Forces acting between the anti-Communists and the Communists, and forced to allow for more complex motives in the enemy (nationalism as well as Communism) and a more dubious view of one's allies (the belligerent bishops and the terrorist warlords). It is apt that the copy designed for *Life* ended up on the streets of Paris – Greene is writing with the repressed anti-Americanism of a de Gaulle, appealing to the liberals in France to rally against the friendly superpower. For that he is willing to flatter their presence in Vietnam: the principal objective is to kill the king ally, the US and its ruinous hypocrisy.

The uncomfortable corollary is that by attacking the Americans in this overt way, he must also be attacking the British propaganda machine which had worked so hard to fabricate the domino theory and the Cold War counterinsurgency/containment jargon of hearts and minds which the US took on board with the outbreak of the Korean War. In killing off American pretensions in South East Asia, by *killing Pyle*, he is unconsciously striking at his brother Hugh. The animus against the kinds of procedures Hugh Greene and the IRD had been cooking up in Malaya is ferocious in *The Quiet American*. Propaganda itself receives a broadside from the outset, with the epigraph from Byron: 'This is the patent age of new inventions / For killing bodies, and for saving souls, / All propagated with the best intentions.'[23] The Janus-faced policy of counterinsurgency, Emergency-style (killing bodies in the jungle while saving souls in the New Villages), and the propagation of Emergency best intentions through the IRD in Singapore: these were to become the model for American intervention in the Asian Cold War – as such they turn out to be the real concealed enemies of the book.

Pyle in fact sounds like an American conjured up, or at least politically informed, by the IRD. He believes in the anti-Communist agenda being sold in the IRD's propaganda drive: he is a disciple of the suspiciously British-sounding York Harding, a fictional Kennan-containment theorist writing Cold Warrior texts with titles like *The Advance of Red China* and *The Role of the West* (*The Quiet American*, p. 24). Pyle believes in the magic of Third Force arguments, a favourite objective of the early IRD. It was precisely the idea that the Asian Cold War could serve a liberal purpose in the world – Third Force decolonizing anti-Communism replacing the 'old colonial powers' – which had been British propaganda policy to tempt the US into intervening in the area. If Pyle's political credences accord with the kinds of material Hugh Greene had been disseminating in Malaya, then the relationship between Pyle and Fowler mimics as well as challenges the propaganda web being woven by the special relationship. It mimics it in so far as Fowler adopts the tone and attitude of a cynical British colonialist advising the naive young American on precisely how to proceed with these damn natives: 'We are the old colonial peoples, Pyle, but we've learnt a bit of reality, we've learned not to play with matches' (*The Quiet American*, p. 174). At the same time, Fowler uses the colonialist *savoir-gouverner* only to advise Pyle against acting too naively according to the Third Force pseudo-liberalism of the Asian Cold War: 'This Third Force – it comes out of a book, that's all. General Thé's only a bandit with a few thousand men: he's not a national democracy' (p. 174). Fowler knows about the kinds of book the Cold War produces to sustain its policies: they resemble the books the IRD was producing, written by British Cold Warriors aiming at drawing the US into protecting British interests.

If Fowler acts at once as a typical British spent force, handing over the colonial reins of power with quiet words of advice, and also more subversively as stripper-away of the propaganda running the Asian Cold War, it is because the contradiction more perfectly mimes the true relationship between British and America interests in Vietnam. Taking Phuong as a super-sexualized figure for South East Asia (Vietnam *plus* Malaya), the struggle is over the long-term survival of those interests as such. Fowler will continue to advise Pyle, because only by IRD forms of persuasion will the US believe its intervention to be a UN-style decolonizing and protective mission, replacing the old colonial powers with its own brand of democracy. At the same time, true possession of South East Asia will fall to the more cynical player of the darker black arts of power, Pyle's dabbling in Third Force terrorism (General Thé's bicycle bombs) trumped by Fowler's secret collusion with the Vietminh (shopping Pyle to the Communists). As such, it should suit long-term British interests to tempt the US into the war of dirty tricks, remove the false glow of righteousness propaganda gives men of power, and thereby trap the Americans into purely cynical *Realpolitik*. Doing so not only serves to corrode the liberal conscience that might resist the lure of informal empire, but would help involve the Americans in self-destructive ways in the murderous violence of an unwinnable war – following the precept that the more unprincipled the warfare is, the more likely it is to encourage addictive bloodlust and a certain tenacity in the face of international and domestic criticism. Fowler seems to be punishing Pyle for the secret dirty war by giving him up to the Communist insurgents. What he is really doing is turning the brother-allied dirty war against the American intruder (who is only really here in the first place *because* of the old colonial powers) in order to get the girl, a submissive South East Asia for British trade.

The real secret of the war, as in the book, is that the black propaganda and criminal terror to which Pyle feels justified in resorting to protect Western democracy have been learnt from British and French example. Though Fowler insists he is neutral, and will not take sides in the Cold War in Vietnam (he fancies himself as a tough and objective reporter, one of the obvious ironies of his unreliable first person), the double plot demonstrates quite the opposite. He is ruthless in protecting his interests in what he calls the 'other kind of war', the war between men and women, and the war between men for women (*The Quiet American*, p. 130). That other kind of war is stylized according to the other war for hearts and minds – it is a pitiless war of mind control and betrayal at which Fowler is an old hand. As a propagandist he must seem to be helping Pyle control the sexual territory, whilst secretly working against him. The act of betrayal is thematically linked to the kinds of martial knowledge the French have as a military force in Vietnam – the French are admired for their cold-blooded use of napalm, for the grace and Machiavellian sangfroid of their bombing campaigns. It resembles the kinds of military action undertaken by the British in Malaya.

Darker than these overt acts of military ruthlessness, though, is the black propaganda which would mimic the enemy in order to betray a friend.[24] Like the SEPs used by Hugh Greene to betray the MCP, Fowler will pretend to be Pyle's friend in order to destroy him. In his report to the government, Hugh Greene had been eloquent on the subject of the propaganda value of surrendered bandits:

> In any ideological war it is the convert and the deviationist who will have the most effect both on his former comrades and those who have been influenced to any degree by the ideology in question. This showed itself to some extent during the German war – but still more plainly since International Communism became the enemy. Wherever the free world has been engaged in any form of psychological warfare against Communism it is the convert and deviationist who have been recognised in the Communist world as the most dangerous enemies, because these people understand the Communist mentality and methods as no-one else can. Malaya is no exception to the rule. (Hugh Greene, 'Report on Emergency Information Services', p. 3)

And neither was Vietnam, except that, as represented in *The Quiet American*, it is a British deviationist who betrays, through mock conversion to the enemy's creed, the free-world ally he intimately understands, whose ideology he knows backwards: 'Sometimes,' Fowler lectures Pyle, 'we have a kind of love for our enemies and sometimes we feel hate for our friends' (*The Quiet American*, p. 196).

Greene's simple inversion of his brother's anti-Communist propaganda strategies is based on the Freudian premise he had explored in *The Third Man*: that the Cold War is, at the level of the political unconscious, a struggle between brothers for the same woman. The struggle occurs not, as one might expect, between ideological rivals, USSR vs. US, but between the allies, deep within the meshes and contradictions of the special relationship.[25] *The Quiet American* takes one further step, though: it can be read more secretively still as being less about the special relationship than about an internal rift in British politics, a civil war between progressive and reactionary forces as the Empire falls to pieces. Pyle is a creature of the kinds of propaganda being nurtured by Hugh Greene in Malaya, with a view to sustaining American involvement. Pyle dead, shot and drowned in the mud of Vietnam, Pyle who'd saved Fowler's life, Pyle trafficking in subversive black propaganda following British-sourced policies: to kill off this monster is to kill off the Frankenstein who made him, the EIS propaganda machine identified with Hugh Carleton Greene.

Or rather what is killed off, cynically, guiltily and Oedipally, is the kind of person who had consented to do the propaganda job for his brother in Malaya – the older brother self moves over to the enemy to betray the younger brother self with his absurd Cold War rhetoric and pro-American idealism. Like civil war in the brother clan after the parricide of the patriarch of empire, the struggle over the captive women (or old colonies) is played out as a totemic para-Freudian tale of self-sacrifice: Greene making a compromised oblation of the Cold War ideologue of his 'Malayan' identity. Pyle shot in the mud of Vietnam pays for the Malay constable photographed by Greene to help his brother in an emergency.

What makes the oblation so compromised is the very fact that the struggle between Pyle and Fowler is an internalization of the special relationship's decolonizing tensions and resentments. This is a sacrificial narrative where the two men *pretend* to fight to the death. The real victims are not the Pyles and Fowlers of the Cold War world, but the soldiers and peasant victims in the jungles and towns in the country. In particular it is the women who strike this message home. In a war so sexualized 'inside' its ideology as to appear to the Freudian Greene as a fight to the death for Phuong, it is Phuong's substitutes, women killed in the war, who most *signify*. In the other kind of war beyond the propaganda for hearts and minds, it is the women who are chosen to stand in for the brother to be sacrificed.

For Pyle, the bystanders who died in the bombing of the Place Garnier died for Democracy; Fowler tells him he doesn't know how to translate that into Vietnamese (p. 200). The arranged murder of Pyle aims to punish him for this by making Pyle assume the role of the proxy in Democracy's Cold War sacrifice. But this is in another sense just a further elaboration of the male fiction of fake victim substitution: the real victims lie elsewhere. Though Phuong is warned away from the Place in time, the bomb is designed to kill women and children: 'This is the hour when the place is always full of women and children' (p. 181). The first victims described form an accusatory *pietà*: 'A woman sat on the ground with what was left of her baby in her lap; with a kind of modesty she had covered it with her straw hat. She was still and silent, and what struck me most in the square was the silence' (p. 180). Greene's Catholic conscience manipulates the image for maximum effect – a close-up click of the dead child, despite the mother's modesty – aimed with anger at the propagators of the Asian Cold War. The image recalls the Malay constable, but has greater iconic power, since it gathers into itself sharp reminiscence of the war-zone horrors Greene/Fowler experienced in North Vietnam: in particular the dead mother and child at Phat Diem. Phat Diem also prompted Greene to Catholic condemnation of the war, with the Dantean vision of the dead villagers crammed into the canal, caught dead in the crossfire between the Cold War forces. The war has unleashed hellish damnation on the Catholic community, silencing the zone round the church – the Cold War's brutal cynicism, for Greene, was stifling the life out of Christian Asia. For the massacre takes place in a Catholic community, and also has a brutal *pietà* at its core:

> Twenty yards beyond the farm buildings, in a narrow ditch, we came on what we sought: a woman and a small boy. They were very clearly dead: a small neat clot of blood on the woman's forehead, and the child might have been sleeping. He was about six years old and he lay like an embryo in the womb with his little bony knees drawn up. [. . .] The lieutenant said, 'Have you seen enough?' speaking savagely, almost as though I had been responsible for these deaths: perhaps to the soldier the civilian is the man who employs him to kill, who includes the guilt of murder in the pay-envelope and escapes responsibility. (*The Quiet American*, p. 53)

The Quiet American has four violent coordinates: the assault on the watchtower where Pyle saves Fowler's life; the Dantean vision of the canal and the *pietà* at Phat Diem; the dead boy in his mother's arms in the Place Garnier; and the murder of Pyle under the bridge to Dakow. The four space-time zones map out Vietnam: Hanoi and North Vietnam (Phat Diem); Saigon and South Vietnam (Place Garnier); and two interzones, the watchtower and the Saigon bridge between Communist and anti-Communist worlds where Pyle drowns. The book seems to be balancing the four: interzone space where the struggle of the males takes place; war-zone north and south where the women die with their children. But the despicable sexual rivalry for Phuong which is Fowler's real motivation, and the savage indictment of the lieutenant accusing him of the crime, both mesh together to form a counter-narrative.

That counter-narrative is something Fowler cannot bring himself to articulate, yet it is there in the text as an open secret, so open that it comes out of Fowler's own mouth, though aimed only against the younger brother Cold Warrior. It is a story about proxy sacrifice. York Harding, the IRD-fashioned ideologue, has had one unfortunate effect on the disciple Pyle: to stylize him into a mind capable of contemplating the ruthless sacrifice of others as somehow standing in for his own: 'I knew that [Pyle] was already forming his phrases in the style he had learnt from York Harding: it was coincidence that the sacrifices were all paid by others, until that final night under the bridge to Dakow' (*The Quiet American*, p. 63). Yet in the final economy of the book, it is Fowler who revels in the sacrifice paid by Pyle for purely selfish purposes. Fowler knows that much about himself: when praised for thinking of the dying Vietnamese guard in the tower, he dismisses the assumption of compassion. Other people's pain stops him feeling at ease:

> I know myself, and I know the depth of my selfishness. I cannot be at ease (and to be at ease is my chief wish) if someone else is in pain, visibly or audibly or tactually. Sometimes this is mistaken by the innocent for unselfishness, when all I am doing is sacrificing a small good – in this case postponement in attending my hurt – for the sake of a far greater good, a peace of mind when I need think only of myself.
>
> They came back to tell me the boy was dead, and I was happy – I didn't even have to suffer much pain after the hypodermic of morphia had bitten my leg. (p. 124)

The deep selfishness of Fowler comes down to this: that he finds hypodermic peace of mind that censors British responsibility for the killing of women and children in the Asian Cold War, responsibility we might call the Malayan hypothesis, the whole IRD bag of tricks tempting the Americans to intervene in Vietnam, in mimicry of British Janus-faced and mock-liberal counterinsurgency. The forgetting of Malaya and the peace of mind over the death of the Vietnamese occur through a fantasy oblation of his 'American' Cold Warrior self. Fowler then, extraordinarily, rewards himself for the lying delusion with a prostituted allegorical substitute for the women being killed, in the shape of Phuong. The real sacrifice, the dead mother at Phat Diem, is censored and rewritten (according to the logic of black propaganda) as an internal sacrifice of the other man in the triangle, the old friend/younger self fabricated by the propaganda of the 'brotherly' special relationship. It is all for the sake of allied solidarity as deeply solipsistic unity of purpose, a peace of mind where the pain of the victims of the hot Cold War can be silenced, invisible, inaudible, untactual.

When Fowler receives a letter from his wife, he reflects on the pain he can read in every line, pain he had managed to forget here in Vietnam, and half admonishes himself for the hurt he is causing her, only to smooth away the idea of her pain with smugly cynical and deterministic abstractions: all possession involves hurt; 'the innocent are always involved in any conflict. Always, everywhere, there is some voice crying from a tower' (p. 130). If he recognizes that his selfishness serves to silence the 'voice crying from a tower', what he cannot acknowledge is how his possession of the fictional creature of his dream of informal empire, the subservient Phuong, is designed to pander to that need to silence. She is the sexual fantasy generated by crusading empire, informal, decolonizing or otherwise: 'She lay at my feet like a dog on a crusader's tomb, preparing the opium' (p. 131). She is the censoring opiate to the dead liberal conscience: 'Phuong bought three more silk scarves. She sat on the bed and displayed them to me, exclaiming at the bright colours, filling a void with her singing voice' (p. 131). That void is the silenced cry from the tower at the core of the Cold War, and Phuong's song is the neo-imperial wet dream censoring the innocent dead. She is the counterinsurgent object of 'special relationship' desire, the American's slave girl owned by the newly potent old colonial power, guilty about something he cannot quite recall.

Vietnam got under the skin of the liberal opposition. It burned there like a guilty conscience. It lay on their pillows at night, breeding visions and nightmare dialogue with the sources of power. For Mary McCarthy, Vietnam became an obsession that took over her world:

> Vietnam had ensconced itself on my pillow. I *thought* about it just before going to sleep, during intervals of the night, and instantly on waking in the morning, spinning out strategies for opposition that grew baroque and fanciful as I became drowsy. Imaginary dialogues with Johnson's apologists, telegrams to senators and congressmen, Portia-like audiences with McNamara, urging him to make his doubts public. Some of this carried over into waking life. Telegrams were drafted and sent; I incessantly argued with anybody I met who was remotely near the sources of power.[26]

The 'I' who argues during the day is being driven incessantly by the imaginary 'it' of Vietnam met at night, the sexless, garrulous lover with 'its' pillow-talk, voices, dramatizations and puppet men of power. Vietnam as scandal and political outrage has taken over the inner vocalizations of the writer's imagination: the novelist's spidery weaving of baroque fancies now recruited to the spinning of 'strategies of opposition'; gifts of scening and dialogue mere interns now, pleading with imaginary political masters. Only in dreams can that distance be bridged, and only then at the cost of such ceding of agency to Vietnam as political Id.

From the outset, the contradictions and insanities of American policy in Vietnam seemed to demand such a wholesale sacrifice of the imagination to the responsibilities involved in 'strategies of opposition'. The self-immolation of the Buddhist bonzes in Vietnam served as a pattern for the commitments demanded of dissenters in the States:

> If we had anybody to thank for saving us from ourselves, that is, from an American victory and its deadly political after-effects, it was the Vietnamese. Ho Chi Minh, the VC [Vietcong], the 'fanatical' bonzes who were setting themselves alight [. . .] They were defending our country, as well as their own, against its enemies in the White House, the Pentagon, and Congress. (McCarthy, *The Seventeenth Degree*, p. 9)[27]

For the novelist to force herself to give her gifts away to 'it', to Vietnam, meant turning herself into and over to the VC as the only true patriots. The real enemy is within the state, is identical with the remotely-near sources of power, 'in the White House, the Pentagon, and Congress'. This perfect inversion of the war establishes the grammar of dissent for the oppositional imagination – readable as a twisting and turning inside out of pronouns. The dissenting citizen performing as 'it' must betray America to save it from itself – and that first 'it' is vocalized as 'Vietnam'. McCarthy's political identity is pronominally turned inside out, therefore – as a citizen she is still part of the body politic ('saving *us* from *ourselves*'), but only as a strategic subject position which is being sacrificed, nightly, so that 'she' may become the voice and advocate of Vietnam.

Implicit in this syntactical and ontological split between American citizen and 'Vietnamese' sacrificial voice is the very division which is breaking the United States in two. If the American 'us' needs saving from 'ourselves', it is because Vietnam on the home front took the form of a 'cold' civil war, happening across the nation in the clashes between police and teach-in students, in the media in the shouting matches between anti-war and pro-war intellectuals, in the endless enquiries and white papers and propaganda battles, and in the heads of each citizen as they hit their pillows at night. The US of 'us' needs saving from our enemy Pentagon selves – both collective voices at cold civil war over the meaning of Vietnam, the meaning of Vietnamerica.

The Vietnamese bonze self-immolation came home with frightening actuality with the death of Alice Herz. In February 1965, President Johnson announced Operation Rolling Thunder, a massive bombing campaign in North Vietnam. On 16 March, Herz, an 82-year-old Quaker pacifist, founder member of Detroit's WSP, set fire to herself on a street corner in Detroit in protest against the bombing. Her last note read: 'I am not doing this out of despair but out of hope for mankind.' She called on Americans to take action before it was too late: 'Yours is the responsibility to decide if this world should be a good place to live for all human beings or if it should blow itself up to oblivion.'[28] She poured cleaning fluid on herself and ignited it, surviving long enough afterwards to tell a fire fighter on the way to hospital: 'I did it to protest the arms race all over the world. I wanted to burn myself like the monks in Vietnam did.'[29] Seven other Americans were to follow her example, including the Quaker leader Norman Morrison, who in November 1965 set fire to himself on the steps of the Pentagon – among the audience a horrified Robert McNamara.[30] The driving force of Vietnamerica not only induced dissenting minds to stage Portia-like audiences with McNamara at night; but to perform real self-napalming sacrifices by day, remotely near the very man himself.

According to his wife Anne, Morrison was inspired to act by the example of the bonzes and by Alice Herz: 'Both of us were moved and awed by the self-immolation of Vietnamese Buddhist monks, as well as that of Alice Herz, an elderly Quaker from Detroit.'[31] What sparked off his own decision was reading an article in *I.F. Stone's Weekly* for 1 November which quoted a French priest protesting at the napalming of his church in Saigon: '"I have seen my faithful burned up in napalm. I have seen the bodies of women and children blown to bits. I have seen all my villages razed. By God, it's not possible!" [. . .] He cursed the war and all its attendant horrors and absurdities. He railed at the Americans in English, as if they were there to hear him' (Morrison Welsh, 'Norman Morrison', p. 5). The horror at the napalm was linked in many protestors' minds with the horror of nuclear war – many were seasoned anti-nuclear pacifists, and feared that Vietnam would trigger a nuclear confrontation. Norman Morrison, according to Anne, 'feared the war would have a corrosive effect on America; he worried it might spill over into nuclear confrontation if Russia or China were pulled into the battle'.[32]

What was most disturbing about the Morrison immolation was his decision to take his one-year-old daughter Emily with him. She was with him, his wife Anne recalled later, right till the end, 'until he released her physically unharmed' (Morrison Welsh, 'Norman Morrison', p. 4). He may have planned to die with her, though, if the note he sent Anne is anything to go by: 'Dearest Anne, Please don't condemn me [. . .] at least I shall not plan to go without my child, as Abraham did.' For Anne, taking Emily to the Pentagon for Norman was:

> reminiscent of Abraham's taking his beloved Isaac up to the sacrificial altar in an unreasonable, unconventional act of faith (as Norman had once called it) before an angel intervened and saved Isaac. [. . .] Had she been injured or died, it would have been unspeakable and maybe impossible to have forgiven him. Emily's presence became a symbol of the many precious Vietnamese children who were victims, if not targets, of the war. (Morrison Welsh, 'Norman Morrison', p. 4)

Defending the country against itself, turning the American self into its VC coun-terpart, emulating the example of the enemy's sacrifices, the liberal opposition was tempted to such extremities: the sacrifice of the girl-child on the altar of the state enemy within.

That year, 1965, was the maddest of them all – the war's escalation, the imagin-ing of incendiary violence, the horror of the news and reels drove Vietnam deep into the heart of the homeland's dream of itself. Robert Bly's poem, 'At a March against the Vietnam War', is zoned and dated 'Washington, 27 November 1965', the month of Morrison's self-immolation, the day the Pentagon told President Johnson that troops would have to be increased from 120,000 to 400,000.[33] In the poem, protesters march against the war, but the protesting feet seem split from the citizen bodies:

> Looking down, I see feet moving
> Calmly, gaily,
> Almost as if separated from the bodies.[34]

The separation of feet from bodies reproduces the cold civil war in the body politic of America, but also, more disturbingly, suggests a dreamlike dissension within the oppositional imagination – as though those marching feet might be marching unto war not peace. The peacenik Bly, simply because he is an American, must also harbour the soldier within his 'representative' citizen body.

The dreamy split between body and feet heralds a darker move into other inner territory, turning Washington into the Mekong Delta. At the 'edge of our eyes: a boat / Covered with machine guns' – it is black, signifying 'that dark-ness among pine boughs / That the Puritans brushed / As they went out to kill turkeys'. The black boat explodes at 'the edge of the jungle', and the Bly voice moves into the incantatory zone of sacrifice:

> We long to abase ourselves
>
> We have carried around this cup of darkness
> We have longed to pour it over our heads
>
> We make war
> Like a man anointing himself

The deep image discovered in the depths of the peace protestors' psyche is their Viet double, the self-anointing grunts pouring the victims' blood over their heads. The impulse that had motivated Herz in radical sympathy with the inno-cent victims of Rolling Thunder has become tainted with the sacrificial pleas-ures of Abraham, a Puritan wedge of self-savouring self-abasement dependent on the death of others on Vietnam's exploding black boat.

Bly saw a continuity between the violence of the war in Vietnam and the traditions of male violence in America – beginning with the killing of animals (Puritans going out to kill turkeys), developing into aggression against rival settlements (defensive violence against Native American tribes), mutating into systematic ethnocide (Native American removal) and outward into the world in the form of colonial, world war and Cold War-imperial military violence. 'We have that in our bodies', he would say.[35] Importantly that violence is present within every American male, just as the 'American psyche' is inside every poet's body: 'since that psyche is inside *him* too, the writing of political poetry is like the writing of personal poetry, a sudden drive by the poet inward'.[36] Inside each citizen is the heart of war's darkness, Mekong Delta visions of black boats, black the colour of the VC, perhaps the torpedo boats which had sparked off the war at Tonkin. The darkness caused by the explosion – metonym for the deaths brought on by the bombs – is condensed into the blood in the 'cup of darkness', the libation cup of sacrifice. The dead VC blood is poured on 'our heads', the heads of the war protestors in Washington, in a staged recall of the kerosene poured over Morrison's body, the cleaner fluid over Alice Herz. Their self-immolation created this sacrificial emblem at the heart of the protest movement. But it is an emblem struck through with divisive meaning: the act of sympathy for the black boat of Vietnam is crossed through with the self-consecrating bloodlust of the war-mongers. The radical act of pacifism, sacrificing the representative citizen body on the Pentagon steps, is feeding off the napalming violence being wreaked on the victims abroad – the protestors and their marching feet harbour within themselves (driven deep inside their bodies by the war's unspeakable violence) the men who make war. Alice Herz has been co-opted to the darkness of the war as fantasized male violence, turning into Emily Morrison, potential 'Vietnamese' sacrificial substitute for the self-anointing priest-victim.

As an act of protest, McCarthy eventually chose to fly to Hanoi, to live under the American bombs alongside the North Vietnamese. She had been asked to go to Vietnam by Bob Silvers of the *New York Review* in early 1966 but had refused, because her husband James West worked for government agencies. But when West told her he was willing to resign, and when Silvers asked her again in January 1967, husband and wife agreed, solemnly at the Deux Magots in Paris, that she must go. She would be the first American novelist to travel to the North, and only the third, after Martha Gellhorn and John Steinbeck, to visit the South. She spent a month in Saigon in 1967 – basis for the material gathered in *Report from Vietnam* – and then travelled to Hanoi in 1968. *Hanoi* was the result. In 1971, Vietnam cropped up again for McCarthy – she covered the My Lai court martial of Captain Medina. All three were collected in the volume *The Seventeenth Degree*.

McCarthy never actually got to the De-Militarized Zone (DMZ) at 17°, the border between North and South – what the title refers to is her own subject position, on the border between the two states, objective liberal reporter on the two home fronts behind the lines. For it is only at this rear position behind the front lines that the war's justifications can be measured:

> The meaning of a war, if it has one, ought to be discernible in the rear, where the values being defended are situated; at the front, war itself appears senseless, a confused butchery that only the gods can understand. (*The Seventeenth Degree*, p. 235)

Although as a war protestor she had opted for support of the North Vietnamese, still her status as novelist of the liberal opposition meant she had to be committed to the careful argument needed to persuade hostile American minds, a commitment based on the enlightened ability to *see both sides to any question*. To write as a liberal on Vietnam would be to write as though hovering above the seventeenth parallel between Hue and Dong Hoi, coasting above McNamara's electronic barrier, the provisional demarcation line between the Democratic Republic of Vietnam (DRV) and the Republic of Vietnam (RVN), observing both sides as though from some notional UN helicopter.

To go to Saigon and Hanoi as a seventeenth-degree liberal witness was not to act the part of Ms Facing-Both-Ways before crossing the line to commitment. McCarthy had already made up her mind. She had sided with the North Vietnamese and would write and report accordingly. But neither was the 17° point of view a mere matter of presentation, describing the simple Saigon/ Hanoi structure of the trips and books. The demarcation-line subject position was more a question of acting the intermediary, of performing the role of liberal witness as mediating vehicle for the expression of the Cold War-boosted confrontation of ideologies. The documentary force of the contrast of the two home fronts depended more for McCarthy on the performative power of this intermediary point of view than on the value-free fact-finding mission it might resemble. The idea of documentary as commitment, as indeed propaganda, went back to its roots in the Spanish Civil War.[37] The documentary in this sense works as an already committed instrument of persuasion, miming the moves of objective reportage (i.e. showing both sides to the question, both rival sets of facts and figures, events and interpretations) only to underline all the more forcefully the need to choose the only possible side for justice. The documentary intermediary performs the 17° role of liberal witness best if the whole voice and style of the author are offered up, publicly, to the side chosen. This meant, in a war marked by Herz's self-immolation, offering up the body to the enemy's bombs, the bombs unleashed by the enemies of the cold civil war US in the White House, the Pentagon and Congress. To be prepared to die in this way *between* the two states is to reveal to the world who in fact are the real victims in this war. It is also to reveal the triangular logic running the enemy's ideology, the ways the American corrupt 'Third Force' system of Cold War management in the decolonizing Third World was founded on the victimizing sacrifice of peasant victims.

For the Cold War theorists, South East Asia was a zone of deadly triangles, in particular the so-called 'Power Triangle' of the United States, Russia and China.[38] The power triangle had become dangerously unstable with the fallout from the Sino–Soviet split: the split occurred following the breakdown of talks between the delegations of the Chinese and Soviet Communist parties in Moscow in July 1963. This initiated a phase of mutual suspicion: 'each of the three powers perceived the other two members of the triangle as a threat to their own security' (Raju G.C. Thomas, *The Great Power Triangle*, p. 4). Asia was seen as a key battleground for the extension of America's containment policy to loose-cannon Maoist China. Asia was the hottest theatre of the Cold War: of the five times the US National Security Council considered using nuclear weapons, four were in Asia. It was a region of extraordinary volatility because '[intertwined] with the obvious Cold War frictions were the pressures of nationalism and anti-colonialism, the politics of neutralism, and non-alignment, together with the deep tensions of Sino-Soviet rivalry'.[39] Korea had been a spectacular failure, as had been the Bay of Pigs and other interventions in Cold War hotspots in the decolonizing Third World. As a result, Vietnam could not fail: 'American retreat in Asia might upset the whole world balance', Kennedy had argued, still stung by the ordeals of Berlin and Cuba.[40] The power triangle of the Cold War thus had to be worked out in detail, on the ground, in Vietnam – and the ground as an ex-French dependency was subject to another triangle: United States, Britain and France. The intervention in Asia, as the South East Asia Treaty Organization (SEATO) revealed, was importantly a contractual arrangement for the decolonization of the old colonial powers' territories according to the Cold War dictates of the *Pax Americana*. The process of decolonization had to be enforced and manipulated by politically motivated aid, counterinsurgency and military firepower, using methods partly borrowed from the French in Indochina and the British in Kenya and Malaya. The decolonizing triangle was turned into a Cold War force-field by the larger Sino–Soviet–US power triangle, its 'balance' depending on securing other triangles *within* Vietnam, the local force-fields which clever 'Third Force' subversion and counterinsurgency, backing frontline search-and-destroy missions and area bombing, could turn to American advantage. Many of the force-fields operated within and around that most haunting of Vietnamese triangles, the Mekong Delta.[41]

The most celebrated triangle within the Delta was the Iron Triangle, a VC sanctuary in War Zone C, Tay Ninh Province, a 60-square-mile area 20 miles north of Saigon, between the Saigon River and Route 13. In 1965–6, the year before McCarthy's visit, Operation Attleboro was meant to combat-test the 196th Light Infantry Brigade in the Iron Triangle; it had expanded by November 1967, when it ended, into the largest US joint operation of the war at that time. In January 1967, Johnson ordered the massive search-and-destroy Operation Cedar Falls, designed to blast the VC from the Triangle. To do so the United States stripped the zone of its peasantry, rehousing them in concentration camps, and bombed War Zone C to high heaven: 16,000 troops moved in to discover an empty landscape, the enemy having abandoned their bases and extraordinary network of underground tunnels.

If it was a zone spawning a multiplication of triangles, Vietnam was also routinely described as the focus of sacrifice. Thomas J. Dodd, Cold Warrior senator, in a February 1965 speech to Senate against the dangers of the peace camp's 'new isolationism', equated escalation of the war in Vietnam with the Cold War sacrificial code: 'More effort, more sacrifice – not less – is the need of the day.'[42] Secretary of State Dean Rusk, at the first Vietnam hearing organized by the Foreign Relations committee, on 28 January 1966, stated that 'the South Vietnamese must believe that they and we are fighting for something worth great sacrifice'.[43] At the second Vietnam hearing, on 18 February 1966, Senator Symington suggested to Dean Rusk that American policy in Vietnam could be summarized as the desire 'to see a peace without sacrificing the honor of the United States' (Fulbright, *The Vietnam Hearings*, p. 289).[44] Implicit in the triangular sacrificial logic of the war was the creeping disease of the Vietnamization which ended it: on the surface a training of Army of the Republic of Vietnam (ARVN) troops to take over US commitments; in practice a replacement of one sacrificial victim with another, American GIs with South Vietnamese fall-guys, brainwashed into acceptance of Dean Rusk's 'something worth great sacrifice'.

In her own mind, McCarthy's journey to Hanoi was a journey to the zone of sacrifice within the 'iron triangle' of the Cold War: she would be reversing the Vietnamizing substitutions being practised by the imperial brotherhood. After the trip to Saigon, she waited in Cambodia for a visa for North Vietnam, and began to sense the edges of the force-field of sacrifice she imagined herself entering. In a tourist trip to the temples around Sim Reap, including Angkor Wat, the huge twelfth-century temple complex dedicated to Vishnu, Cold War paranoia set in, prompted by her fear of the US bombs on Hanoi. Though a Hindu temple originally, Angkor Wat was inhabited by Buddhist monks, brothers to the men who immolated themselves in the protests against Diem's regime in 1962. For McCarthy, the association of jungle, Buddhism and fear of bombs came together to colour the paranoia, culminating in a panic attack as she swam in the pool of the Villa Princière, overlooking the Siem Reap river:[45]

> There, on the edge of the jungle, I was overcome by terror. [. . .] Perhaps it was the vegetation, the sinuous crawling gray tree trunks I had seen during the day, or the long files of smiling Buddha figures, or else it was

the fear I had been suppressing, without knowing it, in Vietnam, now burgeoning like some gross luxuriant plant that choked me. [. . .] My solitude made me conspicuous: what was I up to, alone and palely loitering? I felt followed, stalked. (*The Seventeenth Degree*, p. 29)

Buried in her paranoia is fear of sacrifice: she is Keats' 'wretched wight' in *La Belle Dame Sans Merci*, a white woman acting the knight-at-arms in the war of which Kennedy had predicted: 'if it becomes a white man's war, we will lose it as the French did before'.[46] But she is also the Belle Dame Sans Merci with 'her wild sad eyes' closed shut, a projection of McCarthy's dead self under the dreadful gaze of Keats' 'pale kings, and princes too, / Pale warriors' of the Cold War, there on the war's 'cold hill side', on the edge of its jungle battlegrounds.

Their gaze *is* the jungle, a 'gross luxuriant plant' choking her as the eyes follow and stalk her swimming in the pool – in water taken from a river that flows, through the Mekong–Tonlé basin, down to the Mekong Delta in Vietnam. The gaze of the pale Cold Warriors takes on the form of the stone figures of the smiling Buddhas at the temple of Bayon at Angkor Thom she had visited that day,[47] as well as of the creeping tree trunks which snake over the Bayon stonework. The gaze takes the form of dreaming, alien powers (the heads at Bayon all have their eyes shut, like the Belle Dame) recalling the nightmare of the remotely near sources of American power. As Buddhist symbols, they also stand for the sacrificial death-wish imitated by the Quaker peace resisters in the United States cold civil war. As the jungle tree forms sinuously crawling over Bayon, they are an underground and insinuating life form, aiming to choke her in the VC Mekong waters for her treachery. They are also traditional Western symbols for Asia as alien other, the jungle a darkness to her wretched white imagination. The paranoid fear is perfectly double, crossing a resister's terror at the Cold Warriors' power in the Third World, and an ordinary American's fear of the inscrutable East. At the edge of the jungle, like Bly's black boat at the edge of vision, McCarthy glimpses the schizoid shape of Cold War paranoia, a bi-fold discourse mixing the enemy's otherness with deep and inward American fears. Both East and West mark her out as prey: she is, like the Vietnamese children Morrison hoped to save, the victim, if not target, of the war. When she sees pictures of the 'dread F-111A's', the bombers set to strike Hanoi, by the Mekong whilst waiting to travel to the North, she is sure 'they had a personal appointment with me' (*The Seventeenth Degree*, p. 33). They appear as terrible 'winged retribution figures' designed to kill *her* (p. 34).

The Villa Princière fit of paranoia inaugurates a dream, the nightmare McCarthy habitually had concerning Vietnam:

I never dream of Vietnam, North or South, but I have a recurrent nightmare *concerning* Vietnam but laid in Cambodia, or, sometimes, Laos. I am in the midst of unfriendly, excitable people, brown, like the

Cambodians, but there are some whites, too, perhaps American officers. I have an important message to carry or a report to make to a court of law. It is something about a war crime I have witnessed, and these people swarming around may try to obstruct me. Then I realize I have forgotten the thing I need to report about. It has slipped my mind, and now – the frontier is closed or there is fighting – I cannot get back into Vietnam to find it. Yet maybe it will come back. Something in the countryside here will remind me of it. I am running around, looking. I see a rural railroad station, an army truck, uniformed men in it. 'They . . . ' I almost have it. No. Gone. I cannot remember the rest of the sentence. It is a version of the examination dream. I fail.

Probably this is my secret assessment of how I carried out my Vietnam 'assignment'. Some essential was missing. But I do not know what it was, and indeed that is the plot of the dream: that, being the person I am, I am unable to recover that essential, find the master-switch that will give illumination. I had it once, apparently (in my youth?), and lost it, from sheer distraction. (*The Seventeenth Degree*, p. 30)

The war crime may have something to do with My Lai, or it may be the war itself, a crime against humanity for the liberal opposition. What emerges, though, is less a sharp protest against the war than a buried anxiety about her act of witness. The 'it' of Vietnam is elusive, slippery, forgettable like a guilty fantasy – 'I cannot get back into Vietnam to find *it*.' It might return, though, like the repressed ('Yet maybe it will come back'). The Cambodian setting plays again on the race register: her 'white' act of witness, even though aimed against those white American officers, is obstructed by the 'brown' Cambodians. She cannot bring herself to utter the words which will condemn the white men of war; she will fall apart under interrogation in the paranoid court of law, like the poor witnesses against Medina in 1971. Medina had been charged with cold-bloodedly shooting a woman through the head at My Lai – the brave men who witnessed against him were told she'd *flinched* and therefore may have had a grenade in her hand (*The Seventeenth Degree*, p. 392).

At any rate, McCarthy fears a similar erasure of her truth – but it is an erasure which she is complicit in, by guilty association with those American officers. The erasure is not only a loss of voice, a loss of memory, a loss of 'it'. The very lack of the 'rest of the sentence' leaves 'They' in charge of the syntax of her imagination: '"They . . . " I almost have it.' *They* are paranoid figures for the military in Vietnam, uniformed men in an army truck. *They* are the judges at the court martial within her white woman's body, the men who 'make war / Like a man anointing himself'. Within the iron triangle between 'they', 'I' and 'it', it is Mary McCarthy who is under judgement and erasure, for the sin of acting the intermediary between the US and Vietnam, for daring, as a white woman, to speak, in broken Vietnamerican, the language of the VC. She fails the examination, judged as pure *lack* by both the Vietnamese (Cambodians in the dream) and the uniformed men in the army trucks she means to betray.

In November 1964, a year after Kennedy's assassination, the month LBJ got himself elected, three months after the Tonkin Gulf Resolution was passed, Columbia historian Richard Hofstadter published his celebrated essay on the political rhetoric of fear running Washington, 'The Paranoid Style in American Politics'. The essay gives a prehistory to McCarthyite anti-Communism, recalling similar conspiracy theories, from the anti-Masonic scare stories of the eighteenth century through the Jesuit scare of the nineteenth. But it is the Cold War which is the most spectacular breeding-ground for the paranoid style:

> Events since 1939 have given the contemporary right-wing paranoid a vast theatre for his imagination, full of rich and proliferating detail, replete with realistic cues and undeniable proofs of the validity of his suspicions. The theatre of action is now the entire world, and he can draw not only on the events of World War II, but also on those of the Korean War and the Cold War. (Hofstadter, 'Paranoid Style', p. 81)

The Cold War generated the ideal theatre because it was constructed on the principle most suited to conspiracy theories, namely the 'confrontation of opposed interests which are (or are felt to be) totally irreconcilable, and thus by nature not susceptible to the normal political processes of bargain and compromise' (p. 86). Those opposed interests are given roles in the psychodrama of the paranoid style. The Cold War theatre of action has one leading role: that of the enemy:

> The enemy is clearly delineated: he is a perfect model of malice, a kind of amoral superman – sinister, ubiquitous, powerful, cruel, sensual, luxury-loving. Unlike the rest of us, the enemy is not caught in the toils of the vast mechanism of history, himself a victim of his past, his desires, his limitations. He wills, indeed he manufactures, the mechanism of history, or tries to deflect the normal course of history in an evil way. (Hofstadter, 'Paranoid Style', p. 85)

The enemy as powerful evil genius is the doppelgänger of the Cold War conspiracy theorist, his dark twin: 'It is hard to resist the conclusion that this enemy is on many counts the projection of the self; both the ideal and the unacceptable aspects of the self are attributed to him' (p. 85). As such, the conspiracy is a creation of the paranoid, a projection of unspoken desires bound up in the complex act of 'emulating the enemy', subtitle of this section of the essay. To emulate the enemy is to compose a melodramatic fiction or play woven around the paranoid's own psyche, a doubling of the self engendered by lusts that war in his members. The point of the melodrama is masochistic, clearly: inventing one's own best bully-boy enemy. But it is masochistic in a peculiar way: 'We are all sufferers from history, but the paranoid is a double sufferer, since he is afflicted not only by the real world, with the rest of us, but by his fantasies as well' (p. 86).

The doubling of the paranoid self through emulation of the imaginary enemy establishes the proper ontological grounds for the pleasures of the double sufferer. The two men of the Cold War power triangle are interpellated into being by the machinery of political history, paranoid 'we' and enemy 'they' conceived as rival characters in fictions generated by the State Department, not by solitary paranoids in their dens.

The launching of the second war in Indochina meant that the State Department's paranoia-as-history spilled over into the body politic; even into the minds and members of the peace movement. It was not only that there was something in the air that favoured the toxic extension of the paranoid style to all forms of politics in the United States – the Cuban missile crisis and the assassination of Kennedy could be said to have triggered this. It was also that the very nature of fiction-making during the 1960s Cold War had undergone a cynical sea-change. As McCarthy observed in 'Characters in Fiction', a talk she gave in Yugoslavia in 1961: 'Much of modern literature might be defined as the search for one's own diametrical opposite, which is then used as the point-of-view.'[48]

At the political level, the paranoid style is a fiction-generating rhetoric which seeks to capture an evolving notion of the state's diametrical opposite in order to fabricate a matching national security policy as point of view. Cold War policy, therefore, especially in the hot wars in the Third World, is by its nature always a form of emulation of the enemy. If emulation is this fictionalizing history of the enemy put into violent action, then Vietnam was the paranoid style made flesh, armour, practical dreamwork.

For Johnson and his administration, the war was a complicated mime and anticipation of the other's moves – the word 'other' dominated their policy. Taking inspiration from his own domestic policy, based on his reading of Michael Harrington's *The Other America* on black America in the 1950s, Johnson conceived of the 'other war' in Vietnam, the war for hearts and minds: basically a revamping of the pacification programmes.[49] The 'other war' chimed with Dean Rusk's favourite expression, 'the other side', his formula for Hanoi. At the Vietnam Hearings, for instance, he spoke of the dangers of vacillating whilst the enemy developed its policy:

> So, gentlemen, time may help, but we cannot let time get away from us by having it used by the other side to develop a momentum and an appetite and a danger that will be increasingly difficult to bring under control.

[. . .] we are not on track here where everything is frozen on both sides. We don't know what the other side is going to do in this situation. We do know that they must face the fact that they are not going to have a military success in the South. (Fulbright, *Vietnam Hearings*, pp. 292–3)

This is an extraordinary display of the paranoid style: time itself is subject to the enemy's power, the devious opponent, shape-shifting, treacherously revolutionary in its shifts in policy. At the same time, Rusk's words fit perfectly the activities of the United States in Vietnam: the escalation of the war was precisely this, a development of 'a momentum, an appetite and a danger' which the administration knew would be difficult to control. The savouring of the words, there in the rising rhythms and fake precision given by those indefinite articles, in the sentence's own momentum and frisson, in the secret knowledge of how power feeds off abstract energies, in the little triangle created by the terms 'momentum', 'appetite' and 'danger', all expose the administration's abstract appetite for violence as history, history as paranoid policy in time and against time ('we cannot let time get away from us'). Vietnam was indeed an other war, a war fabricated against Washington's other side so as to generate a self-sustaining, self-anointing momentum, appetite and danger, a fantasy projection of its own power as violent history imposed upon the world.

Before undertaking the potentially self-sacrificial journey to Hanoi, McCarthy studied the home front in South Vietnam. She went with a view partly to expose the propaganda being spread by her opposite number, John Steinbeck. Steinbeck had been asked to cover Vietnam over six weeks in 1966 for *Newsday* magazine, published as the 'Letters to Alicia'.[50] As a propaganda war, Vietnam pitched writers against each other in a literary mime of the ideological struggle between Hanoi and Saigon, though McCarthy was sane enough to realize that the writers' war was an insignificant sideshow. It hardly mattered, even, whether they appeared as saps or not, as long as they were visibly there as representatives of the rival forces:

> I did not think I was going to make a fool of myself, and, if I did, it did not seem to me important to my career (something I never cared about) or to the anti-war movement. John Steinbeck was out there making a fool of *him*self but did not appear to be creating any disarray in the pro-war forces on whose behalf he was traveling. (*The Seventeenth Degree*, p. 22)

But once out in Vietnam, McCarthy felt it her duty to expose Steinbeck's many duplicities, including his rosy picture of the education aid programme.

She travelled to Rach Kien in the Delta, 'a Pentagon pilot project of a few months before', for instance, to check on the 'little school house Steinbeck wrote about, back in January, and the blue school desks he had seen the soldiers painting' (*The Seventeenth Degree*, p. 81). 'The picture he sketched, of a ghost town coming back to civic life, made the officers who had entertained him smile – "He used his imagination"' (p. 81). Rach Kien was briefly a showcase for the Pentagon's pacification programme: a former VC stronghold, it was felt to be an ideal base for a model village to demonstrate to the Delta villagers the superior benefits of Saigon planning and culture. Unfortunately, the hamlet suffered nightly VC mortar attack, and the plan had to be abandoned. But not before it had been visited by the great and the good for Pentagon propaganda purposes: James Mitchener covered it for AFVN radio, columnists and reporters came and went. For it was in hamlets like Rach Kien that the other war for hearts and minds was being fought, with all the crazy fanaticism and fake public spirit that Washington could muster.

The war in Vietnam would not be won, the propagandists would say, in Saigon or on the battlefield, but in the Rach Kien model villages:

> This idea, by now trite (it was first discovered in Diem's time and had been rebaptized under a number of names – New Life Hamlets, Rural Construction, Counter Insurgency, Nation-Building, Revolutionary Development, the Hearts and Minds Program), is the main source of inspiration for the various teams of missionaries, military and civilian, who think they are engaged in a crusade [. . .] the 'other' war, proclaimed by President Johnson in Honolulu, [. . .] is simultaneously pictured as a strategy for winning War Number One and as a top priority in itself. Indeed, in Vietnam, there are moments when the 'other' war, for hearts and minds, seems to be viewed as the sole reason for the American presence, and it is certainly more congenial to American officials, brimming with public spirit, than the war they are launching from the skies. Americans do not like to be negative, and the 'other' war is constructive. (*The Seventeenth Degree*, p. 72)

The satirical edge in McCarthy's prose cuts deep into the official bullshit, slicing through the special pleading disguising the Janus-face of the American war machine: one face the public-spirited official nurturing democracy in the Vietnam fields, the other the ethnocidal killer napalming those same fields back to the Stone Age. McCarthy's inverted commas round 'other' register a suppressed nausea and contempt in her voice, at the same time as mimicking the official repetition of the concept *ad nauseam*. The two faces of power in Vietnam, Pentagon officials and military, are the real subject of the 'Vietnam' chapter of *The Seventeenth Degree*: they are each other's other, each acting as though the other did not exist, yet indistinguishable in the operation of the war. These are the two men of power with their two different wars: the positive propagandist with his statistics and his sociological and anthropological systems analysis of the peasant victims herded into camps, and the hard-headed strategist with his body counts and operations assessments. In between these two men are squeezed the South Vietnamese.[51]

At the heart of the iron triangle of Cold War power in Vietnam was this combination of what McCarthy calls 'Uncle Sam with candy in his pockets' (*The Seventeenth Degree*, p. 99) running a psy-war freak-show of official blandishments, with the Air Force's 'Eye of God': soon, 'all will be razed, charred, defoliated by that terrible, searching gaze' (p. 93). 'The simplest Vietnamese', McCarthy writes, 'could perhaps see a connection that eludes many American intellectuals between the spray of pellets from the "mother" bomb and the candy hurled at children in the South' (p. 309).[52]

Because it was the other war which had become the sole justification for American presence in Vietnam after the collapse of belief in the domino theory of Cold War containment, it is the official hypocrite whom McCarthy zeroes in on with most withering contempt: the sanctimonious Pentagon-spirited technocrat, Pharisee–Pangloss–Tartuffe of the Cold War's endgame in Vietnam. It is the bogus values being sold to the South Vietnamese which are the only motivation for most of the young American soldiers involved in policing both wars, values such as free enterprise. To attack what she terms the 'relentless priggery' (*The Seventeenth Degree*, p. 80) and 'pharisee virtue' (p. 87) being preached to justify the bombing, shelling and defoliating needed satire at least as harsh as this. The troops, she is arguing, are the dupes of the propaganda running the other war of 'Counter Insurgency, Nation-Building, Revolutionary Development'. And that propaganda is not only schizophrenic (the 'officials, brimming with public spirit' as the 'other side' to the perpetrators of 'the war they are launching from the skies'); it is deeply paranoid in its emulation of the enemy.

The advocates of nation-building counterinsurgency were specialists in the new systems-theory-inflected social sciences, McCarthy found: political science, sociology, anthropology, with their jargon buzzwords, 'infrastructure', 'cadre support', 'strategic hamlets'. It was these political scientists who staffed the psychological operations and civil affairs teams which fought the other war. The new disciplines were calqued on Cold War Kremlinology, which had studied the 'behavior of the enemy [. . .] under university microscopes, with the aid of samples furnished by defectors to the Free World' (*The Seventeenth Degree*, p. 122). The study of the enemy for indoctrination purposes was updated by Kennedy's men in the thrusting technocratic culture of the New Frontier, McCarthy argues, in terms of counterinsurgency and special warfare, with techniques borrowed from 'elite French officers who used it in Algeria – with what results we know' (p. 124). The Staley Plan in 1961 perfected the Diem-Nhu 'agrovilles – basically, fortified settlements, also on an Algerian model' (p. 125) – turning them into Strategic Hamlets. Staley hoped to 'transfer the population, wherever moveable, into Prosperity Zones, which were to contain 15,000 model hamlets, for a starter, all heavily fortified and surrounded by barbed wire' (p. 125).

For McCarthy, the issue is clear – the Staley Plan was openly totalitarian, advocating concentration camps for CIA indoctrination and psychological warfare. When Diem fell and was assassinated (possibly triggering Kennedy's own assassination), the Plan was dropped, only to reappear in different form as the Rural Construction programme. This failed, to be replaced by the Revolutionary Development (RD) programme. It is this which McCarthy witnessed at work when she visited the showcase hamlet of Phu Cuong. RD, she saw, was just Rural Construction plus 'the black pajamas':

> the black-pajama uniform proclaims a thing that was always implicit in such conceptions as counter-insurgency and special warfare and in some features of the Staley Plan – plagiarism of the enemy's techniques.

Indeed, the whole concept of the other war was an act of brazen emulation of the enemy:

> Indeed the 'other' war dramatically declared by Johnson at Honolulu is an idea rather tardily lifted from the Viet Cong. Long before the Americans thought of it, the VC was building schools for the peasantry, digging wells, teaching better methods of agriculture. But because the Viet Cong did not control the mass media, the 'secret' of its appeal remained a secret, at least from the military, who are digging the wells, building the schools, under the impression that this grass-roots courtship originated in the big heart of America. It would not occur to a general (unless he were Caesar) that he was plagiarizing from the enemy: to a straight-shooting man of action, the thought is distasteful. (*The Seventeenth Degree*, p. 127)

On the face of it an attempt to demonstrate to the peasantry the virtues and benefits of US free enterprise and consumer culture, in reality RD aped the enemy in an attempt to destroy the rural economy which was seen as a seed-bed of Chinese-style Communism. RD hoped to bribe the Vietnamese forcibly removed from their homes to act as spies and informers on their own people – the so-called Chieu Hoi or Open Arms amnesty programme. Open Arms, McCarthy understood, 'is a typical instance of counter-insurgency thinking and has the earmarks of a CIA project: the CIA has a special rapport with the traitor' (especially if the traitor is an intellectual) as a direct result of the early years of the Cold War: 'the experience of the Cold War and, later, of Cuba opened the minds of the Americans to the uses of the "defector" – a traitor and a deserter combined in one *politically conscious* person' (p. 142). If the war was run by a schizophrenic US, it naturally sought the help of those prepared to betray themselves.

The showcase refugee camp at Phu Cuong housed the majority of the 8,000 villagers forcibly removed from Ben Suc and outlying hamlets in the Iron Triangle – a deliberate use of technology 'to generate a record production of homeless persons' (*The Seventeenth Degree*, p. 94). In that triangle, the 'hostile civilians' are subjected to a nauseating combination of bullying tactics and civic education:

> 'We're teaching them free enterprise', explains a breathless JUSPAO [Joint US Public Affairs Office] official in the grim town of Phu Cuong. He is speaking of the 'refugees' from the Iron Triangle, who were forcibly cleared out of their hamlets, which were then burned and leveled, during Operation Cedar Falls ('Clear and Hold'). They had just been transferred into a camp, hastily constructed by the ARVN with tin roofs painted red and white, to make the form, as seen from the air, of a giant Red Cross. (p. 79)[53]

Counterinsurgency thinking was based on such 'complex self-deception' (p. 100), in a Humpty-Dumpty game of lunatic meanings and pseudo-scientific euphemism. What was being countered was some sane sense of the reality of the totalitarian fictions being imposed on the populations, Uncle Sam blind to the true forces being unleashed by the Eye of God. The villagers herded off their land in the Iron Triangle entered another iron triangle constructed by the Military Assistance Command, Vietnam (MACV): a force-field of psychological warfare uniting the systems-thinking of the new social sciences, the mass 'resources control' strategies of military intelligence, and the concentration, indoctrination and subornation techniques of 'black-pajama' propaganda plagiarized from the enemy.[54]

At the heart of McCarthy's account of the US other war for hearts and minds in the iron triangles of South Vietnam is a girl victim, sacrificial offering to the Eye of God and Uncle Sam, discovered during a trip to a Marine Corps camp in I-Corps district, up near the DMZ, close to the seventeenth parallel:

> The Marine Corps had donated a children's hospital, and in that hospital, right up the road [. . .] was a little girl who had been wounded during a Marine assault. 'We're nursing her back to health', [the Marine General in charge of logistics] intoned – and paused, like a preacher accustomed at this point, to hearing an 'Amen'; his PIO (Information Officer) nodded three times. [. . .] John Morgan, in the London *Sunday Times*, described another little Vietnamese girl up near the DMZ – do they have one to a battalion? – who had been wounded by Marine bullets ('A casualty of war', the general repeated solemnly. 'A casualty of war') and whom he saw carried in one night to a drinking party in sick bay, her legs bandaged, a spotlight playing on her, while the Marines pressed candy and dollar bills into her hands and had their pictures taken with her; she had more dolls than Macy's, they told him – 'that girl is really spoiled'. To spoil a child you have injured and

> send her back to her parents, with dolls as souvenirs, is pharisee virtue,
> whitening the sepulchre, like 'treating' malnutrition in a hospital ward.
> (*The Seventeenth Degree*, pp. 85–7)

John Updike accused Mary McCarthy's protest against Operation Cedar Falls of being 'too reflexive, too pop', too reliant 'upon satirical descriptions of American officers and the grotesqueries of cultural superimposition'. Like Auden, he wrote in a letter to the *New York Times* on 24 September 1967, he felt 'that it is foolish to canvass writers upon political issues'; 'our views, as [Auden] says, "have no more authority than those of any reasonably well-educated citizen."' Updike then wheels out a well-worn Cold War argument: 'in my own case at least I feel my professional need for freedom of speech and expression prejudices me toward a government whose constitution guarantees it.'[55] Updike's disdain for McCarthy's prose hardly makes sense, as though satire couldn't possibly apply to an American officer without it being knee-jerk populism, or the arrogance of 'Pacification (Revolutionary Development)' could be anything else but grotesque in its superimposition. The only argument left is the vague Cold Warrior stance embedded in the line on freedom of speech. This hardly has any logic either, unless you unpack it this way: McCarthy should not bother her head with politics, because writers are mere civilians, and civilians have no authority at all in culture. In any case, her protest could not occur in a Communist country, could it, which surely means it should not be made at all in a free one. Her writing on Vietnam, therefore, is reflexive and pop *because* it is satirical, anti-American and a political protest.

A letter like this could hardly have been written in a country that was not weevily with Cold War prejudice and traditions of insinuating sarcasm. What is truly reflexive is Updike's breezy assumption of the virtues of an apolitical, civilian passivity, even finding a certain comfort in being so indiscriminately generous towards LBJ and the sources of power: 'I differ, perhaps,' he wrote, 'from my unanimously dove-ish confrères in crediting the Johnson Administration with good faith and some good sense', as though the mere crediting it must make it so.

It is a surprise to discover how many of those who supported the Vietnam war effort presumed themselves to be, like Updike, somewhere between the hawks and the doves, as though on some seventeenth parallel between two opposed camps. The LBJ administration conceived of itself in this way: they were advocates of a *moderate* bombing campaign, the president in 1967, for instance, carefully choosing targets which would not offend the Chinese or Russians, limiting strikes for fear of incensing the unanimously doveish public, yet still bombing north of the seventeenth parallel to appease the hawks in his military. An influential 1967 memo drawn up by William Bundy, Nicholas

Katzenbach and Richard Helms, for instance, arguing that bombing should be restricted to supply routes north of the twentieth parallel, concludes by considering the pros and cons of making such a decision public, in the context of both the Sino–Soviet–American Cold War power triangle and the perceived 'credibility gap' between the administration and the public. One of the pros reads: 'A more specific statement would help with "doves" and worriers at home and abroad'; whilst one of the cons reads: 'A public statement might arouse the "hawks" more than some degree of uncertainty would do.'[56] Such mealy-mouthed thinking could, again, be said to proceed directly from the unholy marriage between public-spirited Pharisee virtue and old-fashioned Cold War anti-Communism. Vietnam was fought by a doveish hawk, or a hawkish dove, a Third Force hybrid obsessed with opinion and public relations, yet quite prepared to turn a blind eye to the indiscriminate destruction wreaked by its own Eye of God.

One of the Pentagon people sent to Vietnam as part of the massive analytic drive to reconceptualize the war as doveishly hawkish was Daniel Ellsberg. He spent two years in Vietnam as a Department of Defense (DoD) policy wonk, using analysis methodology he had learnt at the RAND corporation. He was a civilian acting for General Lansdale, who had been Kennedy's Indochina counterinsurgency expert, deeply involved in covert operations in Cuba (including Operation Mongoose), an expert in psychological warfare, and ingenious dirty tricks Cold Warrior. In his paper 'A High-Level Look at the Cold War', for instance, Lansdale proposed a Machiavellian school for political action to educate a 'skilled free world leadership', and the creation of 'a super-elite (under 100 persons) in such a way as to bring about a decisive change in the outcome of the cold war'.[57] Clearly, Ellsberg believed himself to be one of the super-elite in the secret enterprise to change the outcome of the Cold War, as he admitted in one of the curious documents he drew up for the RAND corporation when he returned from Nam:

> Going as a member of General Lansdale's team of irregulars, I expected (though it didn't quite turn out that way) to be in the front lines of the political conflict, in an exposed position. After ten years as a cold warrior, at RAND and in the Marines before that, I had a personal desire to beat the Communists, this once, this place.[58]

One of Ellsberg's assignments was to spend time with the infantry grunts in the paddy fields, and he was sent to Rach Kien, the very same camp visited by Steinbeck and McCarthy in the propaganda wars. He arrived at Rach Kien in December 1966 and stayed with the 25th Infantry Division for a couple of weeks. The shock of the search-and-destroy missions he witnessed there – indiscriminate hut-burning, 'reconnaissance by fire' (shooting up hamlets to see if anyone shot back), useless and wasteful patrols – did much to convince him of the futility and evil of the war, partly motivating him to make the crucial Pentagon Papers leak in 1971. The papers were the result of a secret DoD study ordered by McNamara to consider US decision-making about Vietnam since the Second World War. The study, 7,000 pages of history and documents, was finished in 1969. It was top secret, and only fifteen copies were produced, one ending up with the RAND corporation: this was the copy Ellsberg leaked to Neil Sheehan at the *New York Times*.[59]

The Papers were devastating evidence of the duplicities of the US's Third Force strategy in Indochina, detailing covert operations against the North going back to 1954, the actions taken to sabotage the Accords and ensure no elections were held in order to force their preferred Third Force candidate on the South Vietnamese, the deliberate distortions of events at Tonkin to whip up a *casus belli*.[60] Most of all, they were a deadly display of the rhetoric of self-anointing war-mongering which resulted from the alliance of counterinsurgency thinking (the pacification dove) and unprecedented violence from the air (the napalming hawk), killing 3.8 million Vietnamese in the name of democracy and free enterprise (the estimate made by McNamara, the man who initiated the Pentagon study, and who left the administration quietly in 1968, nauseated by the violence he had helped unleash).[61]

Ellsberg, like McCarthy, was appalled by the filth and squalor of South Vietnam, but also increasingly disturbed by his own double-headedness. He was as well the Cold Warrior technician, coolly breaking down statistics of Killed In Action (KIA) figures to prove a case against ARVN battalions, or discussing pacification with friendly Vietnamese intellectuals with the level-headedness of the RAND social scientist observing native informants:

> All pacification schemes will be <u>mechanical</u>, only <u>buying</u> compliance with benefits and coercion, so long as the GVN [Government of Vietnam] lacks any credibility or respectability: which are unattainable for those <u>mercenaries</u> who, for money or career benefits, sold themselves at the start to the French and have never, since, taken any opportunity to sacrifice, to suffer, to pass up personal advantage, or risk their lives, <u>for their country</u>.[62]

Note how, again, the administration, even from this secretly oppositional point of view, cannot conceive of winning the war without the South Vietnamese being *made to believe in their own sacrifice*. And this despite or because of their collective subject position between the Communist and US ideologies: '<u>The problem of South Vietnam has been that of a people squeezed between two competing authoritarian regimes: not a two-sided civil war</u>' (Ellsberg, 'On Pacification', p. 6).[63] More than anything else came the realization that his own intermediary position was itself a direct result of the fake Third Force manoeuvres of his government:[64]

Indeed, we have always in Vietnam backed one unpopular, authoritarian, minority faction against another:

French and Bao Dai	vs.	Viet Minh
Diem	vs.	Viet Cong
Generals	vs.	Viet Cong

with 'our' faction always unwilling or unable to draw support from the mass 'in between'.[65]

The protesting men, too, are riddled with the 'in-between' contradictions generated by US intervention in South East Asia. Harbouring the Cold Warrior and the witness within the same body, conscious of the hypocrisy of trying to force the Vietnamese to sacrifice their lives for a mercenary and corrupt 'Third Force' faction, yet aware of the chime between the Janus-faced forces they are criticizing and their own masculinist contradictions, it was impossible, especially for a Westerner, not to tip over into the muck of the war.

It was a peace activist woman who cemented Ellsberg's resolve to leak documents to the press. He met her at a Princeton conference on 'America in a Revolutionary World', where he shared a platform with activists of 'the anti-nuclear movement of the fifties and the civil rights and antiwar movements of the sixties' (Ellsberg, *Secrets*, pp. 209–10). There he'd heard Janaki, an Indian Ghandi activist of the *sarvodaya* movement (a movement for people's democracy based on Ghandian ideals), argue against the concept of the enemy. To the RAND bureaucrat, the statement hardly made sense:

> A strange statement. Hardly comprehensible. No concept of the enemy? How about concepts of sun and moon, fire, water? I came from a culture in which the concept of the enemy was central, seemingly indispensable – the culture of Rand, the US Marine Corps, the Defense and State departments, international and domestic politics, game theory and bargaining theory. Identifying the enemies, understanding and predicting them so as to fight and control them better, analyzing the relations of abstract enemies: all that had been for years my daily bread and butter, part of the air I breathed. (p. 211)

Janaki convinced him of the coherence of non-hostile resistance to evildoers, as with the Montgomery bus boycott. Only a Ghandian approach to wrongdoers can resist the temptation to imitate their coercive power. Only peaceful non-cooperation can break the unconscious complicity in extreme state violence:

> Nearly all evildoing, she pointed out, like nearly all coercive power, legitimate and illegitimate, depends on the cooperation, on the obedience and support, on the assent or at least passive tolerance of many people. It relies on many collaborators that are conscious of their roles;

these include even many victims, along with passive bystanders, as in effect accomplices. (p. 213)

It is this advice and example which gave Ellsberg the courage to act against what he came to call the murdering 'lying machine' of the White House war establishment, with its elaborate culture of secrecy and fabrication. It was a woman pacifist who opened his eyes to his own complicity, as Pentagon insider, in the industrial death inflicted on the thousands of victims in Vietnam, a complicity deeply ingrained in the very system of government in Washington. Only insiders courageous enough to act as outsiders could hope to exert enough power on the sources of power in the White House:

> It appeared that only if power were brought to bear upon the executive branch from outside it [. . .] might the presidential preference for endless, escalating stalemate rather than 'failure' in Vietnam be overruled. 'Inside' consulting and advice, as in the Rand mode, or the normal practices of the broader 'establishment' withheld from Congress and the public the facts and authoritative judgments needed for the self-confident exercise of such a power. By that very silence – no matter how frank or wise the 'private' counsel – it supported and participated in the structure of inordinate, unchallenged executive power that led directly in circumstances like Vietnam to its rigid, desperate, outlaw behavior. (pp. 275–6)

The imperial brotherhood of silent, private, secretive insiders, though remotely near the sources of power, had no real power as such to change the habitual paranoid Cold War policy running the Pentagon–White House as if by invisible tradition. It took women to open Ellsberg's eyes to the two men he'd become: the silent liberal and Cold War robot. It was the example of these women which tipped the scales and led to the Pentagon Papers leak, a leak which taught the world how to read Nixon and Kissinger at last, *from the inside*.

Obsessed by the Villa Princière paranoid dreams being generated by the iron triangle, terrified by the prospect of her own sacrifice under the F-111As, Mary McCarthy prepared to fly to Hanoi. Though the first novelist to do so, she was following in the footsteps of other women, women inspired by Alice Herz. As Hershberger has shown in *Traveling to Vietnam*, by 1969 a group a month was making the trip to North Vietnam, over 200 in all. But the first travellers were members of WSP, the organization Herz died for in Chicago, the same anti-nuclear protestors who had inspired Plath and Paley in their struggle against the atmospheric tests, women who saw the relationship between the war, decolonization and the international arms race. Most were also conscious of the relationship between the war and civil rights at home.[66]

The month after Herz's self-immolation, a WSP delegation travelled to Moscow to meet representatives from North Vietnam and the National Liberation Front, and then spent three days in Hanoi, 'the first citizen-initiated contacts with the North Vietnamese' (Hershberger, *Traveling to Vietnam*, p. 3). The meeting led to a joint American and Vietnamese women's organization conference in Djakarta in July 1965, with talks with women from the Vietnam Women's Union and National Liberation Front (NLF). As Hershberger argues, the meeting brought home to the American women the violence being meted out by the Cold War abstractions of the theorists:

> The National Liberation Front cadres provided vivid descriptions of American bombing raids on villages, 'search and destroy' missions, forests and fields defoliated by American herbicides, and the deliberate creation of refugees through the pacification program. In Jakarta, the abstract arguments from Washington that appealed to a 'domino theory', or to the necessity of honoring agreements made with allies to combat communism, gave way to a depiction of the brutality that those abstractions wrought in everyday life. (p. 8)

Returning home to the United States, the delegation pressed the administration to justify the war. For them, the war was clearly a colonizing enterprise, with Operation Rolling Thunder a cynical campaign to sabotage reunification (i.e. the bombing was designed to keep Vietnam divided, sold to the public as retaliation against Communist aggression (p. 15)):

> If the Cold War was to be waged in a poor country struggling to build a nation out of the imperial delineations of the nineteenth century, then, for the travelers to Hanoi, the whole basis of the Cold War was suspect. Strip away the anticommunist rhetoric, they believed, and reveal the colonial roots of the war, and other Americans would join them in opposing Washington's military pursuit of a divided Vietnam with an American-maintained government in the South. (p. 10)

For the WSP activist, the civilian journey to Hanoi enabled a demystification of the war. Countering Washington's abstract arguments and anti-Communist rhetoric with 'vivid descriptions of American bombing' and a display of the war's colonial roots, the alliance between the Vietnamese and American women broke through the logic of the Cold War hermeneutic triangle set up by the men they saw running the war. The very divisions between Vietnam and America were revealed as fake Cold War, as fake as exaggerations of the Tonkin incident, mirroring the false division of the country at the seventeenth parallel, artificially preserved by Operation Rolling Thunder.

If McCarthy's journey to Hanoi in 1968 reprises the originative WSP delegation visit in 1965, it is also haunted by its inspiration, Herz's self-sacrifice.

Impatient with the complacency of American intellectuals about Vietnam, McCrathy saw this complacency as an 'absence of sacrifices' – without having to give anything up, unthreatened at home, '[we the intellectuals] have not withdrawn our sympathy from American power' (*The Seventeenth Degree*, p. 154). To go to Hanoi and suffer the threat of the American bombs would be to make the VC sacrifices *present* to the intellectuals of America, and thus break the link between the liberal opposition's 'habitual standards and practices' and American power. It would be to break, in effect, the unspoken alliance between American liberalism and the Cold War, so long sustained by the CCF, the New York Intellectuals, Trilling, Schlesinger, Niebuhr, Daniel Bell et al., in particular by the ex-Trotskyites (like James Burnham) who had battled so hard in the fashioning of a liberal, anti-Stalinist, Cold War consensus.

The Cold War had accustomed intellectuals to the comforts of habitual standards and practices blessed by American power, even and especially when articulating opposition to Washington. In return, the sources of power promised the intellectuals the absence of any painful sacrifices on their part. Something of the complacency of this contract can be registered in Updike's abdication of responsibility whilst still condemning the war's brutality – it is there in the clubbability of his affection for the men running the war.

The problem for McCarthy, though, was the need for a real, present sacrifice in order to shake American intellectuals out of this Cold War complacency. Might she not be reproducing the government's 'hypocritical performance' at some *other* oppositional level (*The Seventeenth Degree*, p. 161)? Might her journey to Hanoi not be taken to be an invasive, fake, self-anointing sacrifice parasitical on the real suffering of the Vietnamese? Maybe even to speak of sacrifice at all would be to enter into the Delta of Washington's systems of representation.

At all events, Hanoi had an extremely unsettling effect on her sense of self, on the liberal mind she was so proud of, even on her liberal powers to argue subtly, to see both sides to any question. In Hanoi, she underwent what she called an identity crisis, attacking her at her foundations, beginning with the grounds of her being as a child of America. Something about the landscape of North Vietnam recalled her childhood in Minnesota – the cluster-bomb-pitted roads like bumpy American roads before the war, the sense of a pioneer country, the ethnic minorities like Native Americans, the spookily similar schoolhouses – the resemblances conspiring to bring back 'buried fragments of my personal history. I was aware of a psychic upheaval, a sort of identity crisis, as when a bomb lays bare the medieval foundations of a house thought to be modern' (*The Seventeenth Degree*, pp. 203–4).

Travelling to Hanoi to suffer the bombs her own country are dropping upon it, she travels back to the foundations of her own physical body as an American citizen, but also back to a time when such a bombing campaign would have been inconceivable. But there is more: the bomb's destruction reveals more than it destroys, an Ur-Vietnamerica surviving the double suffering of history, and a psychoanalytic return of the repressed 'it' of Vietnam as underground counterculture, both conjured from the buried fragments of McCarthy's personal history, predating the fashioning of the fashionable Vassar liberal, predating American liberalism itself, as an enlightened philosophy and lifestyle based on the rational individual. The crisis has something to do with crossing America with Vietnam, in discovering the Ur-culture common to them both. Also, it may be only by imagining the war as also psychically a bombardment of the real America, as a napalming and cluster-bombing of her Minnesota, that she can begin to connect the liberal opposition and the VC. In bombing her, they bomb her home town. Thus, the Pentagon *they* are the true enemy of America and we are fighting a psychic civil war, in Minnesota as in Hanoi.

The identity crisis becomes more subtle and insinuating as it develops, however. At the Museum of War Crimes in Hanoi, after peering at the cluster-bombs, rockets and Agent Orange canisters, she is given a gift, a ring and comb made from downed US aircraft. McCarthy's ring is 'like a wedding ring', she thinks, dated and zoned to the day and place the plane was shot down. It is a ghastly present. Back at the hotel, she shuts it away in a drawer, where it begins to trouble her mind, 'making me toss at night, like an unsettled score' (*The Seventeenth Degree*, p. 211). She cannot bear to wear it; it would be a form of betrayal:

> repugnant to my nature, to my identity, whatever that is, to the souls of my ancestors, would be to be wedded for life or at least for the duration of this detestable war to a piece of aluminium wreckage from a shot-down US war plane. (p. 212)

She dreams of throwing it away, but, sounding strangely like Lady Macbeth, thinks 'there was no sea anywhere deep enough for me to drop it into. I had to keep it.' The comb she is given is easier to deal with:

> The comb, presenting no problem, a simple keepsake and rather pretty, remained openly on my bureau in the Thong Nhat with my other toilet articles. Yet I now slowly realize that I never passed it through my hair. Mysterious. I cannot explain the physical aversion, evidently subliminal, to being touched by this metal. Quite a few of the questions one does not, as an American liberal, want to put in Hanoi are addressed to oneself. (p. 212)

What is odd is that she finds her own repugnance and aversion mysterious. What could be more gruesome than sporting blood-stained technology as a fashion statement. There is little difference between the rings and the ears collected by GIs in their hunt for body count. What is perhaps more frightening is the fact that she *does* wear the ring for a few minutes to please her hosts, and that she does add the comb, so simple and pretty, to her 'other toilet articles'. Half of her is aghast at the grizzly fetishes made from dead Americans; half of her, polite and well-groomed, accepts the gory trophies as simple, pretty accessories, debutante at the War Crimes Museum.

The real source of her repugnance may lie in the growing identity crisis she is undergoing. To have travelled so far away into the enemy's country, to have recognized and adopted it so deeply as her own, to have made it a substitute Minnesota in this detestable war: the costs are beginning to tell. Only her body reacts against the technological spectacle of American death: the comb cannot pass through her *hair*. Her *fingers* cannot pass through the ring or touch the metal. Buried deep in the subliminal aversion is the fear of contamination: the wrecked metal, signifying lethal technology compacted with the dead flesh of her countrymen, also, weirdly, may have toxic-cybernetic power to kill her. Her fear of the F-111As, the certainty that they were coming to get her, is here answered by the grim wreckage of the planes, the very same planes at the subliminal level. Its metal concentrates into itself, like a fetish, the dead flesh of the airmen, and perhaps also the dead bodies of those the plane had bombed. This at least is what the strange coincidence of Robert Bly's poem 'Counting Small-Boned Bodies' suggests. Perhaps the most celebrated poem of the war, it imagines the US war administration fantasizing about miniaturizing the war dead into displayable objects on their Washington war desks. It ends with the chilling lines:

> If we could only make the bodies smaller,
> We could fit
> A body into a finger-ring, for a keepsake for ever.[67]

McCarthy's guilt goes deeper than this, though. It is the fact that the ring looks like a *wedding* ring that gives it such a taboo power to terrify. For the whole journey to Hanoi had put her husband's career in jeopardy, had forced him almost to quit his work for the government. But also her husband was in the government's pay, therefore was, at the subliminal level, her enemy's friend, her friends' enemy. Writing to James West had become a bizarrely guilty act – McCarthy remembers writing deliberately clear letters, avoiding 'any expression that could sound like code' because the 'North Vietnamese knew very well that the husband they were telegraphing in Paris was an American diplomat' (*The Seventeenth Degree*, p. 38). How twisted the syntax there – not 'my husband' but 'the husband they were telegraphing'. This guilt about her husband is allied to a related fear – her fear of acting the spy whilst in North Vietnam. She avoids asking where trucks and convoys she sees on the roads are going, because she 'did not want to feel like a spy'. Equally, she avoided 'observing my companions and attempting to study their attitudes and behavior, in the manner of a social scientist', because she felt the approach was:

dictated by courtesy to a people whose country was being invaded not only by fleets of bombers but also by reconnaissance planes, monitoring every pigsty and carp pond, while in the South, below the DMZ, North Vietnamese prisoners were being interrogated, their documents, little poems, and diaries read and studied by military intelligence and US political scientists, hopeful of penetrating the medulla of North Vietnamese resistance to find evidence of homesickness, disillusion, war fatigue. (p. 225)

The terrible gaze of the Eye of God is an act of surveillance too, technological twin to the prying Uncle Sams of counterinsurgency rifling through the prisoner of war's personal effects: both are forms of invasion. McCarthy sacrifices her reporter's eyes because they must not resemble the American military gaze. But also, her fear of looking the spy allied with the fact she doctors her letters to her husband seems, again at the level below the threshold of consciousness, in the body zone of aversion and repugnance, to identify him potentially with the Pentagon's snoops and spooks. At the very least, she is monitoring her own marriage out of *courtesy* to the North Vietnamese, acknowledging their identification of James West with the Western power in the sky. If the men running the war were all 'divorced or separated from their wives by more than distance', then McCarthy, too, was prepared to sacrifice those bonds.

More distressing is the realization that the very act of coming to Hanoi, its sacrificial logic, may have been concocted *against* James West. To enter the triangle and die under the bombs would demand a sacrifice of her life, perhaps, but in truth, as she discovered in her fear and trembling at the prospect of the F-111As by the Mekong, she was prepared to sacrifice her feelings for Jim rather than be seen as running away. There on the Mekong, at the heart of the Delta, waiting to fly to Indian country from in-country, she had wracked her body with remorse over the act:

> There was not the slightest doubt in my mind that I was going to my death. The certainty of that had been established as guilt fed apprehension. What I saw was that I had no right to die: my stupid, silly life did not belong to me alone; it was a joint account. Personally (I thought), I no longer cared whether I got killed; it would almost be a relief. I was only agonizing on Jim's behalf. Was this truthful or not? Then, at any rate, I was sure it was. Today, I can wonder whether remorse may not have been the form physical fear was taking in me. But it was remorse in a pure state that I felt. And it was useless to dream now of expiation, atonement: even if by a miracle I escaped death, I had probably killed his love for me. (*The Seventeenth Degree*, p. 35)

The self-sacrifice she was moving towards, because it was calqued on the self-anointing immolation of Herz and Morrison, and because those acts were shaped by the sacrificial logic of Operation Rolling Thunder, must mean that *another* be sacrificed in her stead. At the physical level of fear in the body, it is Jim West's love which must be 'killed' and sacrificed, just as little Emily was to be the symbolic witness-substitute in her father's public suicide. Indeed, in the awful twisted arguments the Vietnam War so often generated, on all sides, it is precisely *because* her death would be his love's death that she must be punished and killed:

> How had I not seen this before? I was a cruel, selfish woman. He had left his family for me. I had not urged it but I had consented. If I got killed, he would never forgive me. And that was *why* I was going to be killed, to show me that my acts were consequent. (pp. 34–5)

According to the rationale of the sacrificial code, it is because you desire to sacrifice another in your place that you deserve to die: acceptance of this is the ultimate sacrifice. The Mekong panic had been pricked into action within her body by the sight of the bombers in the newspaper: there, as clearly as such a tortuous set of psychic facts allows, is the real culprit. The whole war was an act of sacrifice by proxy: the Americans urging the South Vietnamese to accept their sacrificial terms whilst the bombs fell on their countrymen. McCarthy had entered the Delta's force-field of fear and fake self-sacrifice. And it is then that the revelation comes:

> It occurs to me now that you cannot embark on what you think is a good deed without sacrificing someone else to it. Someone close to you, naturally. Or something equally close – an idea, a principle. Good deeds are Molochs. I cannot recall a single instance of pure *self*-sacrifice in my entire history. [. . .] Possibly self-sacrifice, by its very nature, since the self has many extensions, includes the willingness to sacrifice your nearest and dearest. (p. 37)

In analysing the Byzantine self-deception affecting her marriage, McCarthy stumbles on one of the meanings of the war. And as the war was being waged by single men, and as it involved the killing of innocents, like Captain Medina shooting the defenceless village-woman through the head at My Lai, the terms of fake self-sacrifice preached by Washington and urged upon the ARVN and 'pacified' villagers could also be found infiltrating the relationships between men and women, husbands and wives. It is the culmination of the inward logic of the Cold War, where two rival forces combine to act against the 'the mass "in between"', a scapegoat figure they can elect: the trick being that the scapegoat must be coerced into believing she must die. She must *choose* to die. Or rather she may choose who must die in her stead, thus mimicking the fake self-sacrifice of the men in power – therein lies her Cold War freedom. And as McCarthy found, it was in the realization of the horror of this, as when contemplating wearing the wrecked F-111A wedding ring, that a real suicidal remorse is likely to set in, deep in the body zone under sacrifice.

There is no good deed in a dirty war: her self-sacrifice breaks down into a destruction of her marriage. To be 'wedded for life or at least for the duration of this detestable war to a piece of aluminium wreckage from a shot-down US war plane' is to contemplate being wedded for life to a government official her new country must treat as a spy and invader. In the inward narrative of her journey to Hanoi is the story of her identification of James West with the enemies of her country in the White House, the Pentagon and Congress, of her suppressed wish symbolically to kill off his love for her on the altar of her activism. Guilt about this proxy death-wish leaks into her horror at the VC trophy – the dead pilot fused into the plane-metal fetish is her husband as ideological fantasy locked into the dangerous token of their war-broken marriage.

Of crucial importance, though, is McCarthy's refusal to wear the ring of fake self-sacrifice. However compromised by indecision and political bad faith the gesture of refusal may be, it still *counts as one*. For McCarthy had understood the ways the code of proxy sacrifice was being generated by fear of her nation's technology, firepower, invasive Eye of God surveillance allied with Uncle Sam's insinuatingly liberal propaganda. She had learned the deep paranoia and psychosis generated by that fear beside the Mekong in the Delta and on the edge of the jungle by the Siem Reap river. She had learned its *divisiveness*, how it divided her into Westerner and witness, loving wife and husband-killer, just as it divided Vietnam with its bombs. It is because she recognized this that she chose to sacrifice something else as a proxy in her own strike for peace. What she chose to sacrifice was not a dream of her husband's love, nor a child, principle or idea, nor another symbolic maiden on the altar, but the very liberal selfhood her country had co-opted to its war effort in its vile pacification and counterinsurgency programmes.

She came to North Vietnam with this liberal point of view, 'the confidence of the American who knows himself to be fair-minded, able to see both sides, disinterested, objective, et cetera, as compared to the single-minded people he is about to visit' (*The Seventeenth Degree*, p. 311). In other words, the liberal point of view, the hovering subject position above the seventeenth parallel, seeing both sides like the Janus of the war machine, is implicitly an 'assurance of superiority, not personal but generic' over the Vietnamese she had come to support. The liberal virtues go back a long way in America, are part of the cultural material being thrown up by the war, as fossil remains of the Ur-America:

> they are the fossil remains of the old America, detached by an ocean from the quarrels of Europe, having no colonial interests compared to the Great Powers, a permanent outsider and hence fitted to judge and bear witness. (p. 311)

But here in Vietnam, the very virtues she boasted of as a reliable novelist-witness, being able to 'judge, compare, and report back', could not work in a situation where the United States was acting out of colonial interests, in mimicry of the Great Powers. Indeed, modernization theory, the refashioning of Third World societies into modern states as bulwarks against Communist advances, was one of 'the classic protocols of Cold War liberalism', 'a civil religion championed by liberal cold warriors', as Jonathan Nashel has shown (Nashel, 'The Road to Vietnam', pp. 132, 134). McCarthy began to turn against her generic liberal assumptions: 'I found my claim to be a disinterested party starting not exactly to disappear, but to shrink from showing itself, as if ashamed' (*The Seventeenth Degree*, p. 312).

The identity crisis McCarthy suffered was to wake up from the paranoid dream of the double sufferer of history. It was to recognize that the artificial division of the world and the imagination into the Cold War polarities had had a corrupting effect on the American liberal values she had lived by since Minnesota. The polarizing, paranoid vision had turned the capacity to judge and compare into a lifeless lack of commitment. That lack of commitment had been generated by the Cold War. For her generation, 'Stalinism', she writes, 'which had to be opposed, produced the so-called non-Communist Left, not a movement, not even a sect, but a preference, a political taste shared by an age group resembling a veteran's organization, which had last seen action during the Spanish Civil War' (*The Seventeenth Degree*, p. 313). But since this brand of radicalism had 'no appeal for the masses', the non-Communist left 'had no alternative but to be "believing" socialists and practicing members of capitalist society' (p. 313). It was the struggle against Stalin which had turned her generation into Cold War liberals, with two sides within each intellectual, capitalist and socialist, dedicated to nothing but personal salvation and individual peace of mind (pp. 316–17). Political thinking was reduced to a similarly self-cancelling combination of a 'dream of a New Jerusalem' and 'desert-island fantasies' (pp. 313–14). The net effect was that, as a Cold War liberal, potentially merely a 'sample of American society', since made up of so many conflicting and divisive ideological habits, tastes and preferences, 'I had no subjectivity at all' (p. 315).

The journey to Hanoi, finally, precipitated this new and radical form of sacrifice: the sacrifice of the self-cancellingly divisive pseudo-subjectivity of the NCL Cold War liberal. To understand Hanoi outside the iron triangle of the self-anointing liberal-totalitarian rhetoric of fake self-sacrifice meant taking sides against the Janus-sided liberal contradictions: 'for you ought not to be two people, one downstairs, listening and nodding, and the other scribbling in your room' (*The Seventeenth Degree*, p. 316). Yet even this refusal to split according to liberal ideals of tolerance and consensus has its own cost. Maybe, just maybe, McCarthy flew to Hanoi not to take a stand, but to help stop the war so that she could go back to enjoy her 'normal pursuits' (p. 317). Perhaps the whole peace initiative betrays a deep selfishness: 'I have come to recognize that I went chiefly for my own peace of mind' (p. 317). The shame at the very thought, she acknowledges, has changed her for ever, like some roughly discovered, ineradicable curse inside the liberal body and mind: 'Nothing will be the same again, if only because of the awful self-recognition, including this one, the war has enforced' (p. 317).

Nevertheless, to take sides against the sides imposed by the American invasion was to sacrifice liberal disinterestedness in the name of basic human, Vietnamerican justice. The American military command 'demands that the population take sides; anybody who remains in a hamlet designated Viet Cong is liable to execution from the air' (*The Seventeenth Degree*, p. 321). That demand is so brutal, McCarthy found, because 'in my opinion the Americans do not *have* a side in this war, that is, do not have an excuse, surely not that of ignorance. This war is no *Antigone*, where both Antigone and her uncle Creon are right according to their lights' (p. 276). To opt to support the North Vietnamese was not to choose Communism over democracy, to choose one totalitarian regime over another: it was simply to choose to refuse the Cold War terms being imposed upon the Third World, and to opt out of the crudely self-complacent liberal double-headedness which was at such evil work in the Delta and beyond.

To refuse to wear the ring was also to refuse to rescind all agency in the war culture, to refuse to sacrifice all self along with the abandonment of the fake liberal Janus identity – she may, as a liberal, have no subjectivity at all, yet she is still 'aware of a subject, an "I", asserting itself from time to time, in protest or scruple, a subject I did not dislike' (*The Seventeenth Degree*, p. 315). That 'I' discovered after the sacrifice of the liberal cogito to the twin powers in the Delta is no longer their creature, their fantasy construct, their paranoid plaything and victim, but a decolonized subjectivity, rational, vocal, unswayed. And most important of all, it is not a subject huddled deep in the writer's vitals, a thing of shred and patches of texts in the guts of culture. It is not the deep image conjured by the sudden drive inward, as with Bly's self-anointing protest, nor is it the self-savouring emulation of some hypothetical dark force within, as in Dean Rusk's political paranoia. It is free of the cold civil war haunting the liberal opposition at home, as it is disengaged from the tumult of sacrificial bloodletting unleashed on bodies and imaginations in Vietnam. It is also untainted by the double-dealing of the Janus-faced male Cold Warrior/peace protestor, as with the psy-war mole within the RAND corporation, Daniel Ellsberg. What McCarthy found with the turn against her liberal disinterestedness and judgement was women's collective power against the war, the power of the WSP *without* the sacrificial logic that had burned Alice Herz alive. It was also a healing force and subjectivity that would *not* treat her husband as phantom enemy, but would choose to work alongside him in ventures against the despicable war, in an act of recuperation of the bonds between men and women which Cold War misogyny had nearly destroyed.

In many primitive rituals of sacrifice, the priest must perform haruspicy, or the examination of the entrails of the victim, known as the *exta*, to divine the future and reconcile the people with the impersonal powers.[68] In the sacrificial ritual of Vietnam as fantasized 'it', the writer is tempted to sacrifice herself to the Uncle Sam–Eye of God by undergoing self-victimizing and suicidal haruspical processes, a self-anointing and self-annihilating ritual of guilt and paranoia 'spoken' by her alienated, deep and inward guts. The Cold War had corrupted the writer's sudden drive inward into a self-victimizing comedy of blank sacrifice of the *exta*-tic symptoms of its war culture. McCarthy's refusal to wear the war's ring of lethal technology is a refusal to go under in this way. It challenges the passivity of the drive inward and the display of symptomatic *exta*, and proposes a single-minded, self-critical but not self-wounding, harshly satirical and still rational voice of dissent, designed to join a chorus of *public* protest, from the WSP to her husband in Paris, against the war, in a redemptive strike for peace. Instead of the fake Third Force in the fictive power triangle of the Pentagon's dream of the Delta, and against the recolonizing substitution of the United States for the old colonial powers in the Third World, this was a strike for peace energized by a real third world force, an alliance of non-aligned women working for both Vietnam and the Ur-America of revolutionary democracy. In her strike for peace, McCarthy broke through the iron triangle of that paranoia, refused the ring of the warfare state's fake proxy sacrifice and revealed to the world the structures, language and systems of the two men of power, with their Pharisee virtue and their brutal war games, hot and cold.

Reading McCarthy's *The Seventeenth Degree* and Greene's *The Quiet American* together reveals remarkable coincidental material. Both texts see Vietnam as the breaking point for the ideal of liberal objective reporting: Fowler is forced to take sides, abandoning even the radical neutrality of Christian sufferance; McCarthy sacrifices her liberal Cartesian ego in support of the 'Minnesotan' VC. Both come to realize there are no real sides to the Cold War at the level of the citizen imagination, only deep paranoid dreams of selfish peace of mind within state and subject: McCarthy fears her act of protest was simply a way of stopping the 'brutal, brutish onslaught' so that she could return to her quiet intellectual life; Fowler's compassion is a screen for the 'peace of mind' which silences the cry from the tower. Both texts ponder the true nature of the war: for Greene, it is a war fought between brothers for a sexual-economic fiction substituting for the women being killed; for McCarthy, it is a projection of America's cold civil war, visible in the monstrous Janus of the war machine, part Eye of God, part Uncle Sam, feeding off victims censored by propaganda. Both McCarthy and Greene enact something of a crisis of identity through traumatic journeys to Saigon and Hanoi, including dark imagining of violence at the interzones between the Cold War forces. And both seek out the body consciousness of the wars in Indochina, consciousness expressed *exta*-tically in Bly's longing 'to abase ourselves' in sacrificial rituals within triangles, the love triangle of Greene's Freudian plots, and the Iron Triangle/Mekong Delta of Vietnam's endgame for McCarthy.

The reason the two texts so closely mirror each other is obscure and difficult, not simply a matter of an abstract coincidence of feeling about liberal politics in an atrocious foreign war. The middle term is Malaya and the indebtedness of the Americans to British counterinsurgency. If Greene/Fowler and McCarthy feel there might be some original dark mistake they must pay for in Vietnam, perhaps it is Malaya, not My Lai, which needs to be atoned for, the propaganda drive that gave the US the mode and means of intervention. McCarthy was clearly unaware of the British connection – she saw pacification, as instanced in the evolution of the Staley Plan through Rural Construction to Revolutionary Development, as predominantly a French idea, the US imitating the agrovilles of the Diem regime and Algerian concentration camp policy. But for the Americans, the real experts were not the French but the British, and the example was not Algeria but Malaya. Operation Cedar Falls, the Strategic Hamlets programme and camps such as Phu Cuong were explicitly modelled on Malaya's New Villages. The Staley Plan had been developed with them in mind. Why? Because the British had done it. They had successfully steered the colony through to independence whilst crushing the Communist insurgency, paving the way for a successful, post-independence, informal, trade empire.

Sir Robert Thompson, administrator in the British colonial administration during the Emergency, deputy secretary and then secretary of defence in the late 1950s (1957–61), was considered an expert in counterinsurgency and was invited over by the US as head of the British Advisory Mission to South Vietnam. It was Thompson who was most influential, in the Kennedy administration and beyond, in advising the Americans how to combine tough police control and political reform through pacification and use of new villages of the Malayan kind. As Emergency historian Deery puts it: 'US army officers attended the jungle-warfare training school in Johore; the "hearts and minds" campaign was translated into that ugly euphemism, "pacification"; and "strategic hamlets" dotted the South Vietnamese countryside in imitation of the Malayan "New Villages".'[69] Thompson's advisory mission supervised the Strategic Hamlet programme, initiated in South Vietnam in April 1962. Within two years, a staggering 12,000 Strategic Hamlets had been built.

The influence of Malaya on American thinking survived the change of administration. Harold K. Johnson's influential Program for the Pacification and Long-Term Development of South Vietnam (PROVN) report of 1965, which changed Westmoreland's attitudes towards pacification, was based on his partnership, at Fort Leavenworth, with another British expert in Malayan counterinsurgency, Colonel Richard Clutterbuck.[70] Clutterbuck's 1966 book on the explicit lessons to be learnt from Malaya for use in Vietnam, *The Long Long War: Counterinsurgency in Malaya and Vietnam*,[71] as well as Robert Thompson's *Defeating Communist Insurgency*, also 1966, were persuasive in shoring up support for PROVN.

Clutterbuck argued that the Briggs Plan had to be followed through 'to dig out the roots of subversion and guerrilla Communism' (*The Long Long War*, p. 9). The Malayan example could show why the pacification programme in Vietnam between 1957 and 1963 had failed.[72] It could also show the way towards a successful pacification programme – Clutterbuck assumes, with good reason, that the new 1965 policy (for 300 hamlets, not the unmanageable 12,000) is based on sounder analysis of the Malayan example: 'a painstaking intelligence operation to identify Viet Cong agents and sympathizers, establishment of local government with protection that can be sustained, and tangible social improvements, particularly in health and medical care' (p. 75). Thus was born Uncle Sam with candy in his pocket and projects up his sleeve. The ultimate goal to be achieved is the informal trade empire:

> British-owned plantations, mines, and businesses continue to operate; British capital continues to flow into the country. There seems to be no reason why this should not continue to the benefit of both sides, as it has in India, where there now more British people living than before independence was granted. (p. 148)

If Clutterbuck and Thompson were helpful for PROVN, so PROVN finally moved the administration's policy away from blind trust in bombardment and search-and-destroy to centring the war on hearts and minds in the villages: 'At no time should US-FW [Free World] combat operations shift the American focus of support from the true point of decision in Vietnam – the villages.'[73] Malaya is the secret root cause of the shift in policy emphasis which so staggered McCarthy: that the war in Vietnam was now *exclusively* justified according to Revolutionary Development.

Clutterbuck not only recommends many of the propaganda innovations which Hugh Greene did so much to introduce into Malaya: use of SEPs, of broadcast propaganda and leaflet drops, including voice aircraft,[74] especially since the MACV, like the British Malaya Authority, enjoyed, in Clutterbuck's words, 'monopoly of air power' (Clutterbuck, *The Long Long War*, p. 156). He particularly praises the ex-Communist Malayan Chinese head of psychological-warfare, C.C. Too, a man recruited by Hugh Greene (p. 106). The perceived success of the British SEP policy led directly to the CIA's Chieu Hoi or Open Arms amnesty programme, so condemned by McCarthy.

But there is a darker story yet, and it has to do with the other story of counterinsurgency measures in Malaya which served as example in Vietnam.

In a chapter entitled 'Air Support', Clutterbuck recommends use of helicopter patrols and troop-carrying helicopters, for rapid deployment in difficult jungle as transport rather than tactical devices (Clutterbuck, *The Long Long War*, pp. 167–8). They would also be useful for clearing jungle. Clutterbuck urges the example of Emergency starvation measures against enemy cultivation, also potentially for removing enemy cover:

> Helicopters, Pioneers, and the De Havilland Beavers were used for spraying weed-killer onto enemy cultivations. One limitation, however, was that sprayed (as opposed to injected) weed-killer works only through the leaves; the guerrillas were quick to pick off those affected, leaving the roots intact.
>
> Defoliation to deny the enemy cover was not done in Malaya by air spraying. The only areas where this could have been both practical and effective were the likely ambush sites along the roads; but that was more effectively done by hand; and there were always more urgent demands for aircraft. (p. 160)

Though Clutterbuck is against futile bombing of the jungle without proper, pinpoint intelligence on the ground, his reason for this is the cover provided by the jungle itself. All in all, the only conclusion would be to find a weed-killer which would affect the roots of the enemy's plants, and to find a defoliant which would remove cover to create a clean slate for the bombers, once the local population had been resettled. Malaya, in other words, provided the rationale for deployment of 2,4,5-T (Tetrachlorodibenzodioxin), otherwise known as Agent Orange.

ICI had supplied the defoliants used in Malaya. Monsanto supplied the most effective dioxin-based Agent Orange for Operation Ranch Hand defoliation programmes, using a formula developed from British weed-killer example. In March 2005, Judge Weinstein used the British example to help dismiss the claims of war veterans exposed to Agent Orange in their suit against the chemical companies that had supplied it.[75] Weinstein's report contains the following statements:

> The Department of Defense's Advanced Research Project Agency's ("ARPA") Project Agile was instrumental in the United States' development of herbicides as a military weapon, an undertaking inspired by the British use of 2,4,5-T to destroy jungle-grown crops during the insurgency in Malaya.[76]

The first tests took place in 1959, at Camp Drum, New York, using Agent Purple (a 50: 50 mixture of 2,4-D and 2,4,5-T). The use of Agents Orange, Purple, Pink and Blue was authorized by Kennedy on specific advice from secretary of state Dean Rusk in November 1961. In Weinstein's words:

The United States considered British precedent in deciding that the use of defoliants was a legally accepted tactic of war. Secretary of State Dean Rusk advised President John F. Kennedy that herbicide use in Vietnam would be lawful, because '[p]recedent has been established by the British . . . in Malaya in their use of helicopters for destroying crops by chemical spraying.'[77]

From August to December 1961, the US tested in South Vietnam using dinoxol and trinoxol. Again, Kennedy needed reassurance, this time from McNamara, on the use of herbicides to destroy crops ('food-denial' the euphemism): 'This would be the first trial of both the strategic hamlet concept and the complemental food-denial operations since the successful campaign in Malaya', McNamara told the president in a secret memo in August 1962.[78] The first major herbicide shipment arrived in RVN in January 1962; defoliation targets were sprayed during September and October 1962 (Agent Purple); crop destruction targets were sprayed in November 1962 (Agent Blue; Weinstein, 'Agent Orange Liability Litigation', p. 20).

Not only did Malaya provide the concept, methodology, justification and precedent for the use of Agent Orange et al., but the delivery of the herbicides mimicked the voice aircraft and leaflet drops developed by Hugh Greene and subsequent EIS personnel. Indeed, the C-47 sprayings in early 1962 accompanied them, as a Ranch Hand veteran recalls: 'During the early spray missions, Air Commando C-47 [. . .] preceded the spray missions by dropping thousands of leaflets, and conducting Vietnamese language voice broadcasts to the villages below. The communications explained to the population what the defoliant flights were, and why they were necessary.'[79] Nearly 46 million litres of Agent Orange were sprayed on Vietnam between 1965 and 1970. In the 20,000 sorties taken by the Leaf Killers, herbicides were sprayed directly onto 3,000 of Vietnam's 20,000 hamlets, affecting between 2 million and 4 million Vietnamese.

The uncanny feeling of horror produced by Vietnam has a great deal to do with the evil poison of Agent Orange, and its traces can be felt in the fetish objects of terror imagined by Graham Greene and McCarthy. Greene proleptically imagines the agent with this strange MacGuffin, the plastic substance Diolacton used by the lunatic Third Force encouraged by Pyle's Lansdale-style secret service. The term reminds Fowler of condensed milk, and Mr Heng agrees:

> 'It has something in common with milk.' Mr. Heng shone his torch inside the drum. A little white powder lay like dust on the bottom. 'It is one of the American plastics,' he said.
>   'I heard a rumour that Pyle was importing plastics for toys.' [. . .]
>   'Not for toys,' Mr. Heng said. (*The Quiet American*, p. 142)

The relation of Diolacton to milk and toys seals its associations with mothers and children, the key psy-op target of the bomb, as the *pietà* in the square proves. It is a 'concave object like a stick of celery which glistened chromium in the light of the torch' (p. 141), as though a deformation of vegetable nature by technology. Whether Greene knew about 2,4,5-T and its use in Malaya or not,[80] this is an astonishing proleptic imagining of Agent Orange – its most crippling effects are birth defects, the dioxin contamination (how close to Diolacton!) leading to deformed foetuses, spina bifida in children, cancer, lower IQ and more emotional problems for children, and spontaneous abortions and birth defects if the mother was exposed. One of the major routes of human exposure is through ingestion of contaminated dairy products, or mother's milk. The man-made contaminant mimics human hormones in the body responsible for reproduction and development, i.e. *pretends to be natural*. Greene's concave object, chromium stick of celery, reads eerily like an exposed canister of something unspeakable. In the novel Diolacton comes from a drum; Agent Orange was stored in 55-gallon drums.

In its crossing of lethal technology with the natural, the chromium celery looks forward to the horrific ring of airplane metal McCarthy refuses to wear. Symbol of the death from the sky, fusing blood and toxic machine, related in McCarthy's mind and body to the USAF's Eye of God ('all will be razed, charred, defoliated by that terrible, searching gaze'), the ring is a nightmare, abject scrap of debris from her own country's war machine, aimed specifically at damaging her insides, her relations with men, her bond with her husband, her powers to conceive and create: it is a dream of contaminant dioxin, Agent Orange as mother-and-child killer. The ring uncannily summons from her culture's political unconscious the two benzene rings of dioxin, connected by two oxygen atoms, the natural processes of bonding in love twisted by this double-ringed agent, hormone masquerader, toxic destroyer of the bodies it invades.

The long long war of the Cold War came full circle, like the rings of dioxin, in the fields of Vietnam – the dream of contamination in devastated Vienna returned when America learned from Britain the Janus-faced lessons of counterinsurgency. Nabokov's feeling for the plight of mothers and daughters in the nuclear heartland of the US, Plath's fears of contaminated mothers and deep genetic damage by the Cold War sex war, Herbst's suicidal dream of *Pharmakos* as remedy/poison drug come together in the paranoid terror felt by Greene and McCarthy at the unconscious effects of Agent Orange in the body, in the air, and in the jungle. The hounding of innocents intuited by the writers in this book – John Herrmann's vision of the burning of the *Pharmakos*, Nabokov on the death of Lolita, Ginsberg and his mother's death – comes together in the women and child victims of the wars in Indochina, turning on the napalm-inflected self-immolation of Alice Herz. It is a bleak and defoliated vision, but shot through, none the less, with resistance – the brave and necessary resistance of those who refuse to come to the sacrifice, the women who struck for peace.

NOTES

1. His experiences in Germany overseeing radio communications had made him anti-Communist very early on. For the relations between the BBC and the Cold War, cf. Rawnsley, 'The BBC External Services and the Hungarian Uprising, 1956', in Rawnsley, *Cold-War Propaganda in the 1950s*, pp. 165–81.
2. Kaplan, 'Britain's Asian Cold War: Malaya'.
3. Quoted in Kaplan, 'Britain's Asian Cold War: Malaya', p. 202.
4. Its founding director was the Foreign Office undersecretary Christopher Mayhew, who had served in Phantom (Phantom GHQ Liaison Regiment) and the Ministry of Economic Warfare during the war.
5. The secrecy practiced by the IRD had little to do with the material they disseminated – the documents circulated were produced for public consumption. The real IRD secret was the IRD itself. The ground rules it insisted upon with those receiving its information were simple, as Australian historian Philip Deery found, looking at instructions in IRD correspondence: 'all IRD "productions" must remain non-attributable; none of them could carry any printer's name, mark or label to indicate their official origin; and no recipient, even if trusted and a "person of influence", must be "aware where you got them from" or refer to them publicly by title or pass them on to anyone' (Deery, 'Covert Propaganda and the Cold War', p. 614).
6. Orwell did not think his list a betrayal in any way; he only feared the list might be libellous. Kirwan did not think it constituted betrayal, since having your name on the list merely meant that you would not be asked to do propaganda for the government. Cf. Garton Ash, 'Orwell's List'.
7. The IRD was first stationed at Carlton House Terrace, then at Riverwalk House in the mid-1950s. Riverwalk now houses the Government Office for London.
8. Kaplan, 'Britain's Asian Cold War: Malaya', p. 202. Cf. also Lee, *Outposts of Empire*.
9. The Marshall Plan was the thinly disguised model for the 1951 Colombo Plan (for Cooperative Economic Development in South and Southeast Asia) – pitched by the UK and its Commonwealth partners as essential anti-Communist nation-building aid in the region in the name of containment.
10. Joseph Smith, *The Cold War*, p. 55.
11. Wint, *The British in Asia*, p. 217.
12. Quoted in Kaplan, 'Britain's Asian Cold War: Malaya', p. 201.
13. Quoted in Joseph Smith, *The Cold War*, p. 71.
14. Cf. Newsinger, 'Counterrevolution: The Malayan Example'.
15. Harper, *The End of Empire and the Making of Malaya*, p. 154.
16. Sherry, *The Life of Graham Greene*, vol. 2, p. 344.
17. Hugh Greene, 'Report on Emergency Information Services'. Some of the report is quoted in Carruthers, *Winning Hearts and Minds*, p. 94, and it is extensively discussed by Ramakrishna in his excellent book *Emergency Propaganda*.
18. Flight Lieutenant A.F. Deery, 'Psychological Warfare in Malaya' c. 1955, at www.psywar.org/pdf_malaya.pdf, accessed 8 December 2008.
19. Hugh Greene, 'Report on Emergency Information Services', p. 5.
20. *The Quiet American*, p. 93. Cf. Sherry, *The Life of Graham Greene*, vol. 2, p. 357. I am grateful to the following articles for their analysis of *The Quiet American*:

Bonney, 'Politics, Perception, and Gender in Conrad's *Lord Jim* and Greene's *The Quiet American*'; Bushnell, 'Paying for the Damage'; Kerr, '*The Quiet American* and the Novel'; and Whitfield, 'Limited Engagement'.

21. Graham Greene, *Ways of Escape*, p.146. Greene transferred the *Life* piece verbatim into the memoir.

22. Graham Greene, 'Indo-China: France's Crown of Thorns', in *Reflections*, p. 129. First published in *Paris Match*, 12 July 1952.

23. *Don Juan*, canto 1, stanza 132 – it follows a stanza about America as the source of disease.

24. Hugh Greene never explicitly involved himself in black propaganda (what the Americans referred to as 'morale operations') in Malaya – but his report indicates that he was implicated. An enigmatic sentence in his report, buried between details of news and broadcasting propaganda and assessment of enemy reactions to that propaganda, simply reads: '"Black" propaganda. No account of "black propaganda is given in this report' ('Report on Emergency Information Services', p. 9).

25. Pyle's first name, Alden, which Fowler cannot bring himself to use when talking to Phuong (for reasons he cannot quite understand, cf. p. 210), means 'old friend'.

26. McCarthy, *The Seventeenth Degree*, p. 10. I am indebted to the following for the background to McCarthy's work on Vietnam: Abrams, *Mary McCarthy*; Brightman, *Writing Dangerously*; Stwertka and Viscusi, *Twenty-Four Ways of Looking at Mary McCarthy*; and Gordon O. Taylor, 'Cast a Cold "I": Mary McCarthy on Vietnam'.

27. The immolations launched the Buddhist Struggle Movement against Diem's government in 1963. Reprisals against pagodas and priests by Diem's brother Nhu precipitated the coup against Diem.

28. Quoted in Hershberger, *Traveling to Vietnam*, p. 2. Cf. also Swerdlow, *Women Strike for Peace*.

29. *New York Times*, 18 March 1965, quoted in www.angelfire.com/nb/protest/amer. html. The North Vietnamese were moved to name a Hanoi street after her, and ordered a night-long vigil.

30. Cf. Hendrickson's *The Living and the Dead*. Seven days later, on 9 November 1965, Roger LaPorte poured petrol over himself and set himself alight in front of the UN.

31. Morrison Welsh, 'Norman Morrison', p. 4.

32. Interview with the *Charlotte Observer*, 11 April 2003, www.charlotte.com/mld/ charlotte/living/5612485.htm?1c, accessed 8 May 2004.

33. The march was organized by SANE (Committee for a Sane Nuclear Policy) and was designed to mobilize moderate, respectable and responsible opposition to the war in Washington – roughly 35,000 protestors turned up on the day.

34. Bly, *The Light Around the Body*, p. 34.

35. As Bly put it in a 1998 PBS interview: 'The roots of male violence obviously go back to maybe four hundred thousand years of killing animals. And, so in the beginning, men were asked to be violent. And after that, as you know, after the hunter time, then people went into agriculture and the cities began to form. Then there was a surplus of grain and then neighboring people come to steal their grain. And they think there was no real warfare in the hunter-gatherer groups. But once the cities were formed, there was violence. So we have that in our bodies' (interview, www. pbs.org/kued/nosafeplace/interv/bly.html, accessed 28 August 2008).

36. Bly, 'Leaping Up into Political Poetry: An Essay', in *Talking All Morning*, p. 98. First published in 1970. For Bly, 'the political poem comes out of the deepest privacy' (*Talking All Morning*, p. 99).

37. Cf. Rowe, 'Eyewitness'.

38. Cf. Segals' *The Great Power Triangle* and Raju G.C. Thomas's *The Great Power Triangle and Asian Security*.
39. Aldrich, Rawnsley and Rawnsley, *The Clandestine Cold War in Asia*, p. 1.
40. Quoted in Fontaine, *History of the Cold War*, p. 410.
41. Other deltas in Vietnam included the so-called Delta Tango, or Designated Targets: areas chosen by day for attack at night. Also in 1966–7, the special forces operation, Project Delta, consisted of deep infiltration teams, moving into VC sanctuaries in the Delta, working by stealth and imitation of the VC guerrilla tactics, in perfect mimicry of the enemy.
42. Raskin and Fall, *The Vietnam Reader*, p. 36.
43. Fulbright, *The Vietnam Hearings*, p. 5.
44. Cf. also Dean, *Imperial Brotherhood*, p. 243.
45. Built in 1962, King Norodom Sihanouk's guesthouse in Siem Reap is now the hotel Amansara.
46. Quoted in Fontaine, *History of the Cold War*, p. 410.
47. Bayon has fifty-four towers with four enormous faces on all four of their sides, making 216 faces in all – they look like smiling Buddhas with their eyes closed, but actually represent Lokesvara, a Bodhisattva from Mahayana Buddhism, a holy saviour or future Buddha deity who will sacrifice Nirvana for the enlightenment and liberation of his people.
48. McCarthy, 'Characters in Fiction', *On the Contrary*, p. 285.
49. Announced at the Honolulu Conference of February 1966 and reiterated after the Guam conference of March 1967.
50. 'Letters to Alicia', *Newsday*, 3 December 1966–20 May 1967. Alicia Patterson was the publisher of *Newsday*.
51. For an example of the two men at work, cf. Lieutenant General John H. Hay, *Tactical and Materiel Innovations*.
52. A FOR (Fellowship of Reconciliation) peace delegation travelled in July 1965 to Saigon, led by Alfred Hassler, and met Buddhist monk and poet activist Thich Nhat Hanh, who told them 'The right hand of your charity cannot undo the left hand of your bombing' (Hershberger, *Traveling to Vietnam*, p. 21).
53. JUSPAO was the agency which coordinated psychological and information programmes in South Vietnam.
54. Cf. CIA Intelligence weekly report, 'Situation in South Vietnam', 16 January–22 January 1967 (23 January 1967, no. 0334/67) – Declassified Documents Series 1993-002456. Lyndon Baines Johnson Library, available online through the University of Saskatchewan Library website, http://library.usask.ca/vietnam/index.php?state=view&id=890.
55. www.nytimes.com/books/97/04/06/lifetimes/updike-v-vietnam.html, accessed 9 December 2008. Updike was against the war on utilitarian grounds: it wasn't helping the South Vietnamese.
56. Top Secret memo, 'Bombing Strategy Options for the Rest of 1967', 9 May 1967. LBJ Library. Declassified Documents Series 1984-000810, p. 11, www.vietnam.ttu.edu/star/images/024/0240617005.pdf, accessed 9 December 2008.
57. Scheme summarized in a memo for Bundy from Gordon Chase, 'A High-Level Look at the Cold War', 18 June 1963. Declassified Documents Series 1985:001434.
58. 'Some Prospects and Problems in Vietnam', 15 February 1968, p. 1, www.ellsberg.net/writing/Prospects.pdf, accessed 5 October 2006.
59. Sheehan analysed the 2.5-million-word papers in terms of administration commitments, or 'points of escalation' (Ellsberg's own term; Ellsberg, *Secrets*, p. 193).
60. Ellsberg was one of the Pentagon Papers team, specializing in the 1961 decision by Kennedy to send advisers.

61. The death toll outstrips the total number of Americans who ever served in Vietnam (roughly 3.5 million), and does not cover the hundreds of thousands who have died and are still suffering from the Agent Blue and Orange sprayed by the 'Leaf Killers' from their C-123 Dumbos. US forces sprayed an estimated 20 million gallons of herbicides on Vietnam between 1962 and 1971 to deny food and jungle cover to the VC – Vietnam today has 12 peace villages and 500 clinics to help its three million Agent Orange victims (Tran, 'Agent Orange Victims Bring Lawsuit in US').

62. RAND document: 'On Pacification: Comments by Thai and Ellsberg. Working Notes on Vietnam No. 6', July 1969. The comments quoted are dated October 1967. www.ellsberg.net/writing/Pacification.pdf, accessed 5 October 2006.

63. Cf. Fitzgerald, *Fire in the Lake*, and Michael McClintock, 'Edward Geary Lansdale and the New Counterinsurgency', in Michael McClintock, *Instruments of Statecraft*.

64. For Ellsberg on the new villages, cf. *Secrets*, p. 139.

65. 'Vu Van Thai on US Aims and Intervention in Vietnam – Working Notes on Vietnam no. 4', July 1969. Van Thai was one of the many Third Force Vietnamese intellectuals Americans consulted over the years. www.ellsberg.net/writing/Intervention.pdf, accessed 5 October 2006.

66. As Frances Herring of WSP put it: 'the interrelated problem of civil rights and liberties in this country and the rights of all peoples to self determination' ('American and Vietnamese Women Join Hands for Peace' (1965), quoted in Hershberger, *Traveling to Vietnam*, pp. xvi–xvii.) Black civil rights leaders were put under pressure by the LBJ administration to keep quiet about Vietnam, Hershberger argues, so the peace travellers were for the most part white.

67. Bly, *The Light Around the Body*, p. 32.

68. For haruspical rituals cf. Yerkes, *Sacrifice in Greek and Roman Religions and Early Judaism*.

69. 'Malaya, 1948: Britain's "Asian Cold War"?', Working Paper, April 2002. The Cold War as Global Conflict. International Center for Advanced Studies, New York University: 29, www.nyu.edu/gsas/dept/icas/PhillipDeery.pdf, accessed 9 December 2008.

70. Clutterbuck served on the director of operations' staff at Kuala Lumpur between 1956 and 1958.

71. Papers relevant to Richard Clutterbuck's *The Long Long War* are available through Cambridge University library's Janus website, http://janus.lib.ca.ac.uk.

72. 'The Strategic-Hamlet Program in 1962–63 failed to achieve its goal, not because it was in itself wrong but because it was not accompanied by adequate defence, adequate regulations for population control, or adequate local government and police forces within the hamlets' (Clutterbuck, *The Long Long War*, p. 68).

73. Department of the Army, Office of the Deputy Chief of Staff for Military Operations, *A Program for the Pacification and Long-Term Development of Vietnam* (Washington: Department of the Army, 1 March 1966), p. 10 (quoted in Lewis Sorley, 'To Change a War', http://carlisle-www.army.mil/usawc/Parameters/98spring/sorley.htm).

74. Cf. chapter 11 of Clutterbuck, *The Long Long War*, for all these.

75. Cf. Weinstein, 'Agent Orange Liability Litigation', United States District Court, Eastern District of New York, 10 March 2005, www.ffrd.org/AO/10_03_05_agentorange.pdf, accessed 28 August 2008. For Weinstein, as for Kennedy, Rusk and subsequent administrations during the Vietnam War up to 1971, the Geneva Protocol of 1925 did not apply: 'The 1925 Geneva Protocol provision was designed to outlaw poison gases such as mustard gas used in World War I. It cannot be interpreted to encompass the use of herbicides which were not then a known weapon and were far different in their purpose and effect' (Weinstein, 'Agent

Orange Liability Litigation', p. 192). And the changes in the law in 1971 were not retroactive: 'the action of the Senate in ratifying the 1925 Geneva Protocol and the Biological Weapons Convention in April 1975 did not retroactively make illegal United States' use of herbicides in Vietnam' (p. 232).

76. 'ARPA also developed the Hamlet Evaluation System ("HES") which collected the political census data used for estimating population exposures' (Weinstein, 'Agent Orange Liability Litigation', p. 20).

77. Weinstein, 'Agent Orange Liability Litigation', pp. 190–1. Quoting Memorandum of Secretary of State Dean Rusk to President John F. Kennedy (24 November 1961), reprinted in Foreign Relations of the United States, 1961–1963, VIETNAM 1961, at 663, 663 (1988), available at www.state.gov/www/about_state/history/vol_i_1961/z.html, accessed 9 December 2008.

78. Memorandum from the Secretary of Defense (McNamara) to the President, Washington, 8 August 1962: 3. Foreign Relations of the United States, 1961–1963, Volume II: Vietnam, 1962, item 262, www.state.gov/www/about_state/history/vol_ii_1961-63/w.html, accessed 9 December 2008.

79. Dale K. Robinson, USAF booklet 'Air Commando, 1950–1975' (1975), at http://home.earthlink.net/~aircommando1/RANCHHAND.htm, accessed 28 August 2008.

80. It is unlikely that he did. It seems the first use of the herbicide would have been around 1955, when Greene was finally revising the book.

CONCLUSION

Sir Percy Cradock, chairman of the Joint Intelligence Committee, broke open a bottle of champagne on the news of the failure of the KGB coup against Gorbachev, and remarked, with triumph: 'We *didn't* have a war. We *did* win.'[1] The Cold War had to be fought, especially in its early stages with a belligerent and tyrannical leader at the head of the Soviet Union, capable of great evil and addicted to the megalomaniac exercise of sheer power. The struggle for control of Europe and the defence of the Third World against Communism on the part of the Western powers was at this level a frank necessity. It is arguable too that the containment policies pursued by the US administrations did have at the very least the measure of the Soviet Union's Stalinist drive towards ideological expansion, totalitarian control and oppression in the name of collective values only an entrenched bureaucratic *nomenklatura* could enjoy. None of the questions raised in this book about the US and UK during the Cold War can compare with the condemnation that must be levelled against regimes in the Soviet Union and China willing to sacrifice entire peoples to brutal suffering and concentrationary horrors.

What this book does explore are the contradictions forced upon all citizens by the Cold War's nuclear endgames, the sacrificial manoeuvres those citizens internalized under the Cold War's compulsions, and the deadly Janus-faced force that came to inhabit the imagination at the borderline between neurotic inward fear and the superpower-governed public sphere. The turn against the innocent bystander, the 'Third Force' neutral, the apolitical civilian, or any non-aligned presence in the *polis* by the Cold War colossus was compelled by fear of fifth-column subversion and enemy ideology. But it struck its victims as distorted by secret *Realpolitik* and infected by institutionalized violence, partly because of the immensity of the power being wielded: the Second World War pursued by other means; the gargantuan budgets of the military–industrial complex; and the total destructiveness of nuclear weapons. It was the nuclear threat that made each citizen feel as though she were the special target of the Cold War's punitive defence systems. These obscure, unconscious fears were nurtured by the abiding memories of the Second World War, as we have seen with Jameson's *The Black Laurel* and Greene's *The Third Man*. But they were considerably magnified by the atomic, apocalyptic forces ranged on each side of the Iron Curtain, and became public and demonstrable in the worldwide anxieties following the Cuban missile crisis and the struggles over the atmospheric tests, as I hope I have indicated with the Plath and Hughes material.

What those public anxieties revealed were the victimizing structures of the Cold War's ideological control systems, as first instanced in the McCarthyite witch-hunts of the early 1950s, as the Dos Passos–Herbst chapter shows. The Cold War moved into the public realm with the first real resistance to its operations by the peace movements, outstandingly, to my mind, by Women Strike for Peace, who first properly identified the masculinist energies within the nuclear violence at the heart of the military–industrial complex. The genetics and Vietnam chapters sketch out the relations between those anti-nuclear movements and the anti-Vietnam activism which generated the first genuinely radical critique of Cold War militarist ideology. What the Vietnam protestors understood was the direct relation between the state–private networks running the nuclear security state and the sacrifice of millions in decolonizing struggles around the world. What the 1960s also revealed were the cultural forms of the Cold War security state, with the discovery of the CIA funding of CCF-sponsored texts, artworks and events. The literary Cold War may have been fought by something more anarchic and free than a state apparatus, as with the Soviet propaganda structures; but it was fought by writers recruited to the NCL Cold War liberal cause.

Again, one must stress that many writers did this ideological work without shame, and in the best possible spirit. For instance, writers gladly did their British Council stint of lectures in Eastern Europe out of avowedly anti-Communist zeal and with an untroubled conscience about propaganda. Elizabeth Bowen, by way of example, sent a report back to the British Council in 1949 after a lecture trip to Hungary in October 1948 which is quite explicit about the measures the government should take to maximize the people's 'resistance to the régime'.[2] The lecturer, she advised, ought to be 'ideologically harmless' (p. 2), but only the better to act as cultural observer of signs of anti-Communist spirit among the people, as she proves herself to be in her report: 'Apart from the nightmare aspects of enforced Communist government, I thought that the majority of adults were bored and exasperated by its noisy side, perpetual student demonstrations, amplified voices of noisy speakers travelling down the streets' (p. 6). The advice to the British Council is clear and trenchant about the necessity of standing by the Hungarians, using culture as the line of contact with the subject population: 'The lessening of any cultural ties that we *can* maintain with Hungary would be, I am convinced, not only a blunder but a betrayal' (p. 7). And chief among the cultural ties must be books: 'I myself could wish to see a greater import of general modern British literature – fiction, biography, criticism, poetry and *belles lettres* – into Hungary: a further grant for this purpose could not be better spent. Under present circumstances, attractive books would be ideal carriers of the Western idea' (p. 8).

There is no shame here, neither is there any sense of distance from the propaganda role of the British Council: for Bowen, the cultural Cold War was a means of preserving hope for a subject people, of sustaining freedoms under a regime absolutely alien to the Hungarian civilian population. Bowen's cultural espionage (she dutifully counts the tractors she spots in the fields!) is being performed with a secret wartime urgency, hopefully encouraging resistance to the 'nightmare aspects of enforced Communist government' as well as the 'noisy side' of Stalinist cultural indoctrination. The anti-Communist cultural work done by the BBC External service, the British Council and IRD initiatives all had a clear and in its way admirable agenda at its heart: the preservation of the possibility of freedom among peoples denied it by intransigent and punitive totalitarian regimes.

At the same time, with her postwar novels, Bowen gauged the cost of the Cold War for the British citizen in ways that may seem to contradict the jingoist verve of the British Council work. At the opening of *The Little Girls*, Dinah buries a collection of what she calls 'expressive objects' in a cave in her Somerset garden. 'These should', Bowen told an audience at a reading, 'enlighten archaeologists in the far future as to what she and her friend really *were* like.'[3] Memory, the mode of mind most essential to the novelist, is thematized here as a preservation of fetish objects within a crypt in order to preserve them from nuclear holocaust. The exploration of identity and the 'involuntary element of behaviour', which Bowen claims is the core of the novel,[4] depends on a desperate resistance to the nuclear threat; but that resistance becomes pathological, an encrypting and ritual sacrifice of the objects of memorial affection in an Antigone-like cave-as-grave. The threat of nuclear destruction is felt, at this pathological, involuntary level, as a targeting of little girls, or of the (prewar) memory of childhood among women; and the role of the novel, far from being to carry 'the Western idea', is to display the symptoms of the Cold War imaginary. In a real sense, the British Council propaganda and the novel's anti-nuclear troping do similar work, however: both seek to sustain civilian imaginative freedoms against the depredations of the Cold War's lethal control systems, the one using literature as sustenance for 'the genuine life [. . .] being lived surreptitiously' in the East ('Hungary', p. 3); the other using fiction to display the effects of the Cold War on the individual subject's imagination and pathology in the West.

There is a great deal this book has not done: the coverage is clearly selective and focused on a specific cast of writers. I have not attempted to chart the literary Cold War in its responses to the major events of that war, the execution of the Rosenbergs, the Cuban missile crisis, Prague in 1968, etc. Neither have I tried to cover all the possible areas of concern – I hope to publish articles elsewhere on Cold War poetry, on the Black Arts Movement, civil rights and the Cold War, on espionage thrillers, on Cold War theatre. There are writers who ought to have featured even in this limited space: Beckett, Lessing, Ellison, Rich, DeLillo, Coover, Vonnegut, Pynchon, Ballard, etc. Attention needs to be paid, too, to the interrelations between Anglo-American texts and the key dissident books of the Cold War, by Solzhenitsyn, Yevtushenko, Brodsky, Akhmatova, as well as the creative work from the decolonizing cultures of the Third World. A monograph is not long enough for such an enormous set of texts, events and histories. That being said, I hope the book will serve as an incentive to more work on the literary Cold War to supplement the body of critical texts reviewed in the introduction.

For the Cold War was a crucible for modernization in the developing world, as well as for the surveillance systems that have accompanied postmodern technologies and globalization. Invisibly, the operational power of those systems spread over the world as structured by superpower rivalry. As Josephine Herbst wrote in a draft for her memoir:

> Since the second world war we in the west have been told and retold that we are living in and for 'the free world'. But everybody knows this freedom is only relative. If in no other way, we know it by virtue of what we do not know. Power is somewhere in the stratosphere, governing our lives, determining our futures. The individual who prefers to think he has no control over the world situation, is creating that situation, not just interpreting something that already exists. And this type of passivity on a vast scale is something new.[5]

That stratospheric power is a Cold War space, the space inhabited by the missiles, rockets, satellites, and B-52s, at the same time as being the Cold War sublime of spectacular history, like the 'Third Man' regressive forms teased into being in Greene's Vienna. As Fred Inglis argued in *The Cruel Peace*, as a spectacular sublime, the Cold War effectively became a machine for generating a passive and private citizenry.

> The cold war's achievement has precisely been its spectacularity. Politics became a public spectacle that we paid our taxes to sustain. Safe in our private lives, we could remain in our seats and let our politician-actors represent us in the great issues of life's narrative.[6]

The spectacularity of the Cold War was sustained by the display of its technology, by the meshing of that technology with the televisual and communications networks being generated at the same time, and by the recruitment of national cultures to the cause through the recruitment of liberal intellectuals and institutions. The effect was a real freeze on imaginative work, what Inglis has called 'the cold war's frozen sea of feeling and imagination' (*The Cruel Peace*, p. 435).

The victimizing logic of the Cold War was one of the vehicles of the passivity Inglis and Herbst describe, for it relied, as its ground of possibility, on the assumption of a childlike citizen, feminized-infantilized according to the protocols of patriarchy, stilled by the threat of violence, and invited to internalize those protocols in self-sacrificial forms. As Edward Brunner remarked in his *Cold War Poetry*, having noted the frequency of domestic scenes in the poetry of the high Cold War: 'By writing a poetry which sheltered the child, the poets who practised this domestic verse extended protection to those whom the Bomb had most conspicuously and unfairly targeted' (Brunner, *Cold War Poetry*, p. 237). But it was also to acknowledge the childlike status of the poet in an age of nuclear compulsion:

> in the poems of the 1950s [. . .] the civilian has been reduced to a child. When it comes to the threat of the Bomb, the civilian simply has no role to play, no opportunity to intervene except to fret on the sidelines, a figure with no power and no responsibility. (Brunner, *Cold War Poetry*, p. 224)

The constrictions on agency in citizens subject to the Cold War security state were made operational by seductions which invited those citizens to infantilize themselves, specifically through the deployment of a complex set of psychological inducements and entrancements compacted into Cold War Freudianism. The Cold War, as a managerial exercise, administered this successfully through the close fit between the paranoia written into its systems and the nuclear fears being generated among the populace by the war technology.

The inducements generated what constituted a cold civil war in Britain and the United States between those who allowed themselves to be recruited and those who kicked against the pricks. As Suzanne Clark writes in *Cold Warriors*: 'Anticommunism moved liberals to support a project of a security state apparatus; anticommunism found as its object a feminized assortment of targets, most significantly labor unions and civil rights groups' (Clark, *Cold Warriors*, p. 4). Those rival projects relied on coercive hostilities which sustained the larger Cold War oppositional apparatus, drawing all citizens, whether security-minded or feminized-targeted, into its orbit. As Clark argues, from a certain point in the Cold War, all citizens were within the Cold War *polis* of the United States: 'In order to understand postwar modernity, we have to understand the way that all of Western civilization suddenly found itself *inside* American military/industrial history' (p. 6). Becoming insiders in this way constitutes the curious and self-sacrificial basis of the nostalgia for the Cold War illustrated in the introduction, for it reinforces the self-infantilizing by providing a body to float inside, a body fashioned in the likeness of the Janus-faced killer and carer of the Cold War colossus. The dangers of this passive, Cold War, amniotic peace in citizens may strike one as obvious – but they only truly become so if we are sufficiently awake to the present dangers. As Clark warns: 'The Cold War is not over; it lives on in the imaginary where it was so firmly installed through nuclear trauma and phobia' (p. 14). I hope this book will help, in a small way, to disseminate that warning, and to help readers undertake their own journey through the literary Cold War, alive to the continued threats to all our flesh.

NOTES

1. Quoted in Hennessy, *The Secret State*, p. 4.
2. Harry Ransom Center, University of Texas at Austin, Elizabeth Bowen papers – 'Hungary', box 6.2, dated 29 October 1948, p. 3.
3. Elizabeth Bowen papers – *The Little Girls*: notes. Misc. Box 7.4.
4. *The Little Girls*: notes.
5. Beinecke Rare Book and Manuscript Library, Yale Collection of American Literature: Josephine Herbst Papers – Series Ii: B Memoirs. Mss-M-New World. Rough draft pgs. from memoirs.
6. Inglis, *The Cruel Peace*, p. 435.

BIBLIOGRAPHY

Daniel Aaron, *Writers on the Left* (New York: Avon, 1961).

——, 'The Riddle of John Dos Passos', *Harpers* 224 (March 1962), pp. 55–60.

Alex Abella, *Soldiers of Reason: The RAND Corporation and the Rise of the American Empire* (Orlando, FL: Harcourt, 2008).

Sabrina Fuchs Abrams, *Mary McCarthy: Gender, Politics, and the Postwar Intellectual* (New York: Peter Lang, 2004).

Judith Adamson, *Graham Greene and the Cinema* (Norman, OK: Pilgrim Books, 1984).

Anthony Adamthwaite, review of Peter J. Taylor, *Britain and the Cold War*, *English Historical Review* 109: 433 (September 1994), pp. 1035–6.

Advisory Committee on Human Radiation Experiments, 'The Hazards of Radon in Uranium Mines', 19 April 1995, www.gwu.edu/~nsarchiv/radiation/dir/mstreet/commeet/meet14/brief14/tab_e/br14e1.txt, accessed 9 December 2008.

Matthew Aid, 'The National Security Agency and the Cold War', *Intelligence and National Security* 16: 1 (Spring 2001), pp. 27–66.

Richard Aldrich, 'Secret Intelligence for a Post-War World: Reshaping the British Intelligence Community, 1944–51', in Richard J. Aldrich (ed.), *British Intelligence, Strategy and the Cold War* (London: Routledge, 1992), pp. 15–49.

——, *The Hidden Hand: Britain, America and Cold War Secret Intelligence* (London: John Murray, 2001).

Richard Aldrich, Gary D. Rawnsley and Ming-Yeh T. Rawnsley (eds), *The Clandestine Cold War in Asia, 1945–65* (Portland, OR: Frank Cass, 2000).

Vladimir Alexandrov (ed.), *The Garland Companion to Vladimir Nabokov* (New York: Garland, 1995).

Douglas Anderson, 'Nabokov's Genocidal and Nuclear Holocausts in *Lolita*', *Mosaic* 29: 2 (1996), pp. 73–90.

Christian G. Appy (ed.), *Cold War Constructions: The Political Culture of United States Imperialism, 1945–1966* (Amherst: University of Massachusetts Press, 2000).

Judith Arcana, 'Truth in Mothering: Grace Paley's Stories', in B.O. Daly and M.T. Reddy (eds), *Narrating Mothers: Theorizing Maternal Subjectivities* (Knoxville: University of Tennessee Press, 1991), pp. 195–208.

——, *Grace Paley's Life Stories: A Literary Biography* (Urbana: University of Illinois Press, 1993).

Pat Arrowsmith, *On the Brink* (London: CND, 1981).

Steven Gould Axelrod, 'Robert Lowell and the Cold War', *New England Quarterly* 72: 3 (September 1999), pp. 339–61.

Arne Axelsson, *Restrained Response: American Novels of the Cold War and Korea, 1945–1962* (New York: Greenwood Press, 1990).

David Ayers, 'The Long Last Goodbye: Control and Resistance in the Work of William Burroughs', *Journal of American Studies* 27: 2 (1993), pp. 223–36.

Gerhard Bach and Blaine Hall (eds), *Conversations with Grace Paley* (Jackson: University Press of Mississippi, 1997).

Jon Lance Bacon, *Flannery O'Connor and Cold War Culture* (Cambridge: Cambridge University Press, 1994).

Kate Baldwin, 'The Radical Imaginary of *The Bell Jar*', *Novel: A Forum on Fiction* 38: 1 (2004), pp. 21–40.

James Bamford, *The Puzzle Palace: A Report on America's Most Secret Agency* (New York: Houghton Mifflin, 1982).

Murray Baumgarten, 'Urban Rites and Civic Premises in the Fiction of Saul Bellow, Grace Paley, and Sandra Schor', *Contemporary Literature* 34: 3 (1993), pp. 395–424.

Sally Bayley, '"I Have Your Head on My Wall": Sylvia Plath and the Rhetoric of Cold War America', *European Journal of American Culture* 25: 3 (2006), pp. 155–71.

Siegfried Beer, 'Early CIA Reports on Austria, 1947–1949', in Günther Bischof and Anton Pelinka (eds), *Austrian Historical Memory and National Identity* (Edison, NJ: Transaction, 1997), pp. 247–56.

——, 'The Third Man', *History Today* 51: 5 (May 2001), pp. 45–51.

Allen Belkind (ed.), *Dos Passos, the Critics, and the Writer's Intention* (Carbondale: Southern Illinois University Press, 1971).

S. Bennett, *A History of Control Engineering, 1930–1955* (London: Peter Peregrinus, 1993).

David Berry, 'Ted Hughes and the Minotaur Complex', *Modern Language Review* 97: 3 (2002), pp. 539–52.

Jennifer Birkett, '"Waiting for the Death Wind": Storm Jameson's Fiction after the Second World War', in Jennifer Birkett and Chiara Briganti (eds), *Margaret Storm Jameson: Writing in Dialogue* (Newcastle: Cambridge Scholars, 2007), pp. 127–64.

Peter Biskind, *Seeing is Believing: How Hollywood Taught us to Stop Worrying and Love the Bomb* (London: Bloomsbury, 2001).

Alexander Bloom, *Prodigal Sons: The New York Intellectuals and their World* (Oxford: Oxford University Press, 1986).

Robert Bly, *The Light Around the Body: Poems* (New York: Harper & Row, 1959).

——, *Talking All Morning* (Ann Arbor: University of Michigan Press, 1980).

——, interview with PBS, 1998, www.pbs.org/kued/nosafeplace/interv/bly. html, accessed 28 August 2008.

William Bonney, 'Politics, Perception, and Gender in Conrad's *Lord Jim* and Greene's *The Quiet American*', *Conradiana* 23: 2 (1991), pp. 99–122.

M. Keith Booker, *Monsters, Mushroom Clouds and the Cold War: American Science Fiction and the Roots of Postmodernism, 1946–1964* (New York: Greenwood Press, 2001).

Thomas Borstelmann, *Apartheid's Reluctant Uncle: United States and Southern Africa in the Early Cold War* (Oxford: Oxford University Press, 1993).

——, *The Cold War and the Color Line: American Race Relations in the Global Arena* (Cambridge, MA: Harvard University Press, 2001).

Joseph Bouchard, 'Guarding the Cold War Ramparts: The U.S. Navy's Role in Continental Air Defence', *Naval War College Review* (Summer 1999), pp. 111–35.

Brian Boyd, *Vladimir Nabokov: The American Years* (Princeton, NJ: Princeton University Press, 1991).

——, *Nabokov's* Pale Fire: *The Magic of Self-Discovery* (Princeton, NJ: Princeton University Press, 1999).

Brian Boyd and Robert Michael Pye (eds), *Nabokov's Butterflies: Unpublished and Uncollected Writings* (London: Allen Lane, Penguin Press, 2000).

Paul Boyer, *By the Bomb's Early Light: American Thought and Culture at the Dawn of the Atomic Age* (New York: Knopf, 1985).

Carol Brightman, *Writing Dangerously: Mary McCarthy and Her World* (New York: Clarkson Potter, 1992).

Ralph W. Brown, 'Making the Third Man Look Pale: American–Soviet Conflict in Vienna During the Early Cold War in Austria, 1945–1950', *Journal of Slavic Military Studies* 14: 4 (December 2001), pp. 81–109.

Edward Brunner, *Cold War Poetry* (Champaign: University of Illinois Press, 2000).

Eva Bueno, 'Grace Paley's Conversations with Her Father: Patriarchy, Motherhood and the Text,' *Estudos Anglo-Americanos* 16 (1992), pp. 99–105.

Jeannette Buirski, 'How I Learnt to Start Worrying and Hate the Bomb', in Dorothy Thompson (ed.), *Over Our Dead Bodies: Women Against the Bomb* (London: Virago, 1983), pp. 15–28.

Lynda Bundtzen, 'Poetic Arson and Sylvia Plath's "Burning the Letters"', *Contemporary Literature* 39: 3 (1998), pp. 434–51.

William Bundy, Nicholas Katzenbach and Richard Helms, 'Bombing Strategy Options for the Rest of 1967', 9 May 1967, LBJ Library, Declassified Documents Series 1984-000810, www.vietnam.ttu.edu/star/images/024/0240617005.pdf, accessed 9 December 2008.

Alan Burns and Charles Sugnet (eds), *Imagination on Trial* (London and New York: Allison and Busby, 1981).

William Burroughs, *The Ticket that Exploded* (New York: Grove Press, 1962).

——, *Queer* (London: Picador, 1986).

——, *The Soft Machine* (1961) (London: Paladin, 1986).

——, *Word Virus: The William Burroughs Reader*, eds James Grauerholz and Ira Silverberg (London: Flamingo HarperCollins, 1999).

William S. Bushnell, 'Paying for the Damage: *The Quiet American* Revisited', *Film and History* 36: 2 (2006), pp. 38–44.

Judith Butler, *Bodies that Matter: On the Discursive Limits of Sex* (London: Routledge, 1993).

Frank Cain, 'Missiles and Mistrust: U.S. Intelligence Responses to British and Australian Missile Research', *Intelligence and National Security* 3: 4 (October 1988), pp. 5–22.

Duncan Campbell, *War Plan UK: The Truth about Civil Defence in Britain* (London: Burnett Books, 1982).

Elof Axel Carlson, *Genes, Radiation, and Society: The Life and Work of H.J. Muller* (Ithaca, NY: Cornell University Press, 1981).

Lynette Carpenter, '"I Never Knew the Old Vienna": Cold War Politics and *The Third Man*', *Film Criticism* 11: 1–2 (October 1987), pp. 56–65.

Mark Carroll, *Music and Ideology in Cold War Europe* (Cambridge: Cambridge University Press, 2003).

Susan L. Carruthers, *Winning Hearts and Minds: British Governments, the Media and Colonial Counter-Insurgency 1944–1960* (London: Leicester University Press, 1995).

David Caute, *The Dancer Defects: The Struggle for Cultural Supremacy during the Cold War* (Oxford: Oxford University Press, 2003).

Brandon S. Centerwall, 'Hiding in Plain Sight: Nabokov and Pedophilia', *Texas Studies in Literature and Language* 2: 3 (1990), pp. 468–84.

Winston Churchill, 'Sinews of Peace', Iron Curtain Speech, March 5 1946, Westminster College, Fulton, Missouri, www.winstonchurchill.org, accessed 7 August 2008.

Sarah Churchwell, 'Ted Hughes and the Corpus of Sylvia Plath', *Criticism: A Quarterly for Literature and the Arts* 40: 1 (1998), pp. 99–132.

Heather Clark, 'Tracking the Thought-Fox: Sylvia Plath's Revision of Ted Hughes', *Journal of Modern Literature* 28: 2 (2005), pp. 100–12.

Suzanne Clark, *Cold Warriors: Manliness on Trial in the Rhetoric of the West* (Carbondale: Southern Illinois University Press, 2000).

Richard Clutterbuck, *The Long Long War: Counterinsurgency in Malaya and Vietnam* (1966) (London: Cassell, 1967).

Wayne Cocroft and J.C. Thomas, *Cold War: Building for Nuclear Confrontation, 1946–1989* (Swindon: English Heritage, 2003).

Nathaniel C. Comfort, 'Two Genes, No Enzymes: A Second Look at Barbara McClintock and the 1951 Cold Spring Harbor Symposium', in James F. Crow and William F. Dove (eds), *Perspectives on Genetics: Anecdotal, Historical, and Critical Commentaries, 1987–1998* (Madison: University of Wisconsin Press, 2000), pp. 469–74.

Robert Conquest, *The Abomination of Moab* (London: Temple Smith, 1979).

Fred J. Cook, *The Warfare State* (London and New York: Macmillan, 1962).

Robert J. Corber, *Homosexuality in Cold War America* (Durham, NC: Duke University Press, 1997).

John D. Crane and Sylvia Crane, *Czechoslovakia: Anvil of the Cold War* (New York: Praeger, 1991).

F.H.C. Crick, 'The Structure of the Nucleic Acids and Related Substances', *Special Publications of the New York Academy of Sciences*, vol. V (New York: New York Academy, 1957), pp. 173–8.

James F. Crow and William F. Dove (eds), *Perspectives on Genetics: Anecdotal, Historical, and Critical Commentaries, 1987–1998* (Madison: University of Wisconsin Press, 2000).

Michael Curtin, *Redeeming the Wasteland: Television Documentary and Cold War Politics* (New Brunswick, NJ: Rutgers University Press, 1995).

C. D. Darlington, *Evolution of Genetic Systems*, 2nd edn (London: Oliver & Boyd, 1958).

Robert G. David, *The Arctic in the British Imagination, 1818–1914* (Manchester: Manchester University Press, 2000).

Michael Davidson, 'From Margin to Mainstream: Postwar Poetry and the Politics of Containment', *American Literary History* 10: 2 (Summer 1998), pp. 266–90.

——, *Guys Like Us: Citing Masculinity in Cold War Poetics* (Chicago: University of Chicago Press, 2003).

Robert D. Dean, *Imperial Brotherhood: Gender and the Making of Cold War Foreign Policy* (Amherst: University of Massachusetts Press, 2001).

A. F. Deery, 'Psychological Warfare in Malaya', c. 1955, www.psywar.org/ pdf_malaya.pdf, accessed 8 December 2008.

Philip Deery, 'Covert Propaganda and the Cold War: Britain and Australia 1948–1955', *Round Table* 361 (2001), pp. 607–21.

——, 'Malaya, 1948: Britain's "Asian Cold War"?', Working Paper, April 2002, International Center for Advanced Studies, New York University, www. nyu.edu/gsas/dept/icas/PhillipDeery.pdf, accessed 9 December 2008.

Andrew Defty, *Britain, America and Anti-Communist Propaganda, 1945–1953* (London: Frank Cass, 2004).

Marianne Dekoven, *Utopia Limited: The Sixties and the Emergence of the Postmodern* (Durham, NC: Duke University Press, 2004).

Jacques Derrida, 'No Apocalypse, Not Now (Full Speed Ahead, Seven Missiles, Seven Missives)', *diacritics* 14: 2 (1984), pp. 20–31.

Gilles Deleuze and Felix Guattari, *Anti-Oedipus: Capitalism and Schizophrenia*, trans. Robert Hurley, Mark Seem and Helen R. Lane (London: Athlone Press, 1984).

Don DeLillo, *Underworld* (1997) (London: Picador, 1998).

Richard Dellamora, 'Queer Apocalypse: Framing William Burroughs', in Richard Dellamora (ed.), *Postmodern Apocalypse: Theory and Cultural Practice at the End* (Philadelphia: University of Pennsylvania Press, 1995), pp. 136–67.

Michael Dewar, *Defence of the Nation* (London: Weidenfeld & Nicolson, 1989).

John Diggins, *Up from Communism* (New York: Harper, 1975).

George Dimock, 'Anna and the Wolf-Man: Rewriting Freud's Case History', *Representations* 50 (Spring 1995), pp. 53–75.

Thomas Doherty, *Cold War, Cool Medium: Television, McCarthyism, and American Culture* (New York: Columbia University Press, 2003).

John Dos Passos, *The Grand Design* (London: John Lehmann, 1949).

——, *Tour of Duty* (1946) (Westport, CT: Greenwood Press, 1974).

Ann Douglas, 'Periodizing the American Century: Modernism, Postmodernism, and Postcolonialism in the Cold War', *Modernism/Modernity* 5: 3 (1998), pp. 71–98.

Charles Drazin, *In Search of the Third Man* (New York: Limelight Editions, 2000).

Mary Dudziak, *Cold War Civil Rights: Race and the Image of American Democracy* (Princeton, NJ: Princeton University Press, 2000).

John Dumbrell, *A Special Relationship: Anglo-American Relations in the Cold War and After* (New York: St Martin's Press, 2001).

Paul N. Edwards, *The Closed World: Computers and the Politics of Discourse in Cold War America* (Cambridge, MA: MIT Press, 1997).

Daniel Ellsberg, 'Some Prospects and Problems in Vietnam', 15 February 1968, http://www.ellsberg.net/writing/Prospects.pdf, accessed 5 October 2006.

——, 'On Pacification: Comments by Thai and Ellsberg. Working Notes on Vietnam No. 6', July 1969, www.ellsberg.net/writing/Pacification.pdf, accessed 5 October 2006.

——, 'Vu Van Thai on US Aims and Intervention in Vietnam: Working Notes on Vietnam no. 4', July 1969, www.ellsberg.net/writing/Intervention.pdf, accessed 5 October 2006.

——, *Secrets: A Memoir of Vietnam and the Pentagon Papers* (New York and London: Penguin, 2002).

Julia Ehrhardt, *Writers of Conviction* (Columbia: University of Missouri Press, 2004).

Peter Evans, '*The Third Man* (1949): Constructions of the Self', *Forum for Modern Language Studies* 31: 1 (1995), pp. 37–48.

Ekbert Faas, 'Chapters of a Shared Mythology: Sylvia Plath and Ted Hughes', in Keith Sagar (ed.), *The Achievement of Ted Hughes* (Athens, GA: University of Georgia Press, 1983), pp. 107–25.

Quentin Falk, *Travels in Greeneland: The Cinema of Graham Greene* (London and New York: Quartet Books, 1990).

Mark Fenster, *Conspiracy Theories: Secrecy and Power in American Culture* (Minneapolis: University of Minnesota Press, 1999).

Marc Ferro, 'Un Combat dans le film: *Le Troisième homme*', in Marc Ferro, *Cinéma et histoire* (1977) (Paris: Gallimard, 1993), pp. 175–83.

Frances Fitzgerald, *Fire in the Lake: The Vietnamese and the Americans in Vietnam* (New York: Vintage, 1973).

Barbara Foley, *Radical Representations: Politics and Form in US Proletarian Fiction, 1929–1941* (Bloomington: Indiana University Press, 1991).

J.H. Folley, W. Borges and T. Yamawaki, 'Incidence of Leukemia in Survivors of the Atom Bomb in Hiroshima and Nagasaki, Japan', *American Journal of Medicine* 13 (1952), pp. 311–21.

André Fontaine, *History of the Cold War: From the Korean War to the Present*, trans. Renaud Bruce (London: Secker & Warburg, 1970).

Sigmund Freud, *The Basic Writings of Sigmund Freud*, trans. A.A. Brill (New York: Modern Library, 1938).

J. William Fulbright (intro.), *The Vietnam Hearings* (New York: Random House, 1966).

Jim Garrison, *From Hiroshima to Harrisburg: The Unholy Alliance* (London: SCM Press, 1980).

Timothy Garton Ash, 'Orwell's List', *New York Review of Books*, 25 September 2003.

Genetics Conference, 'Genetic Effects of the Atomic Bombs in Hiroshima and Nagasaki', *Science* 106 (1947), pp. 331–53.

Paul Giles, 'Double Exposure: Sylvia Plath and the Aesthetics of Transnationalism', *Symbiosis: A Journal of Anglo-American Literary Relations* 5: 2 (2001), pp. 103–20.

Allen Ginsberg, *Kaddish* (New York: City Light Books, 1967).

——, interview with Eric Baizier, Reywas Divad and Richard Peabody, *Gargoyle* 10 (1978), www.gargoylemagazine.com/gargoyle/Issues/scanned/issue10/ginsberg.htm, accessed 12 August 2008.

——, *Collected Poems, 1947–1980* (New York: Harper, 1988).

——, *Journals Mid-Fifties: 1954–1958*, ed. Gordon Ball (Harmondsworth: Penguin, 1996).

C. V. Glines, 'Operation Vittles: The Berlin Airlift', *Aviation History* (May 1998), http://historynet.com/berlin-airlift-operation-vittles.html, accessed 7 August 2008.

Margaret Gowing and Lorna Arnold, *Independence and Deterrence: Britain and Atomic Energy, 1945–1952*, vol. 1 (London: Macmillan for the United Kingdom Atomic Energy Authority, 1974).

Geoffrey Green, *Freud and Nabokov* (Lincoln: University of Nebraska Press, 1988).

Graham Greene, *The Quiet American* (1955) (London: Reprint Society, 1957).

——, 'Security in Room 51', *Sunday Times* 14 July 1963.

——, *The Third Man & The Fallen Idol* (Oxford: Heinemann, 1972).

——, *The Third Man*, ed. Andrew Sinclair (London: Faber & Faber, 1973).

——, *Ways of Escape* (London: Bodley Head, 1980).

——, *Reflections*, selected Judith Adamson (London: Reinhardt Books, 1990).

Hugh Carleton Greene, 'Report on Emergency Information Services, September 1950–September 1951', p. 1; CO 537/7255.

William F. Hale, 'Measurements of Air-Borne Radioactivity in a Colorado Plateau Uranium Mine', Advisory Committee on Human Radiation Experiments archive website, www.gwu.edu/~nsarchiv/radiation/dir/mstreet/commeet/meet14/brief14/tab_e/br14e1c.txt, accessed 9 December 2008.

Jussi Hanimäki and Odd Arne Westad (eds), *The Cold War: A History in Documents and Eyewitness Accounts* (Oxford: Oxford University Press, 2003).

Steffen Hantke, *Conspiracy and Paranoia in Contemporary American Fiction: The Works of Don DeLillo and Joseph McElroy* (Bern: Peter Lang, 1994).

T.N. Harper, *The End of Empire and the Making of Malaya* (Cambridge: Cambridge University Press, 1999).

Oliver Harris, 'Can You See a Virus? The Queer Cold War of William Burroughs', *Journal of American Studies* 33: 2 (1999), pp. 243–66.

——, 'Cold War Correspondents: Ginsberg, Kerouac, Cassady, and the Political Economy of Beat Letters', *Twentieth Century Literature* 46: 2 (Summer 2000), pp. 171–92.

——, *William Burroughs and the Secret Fascination* (Carbondale: Southern Illinois University Press, 2003).

Woody Haut, *Pulp Culture: Hardboiled Fiction and the Cold War* (London: Serpent's Tail, 1996).

John H. Hay, *Tactical and Materiel Innovations (Vietnam Studies)* (Washington, DC: Department of the Army, 1974).

Cyndy Hendershot, *I Was a Cold War Monster: Horror Films, Eroticism, and the Cold War Imagination* (Bowling Green, OH: Bowling Green University Popular Press, 2001).

Paul Hendrickson, *The Living and the Dead: Robert McNamara and Five Lives of a Lost War* (New York: Knopf, 1996).

Peter Hennessy, *Never Again: Britain 1945–1951* (London: Vintage, 1993).

——, *The Secret State: Whitehall and the Cold War* (London: Penguin, 2003).

Margot A. Henriksen, *Dr. Strangelove's America: Society and Culture in the Atomic Age* (Berkeley: University of California Press, 1997).

Josephine Herbst, 'A Bad Blow', *Scribner's Magazine* (July 1930), pp. 25–32.

——, 'Hunter of Doves', *Botteghe Oscure* 13 (1954), pp. 310–44.

——, *New Green World* (New York: Hastings House, 1954).

——, 'The Ruins of Memory', *Nation* (1 April 1956), pp. 302–4.

——, review of *Scofield Thayer and The Dial* by Nicolas Joost, *Kenyon Review* 105: 2 (Spring 1965), pp. 353–9.

——, review of Granville Hicks' *Part of the Truth*, *Partisan Review* 107: 4 (Autumn 1965), pp. 772–7.

——, *The Starched Blue Sky of Spain, and Other Memoirs* (London: HarperCollins, 1991).

——, *Pity is Not Enough* (Urbana: University of Illinois Press, 1998).

Gregg Herken, *The Winning Weapon: The Atomic Bomb in the Cold War, 1945–1950* (Princeton, NJ: Princeton University Press, 1988).

Ellen Herman, *The Romance of American Psychology: Political Culture in the Age of Experts* (Berkeley: University of California Press, 1995).

Scott Herring, '"Her Brothers Dead in Riverside or Russia": *Kaddish* and the Holocaust', *Contemporary Literature* 42: 3 (2001), pp. 535–56.

Mary Hershberger, *Traveling to Vietnam: American Peace Activists and the War* (Syracuse, NY: Syracuse University Press, 1998).

Richard Hofstadter, 'The Paranoid Style in American Politics', *Harper's Magazine* (November 1964), pp. 77–86.

Duncan Holaday, www.gwu.edu/~nsarchiv/radiation/dir/mstreet/commeet/pm03/pm3brf/tab_c/pm03c2a.txt, accessed 28 November 2008.

Clive Holland (ed.), *Farthest North: The Quest for the North Pole* (London: Robinson, 1994).

Gerald Horne, *Black and Red: W.E.B. Dubois and the Afro-American Response to the Cold War, 1944–1963* (New York: State University of New York Press, 1985).

Rollin Hotchkiss, *Special Publications of the New York Academy of Sciences*, vol. v (New York: New York Academy, 1957), pp. 226–7.

Angela Hubler, 'Josephine Herbst's *The Starched Blue Sky of Spain, and Other Memoirs*: Literary History "in the Wide Margin of the Century"', *Papers on Language and Literature* 33 (Winter 1997), pp. 71–98.

Olwyn Hughes, 'The Plath Myth and the Reviewing of *Bitter Fame*', *Poetry Review* 80: 3 (1990), pp. 61–3.

Ted Hughes, *The Earth-Owl and Other Moon-People* (London: Faber & Faber, 1963).

——, 'The Rock', in Herbert Read (ed.), *Writers on Themselves* (London: BBC, 1964), pp. 86–92.

——, *Gaudete* (London: Faber & Faber, 1977).

——, 'On Sylvia Path', *Raritan* 14: 2 (1994), pp. 1–12.

——, *Winter Pollen: Occasional Prose*, ed. William Scammell (London: Faber & Faber, 1994).

——, *Collected Poems*, ed. Paul Keegan (London: Faber & Faber, 2003).

Joon Ho Hwang, 'Women's Space and Silenced Voices during the Cold War in Sylvia Plath's Poetry', *Feminist Studies in English Literature* 15: 2 (2007), pp. 65–86.

Lewis Hyde (ed.), *On the Poetry of Allen Ginsberg* (Ann Arbor: University of Michigan Press, 1998).

Fred Inglis, *The Cruel Peace: Everyday Life in the Cold War* (London: Aurum Press, 1992).

Storm Jameson, *The Black Laurel* (London: Macmillan, 1947).

——, 'The Novelist Today', *Virginia Quarterly Review* 25: 4 (Fall 1949), pp. 562–74.

——, 'Why I Can't Write About America', *Fortnightly Review* 66 (1949), pp. 381–5.

——, *Journey from the North: Autobiography of Storm Jameson*, 2 vols (London: Collins & Harvill, 1969).

David R. Jardini, 'Out of the Blue Yonder: How RAND Diversified into Social Welfare Research', *RAND Review* (Fall, 1998), www.rand.org/publications/randreview/issues/rr.fall.98, accessed 9 December 2008.

David R. Jarraway, '"Standing by His Word": The Politics of Allen Ginsberg's Vietnam "Vortex"', *Journal of American Culture* 16: 3 (1993), pp. 81–8.

William Patrick Jeffs, *Feminism, Manhood, and Homosexuality: Intersections in Psychoanalysis and American Poetry* (New York: Peter Lang, 2003).

D. Barton Johnson, 'The Labyrinth of Incest in Nabokov's *Ada*', *Comparative Literature* 38: 3 (1986), pp. 224–55.

L.B. Johnson, Speech to Nation, 31 March 1968, American Rhetoric website, www.americanrhetoric.com/speeches/lbjvietnam.htm, accessed 25 July 2008.

Rose Kamel, 'To Aggravate the Conscience: Grace Paley's Loud Voice', *Journal of Ethnic Studies* 11: 3 (1983), pp. 29–49.

Thomas Kaplan, 'Britain's Asian Cold War: Malaya', in Ann Deighton (ed.), *Britain and the First Cold War* (New York: St Martin's Press, 1990), pp. 201–19.

Lillian Kay, 'Cybernetics, Information, Life: The Emergence of Scriptural Representations of Heredity', *Configurations* 5: 1 (1997), pp. 23–91.

Evelyn Fox Keller, *Reflections on Gender and Science* (New Haven: Yale University Press, 1985).

George Kennan, 'The Sources of Soviet Conduct', *Foreign Affairs* (July 1947), www.mtholyoke.edu/acad/intrel/coldwar/x.htm, accessed 7 August 2008.

Douglas Kerr, '*The Quiet American* and the Novel', *Studies in the Novel* 38: 1 (2006), pp. 95–107.

Christine Klein, *Cold War Orientalism: Asia in the Middlebrow Imagination, 1945–1961* (Berkeley: University of California Press, 2003).

Richard Klein, 'The Future of Nuclear Criticism', *Yale French Studies* 77 (1990), pp. 76–100.

Richard Klein and William B. Warner, 'Nuclear Coincidence and the Korean Airline Disaster', *diacritics* 16: 1 (1986), pp. 2–21.

Hans Krabbendam and Giles Scott-Smith (eds), *The Cultural Cold War in Western Europe, 1945–1960* (London: Routledge, 2004).

Mark Krupnick, *Lionel Trilling and the Fate of Cultural Criticism* (Evanston, IL: Northwestern University Press, 1986).

Judy Kutulas, *The Long War: The Intellectual People's Front and Anti-Stalinism, 1930–1940* (Durham, NC, and London: Duke University Press, 1995).

Elinor Langer, *Josephine Herbst: The Story She Could Never Tell* (New York: Warner Books, 1985).

Phyllis Lassner, 'A Cry for Life: Storm Jameson, Stevie Smith, and the Fate of the European Jews', in M. Paul Hiolsinger and Mary Anne Schofield (eds), *Visions of War: World War II in Popular Literature and Culture* (Bowling Green, OH: Bowling Green State University Press, 1992), pp. 181–90.

Peter Laurie, *Beneath the City Streets* (London: Panther, 1979).

Helen Laville and Hugh Wilford (eds), *Freedom's Crusade: State–Private Networks in America's Cold War* (London: Frank Cass, 2005).

John Le Carré, *Tinker, Tailor, Soldier, Spy* (London: Coronet, 1989).
——, *The Spy Who Came in from the Cold* (1964) (London: Sceptre, 1999).
Steven Hugh Lee, *Outposts of Empire: Korea, Vietnam and the Origins of the Cold War in Asia, 1919–1954* (Liverpool: University of Liverpool Press, 1995).
Robert T. Levine, '"My Ultraviolet Darling": The Loss of Lolita's Childhood', *Modern Fiction Studies* 25 (1979), pp. 471–9.
Max Levitan, *Textbook of Human Genetics*, 3rd edn (Oxford: Oxford University Press, 1988).
Anthony Libby, 'God's Lioness and the Priest of Sycorax: Plath and Hughes', *Contemporary Literature* 15: 3 (1974), pp. 386–405.
Liddell Hart Centre for Military Archives's Nuclear History Database, www.kcl.ac.uk/lhcma/pro/p-air02a.htm, accessed 9 December 2008.
Los Alamos Scientific Laboratory for AEC, *The Effects of Atomic Weapons* (New York: McGraw-Hill, 1950).
W. Scott Lucas and C.J. Morris, 'A Very British Crusade: The Information Research Department and the Beginning of the Cold War', in Richard J. Aldrich (ed.), *British Intelligence, Strategy and the Cold War* (London: Routledge, 1992), pp. 85–110.
Catherine Lutz, 'Epistemology of the Bunker: The Brainwashed and Other New Subjects of Permanent War', in Joel Pfister and Nancy Schnog (eds), *Inventing the Psychological: Towards a Cultural History of Emotional Life in America* (New Haven: Yale University Press, 1997), pp. 245–67.
Robin Lydenberg, 'Notes from the Orifice: Language and the Body in William Burroughs', *Contemporary Literature* 26: 1 (1985), pp. 55–73.
Donald Lyons, 'Nabokov in America', *New Criterion* 16: 4 (1997), pp. 18–28.
Mary McCarthy, *The Seventeenth Degree* (New York: Harcourt Brace Jovanovich, 1974).
——, *On the Contrary* (London: Heinemann, 1962).
Barbara McClintock, 'The Origin and Behavior of Mutable Loci in Maize', in James A. Peters (ed.), *Classic Papers in Genetics* (Englewood Cliffs, NJ: Prentice Hall, 1959), pp. 199–209.
Michael McClintock, *Instruments of Statecraft: US Guerrilla Warfare, Counterinsurgency, and Counterterrorism, 1940–1990* (New York: Pantheon, 2002).
Bruce McConachie, *American Theater in the Culture of the Cold War: Producing and Contesting Containment, 1947–1962* (Iowa City: University of Iowa Press, 2003).
Brian McFarlane, '*The Third Man*: Context, Text and Intertextuality', *Metro Magazine* 92 (Summer 1993), pp. 16–26.
Pat Macpherson, *Reflecting on* The Bell Jar (London, New York: Routledge, 1991).

Lucy Maddox, *Nabokov's Novels in English* (Athens: University of Georgia Press, 1983).

John D. Marks, *The Search for the 'Manchurian Candidate': The CIA and Mind Control* (London: Allen Lane, 1979).

Elizabeth Maslen, *Political and Social Issues in British Women's Fiction, 1928–1968* (London: Palgrave, 2001).

Timothy Melly, *Empire of Conspiracy: The Culture of Paranoia in Postwar America* (Ithaca, NY: Cornell University Press, 1999).

——, 'Paranoid Modernity and the Diagnostics of Cultural Theory: Review of John Farrell's *Paranoia and Modernity*', *Electronic Book Review* (2006), www.electronicbookreview.com/thread/fictionspresent/connectivist, accessed 30 July 2008.

Herman Melville, *Pierre; or, The Ambiguities* (1852) (Evanston and Chicago: Northwestern University Press and Newberry Library, 1971).

Salvatore R. Mercogliano, 'To Boldly Go Where No Fleet has Gone Before: Military Sea Transportation Service in the Arctic' (2000), www.USMM.org/msts/arctic.html, accessed 9 December 2008.

M.D. Mesarovic (ed.), *Systems Theory and Biology* (Berlin: Springer, 1968).

Julia Mickenberg, *Learning from the Left: Children's Literature, the Cold War and Radical Politics in the United States* (Oxford: Oxford University Press, 2005).

Diane Middlebrook, *Her Husband: Hughes and Plath – A Marriage* (New York: Viking, 2003).

Rana Mitter and Patrick Major (eds), *Across the Blocs: Cold War Cultural and Social History* (London: Frank Cass, 2003).

Jacques Monod, *Chance and Necessity: An Essay on the Natural Philosophy of Modern Biology* (New York: Vintage, 1972).

Anne Morrison Welsh, 'Norman Morrison: Deeds of Life, Deeds of Death', *Winds of Peace* (January 2000), pp. 4–5.

——, interview with *Charlotte Observer*, 11 April 2003, www.charlotte.com/mld/charlotte/living/5612485.htm?1c, accessed 8 May 2004.

Markus Mueller, interview with René Girard, *Anthropoetics* 2:1 (June 1996), pp. 1–13.

H.J. Muller, 'Artificial Transmutation of the Gene', in James A. Peters (ed.), *Classic Papers in Genetics* (London: Prentice Hall, 1959), pp. 149–55.

——, 'Genetic Effects of the Atomic Bombs in Hiroshima and Nagasaki', in James A. Peters (ed.), *Classic Papers in Genetics* (London: Prentice Hall, 1959), pp. 194–9.

Robert Murphy, 'British Cinema and the Cold War', *Screen* 48: 2 (2007), pp. 267–71.

Timothy Murphy, 'William Burroughs between Indifference and Revalorization: Notes toward a Political Reading', *Angelaki* 1: 1 (1993), pp. 113–24.

Nicholas Nabokov, *Le Cosmopolite* (Paris: Lafont, 1976).

Vladimir Nabokov, *Lolita* (1955) (Harmondsworth: Penguin, 1980).

——, *Pale Fire* (1962) (Harmondsworth: Penguin, 2000).

Alan Nadel, *Containment Culture: American Narratives, Postmodernism, and the Atomic Age* (Durham, NC: Duke University Press, 1995).

James Naremore, *More than Night: Film Noir in its Contexts* (Berkeley: University of California Press, 1998).

Jonathan Nashel, 'The Road to Vietnam: Modernization Theory in Fact and Fiction', in Christian G. Appy (ed.), *Cold War Constructions: The Political Culture of United States Imperialism, 1945–1966* (Amherst: University of Massachusetts Press, 2000), pp. 132–54.

J.V. Neel and W.J. Schull, *The Effect of Exposure to the Atomic Bombs on Pregnancy Termination in Hiroshima and Nagasaki* (Washington, DC: National Research Council, 1956).

J. V. Neel, W.J. Schull, D.J. McDonald et al., 'The Effect of Exposure to the Atomic Bombs on Pregnancy Terminations in Hiroshima and Nagasaki: A Preliminary Report', *Science* 118 (1953), pp. 537–41.

Deborah Nelson, *Pursuing Privacy in Cold War America* (New York: Columbia University Press, 2002).

Judie Newman, 'Napalm and After: The Politics of Grace Paley's Short Fiction', *Yearbook of English Studies* 31 (2001), pp. 2–9.

John Newsinger, 'Counterrevolution: The Malayan Example', *Monthly Review* 45: 9 (February 1994), pp. 19–30.

Guy Oakes, *The Imaginary War: Civil Defense and American Cold War Culture* (Oxford: Oxford University Press, 1995).

A. W. Oughterson, G. V. Leroy, A. A. Liebov et al., *Medical Effects of Atomic Bombs: The Report of the Joint Commission for the Investigation of the Effects of the Atomic Bomb in Japan*, 5 vols (Oak Ridge, TN: U.S. Atomic Energy Commission Technical Information Service, 1951).

Grace Paley, *The Collected Stories* (London: Virago, 1999).

——, *Just As I Thought* (London: Virago, 1999).

David Parent, 'Nietzsche's Arctic Zone of Cognition and Post-Structuralism', *History of European Ideas* 11 (1989), pp. 759–67.

Robin Peel, *Writing Back: Sylvia Plath and Cold War Politics* (Madison, NJ: Fairleigh Dickinson University Press, 2002).

——, 'Body, Word, and Photograph: Sylvia Plath's Cold War Collage and the Thalidomide Scandal', *Journal of American Studies* 40: 1 (2006), pp. 71–95.

——, 'The Political Education of Sylvia Plath', in Anita Helle (ed.), *The Unraveling Archive: Essays on Sylvia Plath* (Ann Arbor: University of Michigan Press, 2007), pp. 39–64.

Ruth Perry, 'Grace Paley', in Janet Todd (ed.), *Women Writers Talking* (New York: Holmes & Meier, 1983), pp. 35–56.

Sylvia Plath, *Johnny Panic and the Bible of Dreams, and Other Prose Writings* (London: Faber & Faber, 1977).

——, *Collected Poems*, ed. Ted Hughes (London: Faber & Faber, 1981).

——, *The Journals of Sylvia Plath 1950–1962*, ed. Karen V. Kukil (London: Faber & Faber, 2000).

——, *Ariel, the Restored Edition* (London: Faber & Faber, 2004).

Heinz Politzer, 'The Liberal Novel', *Commentary* 6 (1948), pp. 95–6.

Stephen Prothero, 'On the Holy Road: The Beat Movement as Spiritual Protest', *Harvard Theological Review* 84: 2 (1991), pp. 205–22.

Ronald G. Purver, *Arms Control in the North* (Kingston: Centre for International Relations, Queen's University, 1981).

Kumar Ramakrishna, *Emergency Propaganda: The Winning of Malayan Hearts and Minds, 1948–1958* (London: Routledge, 2001).

John Ranelagh, *The Agency: The Rise and Decline of the CIA* (London: Weidenfeld & Nicolson, 1986).

Marcus G. Raskin and Bernard B. Fall (eds), *The Vietnam Reader: Articles and Documents on American Foreign Policy and the Viet-Nam Crisis* (New York: Random House, 1965).

Gary D. Rawnsley (ed.), *Cold-War Propaganda in the 1950s* (London: Macmillan, 1999).

Redstone Arsenal, Complex Chronology 1950–55, www.redstone.army.mil/history, accessed 9 December 2008.

Raye C. Ringholz, *Uranium Frenzy: Saga of the Nuclear West* (Logan: Utah State University Press, 2002).

Dale K. Robinson, USAF booklet 'Air Commando, 1950–1975' (1975), http://home.earthlink.net/~aircommando1/RANCHHAND.htm, accessed 28 August 2008.

Neil Roberts, 'The Common Text of Sylvia Plath and Ted Hughes', *Symbiosis: A Journal of Anglo-American Literary Relations* 7: 1 (2003), pp. 157–73.

Nora Ruth Roberts, *Three Radical Writers: Class and Gender in Meridel Le Sueur, Tillie Olsen, and Josephine Herbst* (New York: Garland, 1996).

Ron Robin, *The Making of the Cold War Enemy: Culture and Politics in the Military–Intellectual Complex* (Princeton, NJ: Princeton University Press, 2001).

David Robinson, *Chaplin: His Life and Art* (London: Collins, 1985).

Camille Roman, 'Cold War: Elizabeth Bishop and Sylvia Plath', in Laura Menides and Angela Dorenkamp (eds), *'In Worcester, Massachusetts': Essays on Elizabeth Bishop* (New York: Peter Lang, 1999), pp. 247–58.

Barbara Rose, 'Cultural Paranoia, Conspiracy Plots, and the American Ideology: William Burroughs's *Cities of the Red Night*', *Canadian Review of American Studies* 29: 2 (1999), pp. 89–111.

Jacqueline Rose, *The Haunting of Sylvia Plath* (London: Virago, 1991).

Felicity Rosslyn, 'Plath and Hughes among the Psychiatrists', *PN Review* 29: 3 (2003), pp. 30–3.

John Carlos Rowe, 'Eyewitness: Documentary Styles in the American Representations of Vietnam', in John Carlos Rowe and Rick Berg (eds), *The Vietnam War and American Culture* (New York: Columbia University Press, 1991), pp. 148–74.

Nicholas Royle, 'Nuclear Piece: *Mémoires* of *Hamlet* and the Time to Come', *diacritics* 20: 1 (Spring 1990), pp. 39–55.

Dean Rusk, Memorandum to President John F. Kennedy, 24 November 1961, reprinted in *Foreign Relations of the United States, 1961–1963*, VIETNAM 1961, at 663, 663 (1988), www.state.gov/www/about_state/history/vol_i_1961/z.html, accessed 9 December 2008.

Ken Ruthven, *Nuclear Criticism* (Melbourne: Melbourne University Press, 1993).

Keith Sagar, *The Art of Ted Hughes* (London: Cambridge University Press, 1975).

—— (ed.), *The Achievement of Ted Hughes* (Athens: University of Georgia Press, 1983).

Noel Sanders, 'The Hot Rock in the Cold War: Uranium in the 1950s', in Ann Curthoys and John Merritt (eds), *Better Red than Dead: Australia's First Cold War*, 2 vols (Sydney: Allen & Unwin, 1984), vol. 2, pp. 155–69.

John E. Sater, A.G. Ronhovde and L.C. Von Allen, *Arctic Environment and Resources* (Washington, DC: Arctic Institute of North America, 1971).

Thomas Hill Schaub, *American Fiction in the Cold War* (Madison: University of Wisconsin Press, 1991).

Michael Schumacher, *Dharma Lion: A Critical Biography of Allen Ginsberg* (New York: St Martin's Press, 1992).

W.G. Sebald, *The Rings of Saturn*, trans. Michael Hulse (London: Harvill Press, 1998).

David Seed, *American Science Fiction and the Cold War* (London: Routledge, 1999).

——, 'The Debate over Nuclear Refuge', in Rana Mitter and Patrick Major (eds), *Across the Blocs: Cold War Cultural and Social History* (London: Frank Cass, 2003), pp. 117–42.

——, *Brainwashing: A Study of Cold War Demonology* (Kent, OH: Kent State University Press, 2004).

Hannah Segal, *Psychoanalysis, Literature and War: Papers 1972–95* (London: Taylor & Francis, 1997).

Gerard Segals, *The Great Power Triangle* (Basingstoke: Macmillan, 1982).

Tony Shaw, *British Cinema and the Cold War* (London: I.B. Tauris, 2006).

——, *Hollywood's Cold War* (Edinburgh: Edinburgh University Press, 2007).

Norman Sherry, *The Life of Graham Greene*, 3 vols (London: Jonathan Cape, 1994).

James Smethurst, *The New Red Negro* (Oxford: Oxford University Press, 1999).

James Smethurst, Bill Mullen and James Edward Smithurst (eds), *Left of the Color Line: Race, Radicalism and Twentieth-Century Literature of the United States* (Chapel Hill, NC: North Carolina University Press, 2003).

Joseph Smith, *The Cold War, 1945–1991*, 2nd edn (Oxford: Blackwell, 1998).

Stan Smith, *Inviolable Voice: History and Twentieth-Century Poetry* (Dublin: Gill & Macmillan, 1982).

Michael Snyder, 'Crises of Masculinity: Homosocial Desire and Homosexual Panic in the Critical Cold War Narratives of Mailer and Coover', *Critique* 48: 3 (2007), pp. 250–77.

Lewis Sorley, 'To Change a War: General Harold K. Johnson and the PROVN Study', *Parameters* (Spring 1998), pp. 93–109.

Malcolm Spaven, *Fortress Scotland* (London: Pluto Press, 1983).

Francis Spufford, *I May Be Some Time: Ice and the English Imagination* (London: Faber & Faber, 1996).

L.J. Stadler, 'The Gene', in James A. Peters (ed.), *Classic Papers in Genetics* (Englewood Cliffs, NJ: Prentice Hall, 1959), pp. 244–59.

John Steinbeck, 'Letters to Alicia', *Newsday* 3 December 1966–20 May 1967.

Marjorie Stone and Judith Thompson (eds), *Literary Couplings: Writing Couples, Collaborators, and the Construction of Authorship* (Madison: University of Wisconsin Press, 2006).

Frances Stonor Saunders, *Who Paid the Piper?: The CIA and the Cultural Cold War* (Cambridge: Granta, 1999).

Robin Stuart, interview on PBS website for 1999 film *Meltdown at Three Mile Island*, www.pbs.org/wgbh/amex/three/filmmore/reference/interview/stuart03.html, accessed 9 December 2008.

Eve Stwertka and Margo Viscusi (eds), *Twenty-Four Ways of Looking at Mary McCarthy* (New York: Greenwood Press, 1996).

R.J. Sutherland, 'The Strategic Significance of the Canadian Arctic', in R. St. J. Macdonald (ed.), *The Arctic Frontier* (Toronto: University of Toronto Press, 1966), pp. 256–78.

Amy Swerdlow, *Women Strike for Peace: Traditional Motherhood and Radical Politics in the 1960s* (Chicago: University of Chicago Press, 1993).

Lipot Szondi, *Experimental Diagnostics of Drives*, trans. Gertrude Aull (New York: Grune & Stratton, 1952).

Bryan C. Taylor, 'Nuclear Pictures and Metapictures', *American Literary History* 9: 3 (Autumn 1997), pp. 567–97.

Gordon O. Taylor, 'Cast a Cold "I": Mary McCarthy on Vietnam', *Journal of American Studies* 9 (1975), pp. 103–14.

Peter J. Taylor, *Britain and the Cold War: 1945 as Geopolitical Transition* (London: Pinter, 1990).

Abbott Handerson Thayer, *Concealing-Coloration in the Animal Kingdom* (New York: Macmillan, 1909).

Raju G.C. Thomas, *The Great Power Triangle and Asian Security* (Lexington: Lexington Books, 1983).

René Thomas, 'Molecular Genetics under an Embryologist's Microscope', in James F. Crow and William F. Dove (eds), *Perspectives on Genetics: Anecdotal, Historical, and Critical Commentaries, 1987–1998* (Madison: University of Wisconsin Press, 2000), pp. 293–6.

Robert Thompson, *Defeating Communist Insurgency: The Lessons of Malaya and Vietnam* (New York: Frederick. A. Praege, 1966).

Tini Tran, 'Agent Orange Victims Bring Lawsuit in US', *Herald*, 26 February 2005, p. 11

Tony Trigilio, *'Strange Prophecies Anew': Rereading Apocalypse in Blake, H.D., and Ginsberg* (Madison, NJ: Fairleigh Dickinson University Press, 2000).

John Tytell, *Naked Angels: The Lives and Literatures of the Beat Generation* (New York: McGraw-Hill, 1976).

University of Utah, Learn.Genetics website, www.learn.genetics.utah.edu, accessed 9 December 2008.

John Updike, *New York Times* interview, 24 September 1967, www.nytimes.com/books/97/04/06/lifetimes/updike-v-vietnam.html, accessed 9 December 2008.

Dennis Walder, *Ted Hughes* (Maidenhead: Open University Press, 1987).

Talbot H. Waterman, 'Systems Theory and Biology – View of a Biologist', in M.D. Mesarovic (ed.), *Systems Theory and Biology* (Berlin: Springer, 1968), pp. 1–37.

Tim Weiner, *Legacy of Ashes: The History of the CIA* (New York: Doubleday, 2007).

Jack B. Weinstein, 'Agent Orange Liability Litigation', United States District Court, Eastern District of New York, 10 March 2005, www.ffrd.org/AO/10_03_05_agentorange.pdf, accessed 28 August 2008.

Norbert Wiener, *Cybernetics, or Control and Communication in the Animal and the Machine* (New York: Technology Press/John Wiley, 1948).

——, *The Human Use of Human Beings: Cybernetics and Society* (London: Eyre and Spottiswoode, 1954).

Ray Lewis White, 'John Dos Passos and the Federal Bureau of Investigation'. *Journal of Modern Literature* 14: 1 (Summer 1987), pp. 97–110.

Stephen J. Whitfield, *The Culture of the Cold War*, 2nd edn (1991) (Baltimore: Johns Hopkins University Press, 1996).

——, 'Limited Engagement: *The Quiet American* as History', *Journal of American Studies* 30: 1 (1996), pp. 65–86.

Hugh Wilford, *The CIA, the British Left and the Cold War: Calling the Tune?* (London: Routledge, 2003).

D. Wilkie, *The Cytoplasm in Heredity* (London: Methuen, 1964).

William Carlos Williams, *Paterson*, ed. C.J. MacGowan (New York: Norton, 1995).

Edmund Wilson, *Shores of Light* (New York: Farrar, Straus & Cudahy, 1952).

Louise K. Wilson, *A Record of Fear* (Cambridge: National Trust and Commissions East, 2005).

R.R. Wilson, 'Nuclear Radiation at Hiroshima and Nagasaki', *Radiation Research* 4 (1956), pp. 349–59

Guy Wint, *The British in Asia* (London: Faber & Faber, 1947).

Peter Wollen, 'Spies and Spivs: An Anglo-Austrian Entanglement', in Peter Wollen, *Paris Hollywood: Writings on Film* (London, New York: Verso, 2002), pp. 134–48.

Michael Wood, *The Magician's Doubts: Nabokov and the Risks of Fiction* (London: Pimlico, 1994).

——, '*Lolita* Revisited', *New England Review* 17: 3 (1995), pp. 15–43.

Virginia Woolf, *Orlando: A Biography* (Harmondsworth: Penguin, 1998).

Royden Yerkes, *Sacrifice in Greek and Roman Religions and Early Judaism* (London: Adam & Charles Black, 1953).

INDEX

Abraham and Isaac, 57, 169–70
Acheson, Dean, 36, 40, 155, 156
Agent Orange, 191, 201, 202, 203, 207, 208
air power, 3, 13, 29, 31, 37, 39, 47, 49, 77, 80, 95, 96, 99, 102, 107, 119, 120, 125, 127, 140, 158, 160, 178, 183, 186, 187, 191, 192, 193, 197, 200, 201, 202, 203
Alabama, 136, 137
Alaska, 74, 78, 79, 85, 86, 88, 95, 96, 100, 103
Aldritch, Richard, 11
allegory, 11, 23, 24, 26, 39, 43, 44, 51, 53, 55, 56, 62, 73, 109, 144, 152, 166
Amis, Martin, 2
Angkor Wat, 174
Anglo-Americanism, 11, 29, 38, 40, 115, 150, 156, 212
anti-Americanism, 17, 26, 27, 184

anti-Communism, 5, 6, 10, 14, 17, 37, 57, 61, 65, 144, 152, 153, 154, 155, 156, 157, 159, 160, 161, 162, 164, 165, 177, 185, 189, 204, 210, 211
Antigone, 197
anti-semitism, 21, 43, 99
Arctic, 74, 75, 78, 79, 81, 82, 83, 84, 85, 88, 92, 93, 96, 97, 103
arms race, 12, 14, 17, 117, 118, 120, 169, 188
Army Ballistic Missile Agency, 136, 137, 150
Arrowsmith, Pat, 17
artificial intelligence, 139
Ashby, W. Ross, 139, 141
Asian Cold War, 155, 161, 162, 165, 166, 204, 207
atmospheric tests, 17, 123, 146, 188, 210
Atomic Bomb Casualty Commission, 91, 104

Atomic Energy Commission, 67, 89, 92, 104, 119, 120, 121, 146
Attlee, Clement, 23, 35, 38, 154, 155
Auden, W. H., 25, 184
auto-poesy, 101
Axelrod, Steven Gould, 6

Bacon, John Lance, 6, 7, 8, 11
Bartram, John, 62, 63, 64, 66
Bartram, William, 61, 67
BBC, 9, 151, 153, 154, 157, 204, 211
beam weapons, 95
Bering Strait, 76, 77, 78, 79, 80, 81, 96, 98, 100, 101
Berlin, 10, 12, 19, 20, 21, 22, 23, 24, 25, 26, 37, 40, 41, 42, 44, 45, 46, 49, 50, 118, 156, 173
Berlin airlift, 40
Bethune, Norman, 120
Bevin, Ernest, 40, 41, 156
Bigelow, Julian, 139
Bly, Robert, 170, 171, 175, 192, 197, 199, 205, 207
body paranoia, 4, 10, 14, 19, 20, 21, 30, 31, 32, 34, 35, 55, 58, 75–8, 83, 88, 90, 93–9, 100, 101, 105–16, 119, 120, 124, 127, 128, 132, 135, 138, 140–5, 168, 170–2, 176, 178, 181, 187, 190–4, 197, 198, 203, 212
bombing and the Bomb, 4, 8, 12, 13, 15, 20, 22, 23, 24, 25, 29, 34, 38, 79, 82, 83, 90, 92, 95, 98, 99, 100, 104, 115, 118, 121, 122, 131, 132, 139, 140, 147, 150, 161, 162, 163, 165, 168, 171, 172, 173, 174, 181, 184, 185, 189, 190, 191, 192, 193, 194, 195, 201, 203, 206
Booker, Keith, 8

border zones, 36, 39, 45, 77, 78, 79, 156, 172
Borstelmann, Thomas, 9, 18
Bowen, Elizabeth, 210–12
    Little Girls, The, 211
brainwashing, 55, 84, 114, 160
Briggs Plan, 124, 157, 159, 160, 200
British Council, 210, 211
British hypothesis, 36, 39, 40
British Information Services, 11
Brunner, Edward, 8, 213
Buddhism, 168, 169, 174, 175, 205, 206
Bulletin of Atomic Scientists, 121
Bundy, William, 184, 206
Burnshaw, Stanley, 66, 67, 68, 73
Burroughs, Joan, 143, 144, 145
Burroughs, William, 15, 81, 109–15, 143–5, 148, 151
    Queer, 143–5, 151
    The Ticket that Exploded, 110–14, 148
Bush, Vannevar, 139
butterflies, 89, 92

Cambodia, 174, 175
camouflage, 83, 84, 96, 105
Campaign for Nuclear Disarmament, 1, 2, 119
Campbell, Duncan, 9
Canada, 27, 37, 78, 79, 81, 82, 85, 88
Carlson, Elof Axel, 116, 148
Caute, David, 8
cells and the cellular, 4, 12, 57, 94, 95, 106–47
Central Intelligence Agency, 10, 13, 35, 38, 40, 45, 76, 119, 182, 200, 206, 210
Chambers, Whittaker, 37, 59, 60
Chaplin, Charlie, 91, 104
Chief of Staff Committee, 38

China, 72, 102, 120, 147, 153, 155, 156, 162, 169, 173, 209
chromosomes, 110, 111, 112, 113, 114, 115, 116, 121, 124, 125, 126, 127, 129, 130, 133
Churchill, Winston, 22, 36, 37, 39, 40, 46, 101
citizenship, 13, 65, 66, 85
civil rights, 8, 9, 57, 187, 188, 207, 212, 213
civil war, 5, 54, 55, 56, 68, 128, 142, 155, 164, 168, 170, 172, 175, 186, 191, 197, 198, 213
Clark, Suzanne, 8, 213
Clutterbuck, Richard, 199, 200, 201, 207
Coe, Robert, 67
Cold Spring Harbor, 134, 150
Colombo Plan, 204
colossus, 118, 120, 134, 135, 137, 140, 143, 146, 147, 148, 210, 214
Cominform, 154
Comintern, 45
Committee for a Sane Nuclear Policy, 146, 205
Committee on Biological Effects of Atomic Radiation, 122
Commonwealth, 37, 39, 155, 204
Communism, 2, 3, 10, 13, 17, 36, 37, 40, 46, 48, 50, 51, 53, 54, 55, 56, 57, 58, 59, 60, 61, 67, 70, 71, 72, 75, 77, 99, 105, 113, 120, 153, 154, 155, 156, 157, 158, 159, 160, 161, 163, 165, 173, 182, 184, 186, 189, 196, 197, 199, 200, 204, 209, 210, 211
Communist Party of the United States of America, 59, 60, 71

Congress for Cultural Freedom, 8, 10, 17, 190, 210
Conquest, Robert, 151, 154
conspiracy, 3, 7, 13, 15, 19, 23, 25, 50, 55, 58, 60, 66, 77, 152, 177
containment, 6, 7, 8, 10, 11, 36, 155, 161, 173, 181, 204, 209
Cook, Fred J., 116, 117, 118, 119, 148
Corber, Robert J., 8, 103
Corsham, 9
counterculture, 6, 15, 191
counterinsurgency, 14, 152, 153, 155, 156, 160, 161, 166, 167, 173, 181, 185, 186, 193, 195, 199, 200, 203
counterintelligence, 30, 31, 34, 35, 83, 144, 145
Crick, Francis, 129, 149
Crow, James F., 149
Crozier, Brian, 154
Cuba, 10, 63, 173, 178, 182, 185, 210, 212
cybernetics, 10, 123, 139, 143, 144
cytoplasm, 114, 115, 116, 124, 125, 129, 130, 132, 138, 140

Davidson, Michael, 8
Dawkins, Richard, 138
De Gaulle, Charles, 161
deception intelligence, 83
decolonization, 7, 12, 85, 143, 145, 152, 155, 156, 160, 162, 163, 164, 167, 171, 173, 188, 189, 195, 196, 198, 199, 210, 212
Deery, Philip, 199, 204
defection, 16, 158, 182
defence systems, 79, 80, 210
DeLillo, Don, 2, 3, 7, 15, 17, 212
    Underworld, 2, 3, 17
denazification, 12, 22, 24, 26

Derrida, Jacques, 5, 18
deviancy, 77, 109
DEW Line, 79, 80, 82, 83, 95, 96, 97, 98, 102
Dimock, George, 16, 18
dissent, 9, 11, 70, 119, 146, 168, 169, 198
DNA, 110–15, 123, 124–34, 137–41, 145
Dr. Strangelove, 2, 3, 6, 8, 103, 104, 105
Dodd, Thomas J., 174
Dolores, 88, 91, 94, 96
domino theory, 156, 160, 161, 181, 189
Donovan, William, 26, 35
Dos Passos, John, 11, 17, 47–59, 60, 61, 62, 63, 64, 66, 67, 68, 69, 71, 72, 210
  Grand Design, The, 48–59, 61, 66, 71, 72
  Tour of Duty, 47–51, 72
Douglas, Ann, 7
dreams, 2, 3, 12, 16, 21, 23, 25, 29, 32, 33, 34, 40, 44, 48, 51, 62, 72, 75, 76, 77, 80, 81, 84, 91, 96, 99, 100, 127, 128, 132, 135, 136, 137, 141, 143, 146, 150, 157, 167, 168, 170, 175, 176, 177, 188, 191, 193, 195, 196, 198, 203
drives, 11, 14, 97, 123, 124, 126, 127, 141, 147, 149
Drosophila, 115, 121, 125
Dylan, Bob, 101, 102

Ellsberg, Daniel, 185, 186, 187, 188, 197, 206, 207
Emergency Information Services, 153, 157, 158, 159, 163, 164, 202, 204, 205
Encounter, 10, 149

enemy, 2, 9, 11, 14, 16, 17, 26, 30, 32, 33, 34, 38, 39, 41, 43, 45, 53, 54, 65, 66, 75, 77, 80, 90, 95, 99, 103, 107, 110, 111, 114, 120, 126, 132, 134, 135, 140, 143, 145, 153, 158, 159, 160, 161, 163, 164, 168, 170, 172, 173, 174, 175, 177, 178, 179, 181, 182, 183, 187, 191, 192, 195, 197, 201, 205, 206, 210
English Heritage, 4, 17
Erwinna, 59, 60, 62, 63
espionage, 4, 12, 17, 26, 30, 34, 37, 38, 45, 46, 53, 54, 55, 75, 84, 98, 114, 120, 144, 182, 192, 193, 195, 211, 212
existentialism, 6, 20, 24, 41, 44

fallout, 15, 96, 107, 108, 115, 116, 117, 120, 123, 128, 147, 173
Farrell, James, 61
fascism, 12, 13, 20, 21, 23, 24, 26, 27, 28, 34, 35, 41, 42, 43, 54, 99, 136, 137, 140
Fass, Ecbert, 127, 128, 149, 150
Feather, Victor, 154
Federal Bureau of Investigation, 37, 56, 58, 59, 60, 61, 64, 66, 67, 76, 120, 146
feedback, 21, 114, 138, 139, 140, 142, 145
Fenster, Mark, 15
Ferro, Marc, 43, 44, 46
film noir, 28, 29, 30, 51
Four Corners, The, 88, 89, 91, 92, 96
Fox Keller, Evelyn, 133
Freud, Sigmund, 11, 12, 14, 15, 16, 18, 30, 32, 33, 34, 41, 45, 61, 80, 97, 103, 124, 148
  Interpretation of Dreams, The, 32, 45

Freudianism, 8, 15, 16, 39, 63, 68, 83, 84, 97, 113, 123, 153, 164, 199, 213

Garrigue, Jean, 62
Gellhorn, Martha, 171
genetics, 91, 92, 107, 110–50, 203, 210
genome, 124–6, 132
geopolitics, 4, 7, 8, 77, 78, 111, 144
Ginsberg, Allen, 16, 74–81, 82, 96, 97–103, 105, 203
  Kaddish, 74–81, 98–100, 105
Ginsberg, Naomi, 74–8, 81, 98–102
Girard, René, 14, 18
Gothic, 9, 20, 21, 22, 24, 26, 29, 43, 142
Government Communications Headquarters, 38
Graves, Robert, 53, 54, 71, 127
Greene, Graham, 11, 12, 17, 24–44, 45, 152–67, 198, 199, 200, 202, 203, 204, 205, 208, 210, 212
  Quiet American, The, 152–67, 198, 202, 204, 205
  Third Man, The, 12, 24–44, 45, 152, 153, 164, 212
Greene, Hugh Carleton, 153–64, 200, 202, 204, 205
grey-listing, 17, 67, 68
Gyson, Brion, 114

Hanoi, 13, 17, 165, 171, 172, 174, 175, 178, 179, 188–92, 193, 195, 196, 198, 205
Hantke, Steffen, 7, 11
Harrington, Michael, 178
Harris, Oliver, 103, 143–5, 151
Hassler, Alfred, 206
hawks and doves, 68, 108, 137, 140, 146, 184, 185, 186

Healey, Denis, 154
hearts and minds, 153, 154, 157, 161, 163, 164, 178, 183, 200
Helms. Richard, 185
Hemingway, Ernest, 28, 57, 58
Hendershot, Cyndy, 15, 224
Hennessy, Peter, 9, 11, 18, 40, 46, 214
Herbst, Josephine, 11, 17, 57–73, 203, 212, 213, 214
  New Green World, 61–73
  Pity is Not Enough, 73
  Starched Blue Sky of Spain, The, 73
Herman, Ellen, 14
Herring, Frances, 103, 207
Herrmann, John, 59, 60, 69, 70, 71, 203
Hersey, John, 7
Hershberger, Mary, 188, 189, 205, 206, 207
Herz, Alice, 168, 169, 170, 171, 172, 188, 189, 193, 197, 203
Hines, Barry, 9
Hiroshima, 7, 82, 91, 92, 96, 104, 116, 121, 122, 149
Hiss, Alger, 37, 59, 60, 61
history, 5, 6, 7, 8, 9, 12, 13, 16, 20, 21, 25, 36, 40, 43, 48, 49, 50, 52, 55, 59, 61, 62, 63, 65, 66, 67, 68, 73, 75, 81, 84, 89, 92, 93, 96, 98, 99, 141, 142, 150, 177, 178, 179, 186, 190, 191, 194, 196, 208, 212, 214
Hofstadter, Richard, 177
Hollywood, 8, 28, 45, 89, 91
homosexuality, 77, 81, 84, 111, 112, 144, 145
homosociality, 9, 144
Hong Kong, 156
Hooverism, 77

Hotchkiss, Rollin, 129, 130, 149
House Committee Investigating
    Un-American Activities
    (HUAC), 6, 37, 61, 64
Hrones, John, 139, 150
Hughes, Freida, 147, 151
Hughes, Ted, 11, 12, 91, 115,
    122–33, 135, 136, 137, 140,
    141, 147, 149, 151, 210
    'A Woman Unconscious', 131,
    136
    Gaudete, 127–30, 147, 149
    'Law in the Country of the Cats',
    126
    'Love Song', 126
    'Notes for a Little Play', 128–9
    'Pike', 122–3
    'Poetry and Violence', 125–6
    'Sylvia Plath and Her Journals',
    129
    'Thrushes', 123, 126
    'To Paint a Water Lily', 127
Humbert, Humbert, 13, 81, 82, 83,
    84, 85, 86, 87, 88, 89, 90, 91,
    92, 93, 94, 95, 96, 97, 98, 100,
    104, 105
Hungary, 210, 211, 212, 214
Hyde, Douglas, 103, 154

imagination, 10, 11, 14, 17, 20, 21,
    25, 26, 35, 68, 76, 81, 84, 94,
    99, 103, 106, 120, 123, 127,
    137, 145, 167, 168, 170, 175,
    176, 177, 180, 196, 198, 209,
    212, 213
Indochina, 152, 155, 156, 160, 173,
    178, 185, 186, 199, 203
indoctrination, 21, 22, 88, 101, 181,
    182, 183, 211
informal empire, 163, 167
Information Research Department,
    11, 18, 38, 153, 154, 155, 157,
    158, 159, 160, 161, 162, 166,
    204, 211
information technology, 109
Inglis, Fred, 212, 213, 214
intercontinental ballistic missiles, 79,
    98, 123
internalization, 6, 12, 16, 31, 80, 90,
    91, 96, 99, 100, 120, 144, 164,
    209
International Organizations Division,
    10
interzone, 80, 81, 96, 100, 165
iron curtain, 37, 39, 46
Iron Triangle, 173, 174, 183, 199

Jameson, Storm, 11, 19–26, 41, 42,
    43, 44, 45, 210
    Black Laurel, The, 19–26, 42, 43,
    44, 210
Janus, 11, 13, 16, 17, 42, 68, 161,
    166, 180, 187, 195, 197, 198,
    203, 207, 209, 214
Johnson, Lyndon B., 3, 14, 40, 103,
    167, 168, 170, 174, 177, 178,
    180, 182, 184, 199, 206, 207
Joint US Public Affairs Office, 183
Josselson, Michael, 10

Kai-shek, Chiang, 155
Kaplan, Thomas, 153, 204
Katzenbach, Nicholas, 185
Kay, Lillian, 139, 140, 150, 151
Kennan, George, 7, 36, 37, 39
Kennedy, John, 118, 119, 146, 156,
    173, 175, 177, 178, 181, 182,
    185, 199, 201, 202, 206, 207,
    208
Kenya, 154, 173
Khrushchev, Nikita, 118, 119, 121
Kirwan, Celia, 154, 204
Kissinger, Henry, 188
Klein, Christine, 8

Korda, Alexander, 26, 27
Korea, 150, 154, 155, 161, 173
Kremlin, the, 49, 50, 51, 79, 82
Kremlinology, 5, 181
Krupnick, Mark, 15
Kutulas, Judy, 73

Lafcadio, Peter, 77
Laing, R. D., 15
Langer, Elinor, 57, 59, 60, 61, 62, 67, 72
Lansdale, Edward, 185, 207
Laos, 175
Le Carré, John, 10, 12, 13, 18, 30
    Spy Who Came in from the Cold, The, 12
left liberalism, 54, 61
Libby, Willard F., 120
libertarianism, 52, 61, 63
logic, 2, 12, 13, 31, 43, 44, 49, 137, 147, 161, 166, 173, 174, 184, 189, 193, 194, 197, 213
Long Telegram, The, 37
Los Alamos, 104, 118
Love Canal, 106
Lowell, Robert, 6
Lutz, Catherine, 45
Lysenko, Trofime, 121, 133

McCarthy, Mary, 13, 17, 167–99, 205
    Seventeenth Degree, The, 167–99, 205
McCarthyism, 6, 8, 17, 62, 64, 67, 68, 177, 210
McClintock, Barbara, 116, 133, 134, 135, 150, 207
McConachie, Bruce, 8, 11
McMahon Act, 38, 39
McNamara, Robert, 10, 118, 167, 169, 172, 186, 202, 208
Macpherson, Pat, 16, 228

Malaya, 152–66, 173, 199, 200, 201, 202, 203, 204, 205, 207
Malayan Communist Party, 153, 154, 157, 158, 159, 160, 163
Malayan Emergency, 1, 2, 67, 73, 147, 152–66, 164, 199, 201, 204, 205
Malayan Races Liberation Army, 157, 158, 159, 160
Manhattan Project, 82, 83, 88, 89, 90, 96, 104
Marshall Plan, 26, 38, 41, 44, 90, 155, 204
maternal effect, 125
Mau Mau, 154
May, Alan Nunn, 38
Medina, Captain Ernest, 171, 176, 194
Mekong Delta, 170, 171, 173, 175, 179, 180, 190, 193, 194, 195, 197, 198, 199, 206
Melly, Timothy, 15, 18
Melville, Herman, 78, 81
messenger RNA, 114, 115, 129, 130, 131, 132, 138, 139, 140
Mexico, 3, 57, 60, 71, 81, 88, 143, 145
MI6, 26, 35
Mickenberg, Julia, 8,
Military Assistance Command, Vietnam, 183, 200
Military Sea Transportation Service, 78, 229
misogyny, 55, 115, 127, 128, 134, 135, 143, 197
missiles, 3, 10, 77, 79, 117, 123, 136, 137, 140, 141, 142, 143, 150, 178, 210, 212
Mitchener, James, 8, 180
Mitter, Rana, 5, 18
MK-ULTRA, 144

molecular biology, 111, 115, 121, 124, 137, 139, 140, 151
Moloch, 80, 81, 98, 100
Morgan, Thomas Hunt, 121, 183
Morrison, Emily, 169, 171, 194
Morrison, Norman, 169, 205
Morrison Welsh, Anne, 169, 205
mother worship, 128
motherhood, 16, 74, 75, 76, 77, 78, 80, 92, 93, 99, 100, 101, 102, 103, 107, 108, 109, 112, 113, 114, 116, 117, 119, 120, 124, 125, 127, 128, 129, 131, 132, 134, 135, 144, 146, 147, 151, 159, 165, 166, 181, 203
Muller, Hermann, 115, 116, 120, 121, 122, 148, 149
mutant, 76, 77, 78, 106, 111, 116, 121, 127, 129, 130, 132, 134
mutation, 110, 111, 112, 115, 121, 122, 123, 124, 128, 129, 132, 133, 135, 140, 144
My Lai, 176, 194, 199

Nabokov, Nicholas, 10, 14, 18
Nabokov, Vladimir, 10, 11, 12, 13, 14, 17, 18, 81–97, 103, 104, 105, 203
    Lolita, 12, 13, 81–97, 100, 103, 104, 105, 203
    Pale Fire, 13, 103
Nadel, Alan, 7, 8, 11
Nagasaki, 91, 92, 104, 116, 121, 122, 149
naming, 17, 57, 58, 61, 65, 66, 68, 72, 73, 91
napalm, 163, 169
National Liberation Front, 189
National Security Act, 35, 38
National Security Council, 173
national security state, 2, 6, 12, 13, 17, 30, 31, 35, 40, 210, 213

Native Americans, 64, 65, 67, 89, 171, 190
NATO, 12, 39, 78, 79, 123
neutrality, 5, 11, 22, 25, 63, 94, 111, 153, 163, 209
New Criticism, 61, 63
New Deal, the, 52–61, 66, 71, 72, 117, 118
New Villages, 157, 158, 160, 161, 199
New York intellectuals, 6, 15, 61
Nhat Hanh, Thich, 191, 206
1950s, 1, 6–8, 12, 15, 17, 60, 61, 62, 67, 72, 77, 82, 91, 95, 104, 108–11, 113, 115, 137, 141, 152, 178, 199, 204, 210, 213
1930s, 11, 17, 48, 50, 53, 56, 58, 59, 60, 61, 62, 64–6, 68, 70, 71, 72, 88, 99, 120
Nixon, Richard, 188
NKVD (People's Commissariat for Internal Affairs), 30
Non-Communist Left, 10, 196, 210
Northwest Territories, 82, 85, 96
nostalgia, 2, 3, 4, 16, 214
nuclear accident, 106
Nuclear criticism, 5
nuclear culture, 9, 29, 40, 79, 90, 97, 109, 110, 112, 114, 115, 116, 125, 128, 129, 134, 145, 147
nuclear disarmament, 1, 106, 146
nuclear fission, 90, 94, 98
nuclear holocaust, 135, 211
nuclear power, 4, 40, 90, 107
nuclear threat, 104, 109, 147, 210, 211
nuclear weapons, 5, 6, 38, 40, 97, 101, 118, 122, 123, 140, 173, 210
nucleus, 90, 111, 112, 114, 115, 124, 125, 129, 133, 138, 150

Oak Ridge, 67, 104
Oakes, Guy, 7, 11
Office of Policy Coordination, 38
Office of Special Operations, 38
Office of Strategic Services, 26, 35
Open Arms, 182
Operation Attleboro, 173
Operation Cedar Falls, 174, 183, 199
Operation Ranch Hand, 201
Operation Rolling Thunder, 168, 170, 189, 193
operations research, 14, 139
Orford Ness, 4
Orwell, George, 8, 154, 204

pacification, 157, 180, 186, 189, 199, 200
pacifism, 171
paedophilia, 95
Paley, Grace, 17, 106–9, 112, 146–8, 188
Panama, 144, 145
paranoia, 1, 2, 3, 11, 12, 13, 14, 15, 16, 17, 54, 61, 66, 69, 71, 77, 83, 84, 95, 96, 97, 98, 99, 100, 101, 102, 103, 105, 109, 111, 114, 117, 123, 125, 140, 141, 145, 152, 174, 175, 176, 177, 178, 179, 181, 188, 195, 196, 197, 198, 203, 213
Parmenides, 30, 31
Partisan Review, 6, 61, 62
pastoral, 69, 80, 102
Pax Americana, 173
peace, 2, 5, 10, 21, 22, 25, 36, 50, 68, 80, 81, 103, 104, 107, 108, 109, 118, 119, 126, 145, 146, 147, 166, 170, 174, 175, 178, 187, 195, 196, 197, 198, 204, 206, 207, 210, 214
peace activism, 6, 7, 9, 22, 54, 66,

70, 104, 106, 107, 108, 109, 146, 187, 189, 206
Peenemünde, 136
Pentagon, 118, 119, 168, 169, 170, 171, 172, 179, 180, 185, 186, 188, 191, 193, 195, 198, 206
Pentagon Papers, 186, 188, 206
Phat Diem, 161
Phoenix Park, 153, 157, 159
pietà, 165, 203
Pine Tree Line, 3, 79
Plath, Sylvia, 7, 11, 12, 13, 16, 115, 116, 117, 118–20, 127, 128, 129, 131, 132, 133, 134–7, 140–3, 146, 147, 148, 149, 150, 151, 188, 203, 210
  Ariel, 147, 150, 151, 231
  'The Arrival of the Bee Box', 141–3
  'The Bee Meeting', 141–3
  'A Wishing Box', 135–7
  Bell Jar, The, 16, 127
  'Context', 116–17
  'Death & Co.', 134
  'Fever 103°', 135
  'Getting There', 135
  'Mystic', 141
  'Old Mother Morphia', 134
  'Poem for a Birthday', 135
  'Sheep in Fog', 132–3
  'Stings', 141–3
  'The Stones', 135
  'Three Women: A Poem for Three Voices', 119–20
  'The Surgeon at 2 a.m.', 120
  'The Swarm', 141–3
  'Waking in Winter', 134
  'Who', 135
  'Wintering', 141–3
Plato, 30, 33, 113
political unconscious, 11, 13, 24, 30, 31, 40, 41, 45, 164, 203

Pontecorvo, Bruno, 120

Popular Front, 8, 48, 52, 53, 66, 71, 72

Porter, Katherine Anne, 61, 69

Potomac, 55, 56, 62, 64, 71, 72

Prague, 37, 44, 212

predation, 32, 63, 88, 96, 97, 122, 123, 125, 126, 127, 128, 144, 145, 151

primitivism, 20, 113, 114, 124, 126, 128, 145, 198

Project Agile, 201

Project Camelot, 14

Project Orbiter, 136

propaganda, 5, 6, 7, 8, 10, 11, 13, 14, 17, 21, 22, 28, 30, 31, 34, 35, 36, 38, 39, 53, 54, 55, 61, 72, 77, 84, 92, 102, 110, 112, 117, 144, 152, 153, 154, 156, 157, 158, 159, 160, 161, 162, 163, 164, 166, 168, 172, 179, 180, 181, 183, 185, 195, 198, 199, 200, 204, 205, 210, 211

proxy sacrifice, 13, 14, 165, 166, 194, 195, 198

psychoanalysis, 13, 14, 15, 16, 41, 45, 55, 76, 77, 80, 81, 97, 123, 191

psychogenetics, 123, 124

psychological warfare, 14, 153, 157, 158, 163, 181, 185, 197

Pynchon, Thomas, 3, 7, 15, 212

Quakers, 63, 168, 169, 175

Rach Kien, 179, 180, 185

radar, 4, 47, 78, 79, 80, 81, 82, 83, 98, 101

radiation, 17, 90, 91, 92, 93, 94, 96, 104, 106, 107, 110, 111, 112, 115, 116, 120, 121, 122, 123, 134, 135, 147, 150

radio, 51, 94, 99, 100, 119, 157, 158, 180, 204

radioactivity, 12, 29, 83, 89, 90, 91, 92, 93, 94, 95, 96, 103, 107, 113, 114, 116, 118, 120, 122, 123, 124, 125, 135, 140

radon daughters, 92, 93, 95

RAND, 9, 10, 185, 186, 187, 188, 197, 207

Ranelagh, John, 35, 36, 37, 46, 231

rape, 84, 93, 94, 106, 112, 126, 128

Realpolitik, 23, 26, 28, 30, 162, 210

Redstone Arsenal, 136, 137, 150, 231

Reed, Carol, 26, 27, 28, 29, 32, 33, 41, 43, 44, 46

reproduction, 107, 109, 112, 113, 114, 116, 121, 122, 125, 128, 131, 132, 138, 142, 203

Revolutionary Development, 181, 182, 199, 200

Rieff, Philip, 15

Ringholz, Raye C., 88, 89, 91, 104, 231

rocket, 1, 3, 136, 137, 139, 150, 191, 212

Roethke, Theodore, 135

Roosevelt, Franklin D., 35, 52, 72, 98, 99

Rose, Jacqueline, 135

Rosenbergs, 72, 212

Rusk, Dean, 174, 178, 179, 197, 201, 202, 207, 208

Russell, Bertrand, 154

Ruthven, Ken, 6

Sacco and Vanzetti, 57, 69, 70

sacrifice, 11, 12, 13, 14, 16, 17, 20, 21, 22, 24, 26, 29, 34, 41, 42, 43, 44, 58, 60, 61, 64, 66, 68, 70, 71, 72, 88, 97, 132, 136, 142, 146, 147, 164, 165, 166,

sacrifice (*cont.*)
168, 169, 170, 171, 173, 174,
175, 183, 186, 187, 188, 190,
193, 194, 195, 196, 197, 198,
199, 204, 206, 209, 210, 211,
213, 214
sacrificial victim, 10, 11, 12, 13, 14,
16, 17, 20, 42, 43, 44, 54, 58,
59, 68, 71, 84, 95, 97, 100, 165,
174, 175, 177, 183, 197, 198
Saigon, 102, 161, 165, 169, 171,
172, 173, 174, 179, 180, 198,
206
Salinger, John, 7
satellite, 9, 28, 44, 50, 136, 137,
145, 150, 212
Saunders, Frances Stonor, 9, 10, 11
scapegoating, 14, 22, 42, 54, 70, 71,
194
Schaub, Thomas Hill, 6, 11, 73, 233
schizophrenia, 1, 2, 15, 51, 53, 54,
118, 143, 144, 145, 147, 181,
182
Schofield, John, 4, 17
search-and-destroy, 173, 174, 185,
200
Sebald, W. G., 4, 17
Second World War, 5, 13, 21, 24,
41, 42, 46, 53, 56, 61, 64, 83,
89, 99, 117, 139, 147, 149, 151,
177, 186, 210, 212
secret state, 15, 35
Seed, David, 8, 16
Segal, Hannah, 15, 18
self-immolation, 168, 170, 171, 172,
189, 203
Selznick, David, 27
Shaw, Tony, 8, 233
Sheehan, Neil, 186, 206
Siem Reap, 174, 195, 206
Singapore, 153, 161
Sino-Soviet relations, 156, 173

Smith, Joseph, 155, 204
Smith, Stan, 150
Smolka, Hans Peter, 27
somatic interiority, 22, 24, 45, 58,
69, 92, 93, 94, 96, 106, 107,
110, 111, 112, 113, 114, 116,
122, 125, 135, 138, 140, 141,
142, 143, 144, 145, 151, 198,
203
somatic unconscious, 24, 114, 142
South East Asia, 153, 154, 155, 156,
160, 161, 162, 163, 173, 187
Soviet Union, 4, 6, 9, 14, 16, 17, 23,
24, 25, 26, 28, 29, 30, 34, 35,
36, 37, 38, 39, 40, 41, 42, 44,
49, 50, 51, 53, 57, 60, 74, 76,
77, 79, 80, 95, 102, 114, 118,
120, 121, 123, 134, 142, 144,
145, 146, 153, 154, 155, 159,
164, 173, 209, 210
space program, 136
special relationship, the, 11, 12, 22,
24, 26, 34, 35, 37, 38, 39, 40,
41, 42, 43, 44, 137, 153, 159,
164, 166, 167
species death, 5, 20, 63, 65, 119,
122, 123, 125, 128, 132
Spender, Stephen, 10
Sputnik, 4
Staley Plan, 181, 182, 199
Stalin, Joseph, 36, 44, 52, 54, 121,
154, 196
Stalinism, 10, 61, 190, 209, 211
state-private networks, 8
Steen, Charlie, 88, 89, 91
Steinbeck, John, 171, 179, 185
Stimpson, Catherine, 146, 151
Strategic Hamlets, 199
Strath, William, 9
strontium 90, 107
Stuart, Robin, 148, 234
subatomic, 106, 107, 111

submarine, 123, 127, 149
suicide, 16, 44, 53, 55, 56, 58, 64,
    71, 72, 80, 119, 129, 131, 132,
    135, 136, 141, 147, 194, 198,
    203
Superman, 136, 137, 149, 150
superpower, 6, 12, 25, 26, 31, 34,
    35, 39, 41, 45, 48, 49, 54, 78,
    97, 112, 114, 146, 152, 161,
    212
surrogacy, 14, 78
surveillance, 4, 13, 35, 79, 80, 81,
    84, 102, 118, 141, 142, 146,
    193, 195, 212
Swerdlow, Amy, 145, 146, 151, 205
system, 5, 7, 9, 10, 12, 13, 15, 17,
    28, 31, 32, 35, 48, 50, 52, 53,
    54, 79, 80, 82, 83, 95, 96, 98,
    105, 106, 107, 109, 110, 111,
    112, 113, 120, 121, 122, 123,
    124, 125, 132, 135, 137, 138,
    139, 140, 141, 142, 143, 144,
    145, 148, 151, 173, 180, 188,
    190, 198, 210, 212, 213
systems theory, 10, 139, 140, 142
Szondi, Lipot, 123, 124, 149

target, 2, 14, 43, 81, 97, 104, 109,
    112, 117, 127, 131, 135, 145,
    147, 169, 175, 184, 202, 203,
    210, 213
Taylor, Peter J., 36, 46
technology, 1, 2, 5, 13, 34, 35, 39,
    49, 67, 80, 83, 91, 93, 96, 97,
    99, 102, 107, 109, 112, 127,
    128, 137, 140, 142, 143, 145,
    150, 151, 182, 191, 192, 195,
    198, 203, 213
television, 14
Teller, Edward, 118, 119
Telluride, 87, 88, 89, 90, 92, 104
Templer, Sir Gerald, 153, 157

terrorism, 153, 157, 160
test-ban negotiations, 118, 119, 146
Thayer, Abbott Handerson, 96, 105
third force, 39, 43, 155, 161, 162,
    173, 185, 186, 187, 198, 202,
    207, 209
Third Man Argument, 30, 31, 33,
    34, 40
Third World, 7, 9, 14, 26, 152, 153,
    154, 173, 175, 178, 196, 197,
    198, 209, 212
Thompson, Sir Robert, 199, 200
Threads, 9
Three Mile Island, 106, 147, 148
Tizard, Sir Henry, 154
Tonkin Gulf Resolution, 171, 177,
    186, 189
totalitarianism, 20, 24, 28, 30, 43,
    44, 50, 53, 182, 183, 197, 209,
    211
toxicity, 29, 40, 99, 100, 178, 203
triangle, 11, 12, 58, 68, 72, 152,
    153, 166, 173, 174, 176, 178,
    179, 181, 183, 185, 188, 189,
    193, 196, 198, 199
Trilling, Lionel, 15, 73, 190
Trotsky, Leon, 57, 72, 100
Trotskyites, 11, 57
Troywood, Anstruther, 1, 2
Truman Doctrine, 36, 38
Truman, Harry S., 35, 36, 37, 38,
    39, 40
Tse-tung, Mao, 72, 120, 155

Ulithi, 47, 48, 49, 50, 52, 54
United Nations, 22, 119, 120, 146,
    172, 205
United States, 3, 6, 7, 8, 9, 14, 17,
    22, 23, 24, 25, 26, 28, 34, 35,
    36, 37, 38, 40, 41, 42, 43, 44,
    45, 46, 49, 50, 52, 59, 60, 69,
    70, 74, 75, 77, 79, 81, 82, 85,

United States (*cont.*)
    86, 88, 90, 92, 95, 96, 97, 100,
    101, 103, 104, 105, 114, 117,
    118, 119, 121, 136, 145, 146,
    148, 150, 152, 153, 154, 155,
    156, 161, 162, 164, 168, 172,
    173, 174, 175, 176, 178, 179,
    182, 183, 186, 187, 189, 191,
    192, 193, 195, 196, 198, 199,
    201, 202, 203, 207, 208, 209,
    213, 214
United States Air Force, 203, 208,
    231
United States Army Security Agency,
    38
United States Information Agency, 8
Updike, John, 184, 190, 206, 235
uranium, 12, 82, 83, 85, 88, 89, 90,
    91, 92, 93, 94, 96, 97, 98, 104,
    105

Van Thai, Vu, 207
Vavilov, Nikolai, 120, 121
Vienna, 12, 16, 26, 27, 28, 29, 30,
    31, 32, 34, 37, 39, 40, 44, 45,
    49, 203, 212
Viet Cong, 168, 170, 171, 173, 174,
    175, 177, 180, 182, 187, 190,
    191, 195, 197, 198, 200, 206,
    207
Vietminh, 162
Vietnam, 10, 11, 12, 17, 18, 100,
    101, 102, 152, 156, 158,
    160–204
Vietnam Hearings, The, 174, 178,
    179, 206
Vietnamization, 174
virus, 20, 106, 109–17, 125, 130–5,
    142–5, 149

von Bertalanffy, Ludwig, 139
Von Braun, Wernher, 136
von Neumann, John, 139

War Game, The, 9
war machine, 53, 75, 81, 99, 101,
    180, 195, 198, 203
Ware, Hal, 59
warfare state, 3, 117, 118, 120, 127,
    137, 140, 145, 198
Warsaw, 20, 21, 37, 44, 45
Washington, 36, 48, 53, 54, 56, 58,
    59, 60, 61, 66, 67, 70, 119, 146,
    155, 170, 171, 177, 179, 180,
    188, 189, 190, 192, 194, 205,
    207, 208
Washington, George, 56
Watkins, Peter, 9
Welles, Orson, 27, 33
West, James, 92, 122, 149, 171, 192,
    193, 194, 195, 198, 205
Westmoreland, General William C.,
    199
Wiener, Norbert, 139,144, 151
Wilson, Edmund, 72, 86, 87
Wint, Guy, 155, 204, 236
witch-hunting, 65, 77, 135,
    210
Wollen, Peter, 26, 27, 45, 236
Women Strike for Peace, 145, 146,
    147, 151, 168, 188, 189, 197,
    198, 207

X-ray, 93, 94, 107, 115, 116, 121,
    133

Yalta, 44, 46, 50

zero-sum games, 9, 10, 145